H Holman

Education

Introduction to it's Principles and their Phychological Foundations

H Holman

Education

Introduction to it's Principles and their Phychological Foundations

ISBN/EAN: 9783741187032

Manufactured in Europe, USA, Canada, Australia, Japa

Cover: Foto ©Thomas Meinert / pixelio.de

Manufactured and distributed by brebook publishing software (www.brebook.com)

H Holman

Education

EDUCATION

AN INTRODUCTION

TO ITS

CIPLES AND THEIR PSYC

FOUNDATIONS

BY

H. HOLMAN

(CANTAB.) FORMERLY SCHOLAR OF GONVI
COLLEGE AND ONE TIME PROFESSOR OF E
AND MASTER OF METHOD AT THE UNIV
COLLEGE OF WALES ABERYSTWYT

LONDON
ISBISTER AND COMPANY LIMITED
15 & 16 TAVISTOCK STREET COVENT GARDEN
1896

PREFACE

My aim throughout this book is to give the beginner a clear and intelligible outline of education, as a science only, and at the same time to suggest, but not to discuss, some of its deeper and more philosophic aspects. I hope, therefore, that it will prove both more and less than an ordinary text-book. More, in that I have attempted to discuss, rather than dogmatise about, the principles of education and their origin ; and less, inasmuch as I have carefully avoided summing up every important point in a formula. Those who are likely to read this book will, I feel sure, prefer to do their own work in their own way.

The general conception of the book is, so far as I am aware, an entirely original one. I am fully conscious of the fact that the attempt to set forth a pure science of education, in the sense in which I believe that it should, and can, be done, can at the present moment prove, at best, but a more or less helpful suggestion towards a more perfect solution of the problem. No one could be more anxious or eager to see such a result than myself. That this book should in any way con- tribute to it would be a great joy and gratification to me. Even should it do so at the cost of its own pretensions, this would, I trust, be only a pleasing regret to the fond author of its being.

My ideal has been a very high one, for I have striven to find a scientific basis for pure educational theory, and to directly and systematically develop therefrom the great educational principles ; thus deriving that body of definite and dependent educational truths which constitutes the science of education.

The evolutionary principle is taken as the unifying element, and my endeavour has been to show that the great educationists, from Plato and Aristotle to Comenius, and from Comenius to Herbart and Spencer, have all been working towards such an organism of knowledge.

How far I have succeeded in so ambitious an attempt I must leave my readers and critics to determine. My original indebtedness to the great writers on education is, of course, incalculable ; but I should like to add that I worked out my general view of the science quite independently, and afterwards appealed to the standard works for authoritative confirmation of my conclusions. The authors to whose writings I have referred are mentioned in the text, and most of the books are included in the list at the end of the volume.

I venture to anticipate what I cannot but consider as captious criticism, by protesting that I am no "arm-chair theorist." I have been a practical teacher for nearly a quarter of a century ; and my experience has included the teaching of infants : of boys and girls in elementary and secondary schools, and in private families : and of men and women at a University, and a University College. I have taught an East End gamin the elements of the three R's, and have coached students for honours examinations at Cambridge and other Universities. And I have had charge of the training of teachers, and a short experience as an inspector of schools.

It is from reflection upon the meaning of such experiences, which at least ought to be instructive and helpful, and from a study of writings on education and of the mental sciences, that I have endeavoured to formulate what seem to me to be the great central truths of a pure science of education.

More directly this book is the outcome of lectures given to students in the Day Training Department of the University College of Wales, Aberystwyth : a Teachers' Holiday Course at the University Extension College, Exeter : and the University Extension Students' Summer Meeting at Oxford. I should be very glad to think that it might be of some slight use to those who heard my lectures, and so prove some apology for many shortcomings in them.

I have endeavoured to observe, as far as I could those educational principles which I have laid down as applying to the writing of text-books; and, as my readers will find, I have not hesitated to avail myself of "the principle of repetition."

Since we, unfortunately, have no convenient word in the English language which signifies both "he" and "she," I have been obliged, reluctantly, to continue the egotism of my sex, and always to speak of "man" and

" he." But I should like it to be clearly understood that "woman" and "she" may be read, in such places, by whoever so wills.

I will only add that, whilst I would not echo the delightfully quaint and ingenuous sentiment of an old writer on education, who thus concludes his preface: "If any man shall oppose, and detract from these my labours; forasmuch, as he shall therein (as I take it) shew himself an enemy to the common good of the present age, and of all posterity (the benefit whereof, as God is my witness, I have intended principally in these my endeavours), I can but be sorry, and pray for him;" I can, on the other hand, most heartily subscribe to him when he says, "I oppose myself to none. Shew my oversight in love, and I will amend it. I prescribe to none: no, not the meanest; but only desire to learn of all the learned, to help the unlearned."

H. H.

Woodford Green, *September* 1895.

CONTENTS

CHAPTER I

CHAPTER II

CHAPTER III

CHAPTER IV

CHAPTER V

CHAPTER VI

CHAPTER VII

CHAPTER VIII

CHAPTER IX

EDUCATION

CHAPTER I

THE NATURE AND SCOPE OF EDUCATION

In beginning the study of any subject it is well to have some clear and accurate general ideas about the kind of things with which we shall have to deal; and why, and how, there has come to be a body of knowledge in connection with such a subject. Since, then, we are about to consider the science of education, we will first ask, and endeavour to answer, the question: "What is the science of education, and what is its origin?"

Origin of Education.—Let us begin by discussing the origin of education. Like all sciences, education has grown out of the knowledge which comes from the everyday experiences of what we call ordinary facts. There were children to be dealt with, and it was necessary that they should learn to do certain things for themselves, both for their own sakes, and for the convenience and comfort of their parents. Also persons of all ages found it profitable to learn from each other how to do certain actions, and would, therefore,

notice, and remember, those ways in which it was easiest
to show, and to learn, how to do these things.

Thus there would come to be traditional methods
of what we now speak of as instruction. But these
would have little, if anything, of a plan or system in
them. That is to say, primitive man would, as a rule,
set about showing a child or adult, how to do a certain
action, or would tell him some piece of information
about a certain object, only when the actual necessity
arose.

But later on in the history of the race, when the life
of a tribe or a nation became more complex ; when it
was no longer possible for a man (or family) to do
everything for himself, in the way of providing all he
needed, *i.e.*, when there arose the practice of one man
making, or providing, one kind of commodity only,
and exchanging this for other things which he desired,
which were produced by other persons, who similarly
confined their efforts to the production of particular
objects—when, in the words of economics, division of
labour had arisen—then it was seen to be a good thing
to have young people constantly assisting at some
one of the different occupations, so that they might
both help the capable workers, and themselves in
time become such, by the aid of information and imitation.

Instruction would thus become much more definite and
connected, but it would still be far from anything like
a clear and comprehensive system.

So far, however, there is little more than a rule-of-
thumb way of showing how certain actions are per-

formed, and of giving information to those who are young, or ignorant of some particular subject. When, however, a written language has been invented, and the stores of practical knowledge are recorded in writing, it becomes easier to get some knowledge by reading than by talking, and it is therefore necessary to teach the young, and others, the meaning of the written signs. Now, this work of teaching the use and meaning of writing to all the children of a family would soon become a heavy burden to the parents, and would seriously interfere with the work by which most of them would obtain their means of living.

Hence would arise those who made it their special work in life to impart as much knowledge as possible to the young people who might be given over to their charge for such a purpose. In this way we arrive at the schoolmaster and the school.

The schoolmaster in primitive times was the priest, for he was the person who had both learning and leisure, and a particular interest in imparting knowledge.

A very interesting illustration of this sort of thing in a primitive race is given in H. R. Schoolcraft's book on "The Indian in his Wigwam." In speaking of dancing as a national institution, he says : "Public opinion is called to pressing objects by a dance, at which addresses are made, and in fact, moral instruction and advice are given to the young, in the course of their being assembled at social feasts and dances."

He also points out that the priests, or medicine men, are the learned persons in these savage tribes. He says: "The priests and prophets have, more than any other class, cultivated their national songs and dances. . . . . . They are generally the composers of the songs, and the leaders in the dance and ceremonies, and it is found that their memories are the best stored, not only with the sacred songs and chants, but also with the traditions and general lore of the tribes." He also mentions that the priests cultivated the art of picture-writing, and used it as a system of mnemonics for their medicine and mystical songs.

The following is his account of an instruction dance: " There is, however, another feast instituted, at certain times during the [winter] season, to which young persons only are invited, or admitted, except the entertainer and his wife, and generally two other aged persons, who preside over the feast and administer its rites. The object of this feast seems to be instruction, to which the young and thoughtless are induced to listen for the anticipated pleasure of the feast.

" Before this feast commences, the entertainer, or some person fluent in speech, whom he has selected for the purpose, gets up and addresses the youth of both sexes on the subject of their course through life. He admonishes them to be attentive and respectful to the aged, and to adhere to their counsels: never to scoff at the decrepit, deformed, or blind: to obey their parents: to fear and love the Great Spirit, who is the giver of life and every good gift. These precepts are dwelt upon at great length, and generally enforced by the examples of a good man and woman and a bad man and woman, and after drawing the latter, it is ever the custom to say : ' You will be like one of these!' At the end of every sentence, the listeners make a general cry of haá. When the advice is finished, an address, or kind of prayer to the Great Spirit is made, in which he is thanked for the food before them, and for the continuance of life. The speaker then says: ' Thus the Great Spirit supplies us with food ; act justly and conduct well, and you will ever be thus bountifully supplied.' The feast then commences, and the elders relax their manner and mix with the rest, but are still careful to preserve order, and a decent, respectful behaviour among the guests."

The element of material reward : the experience and special selection of the speaker : the general responses of the listeners : the regulated formality of the proceedings : the ethical character of the instruction : the appeal to concrete illustrations : the religious observance : and the dignified unbendings of the elders so as to share, whilst they control, the pleasures of the youth, and thus cultivate friendly personal acquaintance with their pupils : are all points full of interest and suggestiveness, and they strikingly correspond, in a broad sense, with some of the features of the school-life of to-day.

The work of the teacher would still be very unsystematic. He would constantly be blindly trying to find out some way of doing what he wished ; and after many failures he might be so fortunate as to hit upon a satisfactory method of bringing about what was desired In the course of time such successes would practically provide the means of securing all the results which he was concerned to obtain. Then such methods would be likely to become traditional. Others who wished to do the same kind of work would learn from him, or copy his methods, and so a more or less complete and effective body of rules would be recognised as best fitted to bring about certain practical results. In this way would be developed the art of teaching, in its most primitive form.

Thus we find that in the earliest civilisation of which we have any historical knowledge, viz., the Babylonian, there was a series of tablets specially designed to teach the young and ignorant. These tablets began with syllabaries or spelling-tablets, which were followed by tablets of phrases, and completed with tablets of general information. In the early history of China a book was written which gave detailed instructions as to what was to be taught to boys and girls during particular years of their lives. In the early days of Hindu civilisation the details of the method of oral teaching became traditional and authoritative, and are described in their sacred books.

The art is, at such a stage, purely empirical, being based entirely upon what practical experience has shown to be the most successful way of acting so as to cause children and others, to acquire knowledge in the easiest, quickest, and most effective way. It is also unorganised, for the rules are not put in such an order, and so related to each other, that they each bring about their proper results in the best form and at the best time : thus providing for, depending upon, and co-operating with each other, in such a way that the final result is as complete and perfect as possible—in a similar way to that in which the parts of a watch are connected with, dependent upon, and co-active with, each other in bringing about a perfect measurement of time. But the art is more or less systematic, for there is some recognised order of doing things, both with regard to the complete series of actions, and also with regard to the details of each particular action, however imperfect or mistaken such order may be.

The art becomes more and more developed and systematic, through the discoveries of intelligent workers as time goes on ; but it will remain for some time in the purely empirical stage. Men know how to bring about certain effects, long before they know exactly why those effects are brought about by their actions. The former sort of knowledge is often the result of happy accidents, but the latter can only come from a thorough investigation into the nature of things, and the discovery of the general laws or principles which underlie their activities and interactivities, *i.e.*, we must find out what are the separate parts of an object, what are the qualities it possesses, what are the various things it can do and be, and how it responds to all kinds of influences which affect it. When we have such a knowledge of any class of objects, and have organised it in the sense already described, we term such a body of knowledge a science.

It will be clear that scientific knowledge can in the first instance only come through actual experience of things, and is therefore very likely to arise in connection with an art. For not only does an art require a more or less systematic practical knowledge of objects, and what it is possible to do with them, but the greater the knowledge of the objects the more can the art be improved and extended. It is only as men discover the right way of acting that they obtain what they want. Now the right way is that way which is most in accord with the nature and powers of the object which is being acted upon.

For example, if we have a piece of clay, a piece of wood, and a piece of iron, each of which we wish to cause to take a certain shape, the more we know of the nature of each the easier will it be to effect our purpose. If we have thoroughly investigated the qualities of each, we shall know that water, steam, and fire will make each of them, respectively, ductile; and that, when they have been subjected to such influences, a sufficient amount of pressure properly applied will cause them to take almost any shape.

Such a truth would force itself upon the most earnest, thoughtful, and original of those who practised the art; and they would do all they could to obtain the deeper and wider knowledge which would give them more power and more opportunity. In the history of education such men as Comenius, Pestalozzi, Froebel, Locke, Rousseau, &c., have done this sort of work. In this way there has come to be a body of knowledge of the nature and powers of the things which we have to do with in education which has been more or less completely organised, and forms the science of education.

When a science has been developed, generally through an art, then the art itself takes its highest form ; for there is no longer the mere groping in the dark, but a clear-sighted knowledge of what powers and influences we can use, and what will be the best way in which to use them so as to make the powers of the object acted upon so to respond as to produce just those results we desire, in their greatest perfection and amount. One of the best illustrations of this will be found in the medical art of to-day as compared with that of even twenty years ago, whilst as compared with that of a hundred years ago the advance is simply marvellous; and this progress is mainly due to the great development of the sciences of physiology, anatomy, biology, chemistry, &c. &c.

The science of education has been the slowest in its development, owing to the slow progress in one of the sciences of mind, viz., psychology. So also the art of teaching has necessarily been tardy in its growth. Now, however, the art is rapidly extending and improving, owing to the great strides which have been taken in the advance of psychology, and also to the general recognition that not only must all arts be based upon scientific truths, but that they are most effectively practised by those who have the proper scientific knowledge. Hence it is that technical education (so-called), technical colleges, scientific training, &c., are so much advocated by earnest and thoughtful people.

The Scope of Education.—Next let us inquire into the scope of education. We must fix upon what things we have to deal with, in what sense, and, as far as is possible,

to what extent.   We say "fix upon," because, although
there are great obvious distinctions in nature, yet the
exact points at which we hold these differences to
begin and end are, after all, entirely in our own choice ;
and, so far as these limits are concerned, purely arbitrary.   There are no absolute divisions in nature,
though there are infinite differences upon which divisions can be based.   We can to a certain extent
include as much or as little as we please in any
division, and can call it by whatever name we choose.
But, once having fixed these limits, we are then bound
by our knowledge of the nature and relations of the
things themselves.

Some account of the different ideas of the scope of
education which have prevailed at different times will
emphasise this point, and will help us more clearly to
define our own position.   It must always be the case
that education is directly related to practical life ; for,
after all, it is our life and well-being which we are
always trying to further in all our actions.

The earliest form and object of education were
naturally the domestic.   The aim was to fit the child
for the family life by such training and telling as would
be sufficient for the purpose.   This would of course
involve very little more than an occasional act of
guidance on the part of the parents, as the instinctive
and imitative power of the child would be sufficient
to enable it to acquire most of the knowledge and
modes of action required in the primitive life of the
race.   As civilisation advanced, the parents would have
to do much more in the way of guidance, and the child

would have to make greater mental efforts, with the result that there would be some increase of the general mental powers.

This domestic education would, however, only be a part of a more general education which would follow it, and for which it would largely prepare, viz., the tribal or national education. The life of the family was only a part of the life of the community. Hence the chief aim would be to fit the individual for taking his part in the collective life; for not only would the general life be dependent upon the power and fitness with which each was able to take part in it, but the individual life would be almost wholly dependent upon the collective life for its existence and general well-being. This is especially true of the primitive tribal life, and is evidenced by the extreme rigour and severity of its forms of government. Thus in ancient Persia, which may be described as a military nation, the youths were taught running, shooting with the bow, javelin-throwing, stone-slinging, riding, hunting, the making of long marches, the foraging for food, farming, digging for roots, and the making of fighting and hunting implements. So they provided for their public and private life, and made each a help to the other. Similarly in ancient China the youths were carefully taught the details of the duties and etiquette of private and public life; and the girls learnt from governesses how to manage all the affairs of the house, how to make silks and garments, and how to behave. The need of such teaching is brought home to us in the present day by the disastrous effects of social strife, and it is recognised that education for citizenship is of the first importance to the welfare of a nation.

The next great general phase of education is what we may call professional education. When division of labour arose, then education would take a more special and individual form. In the form of what we now term apprenticeship, and in ordinary and special schools, there would be a special preparation for special work and interests. Previous to this stage of development in the history of the race, every individual would, roughly, have much the same kind of things to do, as all were workers and fighters, though some were leaders and others followers. This special form of education would apply throughout the tribe or nation. The different trades had their regular apprentices, the priesthood had its novices, the knights had their squires, &c.

It is interesting to notice that, in both ancient Egypt and China, whilst education was literary in its character, success in the schools was the recognised qualification for all official posts. In modern times we find that Pestalozzi's first notion of education was to train children in farm-work.

All that education meant with regard to the foregoing would be the training in doing, and the telling of items of information, and was thus chiefly of the nature of what is known as technical education. There was no scientific knowledge, in the sense in which we understand it, though there was much of the elements of sound philosophy amongst the chosen few; and there could not, therefore, be much in the way of scientific explanation and demonstration in teaching.

So long as life remained comparatively simple and limited, it was easy and economical to make education a part of the ordinary life ; but when life became more and more complex and varied, education became more and more separated from the ordinary life, and was transformed into a definite and more or less systematic preparation for the practical life of the adult.

To this end children were taught something of the arts of reading, writing, and figuring; a good deal about the literature of their own country (in ancient times), or of other countries (in mediæval and modern times), since it was the best source of general information, and of anything approaching special knowledge on individual subjects; and with these they learnt more or less of the arts and athletics of the times. But there was very great variety with regard to details, in different countries and at different times; and also there were very different objects in view, according as the administrative power was religious or secular, local or national, private or public. This stage we may call the period of liberal education, inasmuch as the curriculum was somewhat general, and the aim was more or less free from any special training for a particular vocation. Such a stage of development was reached in the history of ancient Babylonia, Egypt, and China.

At this stage of development education has practically remained up to the present day. For, although individual discoverers, philosophers, and scientists, have recognised and expounded the truths of scientific education, there has been nothing approaching a general recognition of these truths, and much less any endeavour systematically to make use of them in teaching, till within the last few years. Teaching as an art has made many departures, and has accumulated a vast amount of practical wisdom, numerous traditional methods, and great successes. The materials contained in these are just those which are necessary for the forming of a science, but at the same time they present the most serious obstacles to its success, for none are more difficult to convince than those prejudiced by the practical success of traditional usages, and no barrier is more difficult to surmount than a machinery which is the growth of centuries.

There is an immense literature of school text-books, of books on school methods, organisation and government, of writings on the function of schools in relation to religion, the state, social life, &c., and of biographies and histories of men and movements connected with education. These make for the earnest student, a rich mine wherein he may find the true ore from which comes the pure gold of truth; but there is much that is worthless, much that simply hinders, and not a little that is utterly false and misleading, which must first be cleared away.

How then, out of these materials, has come the science of education? We may say, in general terms, that after men have learnt, through what their senses tell them, of the parts, powers and practical value, of certain kinds of things, they go on, by the aid of their higher powers of judgment and knowing, to understand

—in a more or less complete sense—that such things have certain qualities and higher powers, that these qualities and powers depend upon the nature of the things, that they have certain relations to each other and to the whole, that each part has its proper work to do with regard to the whole, and that the whole has certain capacities and relations to other wholes of the same class and of other classes. When the whole of the knowledge of such matters has been written, and the parts of it have been so arranged and related to each other as to show most clearly, completely, and connectedly, what is the meaning and value of it, then we have a science. In other words : science is organised knowledge, or knowledge built up into a self-consistent and dependent whole—in a manner similar to that of the watch as above described.

Men have come to consider education in such a way as this, and as a result there is a science of education, but this is a modern product. It is, like all the sciences, necessarily incomplete. Much remains to be done in the way of correction and progress, and something must always so remain.

Before anything like a science of education was possible, people had to decide exactly what they would mean by the word. No doubt the general opinion was largely formed, as all general ideas must be, by the nature of the practical problem which had to be dealt with. Life has become so many sided, the stores of knowledge on all kinds of subject so vast, the nature of such knowledge so profound, and the daily life of an ordinary person requires such power, readiness, and accuracy of well-informed judgment, that only a strong and capable mind and body can fit a person to take a successful part in modern thought and action. Therefore it is expedient that the mind and body should be developed as rapidly and perfectly as possible, solely with a view to getting the maximum of capacity, ability, and power both in their more passive and more active aspects, *i.e.*, with regard to their ready and right response to whatever affects them, and also in respect to those initiating, organising, and interpreting activities which are peculiar to themselves.

We may say that nowadays the mind of the ordinary man has to do what only the mind of the scholar and sage did a few centuries ago ; just as the office-boy of to-day knows more in the way of pure knowledge than did the ordinary philosopher of the middle ages. In short, the intellectual life of this century is as much more comprehensive, rapid, and productive than that of a hundred years ago, as is the present commercial life more comprehensive, rapid, and productive than that of the past.

In primitive times it was possible for a man to know all that was known, and to do all the different kinds of actions that were done; but now no one man knows even all that is known about any one subject, and certainly cannot do all the different kinds of actions required in some complex arts.

The demands upon both mind and body are vastly more numerous and more difficult now than formerly, and this fact has brought about the necessity for a systematic preparation of the mind for purely mental work, as such, *i.e.*, as entirely separate, so far as is possible, from that which causes it to act. This is illustrated in a case where one is justified in saying: "Your reasoning is quite right, but your facts are all wrong!" Similarly the body needs special training and discipline to. fit it to do its own special work most effectively, and thus be able most efficiently to co-operate with the mind.

This then is the way in which education is now regarded. It is, on its practical side, the systematic training of the mind so as best to fit it to do its own proper work, viz., receiving, responding to, recognising, and reasoning about, all that happens to a human being in the form of experience, in the quickest, completest, easiest, and most effective manner possible. And so also with the body and its proper work. Of course the mind and the body can only be brought to work so through being guided and controlled in their ordinary and necessary workings. So that, if we wish to train a mind to the greatest possible skill and power in acquiring knowledge, we must proceed to give it knowledge of the best kind, and in the best way; but we must give it, primarily at least, solely with the object of so giving·it that the work of the mind in acquiring it makes it (the mind) more powerful and independent in getting further knowledge.

If we desire to get the body to do its own work most perfectly, we must guide and control its actions—through giving the appropriate knowledge—in such a way that it gets the power always to act to its own greatest advantage, and to be of the greatest possible

B

use to the mind in supplying it fully and freely with sensations. That is, there must be a specific and systematic method, based upon sound scientific knowledge, for furthering the development of mind and body. Hence, what the science of education has to do is to organise all the knowledge we have, and can discover, as to the nature and laws of the different kinds of things which are involved in the processes suggested.

That the above fairly represents ordinary well-informed opinion on the subject will be clear if we consider what is, and what is not, accepted as true education. Most persons who have thought about the subject would probably agree in denying that the name education should be applied to : (1) the knowledge-giving and mind-developing effects, whether temporary or permanent, of the casual or invariable and inevitable influences which come from personal example, official and other regulations, physical and social surroundings, &c., for these lack the element of organised purpose and system, and if the name be applied to such then everything is education ; or to (2) mere instruction, as such, *i.e.*, pure information giving or telling, in which there is no attention given to what will be the developing effect it has upon the mind, or even whether it has any at all—or imparts any real knowledge—so that in its worst form we call this kind of work cram ; or to (3) mere manual, physical, technical—*e.g.*, carpentry, military drill, engineering—training, as such, *i.e.*, mere instruction and practice in doing certain acts which constitute the technical system of a craft, a profession, or an art, for if such were education, then the learning to make a boot would be education, and the shoemaker who shows an apprentice how to do his work an educator.

On the other hand, most people would agree that the highest and truest idea of education is expressed by the following : "to call into exercise and perfect the powers of the mind" (Dr. J. Ward); "the harmonious and equable evolution of the human powers, by a method based on the nature of mind" (Stein); and "the development of the physical, intellectual, and moral faculties of man" (Compayré). It will be seen that the central idea in the above is that the securing of mental and physical development is the special object of education. Now development includes many things, viz., growth or mere increase in substance, size, or extent : increase of capacity, or power to contain and hold : increase of power, so that work is more easily done, more is done, and heavier tasks are performed : and increase of ability, or power to do more complex, more profound, and more advanced work.

As we have before said, such a progress can only be secured by guiding, controlling, and forming the mind and body through their ordinary workings, i.e., through the knowledge-receiving activities of the mind, and the body-forming activities of the body. The mind acquires the power to act well (in an explicit and independent sense) by acting well (in an implicit and dependent sense) under disciplinary conditions; and the body comes to acquire greater and more perfect forms of activity through habits of right action prompted and guided by right knowledge.

To put the matter in another way, we can say that

a being is properly and completely developed when all
its parts and organs are full and perfect in all their
details, so that the individual can perform all the
actions proper and possible to it with ease, accuracy,
and power. With regard to the mind this will mean
a fully developed power to acquire and to use knowledge.

Definition of Education.—We may sum up what we
have said by giving as a definition of the science : Education is the science of human development, in so far as
that development is purposely determined by the
systematic imparting of knowledge. This represents
the purely scientific view of education, and we will
proceed to discuss it in some detail.

It may seem that this definition is much wider than
the previous remarks warrant, since in the former we
speak of human development, but in the latter of
mental and physical development. But, as we shall
see later on, everything of importance which happens
in the mind influences the whole man, and whatever of
consequence takes place in any part of the man as a
whole influences the mind. Thus mental and physical
development includes intellectual, moral, æsthetic, and
to a large extent, manual, and other forms of special
sense development.

Therefore from this point of view of development,
education is practically unlimited. But from another
point of view it is very strictly and definitely limited,
and must be if we are to have anything of the nature
of a special science. Only that part of mental development which is brought about by systematically dis-

ciplining the workings of the mind and body is regarded as the result of education proper. There must be a definite aim and effort to secure development by subjecting the mental and physical powers to the best influences, conditions, and methods. In other words, the first and only thought, so far as pure education is concerned, is: by what kind of knowledge, and by what methods of imparting it, is the development, as such—without regard (for the time being) to other results—of the mind best secured.

The consideration of what kind of knowledge is most useful, is both a right and a necessary one, and should always be kept in mind ; but it has in itself nothing to do with true education—as we have defined the term—and must always be subordinate to it.

According to the above, instruction must be clearly marked off from education. No system of instruction is a means of education, in the above sense, unless it is directly, definitely, and solely—at least in so far as all other aims are subordinate—used to further mental development. All kinds of instruction may be, but none need be, agents of true education. Of course all true instruction must, to a greater or lesser degree, further development, but it is not therefore an agent in scientific education, in our sense of the term, any more than an action is a moral action because it cannot but have some of the same elements and effects as a moral action. An action is moral only when it is a part of, and related to, the whole of a moral code which is being purposely conformed with. Thus a man, in the pursuit of unworthy ends, may find it expedient to treat certain persons with leniency and generosity, but such acts are not morally worthy, because they are not prompted by moral considerations, or designed to bring about moral ends, in accord with an accepted moral code. So education proper includes only such instruction as is based upon and designed to quicken and extend the powers of mind, in harmony with the proper order of mental evolution.

This endeavour to obtain the greatest, most complete, and most perfect development, as such, of the mind and body is most likely to be effective if made during the period of the general growth and development of the whole being, viz., up to about the twenty-fifth year. During this period all the powers of mind and body are peculiarly plastic and susceptible to all kinds of influences. The practical necessities of life, however, make it impossible that the whole of this time should be given up to education proper, and generally, it ceases at about the sixteenth year, and then a definite training for practical work is begun. Of course, at any time during life we may submit ourselves to mental training which is wholly designed to produce a facility in, and ability for, some special kind of mental or physical activity, *i.e.*, receive education.

Throughout our future discussions we shall, unless something to the contrary is definitely indicated, regard ourselves as dealing with the period of youth which is ordinarily given up to education, viz., from about the fifth to the eighteenth year. This is an important limitation, because the general condition and powers of the individual differ from those of a later period of life, although they also in many ways resemble them. There is a very great difference as to the relative importance and predominance of certain characteristics at certain periods. A youth is more inquisitive and less restrained, more sensuous and less reflective, more energetic and less cautious, than a man; but both have the same kinds of qualities, though they are differently balanced and developed. This makes no difference of quality, but considerable differences of proportion, in educational principles when applied to the one or the other.

In the adult certain powers and qualities are developed which are not possible to the youth, and powers and qualities which are common to both are, in the adult, developed into new and more complex forms. The adult has duties and responsibilities with regard to the life of the community which the youth has not, and these bring new and powerful influences into action upon him. The duties and responsibilities of the parent, the citizen, the employer, the official, &c., have to be taken into account.

So far, however, as the previous education has been real and effective, it is instruction rather than education which will be required for the adult. If right habits of thought have been formed the mind will be able so to deal with the new conditions as to secure further mental progress and development on the old lines. Indeed the individual should be capable of being his own educator in an explicit, thorough, and scientific sense. This will appear more fully as we go on.

With respect to the time taken up by the stages

through which the idea of education has passed before
it reaches such a state of what we know as pure science,
we may say that such stages have been passed through
by many different peoples at different periods in the
world's history. But, speaking in general terms, there
have been deeper, broader, and more intellectual
elements in each movement through the different
grades as civilisation has advanced, so that the highest
form of the idea of what true education really is, is
to-day more comprehensive and complete than at any
other time. History repeats itself, but with a difference
which is usually more or less of an improvement.
Though the Greeks had a very high and beautiful ideal
in education, they had not anything like the scientific
knowledge to help them which we have. We have all
the best of their knowledge and thought to guide and
assist us, so that whilst we need never fall short of
their ideals—for we can adopt them—we can extend
them in many ways.

It is interesting to notice that the forms which we
have called domestic and professional education still
remain, though they have very different positions in
the life of the individual. Domestic education is now
almost wholly social training, whilst professional
education is simply the technical training which is
subsequent to education proper, and preparatory to the
practical life of the adult. Similarly what has been
called liberal education should now be regarded as the
general instruction in knowledge for which education
proper is a preparation, and which should be obtained at
university and similar institutions, or by private study.

The study of the history of education—a most delightful and helpful branch of our subject—shows us that the old ideas and methods have not wholly disappeared, but have been extended and improved, and put into more effective relation with each other, and with the practical problems of life.

Having set forth in some detail what are the origin and scope of education, we can now the better discuss the things which it has to do with. For, after all, it is our knowledge of the nature and laws of the things, or phenomena (as scientists say), concerned, which makes the science of education.

Now it is the development of a human being, as purposely influenced by the imparting of knowledge, with which we have to do. Hence we must know the nature and laws of the human being, and the nature and principles of knowledge. As we shall see later on, to know the human being fully, is to know the nature and laws of knowledge, for the characteristic of the human being is his rationality or power of knowing. But we must also clearly understand what knowledge is—as something involving conditions and powers external to the individual—how it can be best imparted, and how it acts upon the mind. Above all we must know what are the stages of mental, and physical, development, in what they consist, and at what periods in the life of the individual they should usually occur.

It is not proposed to go into all these points in this book, but to consider the more purely mental side of the problem. To do this we must be well acquainted with the nature and laws of mind, and be able to see the relation between these and the special phenomena with which we are dealing, viz., the phenomena connected with mental development—to which we confine ourselves for the present—as brought about by a purposed and systematic disciplining of the powers of mind by special methods of imparting knowledge.

The knowledge of mind, as such, *i.e.*, as different and separate—so far as we are able to regard it as abstractly separate—from all other things, is in itself a science, viz., psychology. Therefore it is only pyschological principles in new relations which we shall now proceed to consider. So that education is what is often called a derived science. But all sciences are more less derived since they all depend upon one another, and, to a large extent, overlap and fade into each other. When, however, we have a class of things which have special characteristics and relations, there is always the opportunity for a special science, even though most or all of the truths which constitute it are already known as parts of other sciences. A new organism of knowledge is a new science.

We may illustrate this by such instances as medicine, which is based upon the sciences of physiology, anatomy, biology, chemistry, physics, &c.; agriculture, which is derived from chemistry, botany, geology, natural history, &c.; and hygiene, which involves physiology, chemistry, physics, medicine, &c. In each of these sciences there is a special class of facts: in medicine all the phenomena connected with the nature, course, and cure of diseases; in agriculture those involved in obtaining produce from the soil; and in hygiene those which concern the perfecting and maintaining of health, and the prevention of disease. Also in each there is a special organisation of our knowledge about such facts. Such is the case with education, and with practically all sciences of modern origin.

Sciences which are, in the more direct and special sense, derivative must necessarily follow the method of those from which they are mainly composed. Education is based upon what are called the moral sciences, viz., psychology, logic, and ethics, so far as the purely intellectual side of man is concerned, and upon physiology, hygiene, &c., with regard to the physical nature of man. It will therefore follow the method of these sciences, which is the inductive method.

We may illustrate this method by the following example. In the earliest days of education all teaching would be directly connected with the objects about which it was desirable for the pupil to know certain things. Although the amount learnt in this way was small in comparison with what is done at the present time, yet it was considerable when we remember the difference of general mental development between then and now. Also it would appear that such a method of teaching was very effective and easy, for ordinary individuals seem to have acquired very great skill and considerable ability in the common arts of the day, as is shown by their implements of war and peace. This appears to be true up to the time that written language was invented and had become, through the aid of printing, a matter of common knowledge. When some of the finest thoughts and knowledge of

the greatest thinkers of the ancient world had been
expressed in printed books, and there had arisen a
very keen interest in them, and a desire to know
them, as being the best that the world of thought
had to give : then it was considered that to know of
these through the books in which they were expressed,
was to know all that was most valuable in knowledge.

Education then, and therefore, resolved itself into a
system of acquiring skill in all the details of the art
of written language, so that the student should be
able to get every possible point of meaning from the
verbal forms.   This kind of learning was made the
more necessary, and difficult, in such countries as
England, because it happened that all the matter
which was thought to be of value was in the Greek
and Latin languages.   So great was the conviction of
this necessity, that for many centuries practically no
attention was given to the systematic teaching of the
mother-tongue.   Only the teaching of the classical
languages was really attended to.   After a time, however, careful observers and thinkers began to recognise
that the results of such teaching were very far from
satisfactory for practical purposes, and, indeed, had
very little permanent value to the average person.
Montaigne says of the scholars of his time : " For the
most part they neither understand others nor themselves . . . . their memories are full enough, it is true,
but the judgment totally devoid and empty."   They
also noticed that there was an amount of time and
energy devoted to the task out of all proportion to the
meagre results obtained, owing to the difficulty of

getting the learners to take a real interest in their work, and to the fact that few acquired sufficient knowledge to be able to read the classical languages with ease and pleasure. Moreover, there was very little occasion for using any language except the mother-tongue in the ordinary affairs of life. And not only was the matter thus learnt out of relation to the common life, but so far as it contained information about men and things, it related to other times, foreign people, and unknown habits and customs, and what it had to tell about familiar objects and acts was not always the truest or best that was then known about them. So that those who obtained their first knowledge of things through a more or less imperfect translation and understanding of the more or less ambiguous and necessarily imcomplete verbal record of more or less imperfect knowledge, were both very ill-informed and, often, very much misinformed.

These points were carefully observed and compared with the results which followed the imparting of knowledge through dealing directly with, and appealing to common experiences of, real objects. Lessons were conducted on the principle of teaching through objects themselves, and the results were found to be highly satisfactory, and far more sound and lasting than those obtained by teaching through written descriptions only. More and more evidence in favour of this method was given by further experience.

Further observation, comparison, and classification of the details connected with the two methods led to the conclusion that the only real difference between

them was as to whether the knowledge was gained
directly through personal experience and thought, or
indirectly through the interpretation of the experiences and thought of others—with little, if any, help
from personal experience—as recorded in written
language; for in many cases the information, the
learners, the teachers, and the general conditions
were for all practical purposes exactly similar. Hence
this was taken to be the reason for the difference of
the results, and it was laid down as a practical rule:
that knowledge of the thing itself through actual
experiences should come before attempting to get
knowledge of it through written words.

Later on, when the nature of mind and its dependence upon the senses for the material upon which it
acts, were scientifically understood, it was seen that the
above practical rule expressed a principle of mental
development, viz., that the mind proceeds from knowledge which comes through sense given material, to
judgments about its fuller meaning, and then invents
signs, *i.e.*, a language, to express and record such
knowledge. This gives the scientific basis for the
principle: development in knowledge is from the
concrete to the abstract and symbolic. From this
great principle many conclusions as to details in
methods of teaching have been drawn, *e.g.*, as to the
place of kindergarten in the education of very young
children, the need of beginning the study of such
subjects as arithmetic through concretes, and the
general value and necessity of sense-training (manual
instruction, &c.) in various forms. And all such con-

clusions have been found to be sound and beneficial, by the excellent results produced by putting them into practice. In this way still more evidence in support of the original principle has been supplied.

The above shows the progress which comes through the efforts of succeeding generations with regard to the practical consideration of the same subject, and also the very great help which the student of a subject can obtain from the study of the history of the development of the present knowledge of it. Where the products are sound, the processes are likely to be scientific ; and, where these are explicit the science itself stands revealed in more or less fulness, and the elements of scientific method are practically complete.

As M. Compayré remarks : " It is profitable to study even the chimeras and the educational errors of our predecessors. In fact, these are so many marked experiments which contribute to the progress of our methods by warning us of the rocks which we should shun. In truth, for him who has an exact knowledge of the educators of past centuries, the work of constructing a system of education is more than half done." With regard to this, it may be said that unless beginners are prepared for the reading of the history of a science by at least an intelligible grasp of the outlines of what is accepted as the orthodox view, they are likely to be very much confused by the conflict of opinions and practices which a historical sketch inevitably reveals.

Professor Foster Watson says : "The history of education is a necessary part of a teacher's training, so that he can enter intelligibly into the continuity of national educational progress. And, secondly, that, as far as possible, disinterestedly, he may have material for judgment for comparing and judging the different present-day ends and co-ordinating them. Thirdly, that, entering into his work with human ends, he may strengthen his manhood by imbibing something of the nobility of aim and endeavour which has characterised the efforts of educators in all ages and all climes." And Dr. Sully maintains that to obtain a sound method it is necessary to reflect upon the observed facts which the history of educational theory and practice involve.

Function of Education.—To make clearer, if possible, our ideas of what true education really is, we may look at it, for a few moments, from the practical point of view. The progress of the human race depends very much upon each succeeding generation being able, as far as possible, to begin where the immediately preceding one leaves off. Now this could never happen if every individual can get all the experience and knowledge of the present generation only by going through every detail of every part of it for himself.

It is true that he must so obtain some one or more examples of each definitely distinct class of experience and knowledge, or he can never realise the meaning of such. The development and history of the individual is in this respect, and to this extent, the same as that of the race, and that of the race as that of the individual. To give a simple illustration of the above : the uninformed dwellers in tropical regions cannot understand that it is sometimes possible for hundreds of persons to travel upon the surface of a lake in the same way that they do upon the solid ground. If report be true, some travellers have lost their heads through trying to convince uncivilised rulers of tropical countries of such a, to us, simple truth. But when we have experience and knowledge of a frozen lake, it is not very difficult for us to understand the accounts of life in arctic regions, if they are put before us in a clear and connected form, and so as to show the relation of the facts of arctic life to those within our own lives.

In this way one who has never been to a certain country can get to know, from the accounts given by many travellers, more about it than even a person who has spent many years there. Similarly, an individual may, in a few years, learn what has taken all the wisest men in all ages all their lives to discover about certain things. Compare, for example, how a young student of chemistry can in a short time become possessed of the latest knowledge of the nature of the atmosphere, such knowledge being the outcome of the work of the ablest thinkers since the very beginnings of the science. We inherit, possess, enjoy, and add to the knowledge of our forefathers, much in the same way as we add to their material wealth.

Now, in educating an individual, the aim is so to develop his mental powers that he may, to as great an extent as is possible, be in intelligent sympathy with some of the highest forms of intellectual knowledge of the day. To whatever degree this can be accomplished, in so far the individual may be said to begin where the race has left off, and, if he has power and perseverance, he may advance the world of knowledge beyond the

c

stage at which he found it. We might say that in this
way the mental power of the individual is, through
education, multiplied by the product of that of the race.

Every one must know from personal experience how
much the mental character is broadened and deepened
through communication with other and greater minds,
and by becoming acquainted with the habits of thought
and modes of life of many men in many countries. So
striking is the effect of such intercourse in developing a
person's individuality that we often say "it has made
a new man of him." To a greater or less degree this
kind of developing influence can be used in educating.
We can bring the mind into intelligent contact with
some of the best thoughts of the greatest minds through
the study of literature, or, in a more elementary way,
by literary selections for ordinary school reading lessons.
In the same way it is possible to become acquainted
with the habits and customs of other men and other
countries through descriptive geography. The whole
world of men and things can, by sample, be brought to
the knowledge of the youthful learner.

This last is a great and significant truth, of the
highest possible value in education. Its possibility
makes the work of educating the young of the greatest
moment to the individual and the nation. The present
generation can thus fit the coming generation to enter
into, and realise, its highest hopes and desires.

The great world of fact and knowledge, which may be
said really to belong only to the human race as a whole,
can, in a sense, be put into the very little world of the
youthful mental life. In seeking to develop the mind

through geographical teaching, the surface and scenery of the whole world, all the most remarkable customs and habits of all nations, and innumerable facts and phenomena of all kinds, are passed in review before the learner. The physical laboratory reveals to him, as in miniature, some of the great and mighty forces of nature which sustain and rule our universe. The biological laboratory puts before him examples of the laws and conditions of life and vital activity. History unrolls the life and actions of the human race before his eyes. And so by things and words, by samples, types, and series, by observation and reflection, this great universe of ours can be squeezed within the four walls of a small class-room. The importance of this truth for the educator can hardly be over-estimated. It is the very corner-stone of systematic development.

Again, we all know from painful experience that if we are left to ourselves we discover a very little truth, after making very many, and often serious, errors. Much loss of valuable time occurs during the process, and still more in undoing the bad effects of the wrong views of things which have been entertained, and of the material losses which may have resulted. It is very difficult, and often well-nigh impossible, to correct an error of judgment which is the result of the individual's own, but mistaken, mental efforts, and which he believes he has found to be confirmed by experience (misinterpreted). Compare, for example, the superstitious beliefs in signs and omens, which arise from mistaking coincidence for cause, and which still remain even amongst the educated, in the form of palmistry, &c.

Errors must always more or less retard true development, for they generally necessitate going over the same ground again. Hence the educator teaches as much truth through truth as he can, carefully avoiding errors, so as to develop a proper mental method which shall, as far as possible, prevent unnecessary mistakes.

Nature if left to itself—*i.e.*, without the guiding and controlling power of reason—produces good and bad in wild profusion, and destroys more than it preserves. It has been well said that nature cares nothing for the individual, but everything for the race. Only the strongest, which are by no means necessarily the best, survive. It needs the care and cultivation which reason alone can secure to bring about the production of much of the best things. Hence the garden as against the wilderness, the orchard apple as against the wild crab-apple, the civilised man as against the savage (when reason looks after itself), &c. Nature, apart from man, orders the individual to his surroundings: man orders the surroundings to the individual, as much as possible. So arises the need of the educator as an agent in the development of the human being.

Man cannot help being informed and developed by his experiences, but he can help his experiences to educate him more easily, quickly, and completely than they would otherwise do it. This is the function of the educator, and, therefore, we should find in the science of education an account of the nature and laws of all the different kinds of phenomena which are dealt with by the educator.

Above all, there will, very properly, be an earnest

endeavour on the part of the educator to bring the learner into practical relation with his surroundings. This is as necessary from the point of view of advantageous living, as it is inevitable from the point of view of living at all. The individual must so act as to get good, and not harm, from his surroundings, and it is, of course, well that he should so act as to get the greatest good from them. But this gives rise to the choice between the greatest immediate good, and the greatest total good in the long run—that which can be obtained during an average lifetime. This consideration is the practical basis of the claim that the earliest years of life should be given up to pure education—i.e., to preparatory development—rather than to the acquiring of certain particular kinds of power. · It is urged that to give proper attention to the former makes the latter easier to secure, and more effective when obtained. Indeed, to get the former most completely we must employ just the same general material and method as for the latter, leaving out only particular details of material and method. If this reasoning be sound, then the educator ought not to try and teach a boy to be a carpenter, shoemaker, accountant, journalist, &c., but to give him such a general physical and intellectual education as will best develop his powers for taking up any of these occupations with the greatest possible likelihood of success.

Similarly with regard to conduct. However important and desirable it may be to form " a Christian character," " a perfection-seeking character," or " a good citizen," these are matters for the theologian, the teacher of ethics, and the sociologist to deal with, and not for the educator, as such. The educator, as such, has no more to do with including such things in his science, than the astronomer, the geologist, and the zoologist, have to do with incorporating biblical teaching with their subjects. One can be taught to be honest, kind, just, &c., without being brought up as a Christian, Buddhist, or Mahommedan, &c. It is not a question of excluding these matters, but of excluding particular views with regard to them. Religion cannot be excluded from teaching, but religions can : whether they should, is a matter to be decided by the public and private conscience.

What particular end we shall set before the individual, or he shall propose to himself, when well-developed powers have been considered and secured, is a different matter from that of obtaining the greatest possible amount of the highest possible mental and bodily powers. It is not a question as to whether one or the other shall be excluded, but as to which shall predominate during a certain period of life. This question really lies outside the limits of the science of education, but it serves to make more clear what is the exact scope of the science. All pure science must confine itself to knowledge, as knowledge, and has nothing to do, directly, with what use is made of it. Such a distinction is very important in connection with the definition of education previously given.

Ideas of Great Thinkers.—Some thoughts from the great thinkers and educationists of the past will show what has always been the highest conception of education, and will give matter for further andlater reflec-

tion. The following are selected from Dr. Barnard's
" Aphorisms on Education " :

"In education there is a union of watchfulness over
the progress of training, and of a course of discipline
for intellectual and bodily development."—*Plato.*

" The mind should be drilled as much as the body."—
Seneca.

"The object of education is . . . . inward development."—*Seneca.*

" Education is to prepare the mind for instruction,
as men prepare the soil before sowing seed in it."—
Aristotle.

" The general problem of education is to develop
children as imperfect beings into perfect beings. The
better part of man is the reason, which must therefore
be the chief object of education."—*Aristotle.*

"The chief problem of education must be . . . . to
develop harmoniously and naturally the various faculties of the soul, so that the pupil himself shall learn
how to investigate further after truth."—*Heydenreich.*

" The design of education is . . . . the development
of what, though undeveloped, is capable of development,
from dependence to independence."—*Karl Schmidt.*

" Man is not clay, which the educator . . . . can
model at his pleasure, but a plant, having its individual
nature and form, and capable only of being cared for
by him as by a gardener, raised up to its full growth,
and brought to its greatest possible perfection."—
Garve.

" As the body must be strengthened before bodily
labour is commenced, so the mind must have grown

before it may undertake the acquirement of art and of science."—*Edwin Bauer.*

" The essence of education consists in this : that each department of human activity is developed in the individual; none of them isolatedly, but each in a harmonious relation to the others."—*Froebel.*

" Examination of the mental faculties and of their reference to instruction is absolutely necessary."—*Quintilian.*

" Mental training must gradually and progressively begin in the same way in which the mental faculties of the child themselves develop."—*Quintilian.*

" The understanding is not a vessel that needs filling ; it is fuel that needs kindling. It is kindled to truth by the faculty of acquiring knowledge."—*Plutarch.*

" Instruction should begin in early youth, and should proceed gradually, according to the development of the capacities."—*Comenius.*

" Sound education stands before me symbolised by a tree planted near fertilising water. A little seed, which contains the design of the tree, its form and proportion, is placed in the soil. See how it germinates and expands into trunk, branches, leaves, flowers, and fruit ! The whole tree is an uninterrupted chain of organic parts, the plan of which existed in its seed and root. Man is similar to the tree. In the new-born child are hidden those faculties which are to unfold during life."—*Pestalozzi.*

To the above it may be added that Locke, Rousseau, Rabelais, Kant, Fichte, Herbart, and Spencer, all insist that the educating processes must be based upon and conform with mental development. This, of course, is possible only in so far as we know the nature of mind, and the different stages of growth and development through which it passes. That there are great differences between the mind of the infant, the youth, and the adult, whilst the minds of all infants, youths, and adults very largely resemble each other—indeed, that they exactly agree as to their general characteristics, though differing greatly as to details—is both commonly recognised and scientifically established. It is for this reason that a common system of educating has been found possible, and that a science of education has appeared and is being developed.

Educational Ends.—Many different views have been held, and are still held, as to what should be the exact aim, or end, of education. From what has already been said it will be seen that very practical views were taken in ancient times. In modern days opinions such as the following are held: "The perfection of our nature" (J. S. Mill): "Complete living" (Spencer): "The happiness of the individual, and the well-being of the State" ("Cyclopædia of Education"): "A perfect citizen:" "A completely moral man:" &c. But such considerations have to do with applied education, and not with education as a science. The only end of education, as a science, is educational knowledge; just as the only end of astronomy, as a science, is astronomical knowledge.

CHAPTER II

MIND, AND THE GENERAL NATURE OF MENTAL LIFE

IN the physical sciences matter and motion are taken for granted, for no one who is sane would think of denying that such things exist, and indeed, there could be no such sciences unless they do exist, for it is our knowledge about matter and motion that constitutes them. We do not begin by asking " Is there matter and motion ? " but we find that it is impossible to be unaware of the phenomena (appearances) which we call by those names, and therefore we give them the names, and try to answer the questions : " What are they ? " or " What are their parts and qualities ? " " What do they do ? " and " How are they connected with each other, and with things in general ? " So with the mind and its activities ; we begin by being forced to recognise something which is different from all other things, and which we call " the mind," and then we go on to find out all we can about it.

What Mind is.—To put this in quite general terms, we may say that all would agree that by " the mind " we mean our power of knowing, and the sum of our knowledge. Of course this does not express all that is meant, nor is it a strictly scientific definition. It is the work of the science of psychology to show in detail the full meaning of the name. But we must begin with some such unquestionable statement, which no sane person can avoid realising the meaning of, or admitting the truth of, about the kind of things which we are going to study. We are unable, so to say, to start from zero, for, obviously, there is nothing to start with, and nothing to be got out of it.

Man is; and man has the power to perform a certain special mental function which is called reasoning. Such is the nature of this truth, that to question it is to prove it; for if one should say: " We do not know that we have reason" (the power of knowing), he really asserts: "I know (my power of knowing realises) that we do not know that we have reason"—an expression which first shows the use of reason and then denies its existence.

Because of this special power of man we say that men know, think, reason, remember, feel, perceive, believe, doubt, decide, will, &c. &c. It is these facts of ordinary life, known to every one in the same way as we know that there are all kinds of animals, plants, &c., which the psychologist has to analyse and try to understand, so that he may be able to build up a science. Now this kind of knowledge about the mind is gained in a way exactly like that in which the scientific knowledge of geology, botany, &c., is obtained, viz., by the inductive method, which has already been described. Every person is able to examine his mind, more or less thoroughly and effectively according to his training and skill in such work. For example, every one can go over again, in thought, most, if not all, of the important thoughts which he had the previous day, and can examine, analyse, and make further judgments about them, as: "That was a foolish judgment, because it did not take into account such-and-such a thought;" "That judgment was a very clever one, for it managed to give exactly the right weight to such-and-such points in the thoughts with which it dealt;" and so on.

Again, we use the word mind as a verb in such sentences as, "I cannot mind it," meaning "I cannot get my mind to recall and think about something which it experienced before." Also, we use such expressions as "I know that my mind is agitated and excited," "I have a very intense feeling of pain, which is very intermittent but quite regular," &c. Some insane persons know that they are mad on certain points. All these things show that the mind is able to observe itself in much the same way as the eye is able to observe physical things.

Psychology is in method similar to the natural sciences; indeed, it is a natural science, for mind is as much an element of nature as, say, electricity or magnetism. It has some advantages over the other sciences, in that mind is always with us, and we can usually observe, analyse, and reflect upon it whenever we wish.

Let us take for granted now what will be made clearer later on, that any one action of the mind expresses, more or less fully and completely, the whole mind, so that if we can thoroughly understand it, we shall have a sound knowledge of the general nature of mind. In the same way as a single dog resembles all dogs of his kind, and this class is similar in all essential points to all the different kinds of dogs, so that we get to know all dogs through observing and getting to understand individuals of a class, and making this the basis for observing and studying other classes; so, also, by analysing and understanding separate states or acts of mind we come to know the whole mind, and we can take this as a basis for discovering the main characteristics of all minds.

Mind Elements.—We will, therefore, try to analyse separate states, or acts of mind. Suppose that a person is sitting in a room which is in semi-darkness, with eyes wide open, but not looking at or seeing anything in particular, with no special thought occupying the mind, and with no individual sensation occupying the attention. Suddenly a very powerful electric light is turned on from a bull's-eye lantern, and the rays come straight to the eyes. What will be the effect of such a condition of things upon the mind? In the case of a very small child there would be what we call a violent shock to the feelings, probably causing pain, the head would most likely be hurriedly turned, the hands would be held up to cover the eyes, and the child would be aware of the great and striking change, as such, from semi-darkness to intense illumination which had taken place. An adult who should undergo the same kind of experience would have the same kind of mental effects, but after the first few seconds of shock and surprise, he would be aware of more than the mere fact of change from semi-darkness to brilliant light. He would doubtless recognise, in a vague and uncertain way, from which quarter the light came; he would know not only that there was a change, but also have some idea of the general nature of the change; and he would connect this change with the shock which he felt. Also, his action to escape the disturbing effects of the experience might be more deliberate. But both the infant and an adult would, at first, have very hazy notions of anything other than the overwhelming realisation of the fact that they were intensely affected by something.

If we suppose the light to be a mild one, and not too abruptly turned on—all other conditions remaining the same—we should find that the infant would give no evidence of having had a shock, and would simply turn its eyes toward the source of the light, out of curiosity as we say; still, however, the chief effect would be the realisation of the being affected by something. But it would also be vaguely aware of the fact that a change had taken place. With the adult, however, the matter would be very different. The change would probably be sufficient to obtain his attention, he would turn his head toward the source of light, if necessary, and definitely use his eyes and thoughts to discover all he cared to about the light. He would be likely to recognise if it was a light produced by electricity; both from its general character as light, and from the mechanical nature of the lamp, &c., which was used in connection with it. Also, he would distinguish between the centre of illumination and the illuminated track. He would also trace, almost instantaneously, the limits or shape of the illuminated track. And this being aware of what affected him, and how it appeared to him, would be the principal effects of the experience.

We will take one other case for the purpose of illustration. We will suppose that the person who has the experience is one who has just before stolen some thing in the room, and has no idea that any one else is there. The chief effect it will have upon him is to cause him to take very definite, decided, and elaborate action. He will endeavour to hide himself completely from the light, if that be possible, and will do a lot of complex and, possibly, clever things to this end ; or he will at once begin to run away, and make all sorts of dodgings, &c., to escape being caught. Or he might immediately set his mind to work to invent some excuses for being there, and to account for his having the stolen article. He will of course be aware, in a more or less definite way, of the kind of light there is, and he will realise that a change in his surroundings is affecting him—indeed, this will be intensified by his fears ; but the greatest effect will be that of causing him to go through a series of thoughts involving actions.

In the above instances we see that there are always three elements or characteristics in a state of mind : the being more or less affected by our surroundings, especially if there is a violent or striking change in them ; the being aware, to a greater or lesser degree, of the nature of the effect which is produced in us by our being affected, and of what it is that so affects us, *i.e.*, what are the different parts, &c., of it ; and the being led to do something, either with the mind or body, or both, in consequence of being affected, and, in some cases, of being aware of the nature of what affects us. We may sum up these three points by saying that mind is always being acted upon by, and reacting on, other things, or acting on, and being reacted upon, by other things ; and that such states of action of mind can be analysed into three elements or characteristics—feeling, knowing, and willing—the technical names for the above described elements.

The elements of feeling, knowing, and willing are always present in every act of mind, but one or other of them has, as a rule, greater force than the other two. Hence we are able the more easily and clearly to understand how they differ from each other, and what conditions are favourable to each. The fact that they are, after all, only three phases, or characteristics, of one and the same thing, must never be lost sight of.

General Nature of Mind.— Mind is, however, much more than a mere collection of feelings, knowings, and willings, or of the results of its activities. We must begin with a mind ; that is to say, there must be the original germ mind, which has all the general powers that ever belong to it, though in an undeveloped state at first—and at last if conditions are never favourable for developing them. Again, mind is a living organism, for it is always in some condition of systematic, purposeful, and progressive activity. Therefore we must think of it as having a continuous existence, for directly it absolutely and entirely stops, it ceases to be, so far as we know of it scientifically.

All normal minds, like other organisms, have their

progressive stages answering to infancy, youth, maturity, and decay. These stages, in ordinary cases, mean a great deal more than mere growth or increase in size. There is an inevitable increase in skill and power, or development. To what extent this development is carried will depend upon the native quality, so to call it, of the particular mind itself, and upon the kind of nourishment which it receives. The indispensable condition for any and all growth and development is exercise. If any power of mind be not exercised, it will inevitably become weak, and will waste away until finally it may be impossible to make it act at all. On the other hand, any power which is constantly exercised, so long as the exercise is not excessive in force or duration, will necessarily become stronger and more skilful in some direction or other. This law appears to be universally true of living organisms.

But it is not a mere heap, or even a mechanically connected whole dovetailed together, so to say; but each part of it, and every one of its actions, grows out of that which precedes it, and grows into that which follows it. If mind were not thus coherent, our lives would never mean much more to us than the experience of the passing moment.

Further, it is not only coherent, but this coherence is both general and special; for the whole of the life history of the mind is a complete and single whole. And besides this, within this complete whole, all those separate items in the whole which are similar to each other, form themselves into a subordinate coherent whole, thus both increasing their own value for the

D

whole, and helping to bring out the significance of other such subordinate groups, and being helped in like manner by them. Thus mind is systematised ; *i.e.*, is a great system consisting of a number of inter-related systems. If this were not so, very little in the way of higher development would be possible, and our mental life would consist of little more than circles of repeated experiences.

Finally, all parts, acts, elements, items, &c., of mind are so inter-related, inter-dependent, and inter-active, that they always act as a whole, and always make up a unit. So mind is unified—*i.e.*, it is a unit which is a unity. This it is which enables us to always speak of our "self" as being always the same individual. It is necessary to get some idea of the nature of mind, as thus described, now, although it cannot be fully understood till the whole of the outlines of psychology has been intelligently studied, because it may at least serve as a warning against some misleading and very mischievous ideas on the subject.

Again, we may say that all minds are very much like each other with regard to all their general features and facts, though very much unlike as to the details of these. Minds are both infinitely like and infinitely unlike each other; but it is the likeness, and not the unlikeness, which is ordinarily predominant, and is always most important and significant for us. Were this not so, the world would be a chaos, so far as man is concerned in it.

There are many different forms of mental activities besides those already mentioned—*e.g.*, remembering,

imagining, attending, perceiving, &c.; and it is necessary to have a general name for all these. The word
which is commonly used as the name for any and
every form of mental activity is consciousness. Any
activity of the mind is, therefore, called "a form of
consciousness," or "a state of consciousness." We say
that a person is conscious of a thing when his mind
so acts as to take account of it.

Definitions of Psychology and Mind.—Mind may be
studied from several points of view. It may be regarded as a something which has the power of knowing,
and one may try to discover what it is that makes
up this something which has the power to know.
Such a study of mind is a branch of metaphysics. Or
mind may be thought of as that which shows us by its
power of reasoning how all things are related to each
other, and may be studied for the purpose of knowing
how it thus relates, and gives a proper value, to all
the parts and powers of the universe. This view of
mind gives us philosophy. Again, we may look upon
it as a living organism, or a kind of living machinery
whose parts are so made as to work together in the
best way to do a certain kind of work. From this
point of view it will be studied for the purpose of
finding out what causes it to work, what is the exact
detail of its working, and what is the nature of the
products of its work. This it is which constitutes the
science of psychology.

Hence we may define psychology as the science of
states of consciousness. Notice that we do not say
"the science of mind," for this is too wide, since it

would include metaphysics, philosophy, logic, and ethics, all of which have to do with some side of the study of mind. Compare with this the fact that the study of the body includes the sciences of physiology, anatomy, biology, medicine, &c.

As the metaphysician, philosopher, and psychologist, each takes a different standpoint in the study of mind, so each has a different idea—with regard to his particular science only—of what mind is. For the psychologist, mind is the permanent unity of consciousness. This expression will doubtless have some definite meaning after what has already been said, but it can only be fully and clearly grasped after much fuller and deeper study.

How to study Mind.—Some further details about the three great elements, or characteristics, of mind are necessary before we proceed to consider that which most concerns education, as such, viz., the development of the mental life. These will be described as briefly as possible, and the student will be left to do what we may call the laboratory work for himself. He must deliberately and carefully set himself to observe and examine his own states of consciousness; he must, as far as is possible, observe the signs, in the acts and general behaviour of other human beings, which seem to be evidence of their having similar mental experiences to his own; he must ask for information from other persons as to their experiences; and he should endeavour to test his conclusions by simple experiments. For example, after trying to study a subject, when tired, and having observed the mental effects, he should see how far his analysis agrees with subsequent analyses of his experiences, under, as nearly as possible, similar conditions.

This looking into one's own mind is called introspection. If one thinks about it a moment, it will be recognised that to try to observe a state of mind while it is actually going on, introduces a new element into the state of consciousness, and more or less changes the original state. A person cannot try to observe a state of anger, without at the same time becoming less angry and more reasonable, and so, very much altering that which he desires to look into. It is therefore necessary always to allow for this, and to put ourselves through such experiences again, if we can, carefully avoiding any effort to observe them at the time, but trying to recall them, as soon after as we find most effective for the purpose of analysing and studying them.

Sensations and Presentations.—Before noticing the details of feeling, knowing, and willing, it is desirable to say something about the conditions which may be said directly to influence the mind, and which cause the mind to re-act upon such influence. Everything in the physical world is, to a greater or lesser degree, in a state of activity in one form or another. These forms of activity we call molecular (*i.e.*, of the smallest conceivable particles of matter), molar (*i.e.*, of ordinary large or small bodies), electrical, chemical, magnetic, &c., motion or force. Under favourable conditions, the activities thus exercised will affect some one or more of our senses, through the special machinery which they have for receiving and discriminating them, *e.g.*, a coloured object acts upon the eye by means of waves of light, an odorous object acts upon the sense of smell through minute particles which chemically stimulate the delicate membrane in the nose. Our sense organs being thus put into a special condition of activity by these external stimuli, they therefore affect the nervous system, and cause it to act in a particular way. This nervous, or neural, activity, is generally passed on to the brain or spinal cord. Answering to and interpreting for the mind these activities of the body, there is an act of consciousness. Such is the most usual way in which a state of consciousness is brought about.

We cannot say that the consciousness is caused by the bodily activities in the same way that the bodily activities cause each other; neither can we say—in the sense of being able to demonstrate the fact—that consciousness is added to the other activities from some other source. Therefore we must regard them as being equally fundamental though inseparable. Hence we speak of them as being correlated, or of having a kind of parallel dependence upon each other, and not a sequent dependence (one thing following or coming from another as a result of the former having occurred).

If we regard the bodily and the external activities as making up a group by themselves, apart from the act of consciousness, then we speak of such as an impression. If we think of the impression and the accompanying act of consciousness as forming one thing, then we call such a sensation. A sensation, therefore, is the condition of

mind which accompanies a definite activity of either of
the senses. Sensations may be looked upon as the food
of the mind by which it keeps itself alive—*i.e.*, thinking
—and out of which it builds up its knowledge, and
finally produces its highest developments. It has been
well said that nothing is in the mind which was not
first in the senses—or, we may say, in sensations.

But when once thoughts have begun to accumulate
in the mind, through its re-action upon the influences
of impressions, then these thoughts themselves are re-
acted upon, as individuals, by the mind as a whole,
and thus minister to mental growth and development.
Any sensation, or thought, &c., that is in this way
taken account of by the mind is called a presentation.
In other words, a presentation is anything which can
enter into and become a part of the mental life.

Feeling.—Feeling is an element, *i.e.*, it is such that we
can get nothing from it which is other than itself. No
one can ever know what feeling is unless he has
feelings, any more than a man blind from his birth can
know what colour is. It is, therefore, impossible to say
exactly what it is. We can really only say that there
is that which is different from all other things that we
know, and which we have named feeling, and then try
to find some general expression which shall serve to
mark it off as clearly as possible from other elements.
For this purpose we may say that feeling is the expression by mind, for mind, of the value of the fact
that we live and move and have our being : that virtue
has gone out of or come into mind : of the realising of
general or special (local) well-being or ill-being, comfort

or discomfort, pleasure or pain : which must, to a greater or lesser degree, accompany every act of consciousness. It is, so to say, the general tone of a state of consciousness which results from the nature of that which acts upon the mind, and from the nature of the reaction which mind itself makes. Feeling, therefore, is always connected with a presentation, and will largely depend upon, and vary with, the general character of the presentation.

For this reason we speak of various kinds of feelings, which are connected with different classes of presentations. Those feelings which accompany sense presentations are termed sensuous feelings. A change to pleasant coolness from too hot surroundings gives the feeling of being refreshed or invigorated; whilst the change to pleasant warmth from too cold surroundings gives the feeling of being comfortable or being sheltered. Having too little light for any length of time, when in a wakeful condition, gives the feeling of being depressed or being mournful. Experiences make us feel gay, sad, heavy, excited, &c. Sometimes we have feelings of repose, unrest, exhaustion, weariness, strength, weakness, &c. The general body sensations make us feel ill, well, lively, sleepy, &c.

Then there are the feelings which accompany the activities of the mind itself, and which are called intellectual feelings. If we judge that things are going smoothly and satisfactorily we feel content, happy, satisfied, hopeful, &c.: if we judge that matters are progressing badly, we feel discontented, troubled, dissatisfied, &c. When our thoughts flow on easily and harmoniously, we have feelings of mental ease, &c. The frequent repetition of an experience calling for a similar judgment each time gives the feeling of familiarity; and, if it is too often repeated, it may cause the feeling of being bored. Experiences which seem to demand judgments that are at first sight contradictory, unusual, or strange, give the feelings of surprise, contrast, conflict, &c. Presentations which do not seem worth the trouble of judging about at all are accompanied by feelings of triviality, contempt, insipidity, &c. If after some difficulty we are able to solve a mental problem, we get such feelings as those of reconciliation, harmony, success, power, &c.

Besides the above there are the feelings which go with the appreciation of the forms of things, i.e., with regard to their beauty, or otherwise. These are known as the æsthetic feelings. Also, there are those which belong to the appreciation of the value of conduct, i.e., of acts as related to an ideal standard. These are called moral feelings. The former include such feelings as those of harmony or balance of outline and parts, rhythm, discord, &c.; and the latter embrace such as the right, the wrong, the good, the bad, the pure, &c.

Underlying and accompanying all these different kinds of feelings, there is always much or little of the element of pleasure or pain. The former seems to accompany all those states of consciousness in which the stimulus is not too violent or too feeble, unduly prolonged or too abrupt; and where the presentation contains nothing that is in itself harmful to mind, and where the mind itself is in a sound condition. The latter is present when the stimulus is either too violent or too feeble, too prolonged or too abrupt; when the presentation contains something which is in itself harmful to mind; or when the mind itself is in an unsound state.

It is found that by repeating pleasurable or painful sensations of small intensity, at suitable regular intervals, there is an accumulation of the pleasurable or painful effects of the later stimulations. Compare, for example, the fact that prisoners have been driven mad by the agony produced by the constant falling of drops of water upon their heads.

Intensely pleasurable or painful feelings appear to affect the whole brain, so that it becomes generally active, and all parts of the body are stimulated and affected by the state of feeling. Thus a person who has received some very gratifying news may be so intensely glad that nothing short of jumping, singing, shouting, laughing, and dancing, seems able to express his joy.

Emotion.—It often happens that the element of feeling in a state of consciousness is so intense that it may be said practically to monopolise the mental condition at the moment. If, for example, a person has a keen sense of justice, and he is treated with very great injustice, it generally results in his becoming very angry; and so great is the mental conflict, so acute the feeling of disgust, pain, outrage, &c., that he realises little else at the moment but the intensity of his feelings. This is usually accompanied by an overwhelming tendency to do something to remedy or revenge the wrong. But so absorbing are these two factors that there is no power to exercise the judgment properly. The result is a kind of blind energy of action, which is often most disastrous. It is for such reasons that we speak of anger as a short madness.

A good evidence of the effect of such an excess of feeling upon the judgment is the fact that an angry person will often declare that he was never cooler in his life. So, too, love, hatred, &c., so prejudice the judgment, that all kinds of pervertings, ignorings, exaggeratings, and so on, take place in our judgments, without the least desire or intention that they should, indeed often in spite of an effort to prevent them.

Emotion may be defined as an excess of feeling. In every emotion there is a disturbance of the mental balance through an excess of feeling, so that feeling itself and willing are violent and absorbing, whilst knowing (in the form of accurate judging) is always prejudiced and sometimes almost entirely destroyed. Any of the previously mentioned feelings may become emotional in their character. Gaiety may be intensified till it becomes a frenzy of delight, sadness may turn to melancholy, illness to agony, hopefulness to yearning, trouble to despair, surprise to wonder, strangeness to terror, contempt to loathing, success to conceit, beauty to voluptuousness, rhythm to monotony, purity to prudery, &c.

Passion.—In some cases individuals possess or acquire a habitual inclination for, and susceptibility to, certain kinds of emotion. Some persons soon become absorbed in the emotions which music arouses, others are carried away by the beauties of scenery, some become exhilarated by physical activity, &c. When there is such an invariable disposition to an emotional condition, we say that a person has a passion for such-and-such things. Hence we may define passion as a permanent tendency to a particular kind of emotional outbursts. Thus, a man who constantly gets angry is said to have a passionate nature.

Feeling as Egoistic and Altruistic.—A very important feature in the development of feeling—viz., the change of its general character with regard to the object to which it directs the general activity of the individual—must be carefully considered. At the beginning of life, when there is only the power to regulate action to a very limited extent, every feeling seems to demand merely its own satisfaction ; for if it is painful, there is a struggle to get relief, and if it is pleasant, there is an endeavour to prolong it. The healthy little child screams and struggles most lustily when what it likes is taken away from it, or when what it dislikes is given to it, or when what it desires is not given to it.

It is often said that a very young child is most utterly and absolutely selfish. This is true, if we do not understand the word selfish to mean that the child chooses its own good in preference to the good of another. It is unable to make such a choice, for it has neither the knowledge nor the judgment required. But it most decidedly and invariably seeks what seems to it desirable. And this is, at this period, most proper and inevitable, for its feelings practically make up all that it knows, all that can make it act, and therefore all that it has anything to do with, in so far as its own consciousness is concerned. Its life consists chiefly of feelings, often very intense (emotions), and it is necessary that these should be properly attended to. The whole of the individual's life is, so to say, self-centred. There is no reference to anything outside his own conscious experiences, as indeed there cannot be, for nothing of the outside is so known as to lead to such a reference.

Feeling which thus appears only to direct the general activity of the individual to the securing of his own advantage, so as to provide in the most direct way for self-preservation, is said to be egoistic. There is always more or less of this characteristic in every state of feeling—since, after all, feeling is of the self, through the self, and for the self—but it may be mainly passive or active. In its active form it may be either spontaneous, as in early life, or selective, as in later life.

When knowledge of the external world begins to be definite and clear, and when through the feeling of relation the individual recognises that he is but a part of the great world around him, from which he receives so much and to which he gives much, then his feelings take a broader reference, and embrace more than the self-centred interests of his own life. For example, a child learns that its feelings of pleasure are largely due to certain actions of its mother or nurse. Then there is no longer the mere realising of a pleasure and the effort to prolong it, but there is also, in the total feeling, the germ of the element of what adults call the feeling of gratitude towards the mother or nurse. Such a disposition to include other persons and things, as parts of the conditions which make up, or bring about, one of the feelings, extends to more and more objects as time goes on.

Not only do we thus include them as parts of the conditions of our feelings, but there is also in our feelings an element which makes for pleasure, or pain, according as we think that others are well affected, or ill affected, towards us. Thus if a child is scolded whilst being given some toy which it has been crying for, the influence of the former action may over-ride that of the latter, so that the little one is still unhappy though it has obtained what it desired.

Because of this realising of our relation to and dependence on others, it will often be the case that a child will cry if it hears another cry, or sees signs of pain and distress. This is doubtless because the grief of another is disturbing to itself. The consequence of such a state may be either that the child tries to get away from the sound and sight of the distressed one, or it may try to soothe or succour him. In either case there is probably as much, if not more, anxiety to get relief for oneself as for the other. It is most likely that there is the wish to relieve another so as to relieve oneself from being disturbed by him.

The taking more or less account, in this way, of the feelings of another, in so far as they tend to help or hinder our own feelings, is what is ordinarily called sympathy, *i.e.*, the feeling with another. Because it includes feeling for oneself as well as for another, it is classified as ego-altruistic feeling. There is, so to say, a transferring of the consideration of oneself to the thought of what some other must be feeling, through the same or similar conditions, because the condition of such an one may, or does, affect us. The different feelings which come under this class are commonly known as the sentiments.

Love, hatred, jealousy, respect, reverence, admiration, shame, dishonour, &c., are all feelings which involve the taking account of others and their feelings, in relation with our own, and are, therefore, sentiments. Shame, for instance, generally arises from our realising what others feel towards us because of what we have done, so that the thought of their feelings towards us causes us to experience this special kind of feeling.

Now this reference to the feelings of others may go so far as almost to entirely shut out any reference to our own feeling, other than to the feeling of wanting to help another. It sometimes happens that a person who is himself unable to swim is so moved by the appeals for help of one who is drowning, that he will jump into the water, with the idea of rendering assistance. In such an action there is rather an absorbing of oneself in the feelings of another, than the realising of what the experience means for oneself. A feeling, which results in taking no account of oneself in the realising of the feelings of another, is termed altruistic feeling. It is shown in cases of pure disinterestedness, self-sacrifice, self-devotion, heroism, martyrdom, &c.

Knowing.—Knowing is, like feeling, an original and fundamental power of mind. It is also an element.

It is the power by which mind takes account of what happens to it, in the sense that it gives to each of the experiences, their parts and powers, a meaning and value for mind itself, so that it becomes acquainted with its own nature and the nature of the physical world : is aware of the repetition of experiences like to those it has had before : is able rightly to appreciate the relation of the different details of experiences, and that which gives rise to them : and can guide the activities of the body, and of itself, in relation to their surroundings and well-being.　It is the mental realisation of likeness and difference—assimilation and discrimination.

Just as vitality is both the result and the being of a living body, so knowing is both the special result and nature of mind.　Knowing expresses the highest value of mind's activity.　It is the purely mental part involved in an experience, and it remains for mind after the experience as such has passed.

Attention.—It has already been pointed out that mind reacts, according to its own proper nature, upon every influence which acts upon it.　It may also be looked upon as taking action on its own behalf, either in answer to some stimulus or by way of exercising its powers on its surroundings.　These reactions and actions may be regarded as the efforts made by mind itself to take in, and appreciate, whatever it can. Like every other organism, it is always taking in and giving out different kinds of material.　This definite and purposeful working of mind is called attention. That is, attention is the activity of mind as engaged in putting or keeping itself in inter-activity with some influence, so as to take it in and take account of it. It is the minding of experiences. Thus it is that, since mind is always more or less active, knowing is always being increased both in extent and power. From this point of view knowing is the taking in, realising, estimating, retaining, reproducing (in the sense of knowing again), relating, and reasoning about, all that happens to the mind.

Nothing has any permanently valuable effect upon mind which is not attended to. Indeed, in the widest meaning of attention, nothing can enter into the mind at all unless it is attended to. Attention in the mind may be compared with digestion in the body. As in digestion appropriate material is received into the body, submitted to bodily activities, transformed into that which can become a part of the body, and then assimilated, *i.e.*, made an actual part of the body; so attention is the receiving, transforming, and assimilating activity of mind. In the case of attention, however, this kind of activity is not limited to one definite circle of work and result, but the mind is able to attend to the first results and get further and higher products from them, and to carry on this process.

When attention is chiefly given up to the more passive reception of presentations, and the activity is mainly called forth by the force of the external stimulus, it is said to be involuntary; and when it is actively engaged in seeking for and securing presentations, and its activity is initiated by the mind itself, it is termed voluntary. There is, however, always a passive and an active element in attention, and it

E

depends upon which element is predominant as to whether we speak of the attention as involuntary or voluntary.

Pre-adjustment of Attention.—Attention is found to be far more rapid in its workings, and far more full, precise, detailed, and accurate, when the mind has some idea of what is the kind of experience which it will soon be subjected to. The mind, so to say, gets itself ready for the experience, and the details of the presentations are very freely and fully received, and very readily and completely appreciated.

For example, if a person is in a room in which another person, whom he has met only once before and not noticed very particularly, is present, a whole evening might pass without the former recognising the latter, even though he sees him several times. But if he is reminded of the previous meeting, and told that the new acquaintance is present, recognition is likely to take place. Should he especially wish to see him again, or should he be told that his new friend is standing in a particular group of persons, the recognition would probably be immediate.

Similarly, if, without any suggestion of what is coming, one is asked to try to identify, say, something that is momentarily flashed upon a lantern screen, frequent failure will take place. But if one is told that a letter of the alphabet, or some one or more of the number figures from 1 to 30 will appear, then success is more likely. And if there be still further limitation to, say, one or other of the first twelve letters of the alphabet, then it will probably be more or less easy to tell exactly what is shown each time.

This getting ready of mind to receive a certain kind of experience is termed the pre-adjustment of attention. Not only does the mind adapt itself in the best way for receiving what is to come, but it confines its power of attending to the particular matter in hand. There is an absence of any distraction, a concentration of power, and the greatest possible readiness to receive and appreciate. The result of this is that the time taken to recognise the nature of a presentation is sometimes reduced to as little as one-seventh of what would be taken without any pre-adjustment of attention. In this way, therefore, knowing is extended and made more thorough and complete.

Memory.—That the fact of having experiences leads to an increase of knowing is due to the elements of continuity and coherence in mental life. Mind has the native power of being able to bind together, retain, and re-use the results of acts of consciousness. This power to retain, which is called memory, is not a special or separate power, but is a general basis, like attention, of mind and mental life, as such. Without memory and attention, mind, as known to us, could not exist. They are of the very essence of mind as a distinct entity, i.e., that which is known to us as a something different from all other somethings, and having its own proper constituents, qualities, and functions.

Memory, like all the mental powers, has two aspects, an active and a passive. We cannot help remembering, or holding in mind, things that happen to us. There are some events which, as we say, we shall remember to the day of our death. By this we mean that they will constantly recur to us, without our making any effort to bring this about, or even in spite of our trying to prevent it, and we shall think about them, and realise over and over again much of the pleasure or pain that they gave us when they actually happened. This is more than the mere holding in mind, which is the more purely passive side of the matter, and is called reproductive memory, or simple remembering.

Since, however, things are held in the mind, we can use our mental energy for the purpose of bringing them into clear consciousness at any particular time. We sometimes are asked, or set ourselves, to try and recall what took place at a certain time and place, and we are usually able to do this with considerable fulness and accuracy. This is the more active side of memory, and is termed recollection.

Whatever is thus again brought into clear consciousness, either through an involuntary or voluntary activity of memory, is known as a re-presentation. To this power of re-presentation is due, primarily, all the higher developments of reason, as we shall see in our later considerations.

It is probable that anything which has once consciously entered the mind never absolutely and entirely leaves it, although it may not appear again unless some very violent mental disturbance takes place, and we may quite lose the power of recalling it when we wish. This losing of the power to recall an experience is known as obliviscence. A good example of this is seen in the fact that Dr. Livingstone was unable to ask for water by its English name, after a long period of speaking nothing but African languages. The more vivid, forcible, interesting, and frequent an experience is, the less likely is the mental effect to sink into such a state of forgetfulness. Repetition in due amount and at proper intervals is probably the most important agent in securing a full, accurate, and ready memory.

The powers of memory are at their greatest from about the tenth to the twentieth years, and during this time a really wonderful amount of work is done. There is a remarkably rapid growth from birth to about the fourteenth year, after which there is a very gradual but steady decline until the thirty-fifth year, when there sets in a much quicker falling-off.

Sub-consciousness.—In connection with memory we have to deal with a rather remarkable fact in the mental life. Probably most of the stimuli which affect our bodies, through the senses, escape being attended to, and therefore do not enter into clear consciousness at the time; *i.e.*, we are not definitely aware of them at the moment when they are acting upon us. One or two every-day experiences will serve to illustrate this. We say that a cat can see in the dark, by which we mean that a cat's eyes are so much more susceptible to light than ours, that they can see things in a state of light in which we are unable to see them. But the same light stimuli which are acting upon the cat's eyes are affecting our own, although we cannot ordinarily appreciate them. Some men, however, by long and careful practice have become able to see down wells or up into the skies, and can tell what is there, when one who has not so trained himself is unable to do so. So a deaf person learns to know, through the effect on his own face and through putting his fingers on the throat of a speaker, certain spoken sounds. Again when the attention is absorbed, we are, at the time, unaware of influences which would, under ordinary conditions, impress us very forcibly, as when a person who is reading a thrilling narrative is entirely unaware that some one is speaking to him in loud and earnest tones.

Though some stimuli are thus unattended to, and do not enter into clear consciousness at the moment, yet some of them do influence the mind, and the effects of such influence may afterwards appear in the mind as a re-presentation. An experience like the following may occur : a person is anxious to attend a certain concert, but does not know the exact day. Hurrying along the street one day, and engaged in earnestly thinking about some subject of study, he may pass a shop window in which there is a notice about the concert. At the time of passing the window he is quite unaware of the notice. But in about a minute afterwards he stops thinking of the subjects which occupied his thoughts, and then there leaps into his mind the thought: " Why, I saw a notice about the concert in a window which I have just passed ! "

A striking example of sub-conscious mental activity was, not long ago, reported in the newspapers. An uneducated charwoman, a patient in one of the public hospitals, was found to be repeating one of the psalms in the original Hebrew, when she was delirious. Inquiry revealed the fact that she had been employed to look after the room of a Jewish Rabbi, and had constantly heard him repeating this psalm. She could hardly have attended to it in any real sense, yet it had become lodged in her memory in a very complete and consecutive way.

Influences and their mental results (until they appear in clear consciousness as re-presentations) of which we are unaware at the time when they actually occur, make up what is known as sub-consciousness. Mental phenomena of this kind are, we may say, on the margin of consciousness, for they are neither quite in, nor quite out of, the ordinary consciousness. We may regard every activity in the universe which surrounds us as exerting a sub-conscious influence upon us, which may force itself into consciousness in the manner just pointed out, or may enter into clear consciousness through being attended to in the ordinary ways.

Association.—Not only is this growth, or mere increase in quantity, provided for by the original nature of mind but the development of knowing into its higher forms is also provided for by the native capacity of mind. Memory is not only a power, but also a system. Mental effects are retained and reproduced in the mind, but more than this, they are combined in definite and helpful ways. Thus all those elements in our varying experiences which resemble each other in their value and meaning for mind, are grouped together by mind itself, in such a way that each addition serves to bring out more clearly and fully the value and meaning of all that has gone before, whilst its own significance is more completely realised because of what already exists in the mind of a like nature.

Every time a child sees and attends to the presentation of, say, a horse, its previous impressions as to what a horse is like are made more vivid and clear; and the next time it has a similar experience it will receive more from it because of what has gone before. It is in this sense that we speak of seeing more in a picture every time we look at it, of realising new beauties in a sonata on each occasion of hearing it re-played, and of finding more meaning in a book at every fresh reading of it. Such a collecting of mental results into groups we call association, and the above form of it is known as association by similarity.

But not only are the results of experiences associated, because of their similarity, by an original impulse due to the nature of mind; they are also associated because of their occurring in the same act, or immediately following acts, of consciousness, or because they are recalled to mind and thought about at the same time, or immediately following each other.

For example, if one is always aroused in the morning by a rapping on the door, then the idea of getting up will usually be accompanied with the idea of hearing a rapping on a door. Indeed, this may go so far that one may get to think that he ought not to get up, and fail to do so, until a rap is heard. Similarly, with the successive actions of dressing; each of these calls up the next so clearly and inevitably, as a rule, that a person does not stop to think what is next, but, as we say, remembers without thinking.

So also with respect to thoughts which occur together or successively, the recurrence of one is likely to recall the other. The whole of the points of an argument that has been studied, or of a speech that has been heard, can often be recollected if we are able to recall one or two of the most important and central ideas. This kind of association is termed association by contiguity.

Attention and Association.—A little reflection will show that association is very largely dependent upon attention, with regard to there being such-and-such associations at all. Not all like or following experiences are grouped together, but generally only those which have some special force or interest both of which will cause, or be caused by, special attention. The amount of attention which the mind gives will depend upon : its own freshness, fulness (previous knowledge, which enables it to attend effectively) and vigour at the moment : the force, clearness, and interest of the experience : and the general bodily freshness, vigour, and accuracy of response—if there be sensation involved.

Attention and association are the two most essential features of knowing, as such, for attention marks off the points of likeness and difference in every presentation, and association so groups and re-groups such points that the highest possible mental value is obtained from them. This grouping is not only a classification, but, by the aid of thought—the highest form of attention—it is, in its highest form, a constructive arrangement, for it gives new products and powers. We may compare the whole process to the following : a man (mind) is set down before a heap of rags (experiences), which he wishes to make use of (knowing). He first notices (attention) that some of the rags are alike in colour, some in material, and some in both (attention and association). He proceeds to put them into groups according to colour and material (association). He then thinks that they may be used to make new material (higher attention and association). He therefore reduces them to their elements and re-makes them, by delicate machinery, into new and useful forms (highest forms of constructive attention and association).

In short, we may regard attention and association as two features of knowing. Between them they reduce to order and significance the mental life. They crystallise, systematise, and unify the mind, so far as knowing is concerned. Attention is the interpreting power of mind, for it brings out the mental significance of experiences. But it would be impossible for it to do this to every detail, or even to every whole, of experience. It is, therefore, also a selecting activity, choosing to exercise itself upon that which is likely to be most fruitful to the mental life. As we have already seen, it is the adjusting activity which puts mind in the best attitude for receiving and responding to presentations.

Finally, it is, in its highest form, the relating agent, for it finds out how experiences are related to each other by discovering the points of likeness and difference in them, through comparing them ; and as a result of this, a higher unity of meaning is formed. Thus, by giving careful attention to actions which strike us as being most satisfactory in their effects, both with regard to the doer and those whom the actions affect, we notice that they are based upon motives which we hold to be of the most worthy kind, and that they involve a method of dealing with persons and things which is equally admirable. We proceed, therefore, to abstract such elements from the persons and the actions, and build them up into separate units which we name right, virtue, equity, &c. It is the special work of attention to find in the world of experiences, which would otherwise be an infinite chaos, all the units and unities of meaning that it can. Only so can our mental life be rational. Such processes constitute the highest activity of knowing, viz., reasoning. Throughout these processes attention is accompanied and aided by the two forms of association.

Of the highest forms of knowing we shall speak in more detail in later chapters.

Willing.—Willing, like knowing and feeling, is elemental. It may be said to express the activity of mind. Since mind is a living organism, it must do as well as be, and this doing, as such, is the willing. No living thing, nor, in fact, any kind of thing, can ever be wholly passive or wholly active. There is always, and everywhere, action and reaction. It is not sufficient for the mind to be surrounded by countless forms of activity. It must take in some of these in a more or less sympathetic and responsive manner, or the influences might as well not exist at all, so far as the mind is concerned, for they can never exist, in any significant sense, for it.

Mind has native energy which can be stimulated, but cannot be commanded without, so to say, its own consent. It is this consenting or resisting power of mind which is referred to when we speak of willing. Even a little child can, and does—as a teacher too well knows—sometimes decline to receive the most enticing and favourably conditioned influences. This does not mean that the mind can cease to be active, for that would be mental suicide, but that it can be, if it chooses, more or less receptive, and can choose for itself what it will thus attend to.

But the native energy of mind has higher duties than these, for it is able to be predominantly active, *i.e.*, aggressive and initiative. Mind can guide and control its own activity, to a greater or a lesser degree, according to the suggestions of the knowing and feeling powers. But we can never leave out of account what we call the force of circumstance—*i.e.*, the fact of other forms of activity—which must always more or less limit mind-activity and self-control. This is the essence of our idea of a rational being as distinguished from an automaton. The latter can do, and must do, only certain things in a certain way, under certain conditions; whilst the former may do one of many things, in one of many ways, under given conditions; but there is a limit to these alternatives, for the reason mentioned above, and because of the limits and laws of mind's own nature.

We may therefore express in a paraphrase the mean-

ing of the term willing by saying that it refers to the
general self-activity of mind which guides and controls,
to a greater or lesser degree, its particular activities.
Before inquiring more closely into what may be said to
constitute this guiding and controlling self-activity of
mind, it will be helpful to consider the matter from the
point of view of its being predominantly passive or predominantly active in the mental life.

Active and Passive Willing.—Attention is a form of
willing, and when we spoke of attention being sometimes due chiefly to the force and vividness of an impression, we were really referring to a case in which
willing is predominantly passive. When, on the other
hand, we spoke of attention as selecting, adjusting, and
relating, we were concerned with acts of consciousness
in which willing is predominantly active. As we then
pointed out, the selecting, adjusting, and relating attention are forms of knowing which largely depend upon
previous knowings. It is clear, therefore, that the
active and highest form of willing depends mainly
upon knowing. Hence it must be a later development,
since knowing is itself a development. In this higher
form willing is a late development, whilst in its wider
sense of mind's self-activity it is from the very beginning of mind.

Spontaneous or Automatic Willing.—There is an almost
entirely automatic element in every act of willing. If
this were not so, we could not receive the influences
which act upon mind, because it is necessary for us
to be disposed to take them in without, at the very
first, our having a conscious desire to do so. How

could a little child be actively eager to take in an impression of which it has had no previous experience whatever? Of course we are now speaking of that consenting of the mind which is really based upon knowing and feeling.

In one sense the mind of a child is overwhelmingly disposed to receive, since its native energy seizes any and every chance of exercising itself. But this is a sort of working in the dark. In receiving all kinds of influences in such a free-and-easy manner the mind is chiefly passive, for it presents no barrier to their entrance, and simply responds in a very vigorous but more or less indefinite way.

This is also true of an adult under some circumstances. If a person suddenly finds himself in new surroundings, he will often try not to give, at once, any definite meaning to his surroundings, but will simply stand quite still, and allow them to make whatever impression they can upon him first, as in the case of one who, having some rather complicated machinery shown to him, says: "Wait a moment; let me get a general impression of it first;" or, in that of a student who first reads quickly through a chapter to get a general impression of what it is about before seriously thinking about its meaning. So far as such effects depend, from the mental side, upon our allowing ourselves to be acted upon, the willing is said to be automatic, or spontaneous.

This spontaneous or automatic element is the basis of the higher forms, for here as elsewhere we cannot start from nothing: something must happen to begin with, and from this comes more and better. Just as in feeling and knowing the first occasions for such activities are found in the bodily activities, so the first exercise of will, in the above sense, accompanies, follows, and precedes muscular movements. The healthy baby is full of bodily vigour, and kicks and vocalises with great frequency and force. Answering to this there must be those activities of mind which take account of the sensations accompanying them. Before long the little one learns to withdraw its body from anything that is too hot, or too cold; and soon, also, learns to grasp and shake the rattle which it likes to hear. But the last named is a comparatively rare kind of activity when compared with the never-ceasing variety of the more passive kind.

Instinctive Willing.—Actions with a purpose which is clearly known and due to the mind itself also have their origin in something which is a good deal less than that which it later becomes. Man as an organism has a certain system of needs which must be provided for from the very commencement of life, or he will die. It is found that the young of mammals are from the first able to perform the series of actions necessary for obtaining the mother's milk; a young chicken can so nicely adjust its actions as to pick up its food immediately after leaving the egg; birds provide themselves with nests for the breeding season; and so on.

Now such actions as these really involve a system of willings, but they are not known to the individual as being connected with one another and the result. So to say, it is necessary for a conscious being to know

how to do some things before he is able to learn how to
do them. He must be able to will right actions, in the
right order, and at the right time. We do will in such
a way, but we do not know that we are doing so.
Such willing is named instinctive. It is most common
in early life, but is always present in a greater or lesser
degree throughout life.

There is still another feature in the progress of willing from the more purely passive and automatic to the
predominantly active and selective. Human beings are
not only very receptive with regard to the influences
which objects exert upon them, but they also respond
very readily to the impressions which the actions of
individuals make on them. The response is often so
full and forcible that it results in a reproducing of the
actions in their own persons. A little child who is
listening to a story, told with dramatic skill, will frown
when the narrator frowns, smile when he smiles, and
even start backwards if he does so. In like manner,
highly sensitive adults will imitate the actions of others.

It is because of this tendency to carry out the
suggestions which actions convey to the mind that we
find that children copy so closely the peculiarities of
their parents with respect to speech, facial expression,
gait, general body pose, &c. We may call this imitative willing. At first it is mainly automatic, but later
it is entirely due to self-activity. It is the basis of
much, if not all, of our highest constructive thought,
e.g., compare how Brunel got his idea for the Thames
Tunnel from the boring of an insect.

Having examined the more passive elements in willing, we shall be able better to understand what is involved in the higher forms, where self-activity is the chief factor. But let us always bear in mind what is always true, and very important, viz., that there is always a more or less developed germ of the higher forms in the lower, and that the lower are the basis of, and, in however slight a degree, accompany the higher.

Elements of Willing.—Willing, in its higher form, and in the sense in which we always think of it as belonging to a rational being, is made up of several factors, each of which depends upon the more highly developed powers of mind. Let us try to analyse an ordinarily simple case of willing. What is involved in a person's willing to learn swimming? The first thing we should inquire about, with regard to it, would be the reason for such willing. We should take it for granted that there was something which caused the person so to will, that some experience had happened to him, or he had heard of some other person's experience, either in the way of harm or advantage, which led him to judge that it would be well to learn. This we call the motive for the willing. As we have already seen—in the discussion of feeling—a most common and powerful motive is feeling. The fact that we know that a feeling is likely to do us good or harm causes us to consider how we can best obtain the largest amount of good, or the least extent of harm. Also, through the association of one feeling with others, an experience may lead us to think of a series of other feelings, desirable or undesirable, which we may enjoy or escape by a certain course of action.

F

Because particular feelings are so related to the general present and future well-being, or ill-being, of the individual that they command our special attention, we say that they have interest from this point of view. All feelings, as such, have a direct interest for us in that they are desirable or undesirable, and they may have a remote and complex interest for us, inasmuch as they have more or less important bearings on our future conditions, plans, hopes, &c. This element of interest in our feelings is, therefore, a motive for willing, in every case.

Interest may be called the initiating element in willing. If the influences which act upon us do not definitely affect us through arousing in us thoughts and judgments about the definite feelings of pleasure or pain which they involve, or through suggesting the likelihood of such, then we say that they have no interest for us, or that they do not appeal to us. In such cases there will be no motive for willing. But, whenever influences affect us so that there is a strong, and practically irresistible, impulse to attend more or less rigorously, then we say that they have interest for us.

Interests are either original or acquired. The activities which are necessary to the mental and physical life have very great interest for us, inasmuch as any failure in them generally brings acute pain, whilst their proper performance insures a very large amount of pleasure. Thus thinking, knowing, feeling, &c, eating, drinking, working, &c., always have interest for us. And we also find that things connected with the forms and modes of life and thought to which we have become used through frequent and continued experiences, have special interest for us. Just as a healthy body insists upon more or less exercise, which brings about the need and longing for nourishment, so the mind demands exercise, for there is a native curiosity or desire to know, which can only be satisfied by some form of knowledge.

The expectation of pleasure or pain, the desire to bring about some mental or bodily condition to agree with our ideals, the tendency to continue customary actions, the attractiveness of novelty, &c., all serve to arouse and sustain interest, whilst too much sameness (repetition without variation), exhaustive knowledge of a thing or a phase of it, defect of knowledge, slowness of progress, &c., all tend to decrease or destroy the interest in experiences.

In a very broad sense it is true that all motives are feelings, since we cannot have any form of mental experience without its particular kind of feeling, which gives it its special value for us, and which largely decides the nature of the willing. But, in that sometimes we have mental states in which the purely intellectual is very predominant and feeling quite subordinate, and that these mental states lead, as motives, to some form of willing, it is as well to regard knowing as also acting as an impulse.

In most, if not all, cases there would be some amount of thought before any judgment on a particular matter would be reached. A person would probably discuss whether, say, a particular advantage would repay the effort and time taken to obtain it, or whether he could not better occupy his leisure, and so on. There would be a sort of general mental debate about the subject. This is known as deliberation.

The end of this deliberation would be that some one or other of the various alternatives which presented themselves to the mind, would be taken as the best. This is choice. Choice will be according to knowing, for one would certainly choose that which, in one way or another, he thought, from his knowledge of what is involved, would be likely to be for the best.

As a result of the above, the mind takes up a certain general attitude toward a matter. We may describe this by saying that there is a wanting of, or wishing for, something. This is desire. But this does not include the real force that there is in true willing. One might very much desire to be able to swim across the Atlantic, but would not be likely to think of willing it, because it would be held to be impossible. Again, a person dying of thirst in the Sahara would desire above all things to have a drink of water, but, if he were convinced that there was none within thirty miles of him, he would not will to get some.

The next point, therefore, is to feel convinced that a certain course of action will accomplish what is desired. Then the mind is, so to say, seized on, and possessed by, the idea of carrying out such a series of actions, and such is the power and force of a true willing that the body is so influenced by it as to perform the appropriate physical actions. Of course we may will to bring about a purely mental result, in which case further mental actions will follow. This part of willing we call impulse, which is the mentally demanding and striving for that which is desired, and includes the representation of a motor series, *i.e.*, the bringing before the mind the idea of those actions which, we judge, will accomplish what we desire.

Since we cannot usually carry out the actions involved in a willing in a very short time, it is necessary that the mind should maintain its conditions, or renew it at intervals, for some time. The doing of this constitutes resolution.

Habit.—A very important and valuable feature in willing is that, after a sufficient number of repetitions of a similar kind of willing, it at last becomes automatic. We have numerous instances of this in our everyday life. Consider, for example, how slowly, and with what difficulty, one at first learns to will the proper position, force, direction, &c., of a motion in learning to play lawn-tennis, but how, after careful judgment and much practice, all these things are done immediately at the mere suggestion given by the position of a very rapidly moving ball. Those of the higher kinds of willing which have become automatic form what we call habit. We must carefully distinguish this from the spontaneous, or automatic, willing, which is from the beginning of the mental life. Spontaneous willing is primary, or original, automatic willing; whilst habit is secondary, or derived, automatic willing.

Habit is an economising agency in mind. When a series of willings, and the actions which accompany them, have become habitual, then the mental energy which would otherwise have been occupied in giving the necessary attention, judgment, &c., to the matter is set free for elaborating and perfecting the details of the whole, or for occupying itself with something else. Thus, further and higher progress is made easier and more rapid.

Both the lowest and the higher forms of willing are thus automatic. The former is necessary to existence and the latter to a high development. The latter is the result of much thought and experience, but the former precedes, though it also continues to accompany, the higher mental life.

Character and Individuality.—As more and more habits are formed and become permanently established, the whole of the mental life, and therefore the usual modes of thought and action, become coloured by them. Thus the tradesman is inclined to regard everything from the profit-and-loss point of view; the sailor acquires an almost irresistible tendency to be continually going from one part of the world to another; the politician thinks of matters as occasions for speeches or acts of parliament; and so on. Again, we speak of persons as resolute, fickle, moody, lively, musical, autocratic, &c. This tendency always to act with a certain kind of bias we call disposition.

The total effect of the various habits which a person has formed, and of his original dispositions and powers —*i.e.*, the sum of his fixed qualities—makes up his character. Character, therefore, is the name for that general consistency of will and action which arises from the formation of habits, and which gives to a person those special differences of mind and body which mark him off from all others.

Now, character expresses the individuality of a man, and therefore all that is of the highest value in him as a rational being. It is, as we have seen, the outcome of the higher willing, which can only come from the self-activity of the individual mind. That only is counted as belonging to the individuality of a man which comes from his own judgment and feeling. Thus we say of a man who merely copies the habits of another, or is always content to do what some other person suggests or commands, that he has no individuality, no character, no will of his own. Only when the mind has the power of acting for itself in judging about the experiences which it has, and in willing for itself according to these judgments, can it be considered to have reached the higher form of willing, and to have attained to that level of independence of mental activity which is proper to the human being.

The Normal.—All pure science is really ideal, for it always assumes normal beings and conditions. In education we understand a normal being to be one who has all the mental and bodily powers in a thoroughly sound and satisfactory form. By normal conditions we mean such as are exactly suitable in all respects. We never actually meet with such perfection, but average persons and conditions approach more or less closely to it.

The idea is got by idealising what we know of the real. This is then used as a standard of judgment, and is as necessary as helpful. It is only through the ideal that we can fully understand the real.

CHAPTER III

GENERAL PRINCIPLES OF EDUCATION

HAVING passed in review some of the most important truths concerning mind and the mental life, we must now try to set forth what are the kinds of principles and conditions the observance of which will be most likely to bring about, most completely and perfectly, the greatest and best development of the mental powers and activities. Not only must we know what are the kinds of principles and conditions which will do this, but we must obtain as complete a knowledge of their nature as we can. We are not now concerned with the ways in which we should apply such things so as to bring about the development most successfully, these belonging to the study of the methods of education, but only with the nature and kinds of that which we should apply. Knowledge for knowledge's sake is what we now seek. The question of how we ought to use such knowledge for practical purposes is an entirely distinct matter. We are still in the region of pure science, or of organised knowledge, as knowledge.

From what we know of the nature of mind, and of the influences which act upon it, and also from the teachings of experience, we find out what are the best influences and conditions for mental development. To find out the nature of mind is, to a large extent, to find out what is best suited to its well-being, just as to know the nature of a plant is to understand what it takes into its system, how it takes it, by what means and in what ways it uses it, and what kinds and conditions of things are best for it.

Growth and Development.—Before dealing in detail with the means of securing development, we must distinguish clearly between development and growth. By growth we mean mere increase of size, or extent, or volume and strength of the organism; whilst by development is to be understood an increase in the ease, quickness, accuracy, and completeness of the organic activities, and an increased ability to do more difficult, more profound, and more complex actions. Both the mind and the body of an idiot increase in extent and power, but they do very little in the way of taking on new and higher forms of activities. There is a good deal of growth, but very little development. Growth involves very little more than the increase of strength which ordinarily accompanies the increase of size, but development includes the increase of skill which usually comes with the increase of strength.

The Principle of Stimulation.—Inasmuch as mind is a living organism, its very being depends upon, and is expressed by, its activity. Now this activity not only requires something to act upon, but it must be acted upon by something. Hence there must be stimulation as a means to and condition of mental development.

But too much or too strong stimulation would be destructive, and too little or too weak would tend to mere growth. There must, therefore, if possible, be a properly proportioned amount and force of stimulation. And not only must there be such an appropriate quality and intensity of stimulus, but these must vary with the gradually increasing power of mind.

These points are so fully illustrated by our ordinary experience, that it will not be necessary to do more than refer to the usual mental work of childhood, youth, and manhood, the evils of unsuitable work, and the doing too much or too little, as showing their importance.

The kinds of stimuli which must be used will, of course, be all those which influence any part of the mental life. Of these we have already said something, and shall have more to say in our later discussions. Broadly speaking, they are the sense activities, and the mental activities themselves.

As we have previously remarked, nature does very little, if anything, in the way of carefully providing for the needs of each individual in such a way as to procure its most perfect development. Neither could the very young, inexperienced, and immature individual provide for its own needs to the greatest advantage, even if it had the necessary knowledge. Stimulation there would undoubtedly be, but it would more often destroy by its excess, or defect, than preserve and perfect by its special fitness. Hence the need of the educator who shall influence the influences so as to further, to the greatest possible extent, the well-being of the person concerned. The educator is, therefore, an indirect stimulus to proper mental development, through his regulating influence upon the direct stimuli. He does not supplant natural influences, but supplements them, and makes them most effective by guiding and controlling them.

Another point which needs very careful consideration is, how long the mind can go on working consecutively, so as to do its best work during such time; and thus, in the long run, do the greatest total amount of its best work. Too little or too much energy in mental work, if continued too long or not long enough, is generally wasteful, and likely to be harmful. Just as in the industrial world it is being shown that more and better work is, as a rule, done by those artizans who work eight hours a day, than by those who work twelve, fourteen, or more hours a day; so we find that thinkers who work too many hours a day accomplish neither so much or so satisfactory work as those who spend less time at their tasks. Stimulation must, therefore, be regulated accordingly.

There is in mental work what the political economist calls the law of increasing returns, and the law of diminishing returns. The more we increase the mental energy, up to the point of its greatest working power, the greater and better will be the results which are obtained. The mind can go on working at such a rate for a certain length of time only. So far, we have the law of increasing returns, in answer to the supplying of increasing stimulation, up to what we may call the law of continued greatest returns, which depends upon the maintaining of the proper stimulus.

After this there comes the falling-off. Although the same amount of stimulus is applied, the results continue to decrease. This is because mind is like other living organisms in requiring time to replace the loss of energy which takes place in its ordinary working. As in all organisms, so in mind, there is a rhythmic rise and fall of energy, under ordinary conditions. Therefore as the supply of mental energy is gradually exhausted, no amount of stimulation can cause the mind to maintain its previous efficiency. A very intense stimulation may cause spasmodic bursts of energy, but this will only the more quickly and severely exhaust the mind. This is the law of diminishing returns. At first the decline is very slight and slow, but after a time it becomes very considerable and rapid, and if allowed to go on, becomes destructive to the extent of causing death. It is important to observe that, after a certain amount of exhaustion, the mind seems to lose the power of easily recuperating itself, and there arises a state of general mental debility, which is accompanied by a feeling of lassitude and depression, and which may develop into something more serious.

A good example of these laws is seen in agriculture, in connection with which they were first expounded. The soil is always being acted upon by all kinds of chemical, physical, and other forms of activities, and cannot but produce something or other. But if we want the most and best products from it, we must cultivate it, *i.e.*, supplement, guide, and control the forces and influences which act upon it. Cultivation has, however, its limits, because the productiveness of the soil has its bounds, and depends upon conditions which the proper amount of cultivation alone can make most effective, but as to which too much help becomes a hindrance. Thus the more we stimulate the soil by draining, digging, ploughing, manuring, weeding, &c., up to a certain point, the larger and better are the crops. This greatest productiveness could not, however, go on indefinitely. Even though we had eternal summer, there could not be crop immediately succeeding crop, and all of the best. The land must lie fallow occasionally, as well as have change in the crops it produces. Thus the land illustrates the laws of increasing returns and continued greatest returns.

The soil also shows how the law of diminishing returns applies. If crops were made immediately to succeed each other for an indefinite time, they would, gradually at first and more rapidly later, decrease in quantity and quality. Too much draining makes the land too dry; too much digging or ploughing would prevent the proper atmospheric influences working successfully, or turn up the worst part of the soil; too much manuring would cause a too rapid growth or prevent it altogether, &c.; and thus each and all would diminish the value of the final results.

There appears to have been no systematic attempt to work out the quantitative side of these laws with regard to mental work. That is, we have few reliable statistics, gained by scientific observation and experiment, which show what may be regarded as the average amount of mental work, at as nearly as possible the highest rate of energy, which the child, the youth, and the adult, can perform, so as to get the best possible results. Nor are there any authoritative opinions as to what amount constitutes harmful overworking, or underworking, of the mind. It is a matter for serious regret and reproach, that the highest and most valuable form of human energy has not received the attention which has long ago been given to mechanical and animal activity. The importance of such knowledge in guiding our efforts to develop the mind to the greatest advantage is obvious.

In all probability school children are still being very much overworked with regard to the mind-effort required from them during the daily school hours. Much more play and manual recreation, and less continuous mental work, would be likely to give considerably better mental results. Mr. Edwin Chadwick, who has given special attention to the subject, holds that children from seven to eight years of age should not work more than from two and a half to three hours a day; those from eight to ten years old, from three to three and a half hours; from ten to twelve, about four hours; from twelve to fifteen, between five and six hours; and from fifteen to eighteen, never more than eight hours, allowing intervals for recreation out of these times. He maintains that children who only attend as "half-timers" make as good progress as those who attend full time, in elementary schools.

The Principle of Nourishment.—That which most

stimulates and supports activity in an organism is nourishment. From one point of view, we may look upon all organic activity as being, for the most part, the expression of the need for, and the using of, nourishment. That which lives is constantly seeking and assimilating food. This kind of action is always going on, but the energy and power thus obtained are used for higher purposes than the mere continuation of the processes involved. A plant, for example, develops graces of form and colour which, so far as is known, have no direct bearing on their preservation or reproduction; and a man, in all points in which he is more and better than an intelligent animal, has gone beyond the bare requirements of providing only for the continuation of life. In considering what is required in the way of nourishment, we must, therefore, bear in mind the highest forms of mental life which are known to us.

The proper nourishment for the mind is such influences as will occasion and promote the best conditions of feeling, knowing, and willing. As we have already pointed out, these ends will be best secured by those influences which give the highest forms of knowledge.

It is clear that in bringing influences to bear upon the mind for the purpose of obtaining the most desirable states of feeling, we must, as a rule, take the bodily conditions into account very largely. For the present, however, we will take all the details of the bodily activities for granted, and only consider the mental element which accompanies them. It is, of course, desirable ordinarily to have neither an excessive nor a defective amount of feeling. But this must not be allowed to become a monotonous uniformity. And it is not likely to be so even if we try our hardest to make it, for the conditions by which we are surrounded change too frequently, and with too great variety of quantity and quality, to allow of it. We need not, therefore, except as to the artificial conditions which we ourselves set up, trouble ourselves about preventing sameness, but rather take steps to regulate the variety.

This consideration may be said to demand and justify the schoolroom and the study, with their limitations and rules. In the open air we are affected by too many and often too forcible influences. Strong and very varied feelings very rapidly succeed each other, so that their value, as feelings, is not fully appreciated, and there is little of connected and systematic relating of them to each other and the rest of the mental life. It is as though one should try to get the greatest amount of the pleasures of taste from wines by sipping as many different kinds as possible in a given time. Epicures have learnt that the rather slow and continued sipping of one kind at a time gives the greatest pleasure, through a kind of accumulation of effect.

So in the school the conditions which arouse feelings are limited, connected, and controlled. Both intense excitement and apathy are regarded as evils, and guarded against. But quiet and fervour are both used as occasional helps.

Feelings thus regulated may be regarded as being the most assimilative, and, therefore, the most nutritive. We can hardly regard any feeling as being wholly non-assimilative, for its very existence shows that it has entered into mind. Still, some feelings cause a state of mental conflict, and, so far, may be classed as non-assimilative.

The Principle of Pleasure.—As has been pointed out, feelings which are in harmony with the general mental condition (if normal) produce a state of pleasure. We may conclude, therefore, that pleasure is, as a rule, most helpful to the good development of mind, and that pain, as a rule, is a barrier and hindrance. So that it is necessary for us to give mental nourishment in such a way that it shall cause as much pleasure and as little pain as possible.

It should be noticed that here we are dealing with what applies to the nourishment itself, and not to the means which it may be necessary to employ in order to get the individual to receive it. The latter subject, which involves the question of rewards and punishments, we shall deal with later on.

At the same time, we must recognise that sometimes it will happen that the mental food which is, in the long run, the best for us is not always of a very attractive or even unobjectionable kind. Just as in the bodily food we now and again have to include medicinal supplements, correctives, &c., which are by no means pleasant, so also mental experiences have at times to be profitable rather than pleasurable. But such inevitable necessities are frequent enough, and

G

the ordinary difficulties, dangers, and drawbacks attending pleasurable experiences are real enough, to render it unnecessary that we should try to make mental nourishment difficult or distasteful to the receiver, simply for the sake of trying to avoid having things too easy for him. The endeavour to get the highest and best progress and development at a reasonably rapid rate, can never allow the individual to have a too easy or too pleasurable time.

If we desire, and strive for, pleasure for its own sake, either in the form of excessive indulgence in those feelings which we most enjoy, or by trying to avoid all the mental efforts we can (intellectual sloth)—a state of mental over-feeding, or under-exercising—we shall have too much pleasure, and shall be mentally degraded thereby. But this is fatal to progress and development of the best kind. So if we gain development during steady persistence—either willingly or unwillingly—in receiving more painful than pleasurable feelings, it will result in a one-sided, limited, and often mischievous mental character.

It is important to recognise that we can bring about an almost infinite variety of feelings in an individual, because we can affect the body in such ways that consciousness can hardly fail to take account of them, though remarkable cases occur in which a person, by sheer force of willing, can remain for some time more or less insensible to physical influences. Both phases are strikingly illustrated in a hypnotised person, in whom, it is held, a concentrated energy of willing has been produced. Such an one can be made to become practically insensible to the ordinary painful effects of having a long pin thrust into him, or can be caused to suffer the most acute and agonising pains from a suggested toothache. This is of course a very extreme example, but, to a much less extent, similar results occur when the attention is directed either positively or negatively towards certain physical stimuli.

At the same time, it must be observed that we do not communicate the feelings, but bring about the conditions which are ordinarily accompanied by them. For, unless the consciousness is receptively and responsively active, there is very little, if any, feeling.

As in feeling so in knowing, we cannot give the individual knowledge, as such, directly; we can only supply the conditions which are most likely to result in his acquiring knowledge. And it is perhaps a good deal more true of knowing than of feeling that the individual can resist, more easily and successfully, the endeavour to influence him; though it is also the case that there are some conditions in which it is practically impossible for him to do so. The fact of having a feeling involves the receiving of some knowledge—the knowledge of a change, of the general effect of this change on the mind, of the general nature of the object or objects, if any, involved, &c.

But, however much one may try to reject a certain kind of knowledge, or the receiving of knowledge under certain conditions, there must always be the taking in of knowledge so long as the consciousness is alive. The mind begins to die in commencing to cease to know. The vital activity of mind expresses itself in the effort to take in mental nurture, *i.e.*, knowledge.   There is an inevitable appetitive activity in mind, which we may term its native curiosity.   However difficult it may be to direct a mind so as to lead it to get the kind of knowledge we may desire it to have, and to get it in a certain way, it is impossible to prevent its obtaining some sort of knowledge, in some way or other.

The principle of pleasure has, of course, by far the most to do with the development of feeling, but, as supplying the best condition of the mind for acquiring knowledge, it has to do with the development of knowing also.   The will is probably least affected by it directly, but it is at least freed from being distracted when otherwise concentrated.

The Principle of Inter-relation and Inter-dependence.— One of the most essential points in education is the determining what relation of subjects is the most effective.   Since we have to form a mind whose great general characteristics are continuity, coherence, system, and unity, it is clearly of great consequence so to arrange the influencing conditions as to harmonise with these characteristics.   In short, we must strive to obtain continuity, coherence, system, and unity amongst the knowledge agencies, for only so can we helpfully influence the mental development in these respects.

The problem then is : what subjects ought to be secured for the purpose of producing the most and best knowledge in the growing mind ; in what way, and in what order, should these subjects be allowed to influence the mind; and at what periods in the mental life ought the different subjects to be made use of? The first two points we will briefly consider now, leaving the fuller treatment of them, and a discussion of the third point, for later chapters.

To get a really well-developed mind, we must, as far as possible, exercise and nourish every one of its powers. To do this it is necessary to bring every kind of influence to bear upon it. It is obviously impossible to do this in detail, but it is possible to subject the mind to some of the most important, common, and representative kinds of influences, and thus bring about a more or less general and harmonious mental development.

As we have already pointed out, we can, so to say, bring the world and its activities, in miniature, before a child in the schoolroom. We can give it knowledge of æsthetic phenomena by pictures, vocal and instrumental music, sculpture, &c.; of the human and ethical through literature, history, and the moral sciences, &c.; of the animal and material through the physical sciences and the manual arts, &c.; and so on. School laboratories, models, &c., extend, by type, the ordinary personal experience of the individual in such a way that all knowledge has a solid basis in the real; whilst diagrams, pictures, and school-books supply information which can be interpreted according to the knowledge gained by such experiences, and which, therefore, has rational reality and real significance.

The family and the school supply the experiences which can be made to convey knowledge of the social world. Thus the purely intellectual, the ethical, the social, and the physical powers of man can all be developed.

The ideal should be : to get such conditions to act upon the individual, and for him to act upon, that the mind may become all that is possible to it, in the highest form and to the greatest extent. The mind should be so exercised and developed by the conditions which surround it, that it becomes able to take up an intelligent attitude towards all forms of knowledge. It should acquire such powers and methods that it will seldom, if ever, be entirely at a loss in dealing with new combinations of experience and fresh forms of knowledge. Only the difficulties of detail will, as a rule, trouble such a mind, except in the region of discovery. We must, in short, make use of all the different kinds of knowledge influences as conditions for securing the greatest and best mental development.

In considering the way and order in which such conditions should be made to influence the mind, we have to deal with the manner and sequence in which we should use the different kinds of knowledge influences of which we know, i.e., the method, order, and relation we should employ in trying to get the individual to understand the knowledge which belongs to the different sciences and arts.

Attention has been drawn to the fact that all new presentations depend very much for their meaning and fulness upon what is already in the mind, of a like nature, through the accumulation and interpretative effects of re-presentations. Thus new knowledge depends upon and is largely formed by the old. Care must, therefore, be taken to connect, as far as possible, one subject of knowledge with another, in the sense of making the one grow out of and develop from the other. Thus all subjects of knowledge should be inter-related, and dependently developed. For so the greatest amount of help is given to the developing mind, because its own nature is thus most nearly conformed with. The working out of a system of knowledge subjects, related with a view to secure their greatest values as developing influences, is known as the theory of cor-relation, co-ordination, concentration, or, as we have termed it, inter-relation and inter-dependence of sub-jects of instruction.

The first point to be decided upon, with regard to such an inter-relation and inter-dependence of subjects, is : what is to be the knowledge subject whose develop-ing influences are the very first to be used. A little thought will convince us of the supreme importance of deciding rightly as to this. Also, from the subject which is selected for this purpose we must develop the succeeding subjects, and this development should be as easy, simple, and direct, as we can possibly make it. Comenius says: "All the studies must form one whole; must proceed from one root."

Let us consider what principle should guide us in making the selection. Whatever form of influence first affects the individual, and is most freely responded to by him, is clearly the one which has the greatest fitness in many ways. And if we find that the history of the race goes to show that what is true of the infant of to-day has been true in a larger sense of the infant race, and that out of the results of such influences have come all the various knowledge subjects, then we may be satisfied that we have found the right subject to begin with.

There can be no doubt that the first kind of influences by which an individual is affected, and to which he most freely responds, is that exercised by all kinds of physical objects and forces. As a result of this he soon becomes able to recognise one object from another, and to know something about the concrete nature of objects, *e.g.*, that an object is hard or soft, cold or warm, sweet or bitter, &c. And it is from this kind of knowledge that the more detailed and more scientific forms are developed. It is from objects that we get our concrete notions of form, colour, number, &c., and it is in relation to them and their activities that language is first used. We transfer the names of bodily activities to mental ones when we say that we see (the eye) the truth of an idea; we grasp (the hand) the meaning of a remark; we overthrow (physical act) an argument, &c.

Now, this knowledge of objects gained through our experiences of their parts and powers constitutes, in its higher forms, the various physical sciences. It thus appears that scientific knowledge, in its simplest and most primitive form, is the proper subject to be used as the very first kind of knowledge-influences for mental development. It will consist of a simple and direct arrangement of knowledge about those common objects which surround the individual, in such a way as to lead most easily and directly to other forms of knowledge.

For example : at first the child, during the time that it is unable to talk, is merely brought under the more or less systematised (household arrangements and nursery toys) influences of objects. When it is able to speak, language symbols are used to help to make clearer, fuller, and more lasting the effects of these influences. Number names, object names, action names, quality names, &c., are used as freely and fully as possible. All this, however, in the form of talk only. So is laid the foundations of arithmetic and the mathematical sciences, of reading, grammar, and literature, and of the physical sciences. Later on, as the bodily powers develop, the child is taught how to make its own records, through imitative outlines and forms, and written language symbols, and in this way it may be said to be introduced to drawing, painting, sculpture, and history. The experiences connected with the local surroundings lead on to geography and natural history, botany, &c., in their wider and deeper meaning.

Froebel seems to have realised this truth, and sought to put it into practice in his kindergarten. The most valuable element of the kindergarten system is the systematic way in which it aims at developing the higher forms of knowledge from the ordinary playful activity of the child, and its inevitable observations and impressions of the common objects by which it is surrounded. Objects and actions are arranged and grouped in a connected and significant manner. Froebel insisted that life always forms a complete whole, and that the idea of education as a mere collection of subjects of instruction was a false and mischievous one. There must be unity throughout the process.

The kindergarten gifts satisfy the child's desire for playful activity, and also serve as knowledge influences as to form, colour, material, number, and names: as developing agents as to powers of observation in seeing likeness and difference : as simple thought exercises in judging how to arrange sticks, wires, strips of paper, &c., to imitate the form, size, pattern, &c., of given models, and in creating original variations on these : and as opportunities for simple information as to the qualities and powers of common things.

This is the idea of organic growth, as against that of mere accumulation of parts: the idea of the development of the inner according to its own proper nature, through the assimilation of the outer, according to its proper nature, as against that of merely plastering the external on to the internal : the idea of true development as against that of mere accumulation.

The above will serve to indicate the nature of the principle involved in the correlation of studies. To discuss the subject at length would require a separate book. There has been a considerable amount written about the matter, and much of the best work of recent writers has dealt with it, some of them having worked out a detailed syllabus of work to illustrate, and practically realise, the right application of the principle.

Reflection will show that such a system also accords with the progressive activity of attention, since it is a continual increasing of the breadth and depth of mental assimilation and discrimination of the elements of experience, and the resulting classifications into new and more significant groups. Moreover, an orderly and constructive arrangement of knowledge influences will not only aid, but will practically compel, an orderly and constructive mental association of knowledge. In brief, system and unity in the product are most likely to be produced by system and unity in the processes.

Educational Values.—Some aspects of the value of the mental nourishment with which we seek to develop the mind, demand further notice. Some knowledge subjects are specially rich in mental nourishment, or are particularly well suited for exercising mind in a gymnastic sense; some have a sort of tonic effect upon the whole mind; and others are most valuable as helps in practical life. These are generally spoken of as educational values. According to our definition of education, we cannot regard the last of them as being strictly educational, except in so far as they provide stimulative interest.

As a matter of fact, there is no knowledge subject which has not got more or less of all the educational values, but just as some bodily foods contain a greater amount of flesh-forming and heat-giving properties than others, whilst all contain more or less of each, so some knowledge subjects possess a high degree of one kind of educational value, and very little of the others. We must, therefore, make a proper selection of subjects according as we desire to produce certain effects upon the mind.

The principle of inter-relation and inter-dependence is primarily and chiefly concerned with the development of knowing; but its organising effect is general, and, therefore, it greatly assists in the developing of feeling and willing.

Discipline Value.—We have taken development as the end of true education, and, therefore, the chief element of value for us in any knowledge subject is its power of exercising, calling forth, and enriching the powers of the mind. As an athlete who desires to get the greatest possible results from his bodily powers systematically arranges his diet and his exercise, so that both are in harmony with the nature, and proportionate to the strength, of his body; so we must nourish and exercise the mind on a definite and sound system. To submit the mental life to such conditions is to discipline it, and those knowledge subjects which seem to us to be best suited for this purpose are said to have great disciplinary value.

If it be true that nothing is in the intellect which was not first in the senses, and, therefore, that all our highest forms of knowledge are based ultimately upon sense-given material, it is clear that the most nourishing knowledge subjects will be those which deal with our concrete experiences, such as the physical sciences. But it must not be forgotten that mind feeds upon itself, so to say, by getting higher values out of the thoughts that come more directly from experiences. The proper feeding of the mind upon such knowledge influences will, so to put it, make the general mental structure solid, sound, and powerful. By a wise selection, a proper amount of the various nourishing elements will be given; the mental growth will be fully provided for;

each power of mind will have its proper nutriment; and there will be no unnecessary waste of energy in receiving and assimilating the mental food.

All knowledge subjects which are largely taught through the directed and controlled activity of the individual himself, in connection with physical objects, have a high disciplinary (nutritive) value. And it is from this point of view that what is known as physical and manual education is so valuable in its bearing on the intellectual life.

But there is also the essential and all-important element of exercise, as such, in the discipline value of knowledge subjects. It has been insisted that exercise is the very foundation of development. It is a condition of life itself, for the stagnant decays and dies. Exercise not only develops power, but, if rightly organised, it teaches the most fruitful and easy methods of applying power. The gymnast learns exactly how and when to use his force so as to get the greatest effect with the least effort. Thus a small and not very strong but well-trained woman can, by carefully arranging and balancing the weight of four big men, and by properly applying her strength, lift them and the chair on which they are seated clear from the ground. Similarly, a well-trained mind can use its powers to the greatest advantage, and perform tasks which would otherwise be impossible.

There is of course a good deal of exercise in the receiving and assimilating of nourishment, and, so far as the nourishment is carefully ordered, both as to its kind and the manner in which it is given, the exercise which accompanies it is of the highest value. It is, however, possible to arrange that exercise, as such, shall be the predominant element in mental activity. To do this, we must as far as possible leave out the more purely nutritive elements. This we are able to do in what are called the formal or abstract knowledge subjects, *e.g.*, mathematics, grammar, logic. These subjects deal not with concrete things, but with the systems of symbols which we have invented to represent them, and the processes which are possible with these. Thus the nutritive element of ordinary concrete experience is at a minimum, whilst the activity of mind itself is at a maximum in dealing with such matters. By orderly and systematic courses of mental training in these subjects the power and skill of the mind are greatly increased. For example, if Euclid is intelligently and thoroughly taught, the mind is likely to get a power and habit of carefully testing the coherence, consistency, and soundness of anything which is offered as demonstration or proof. This is the kind of discipline obtained from the deductive sciences.

Physical science subjects are not only of high disciplinary value from the nutritive point of view, but also from the point of view of pure exercise. For in dealing with pure, as opposed to practical and applied science, we have for the most part to do chiefly with the rational elements of experience—with general truths and principles. The mind is constantly exercised in that which is for mind only—the meaning or interpretation of experiences. And the discipline thus obtained is particularly valuable, because it is in such work that the mind gains the power and habit of fully and accurately receiving and responding to stimuli, of judging relations rightly, and of making those universal judgments about phenomena which, when properly expressed, we call laws or principles.

Any want of precision or completeness in rightly appreciating and interpreting the material dealt with leads to wrong general judgments, and the error is pretty certain to be shown up by later experience, especially if we pursue a course of action based upon the supposed accuracy of such general judgments. If, for example, a person interpreted his observations of a large plain so as to form the judgment that as a whole it was perfectly level, and proceeded to make a canal across it strictly according to this judgment, he would find that his ideas were in conflict with facts; for, owing to the real nature of the earth's surface engineers have to allow about eight inches per mile for the natural curvature of the land.

The consequences of such results are: observations and judgments are made with great care and caution: experiments are repeated: judgments are thoroughly tested: a severely critical method of thought is cultivated: and universal judgments are accepted only after searching and repeated trials. So mind acquires a power and habit of self-criticism. This is the discipline of the inductive sciences.

It is interesting and instructive to compare these ideas on the regulated nutrition and exercise of the mind with the facts of bodily life during infancy. In the first year or so of physical life the infant does little more than eat and take exercise, and it is according to how wisely and thoroughly these are regulated by those who have charge of the child, that the health, vigour, and development of the body are secured.

Culture Value.—While it is of great moment thus to provide for the development of the mind, as such, it is not less important that great care should be taken as to the general nature and character of the development which is brought about. We must attend to the content of the developed powers, or we may after all produce only a sharp and shrewd mental machine instead of a full, powerful, and great mind. Further, we want not only a full and deep mind, but one that is well balanced, whose powers show grace and beauty in process and product, and whose general nature and character are lofty and noble. We want to obtain the highest value of man, as man, from the purely educational stand-point, *i.e.*, with regard to the most perfect development of his powers.

Now, the harmoniously developed and cultured mind is generally accepted as the highest form of mind. Hence we must make use of those knowledge subjects which thus fill the mind with a rich content because they have high culture value. It is a question of the civilised man as against the savage, and of the philosophical and practical man as against the purely practical one.

Before we can decide as to which subjects possess a high degree of culture value, we must agree as to what is to be regarded as a cultured mind. We have already spoken of balance of mental powers, grace and beauty of mental processes and products, and high and noble qualities. To these we may add intellectual sympathy, in its broadest and deepest sense. By this we mean an appreciation of, desire for, pleasure in, and love of, all forms of truth, beauty, and goodness, wherever found. To put it in quite general terms, the most cultured mind is the mind which has all the highest products of the best mental cultivation in their most refined forms. It is the highest mental expression of humanity, and, therefore, will proceed mainly from the influences of those subjects which are more directly concerned with the human being as such.

Subjects which have a high culture value will appeal to the whole mental nature. They will give an organic tone to the mind. The mind will, so to say, give forth the effects of a full, powerful, but well-modulated orchestra, as against the empty roll of a drum, or even the less full beauty of a well-played solo. And such results are most fully and easily brought about by those subjects which deal with the universal elements in human life. Subjects like geography, history, literature, philosophy, music, and art, which contain records and expositions of the most important, refined, and spiritual results of human life, thought, and action, enrich and ennoble to a very large extent the mind which is sympathetically subjected to their influences.

Utility Value.—Practical life is, after all, our chief concern, as all our knowledge is derived from it, and to it all the powers which knowledge gives are again directed. Life, indeed, consists in living, and all our efforts to further human development in the individual and the race would be but lost labour, if it did not result in a fuller and richer living of our lives.

In the first chapter we urged that the present conception of education has arisen from the necessities of modern life. It is for the life of a community that we are fitting the developing individual, and we may say that it is by the social life, through the means which it provides and the efforts which it makes—as in national systems of schools, &c.—that education is possible. The individual, so to speak, absorbs the social life by which he is surrounded; he lives upon it, and has later on to live for it. A person is acted upon by society, but he also reacts upon it, and it depends upon the manner of his reaction whether it be to his advantage or disadvantage; for if he acts in harmony with his social surroundings he will gain˙ thereby, and if his actions conflict with them, he will suffer for it.

Clearly, therefore, the general well-being, present and future, of the developing being depends upon the way in which each and all of his actions are related to his social surroundings. He has to endeavour to make himself a part of the social whole, and in doing so he will make the social whole more helpful to his own individuality.

Although, as we have said, education, as such, has nothing whatever to do with the use which we make of our developed powers, yet it is of great importance to discover definite reasons, should such exist, for choosing between two or more knowledge subjects which appear to be equally good for purely educational purposes. If one subject is likely to prove more practically useful, and also more interesting than the other, it should be chosen.

For example, let us suppose that the educational values of the French language and the Chinese language are equal. Is there any reason for selecting the one rather than the other, when educating an English boy who is likely to spend his life as the ordinary Englishman does? Surely there are a good many reasons for choosing the French language. The mode of thought expressed by it very closely resembles that of the learner; the letters in which it is written are similar to those used in English; many of the words very closely resemble each other in the two languages; French literature is finer, more advanced, more extensive, &c., than the Chinese; the nations have a good deal more intercourse; and so on.

Again, in physical education the powers of the hand could be developed by finger drill, exercises in grasping, &c.; but it is decidedly more advantageous to get the same kinds of results through carefully arranged exercises in handling tools, playing the piano, &c. So also we shall judge with regard to applied science and pure science. If we can get all the educational results we desire from the applied science, then this is a strong reason why it should be chosen, rather than the pure science.

The utility value of a subject is therefore a deciding element in cases of choice between subjects having nearly equal educational value. Other things being equal, or nearly so, we should always choose the subject which has the greater utility value. And not only so, but it is well to give all subjects some utility value by relating them to practical life, so far as this does not prejudice the progress of development. Fortunately, there is no real inconsistency between the two, and very seldom is there even a conflict between them. Those knowledge subjects which have the greatest educational values have generally also great practical value, and, therefore, very great interest.

It is the utility value of subjects which has, for the most part, hitherto been considered in drawing up schemes of instruction for schools. Hence we have the "modern side," which is professional and commercial in its aim, in our public schools; whilst even the "classical side" has utility value, since the fact of having done well in it is accepted as a qualification for teaching in such a school, and a knowledge of the classical languages is also regarded as necessary for most of the learned professions.

There is no objection to—indeed there is every reason for—taking account of what the future life of the individual is going to be, especially towards the end of his course of education, so long as this consideration takes the secondary, and not the primary, position. If it takes the first place, then we are making schemes of useful instruction, and not a system of pure education; and it was in this sense that we previously said that technical schools and colleges, professional training institutions, &c., are not places of education, as such. It will be seen that the questions connected with the educational values of knowledge subjects are very closely connected with the correlation of subjects and also with the general development of the knowing powers of the mind. The elements which make up the values may be said to have special influence in developing the individual. Discipline affects knowing most, culture influences feeling chiefly, and utility has, probably, through interest, the greatest effect upon willing.

The Principle of Repetition.—For knowledge to have real existence for the mind it must be a permanent possession, *i.e.*, the results of knowledge-giving influences must be firmly retained by the memory. Extraordinary experiences impress themselves deeply upon the mind by their unusual character or force. Ordinary experiences are best fixed in the memory by careful repetition, for such is the native capacity of mind for retaining the effects which are produced in it, that the mere recurrence of events serves to fix them in the memory.

How necessary it is to get the memory to do its work thoroughly will be recognised when we reflect that every new experience owes much, if not most, of its meaning and value to the action of the knowledge gained from former experience. That is, the worth of a presentation depends largely upon the work of representations, and the fulness and force of the representations will be according to the faithfulness and freedom of the memory. Also, old thoughts and experiences must be constantly reproduced in consciousness if we are to obtain from them all the knowledge that is possible. Hence, education must point out the conditions which best secure the most extensive and accurate memory.

Repetition acts upon the mind in two ways. It causes the details of the activities which are necessary for the response, or series of responses, to a given stimulus to become easy, certain, and more or less fixed ; so much so, that in some cases it is very difficult to prevent them from acting at the wrong time. Thus, if one has been much and frequently amused by a humorous parody of a serious poem, it is sometimes impossible to prevent the mind from re-presenting the parody even when the original is given with solemn surroundings. In other words, memory habits are formed. Again, repetition causes the mental results of such repeated activities to become more full, clear, fixed, and easily revivable.

Just as an original impression is more or less firmly fixed in the memory according as it is more or less vivid, clear, forcible, and interesting ; so also will any repetition of the experience serve still further to impress it upon the mind in proportion as it has one or more of these qualities. Perhaps the most important point with regard to repetitions is the keeping up of the interest. If the same materials and method are always used, it will become increasingly difficult to impart interest and secure attention. Hence, novelty should be introduced in sufficient amount to give interest and obtain attention, without causing distraction from the real point of the experience. It must also be remembered that repetition itself, however varied the conditions, will become uninteresting if it be too frequent or too long-continued.

Another valuable aid in securing good memory is to

use every simple, direct, and helpful form of association that is possible, without being burdensome. The putting of the points to be remembered in a well-arranged visual or aural group, which answers to a scientific sequence (where possible), will often be of great assist-ance—through association by contiguity. Also the matter in hand should be carefully explained and made clear to the intelligence, so that association by intel-lectual similarity may aid the memory.

It must never be forgotten that memory is not a kind of separate mental machinery into which it is possible to cram all sorts of odds and ends by mere dint of pushing. Clear understanding and thorough mental relation form the best and surest basis of exact remembrance. At the same time, there is the passive and mechanical side of memory, which must neither be neglected nor presumed upon. There must be a proper amount of exercise given according to a good system. Such a system will be based upon a proper correlation of our knowledge about classes and individuals.

The principle of repetition is, perhaps, the most general, as it is certainly one of the most important and valuable of all educational principles. It should govern the application of all the other principles of education. All the higher forms of life, and all their higher functions, seem to depend very largely upon this principle.

The Principle of Preparation.—Very little more need be said about the value of getting the mind ready for what is coming. To bring into consciousness the most appropriate re-presentations just before a particular presentation takes place, is to put the mind into a condition in which its highest powers of receptivity and responsiveness are active.

The effects of good mental preparation would be well illustrated in the case of two persons attending a lecture in the middle of a course. If one of them has been to all the previous lectures, has clearly and completely grasped what has already been said, and has given some thought to its bearing on the lecture in question, whilst the other has done none of these things, and knows hardly anything about the subject, then the amount of knowledge which the former would be likely to obtain from the lecture would be many times as much as that which the latter would probably get.

To have plenty of ideas on a subject is not of so much value as always to have them ready when wanted. How often do we think of the right thing to do when it is too late to do it; of the witty or wise reply when it is too late to give it. We have been taken off our guard as we say, *i.e.*, the mind was not prepared to bring all its resources to bear, because its attention was not pre-adjusted.

Not less important is the securing of sufficient time for the mind to adjust itself for each item in a series of continuous experiences. This kind of preparation is likely to prevent many mistakes of assimilation and discrimination which might take place in a hurried, and, therefore, superficial and uncritical relating of the presented to the re-presented. Too often one finds that a hasty endeavour to acquire knowledge quickly has resulted in many errors and much confusion of thought, and that much time and effort are required to correct the mistakes made.

In the young it is often necessary or expedient to establish, if possible, a favourable or unfavourable disposition towards a coming experience. This is especially the case with regard to moral estimates of actions and individuals, and is also helpful in connection with scientific phenomena, &c., because of the overwhelming influence of feeling in the child's life. But such preparation needs to be used with very great judgment and caution, and in ever-decreasing amount. The only justification for such a course is, that we are fully convinced of the fitness of the pre-disposition, and that it is necessary thus to guide the mind which has not yet got the power to guide itself in right judgment.

It should, however, always be the aim to secure, as far as we can, an unprejudiced attitude towards the expected experience. When the individual begins to think for himself, it is difficult to persuade him to allow for, or to exclude, preconceived notions about new experiences, and it is still harder for the adult to discount what is called the personal equation, *i.e.*, the effects of his habits of thought: of his personal likings and dislikings : of his practical interest (if any) : of his general condition of mind and body at the moment, &c., in the forming of a judgment.

So far as we are able thus to prepare the mind, by bringing into consciousness all those ideas, and into activity all the powers, which are likely to make the presentation more readily, fully, and accurately interpreted and assimilated ; and, further, exclude or lessen the effects of all the ideas and powers which hinder the reception, or prevent the estimate, of a presentation; so far shall we obtain knowledge more swiftly, surely, and soundly.

The Principle of Interest.—Since self-activity is the basis of development, willing the source of self-activity, and interest the most powerful motive to willing, it is clear that the quantity and quality of development will largely depend upon the force and nature of the interests which affect the individual.

We have said that individuals can, if they will, render themselves almost entirely unresponsive to feeling and knowing influences, in particular cases; and they can remain more or less unaffected by them for considerable periods of time. Children who seem to care for no reward or punishment, and decline to receive nearly all kinds of knowledge are by no means unknown; whilst those who exhibit these tendencies at certain times, and with regard to particular subjects, are far too common. It is, therefore, of the greatest importance that the active consent and co-operation of the individual who is being educated should be secured.

Now it is a common and true saying, that what a person is interested in he will do his best work at. The thing to do, therefore, is to arouse, in the person being educated, interest with regard to the influences and phenomena which are educating him. The interest may be either in favour of or opposed to a certain thing. We may be interested in knowing or not knowing, having or not having, a certain experience or series of experiences, mental or physical. But directly we are interested, one way or the other, the attention is fixed, desire is excited, the mind acts, knowledge is gained or used, plans are in some cases formed, and, if necessary, physical action is taken. In short, interest secures purposive activity of mind, body, or both, towards some definite end—even if the activity be only that of restraint. It is an unfailing stimulus to willing.

It is this condition of active interest in educative presentations that it is most necessary to obtain. In proportion as this is strong, so is the educative effect great, and in so far as it is weak, the developing result is small. Every one recognises this in particular cases. Not a few of the most famous persons in the world's history were thought to be more than ordinarily stupid, until having had the chance of devoting themselves to a subject which had an absorbing interest for them, they soon developed powers which greatly surprised and benefited the race. Whilst not all have the genius which thus excels, yet wherever interest is present, there, at the least, the best energy is given to a subject, and, consequently, the greatest effects possible to the individual are likely to be produced.

Herbart, the great psychologist and educationist, has treated this matter very fully, and points out that wherever interest is aroused it is accompanied by just those conditions of mind which make for development. Observation occurs, because the mind realises that there is an opportunity for gaining additional pleasure or profit, or for preventing some pain or loss. So long as this, the opportunity, remains unfulfilled, there is a

condition of expectation. If there is further delay, and
the mind gives most of its attention to the expected
results, then there is a desire which passes into
demand.   And demand, whenever real, expresses itself
in action.

This series may occupy an appreciable, and even
considerable, amount of time—it may be weeks or
months in the case of a somewhat phlegmatic and very
reflective adult—in its completion, or it may occur
almost instantaneously.   It is sometimes very clearly
marked in the case of an infant, who first gazes at some
object with a kind of curious and surprised look, then
stretches out its hand and waits for its mother or nurse
to give the thing to it, and if it does not receive it,
then begins to struggle violently to get it.

The great value of such a state of interest is, that it
influences the individual as a whole, *i.e.*, the self.   For
the time, the whole being is practically concerned with
nothing except that which interests it.   The one and
only thing which it then longs for is to have or not to
have that which has so entirely taken possession of its
attention.   All the energy of the self is given up to
the endeavour to obtain the desired end.   There is a
conviction, more or less explicit, that unless the end is
secured the self will suffer, either negatively (through
loss of pleasure) or positively (through incurring pain).
So that, if the end is gained, there is a feeling of self-
realisation, that is, with regard to the experience, the
self is what it ought to be.   This is best illustrated, in
its extreme form, in the cases of faddists, enthusiasts,
religious devotees, &c.

Two great classes of interest are noticed by Herbart, viz., those interests which are connected with knowledge, and those which belong to sympathy. The former depend upon the fact that the mind appreciates and imitates in ideas the nature and laws of all that is not mind, and brings these ideas into such order and system as seem best to express the relations of the objects of the physical world. It also knows itself. The interests connected with sympathy arise from the fact that we can know of, and share in, the feelings which are experienced by the society in which we live, and also by the human race as a whole.

He himself says : " The first kind of interest—that in the objective—is felt partly in the comprehension of objects, partly in the grasping of their independence according to law, partly in the approval which their harmony and adaptation to an end win from us. The second kind of interest—in the subjective—devotes itself partly to men as individual beings, partly to society, and partly to the relation of nature to humanity. In all these aspects the characteristic of this second kind of interest lies in the sympathy, in the concentration on human feelings (whether personal or those of others). Quite foreign to this, on the contrary, is all mere observation, however interesting, of human beings ; this belongs to the first kind—the objective. Both kinds touch at their highest point and meet together in religion, for its object is providence." From the sympathetic interests come social, political, and religious ideals.

The interests which belong to knowledge are three.

Firstly, the empirical interest, or the interest which the individual has in experiences, as such; in the changes, variety, novelty, &c., of the phenomena which surround and affect him; in the details of these phenomena (including his own body); and in the action of himself and other objects. Secondly, the speculative interest, or the desire and effort to understand these empiricals, by trying to see in them order, relation, system, law, and unity. Thirdly, the æsthetic interest, or the disposition to discover ideal values for our rational knowledge of things, in the form of beauty, harmony, goodness, design, truth, &c.

The interests which are connected with sympathy are also three. Firstly, human interest, or that which we have in knowing ourselves as human beings. We want to know what it is that constitutes our own feelings of joy and sorrow, &c. Thus we come to know what are the expressions of human feelings in others, and, therefore, what is human. There is the desire to understand what is truest and highest in human nature, and this results in an effort of imitation. Thus may arise a sympathetic union with the whole human race. Secondly, the social interest, or the interest which the necessities of everyday life as members of a community have for us. There are obligations of self-sacrifice, subordination, co-ordination, compromise, &c., which cannot be escaped if one's life is to be as comfortable as may reasonably, and rightly, be desired. This is the practical side of human sympathy. Thirdly, the religious interest, or that which leads man to seek to know his own place in nature, and which leads him to recognise his position of dependence. Thus is caused a feeling of humility: of reverence for the higher and greater: of the infinite worth of things: of infinite purpose: and of infinite cause.

Here, then, we have an analysis of the native springs to action, mental and physical, in a human being. It gives us a view of the opportunities and duties of the educator, and shows very clearly what kind of experiences and material must be provided. These are the ways in which the real self of the individual can be reached in the easiest, most complete, and most effective manner.

These general interests are proper to human beings as such. They make up what we have termed original interests. A human being cannot help but have them in more or less completeness. Again, therefore, we see the necessity of many-sidedness of educative influences to satisfy this many-sidedness of interest. Knowledge subjects must be correlated so as best to harmonise with, and aid the development of, such mental characteristics. Here, also, is again shown the function of the educator—to present the whole world of mind and matter in miniature, so far as that is possible, to the growing mind. He is a selecting and stimulating agent.

It is the general disposition or tendency to be thus interested which exists in every human being, and not a particular form of interest in a particular subject at a given time. The latter must be brought about by the art of the educator, and is a subject which is treated of in considering the methods of education. Both general and particular instances of interest depend upon the strength, variety, novelty, familiarity (if not excessive) of presentations, and also upon the general complex in which they occur. Thus a soldier in full uniform, who would attract no special attention in a regiment, would command particular notice in a small crowd of civilians.

We must, therefore, take care that these qualities are present in the educating influences which we employ. And not only should they be used, but they must be constantly and carefully selected and applied. Anything like a mechanical repetition of certain prescribed forms of them is not likely to be very helpful. Some modification or other will nearly always be necessary, and this must be a matter of thought and judgment. Nevertheless, there is a danger of having too great variety, which would distract the attention from the main points, and so prevent systematic assimilation.

Interest is both a cause and an effect of knowledge. The original interests urge us on to acquire knowledge, and when we have obtained it, there is generally a desire to obtain more. This is well seen in the bright child whose education is conducted under free and kindly conditions. No sooner does it gain some slight information about an object, than it immediately follows up the matter with question after question as to the " why " of every detail, and soon exhausts the fund of knowledge, or the power of simple expression, of the ordinary adult.

Hence, if the disciplinary element in educational influences is well and wisely used, the mind is interested in having purely mental exercise, as such, and finds delight in trying to work out simple, appropriate, and properly graded, intellectual problems, puzzles, conundrums, and catches. The keenness, excitement, and pleasure, which children show in well-managed exercises of this kind are evidences of their value. This is also true in the case of the culture elements. The dramatic and artistic reciting, or reading, of suitable pieces of classical literature: the showing and explaining of beautiful pictures: and the artistic rendering of the best music, all satisfy a native capacity for enjoyment, and create the demand for further experiences of a like kind. For example: a well-told tale of thrilling adventure in Africa often causes boys to eagerly read such books as the life of Livingstone.

In the same way the fact that certain forms of knowledge have great practical utility gives them special interest. If the ordinary rules of arithmetic are used in connection with everyday transactions; if manual exercises are illustrated through common household articles; and if drawing is taught from suitable objects, there is likely to arise a desire to extend the knowledge and power thus obtained.

Above all, where interests of these kinds are produced, or exist, they both stimulate to action and reward the activity. A person who is thus really interested in a course of action desires no further reward than the satisfaction of doing that which he keenly wished to do, or, at least, he can be content without more. Thus interest is an end in itself and is the most disinterested (in the material sense), satisfactory, complete, effective, and worthy end. It is, therefore, the chief aim of the educator to make interest an indispensable and sufficient end of educational action. With such a stimulus it is easy to impart mental nourishment and discipline, indeed, it would be difficult to prevent them from being obtained, since the appetite and activities of the mind are in a state of vigorous aggressiveness.

Interest is more particularly connected with the development of knowing; but since it is generally based upon, and always connected with, the feelings, it has much to do in their development also. And inasmuch as it is almost invariably accompanied by willing, in a full and vigorous form, it does much to further its progress.

Interest may be said to be a most effective, because pleasant and impressive, substitute for repetition. Dr. Sully remarks: "The permanence of an impression depends on the degree of interest excited by the object and the corresponding vigour of the act of attention. All strong feeling gives a special persistence to impressions, by arousing an exceptional degree of interest. Where a boy is deeply affected by pleasurable feeling, as in listening to an attractive story or in watching a cricket match, he remembers distinctly. Such intensity of feeling by securing a strong interest and a close attention, ensures a vivid impression and a clear discrimination of the object, both in its several parts or details, and as a whole. And the fineness of the discriminative process is one of the most determining conditions of retention."

Dr. Bain says: "Any kind of ₁knowledge . . . . that is obviously involved in any of the strong feelings or emotions . . . . is by that very fact interesting.

Now a great many kinds of knowledge are implicated with those various feelings. To avoid pains, and obtain pleasures, it is often necessary to know certain things, and we willingly apply our minds to learn those things. . . . . A vast quantity of information respecting the world, and respecting human beings, is gained in this way; and it constitutes an important basis of even the highest acquisitions."

The elements of novelty and variety need special emphasis in the case of the young, though even with them there is the danger of excess. The educator must beware of the peep-show order of excitement, where so many things are seen in so short a time, that practically nothing is seen.

Miss Edgeworth tells of some Esquimaux who were taken for a walk through the streets of London: " When their walk was ended, they appeared uncommonly melancholy and stupefied. As soon as they got home they sat down with their elbows upon their knees, and hid their faces in their hands. The only words they could be brought to utter were, ' Too much smoke—too much noise—too much houses—too much men—too much everything ! ' "

At the same time, monotony is never so monotonous as to the young. Whatever else the educator can afford to neglect, the arousing of interest must always be carefully provided for and earnestly striven after. We may truly say that the first and last condition of effective education is interest. It is the foundation and mainspring of successful effort on the part of the pupil. It is the educational philosopher's stone which turns everything into gold. Through the earnestness and devotion of teachers, and the interest excited thereby in their pupils, systems which are in themselves incomplete and largely unsound have been the means of producing the very highest and best educational results. Where interest is absent the most scientific and complete system of education will be likely to prove flat, stale, and unprofitable.

Some of the most interesting elements in a subject are its pleasure-giving power, the occasion for self-activity, the sense of power which comes from successful work in it, the opportunity it offers of adding knowledge to what we already possess, the stimulating combination of the novel and familiar which it may involve, and the attractiveness and impressiveness of the points of beauty, strength, strangeness, greatness, complexity, unity, power, and so on, which may be present in it. Each and all of these should be realised, in their proper place and proportion, for educational purposes.

The Principle of Habituation.—Inasmuch as habit can only be the result of complete and thorough mental adjustment to, response to, and grasp of, the details of certain operations, we may regard habits as the expressions of the perfection of mental development in the matters which they involve; for with regard to them mind does the very best that it can do, with the least possible effort. For this reason, they have very great educational significance. They point to what we may call practical mental perfection, and, therefore, are the best possible points of departure for higher developments.

The educator regards habit as a kind of self-registering index of mental development. Whenever he has reason to believe that educational discipline and nurture have resulted in the formation of a habit, he considers that he has completed the present work of development in that case, and only has to provide against any subsequent loss of power or skill. For the same reason he is always aiming at producing habits. Not, of course, in the sense of reducing everything to a definite and invariable form; but in the sense of making materials and methods so familiar, and so subject to control, that they no longer present mechanical difficulties; and, therefore, they leave the mind free for making those higher judgments which really express the true self, and show us to be anything but the slaves of habit. It is a good thing to definitely cultivate the habit of being superior to habits.

Only when the mind has acquired accurate habits in dealing with materials and methods, in the above sense, can there be anything of much value in the way of power to solve new problems, complex cases, or real difficulties for oneself. Neither can there be much in the way of original discovery in the world of thought. Education cannot give the native power which is necessary for such work, but it can and does give the mind the best possible preparation for using it. It cannot make the material, but it can make the material into the best and most powerful machine.

Two of the most important ways of forming habits of thought are those of limitation and exclusion. By limitation is meant the keeping steadily in mind the particular kind of knowledge desired, and a special method of obtaining it, and then persistently pursuing the end and the means. But this must apply only to the making of some particular end a predominant, but by no means the sole, purpose of action for the time being. By exclusion, therefore, we mean the power to keep the mind from thinking about those matters which are opposed, or foreign, to a subject which we specially wish to keep in mind.

Dr. Sully gives the following as the main conditions for the formation of a habit:—" A sufficient motive force brought to bear at the outset, in order to excite the requisite effort. . . . . A prolonged repetition of the action in connection with the appropriate circumstances. . . . . An uninterrupted continuity of performance in like circumstances."

Locke offers some wise advice on habit when he says: "Another thing you are to take care of, is, not to endeavour to settle too many habits at once, lest by variety you confound them, and so perfect none. When constant custom has made any one thing easy and natural to them, and they practise it without reflection, you may then go on to another."

Thus if we wish to learn a living language for conversational purposes, it would be a good plan to live amongst those who speak it, until we had gained some facility in its use. It would require very considerable effort to resist the temptation to use the mother tongue; but it is necessary to the greatest success of the endeavour that this should be done.

All that has been said about the principle of repetition applies to the principle of habituation. As was
then pointed out, the result of appropriate repetition
is the formation of a habit. Therefore all the conditions required to obtain a good memory habit are
required for other mental habits; indeed, we may say
that all mental habits are but memory habits with
varying contents, for they consist in remembering
certain thoughts, feelings, and actions, in definite
orders and relations. The principle of pleasure also
applies, for it is much easier to form a habit under
pleasant than under unpleasant conditions. The
former further, but the latter obstruct, the establishing of those conditions which make habits.

A good illustration of the growth of a habit, and of
its value as an economising agent in our mental life,
is found in the case of the use of the limbs in walking. Walking requires very considerable judgment in
the co-ordinating of the actions of a great many
muscles, and also in the adjustment of the actual
movements of the limbs. The latter is brought home
to us with intensely disagreeable emphasis if we suppose that we are walking on level ground, when, as a
matter of fact, there is a sudden fall of the ground in
the limits of the stride. The very severe and general
shock felt is due to the want of proper adjustment.
When the child first tries to walk, the whole of its
little body labours heavily, and the great concentration and effort of thought is shown by the set face
and steadfast gaze. Each leg is lifted very slowly
and with great care and consideration, and is advanced

and set down again with equal deliberateness. It hails the successful issue of a short journey with excited expressions of joy and relief.

Later on the actions become so entirely a matter of habit, that if one stopped to consider how each detail in the process was performed, he would probably be unable to carry it out without stumbling a good deal. It is only when recovering from an accident to, or during a disease of, one of the limbs, or in walking in a strange room in the dark, that the details of movement become again explicit. Thus what at first engaged the whole of the power of attention, finally requires practically no attention at all; so that whilst walking from one place to another through various streets and turnings, one usually gives his attention to all kinds of subjects other than that of his own walking.

But it is interesting, and most important, to notice that if a person desires to adopt a new style of locomotion such as dancing, then all the conditions of laboured details and slow conquest, which may finally result in the ease of habit, have to be gone through. And even the delights of success in the efforts are not usually wanting. So like is the man to the child, and the child to the man—with a difference of power and progress all in favour of the man.

The above illustration indicates the place and function of habit in mental development, as well as in physical, and, therefore, its educational value. It has been said that to educate a child is to lead it to acquire good habits. So long as this is understood to mean that each habit is to be regarded as a completed item of development, which is to be the stepping-stone to higher development, there is much truth in the expression.

The principle of habituation applies to the development of feeling, knowing, and willing, though it has most to do with willing, in that it is chiefly realised through acts of will, and results in a more or less permanent form of automatic willing.

The Principle of Self-activity.—It has been urged that the highest value of the individual is expressed by his character, and that his character is the result of his independence, or rather self-dependence, of judgment, and of actions based upon these judgments. Hence the educator should always endeavour to lead the individual to take action on his own behalf. This kind of action we speak of as spontaneity, initiation, and self-activity, in their higher meanings.

This principle has been so generally recognised that a number of educational maxims have been invented to express it, *e.g.*, educate a child so that it may be able to educate itself; so govern the pupil that he may learn to govern himself; so help the learner that he may become able to do without help; show the scholar how to find out knowledge in such a way that he may be able to find out without being shown; the duty of the teacher is to enable the student to do without him; and, never do for a child what it can do for itself.

From what has been stated with regard to the principles of interest and habit, it will be seen that they have a very important relation to self-activity.

The former is, indeed, practically the only kind of stimulus which can secure a real and effective self-activity. For self-activity in its highest and truest sense, there must be clear and explicit judgment and willing. The individual must realise that there is something which is worth striving for, and must, of his own free will and with set purpose, make the necessary efforts. This is the only kind of activity which both expresses and realises the self.

Habit is valuable to self-activity in that it affords a foundation and occasion for it. When an habitual action is going on under somewhat new conditions and surroundings, there is often the necessity for further judgments with respect to the modification of some detail, or details, so as to ensure the success of the action. As the self is largely determined by the habits of the individual, there will be every reason for it to take some interest in what is after all its own realisation. At the same time it must be recognised that habits generally do more to supplant self-activity than to stimulate it. But the higher habits express the self, for they are the most permanent elements of it, and have, as a rule, been formed by self-activity.

Self-activity is the chief means of increasing the strength of the individual. Mere passive response does little in the way of invigorating the self. As in the physical life it is not being acted upon, but the vigorous acting on other things, which hardens and strengthens the bodily powers, so in the mental life it is self-activity, and not the mere fact of being acted upon by influences, which is most developing. Things which are learnt mechanically in early life are found to be amongst the subjects least thought of in later years.

The very great value of self-activity in developing the highest powers of an individual is thus expressed by Kant: "All the natural endowments of mankind must be developed little by little, out of man himself, through his own efforts." The practical importance is also urged by him in these words : "It is no help to a man that in his youth he has enjoyed an over-abundance of motherly tenderness, for later on he will have to meet all the more opposition from all sides, and constantly be receiving rebuffs as soon as he enters the business of the world."

A strikingly suggestive illustration of the ill-effects which may arise through neglecting this principle of self-dependence is given by Professor L. C. Miall, in an article on " Helplessness and Handiness." He says : " The new boy at school! I look back forty years, and see him standing in the midst of a crowd of noisy urchins, turned into the lavatory to wash for dinner. He was dressed, I rather think, in black, and I have a suspicion that his father was a clergyman, lately dead. I remember his pale face, his neat dress and hair, and his white hands. . . . .

" The new boy, when he finds an unoccupied basin, goes timidly up to it, without taking off his coat, dips his fingers in, and wets his face. Then he stands still as if waiting for the maid to bring a towel. But there is no maid, and when he realises that his wet face and hands will not be dried for him he bursts into tears. The poor mother who saw day after day that he was washed and brushed, and fondly hoped that she was giving him habits of tidiness—how little she realised that her boy of eight or nine would endure the misery of the helpless!"

What have been termed the pleasures of pursuit, the sense of power, and the delights of conquest, all belong to self-effort only. It is self-activity which expresses the investigative and speculative interests. Discoverers, inventors, and original thinkers, and doers of every sort, are those who unite great original, and highly developed, powers of mind with intense and aggressive self-activity. So far, therefore, as we aim at producing the highest powers of mind, we must encourage and give every opportunity for the exercise of self-effort.

It has been well said that the self is the man. We may add to this the assertion that the self is expressed in the general nature of the individual's willings. If this be so, it is clear that the highest aim of education is to develop the power of willing to its highest, fullest, most free, and most effective, form. The last three educational principles—viz., interest, habituation, and self-activity—are all concerned with this aim.

Most thoughtful people would agree that the highest kind of willing is the power to will to know and realise the highest ideals of the good, the true, and the beautiful. To lead the pupil up to such a level should be the ideal always before the educator. Not, let us again urge, that he should necessarily try to develop the will through some particular religious creed or moral code: or through some exclusive view of a science: or by means of a special school of art. There are plenty of general principles, and points of detail, which are common to all special systems, and amply sufficient for the educator's purpose. Particular views on such points are matters for the individual's own judgment and conscience, as governing his own private ideals and conduct as a member of a community.

Of the conditions necessary to develop such self-activity, we have already said a good deal in treating of the principles of interest and habituation. We may add that, when some power and skill have been gained by the individual in a certain kind of knowledge and its use, a specially arranged opportunity for discovering —from the individual's standpoint, but of re-discovering from the racial point of view—should be offered to the individual, and his interest and curiosity aroused with regard to it. The special arrangement will consist in bringing truths or phenomena before him in such an order of simple logical progress that all his former experiences and knowledge which are connected with the present will be vividly aroused, and his observation and judgment led on so connectedly and inevitably that, under ordinary circumstances, he cannot fail to make new judgments.

Hence the developing mind should be constantly required to repeat, without aid or guidance, processes which have been made more or less familiar. It should also have opportunities and inducements to work out special adaptations of its powers and knowledge. Easy and carefully arranged problems should be given, so that after there has been guidance in the method of discovery there may be something, however simple and slight, in the way of original discovery—from the individual's standpoint. During the later period of development it is even desirable, as Milton advised, that the youth should have a knowledge of the science of education, and the art of teaching, so that he may the more readily and effectively co-operate with the educator, and also be able to educate himself.

Self-activity is self-realisation, and no item of development has really become a possession and part of the self, in the fullest sense, unless it is mainly the result of self-effort, and is also capable of producing further self-activity. This therefore is the test of a sound and successful development: that what is so developed is itself able to help in making still greater progress. The greatest success of the educating process is to make the individual realise, care for, and seek to further develop, his higher self.

We have pointed out that willing proceeds from the automatic and instinctive to the self-initiated and reflective. The influences used in developing it should therefore be firstly imperative, then indicative, and lastly suggestive in character. Imperative at first because the individual has neither the knowledge nor power to choose for himelf, though his needs are very great and his person subject to the most serious dangers; but he is able to respond to influences and to benefit thereby. Later on, the influences should be chiefly indicative, and only occasionally imperative, because the physical and mental activities and powers are getting stronger and more skilful, and the powers of imitation great, and also because the more he does for himself the better it is for his further development. And, finally, the educating influences should be mainly suggestive so that self-dependence and self-activity may be developed to the greatest possible extent.

By imperative influences we mean influences applied with such intensity and directness, and under such conditions, that they practically force their effects upon the individual. The educator would use his authority as such an influence, and would say: "You must do so-and-so," "You must call this such-and-such," "You will see a blue colour," "This feels rough," &c. Of course all these influences are to be used wisely, and without any suggestion of harshness—which the name might seem to imply. The influences of cold, heat, wind, water, and solids, when these act upon the body, are imperative in causing certain of their qualities to be known.

Indicative influences are such as most readily and fully give the material for supplying what is needed to develop knowledge and power. Thus, if the educator is seeking to develop knowing through the acquirement of knowledge about a camel and the adaptation of its body to its surroundings, he will get a good picture of a camel in its native country, and a series of separate and enlarged pictures, if necessary, of the details which he wishes to be noticed. These he will introduce to the learner in a well-arranged order, and draw from him, by appealing to his observation, previous knowledge, and judgment, as much as possible of what he desires should be known. Thus the influences are mainly indicative in their character. Some things will have to be told, but these should be as few as thought and ingenuity can possibly make them.

Those influences are suggestive which excite the curiosity, arouse the interest, or direct the energy of the individual to a certain matter, and then leave him as nearly as possible to his own resources, both in the providing of the necessary material and in finding out how to use it so as to secure the desired end. For example, if a boy saw a toy-boat for the first time and was so interested in the sailing of it that he very much desired to own one, he would almost certainly set about making one for himself, if he had learnt how to use the necessary tools and could obtain the material required. Again, if such a lad was very curious about the working of a simple piece of apparatus, he would probably find out what he wished to know if he were allowed to experiment with it. Similarly, if he were asked to make for himself, from a model, a piece of simple apparatus to illustrate the morrow's lesson, he would be likely to find out for himself a way of doing it.

It will be allowed that knowledge so gained is likely to have a much more powerful and lasting effect upon the developing individual than that which comes to him from being, so to put it, fed with a spoon. He will learn many things in the way of observation and judgment on his own actions, &c., which it is impossible for him to learn otherwise, and he will gain more power and skill than in any other way. He puts the whole of his little self into the business, and he comes out of it with a stronger and a bigger, because with a successfully realised ideal, self.

By "a successfully realised ideal self" is meant that a new form of the self, which was previously looked upon as a desirable improvement upon the then condition of the self, is brought about. Thus a man may say, "My ideal of success is to write a novel which shall cause a sensation in the literary world;" and he may manage to write it. An ideal, in this more practical sense, is what one would wish to have, do, or be, in the more or less immediate future.

Character and individuality are themselves developing complexes, and hence comes the essential importance of the developing of self-activity, which means self-dependence, self-respect, self-responsibility, and the power of self-culture.

The principle of self-activity, like that of habituation, applies more particularly to will, but, for the most part, to will as concerned in knowing; and therefore it has most to do with the developing of these two sides of the mental life. It has also to do with feeling, in that we can, as we say, throw ourselves heartily into the excitement of the moment, and so cause the mind to .revel in a form of feeling; and, on the other hand, we can by an effort of will remain almost impassive to what would ordinarily exercise considerable influence upon our feelings.

The Inter-relation of the Principles.—It should be carefully noted, as being entirely in harmony with

K

what we may call the central truth of our view of education—*viz.*, that it seeks to know what are the principles and conditions which best develop mind according to its own proper nature, in view of its greatest possibilities—that the educational principles which we have now set forth are all, like the powers of mind itself, inter-related and inter-dependent.

The principles of stimulation and nourishment are the first and last conditions of influence upon development. Without them nothing of permanent value can be done. The principle of pleasure is the great lubricating, friction-reducing condition, and should be realised in every one of the other principles. It is a general law in this sense. The principle of repetition is the great organising, perpetuating, strengthening, and perfecting agency. It also is a law which should be applied to every other law in education. Repetition fails to be effective if pleasure does not accompany it, and pleasures become fuller and richer when wisely repeated.

Of the principle of inter-relation and inter-dependence nothing more need be said in this connection, since it both directly expresses and reflects, and seeks to realise, the nature of mind in the conditions of the developing influences. The principle of interest is the highest and most definite form of the general principle of stimulation. Interest is the great motive power of the activities which produce all the higher forms of development. The principle of habituation follows from the principle of repetition. It is the principle which leads to the greatest effectiveness and economy of mental power.

The principle of self-activity is the highest and most fruitful outcome of all the others. When self-activity appears it can regulate, reinforce, and realise—to a greater or lesser degree—all the developing conditions. The development of a satisfactory form of self-activity is the completion of the purely educative processes, for then instruction as to the practical application of knowledge and power to the affairs of life may begin.

From another point of view, the inter-relation becomes even more emphasised. The principle of pleasure has chiefly to do with the sensuous feelings, but also with the intellectual; the principle of interest is based upon feeling and knowing, and principally affects willing; the principles of inter-relation, preparation, and repetition have most to do with knowing, but also largely influence willing; whilst the principles of stimulation, nourishment, and self-activity affect the whole mind generally. Thus it appears that the principles involved all, more or less, influence those mind elements of feeling, knowing, and willing, which constitute the mental unity. It follows, therefore, that the principles themselves must be inter-dependent and united.

Some General Remarks.—Let us, here, and constantly, remind ourselves that educational principles besides being based upon psychological truths which have been arrived at by observation, experiment, and reflection, have also themselves been more or less fully discovered, in their empirical or experiential form, by observation, experiment, and reflection upon the developing being whilst under the influences of educating processes. The fullest possible evidence of the entirely practical element of proof, as to the soundness of the principles, is found in the history of education, and in the actual systems and methods at present used in our schools.

A most essential point for the young student to insist upon is that both the psychological basis, and the practical soundness, of the principles ought to be more or less fully demonstrable, and demonstrated, from the concrete point of view. In other words, the intelligent learner ought to be able, under proper guidance and after reasonable endeavour, to recognise the mind elements and their activities in his own mental life, and the signs of their workings in the case of others ; also, he should be able to observe the application, and estimate the effect, of the principles, as used in the actual education of the young.

Not only ought he to be able to recognise the elements of the principles and their activities as involved in the work of those who are educating and being educated, but, to apply the principle of self-activity to his own case, he should learn how to exemplify them in educational method, and realise them in educational practice. In other words, he must regard as part of the proper study of education the observation and analysis of the work of a skilled educator, and the endeavour to imitate and originate similar work of his own. That is to say, what are called model-lessons and criticism-lessons are the laboratory work, and an indispensable part, of the study of education.

No better advice could be given to young students of education than to take "a child, and set him in the midst of them." With the guidance which the experience and knowledge of others can give them, they may hope, through a study of children, to obtain a really scientific grasp of educational principles, but not otherwise.

Two cautions may be useful to the beginner in helping him to avoid some misconceptions. Firstly, he should be very careful not to attempt to carry further than the immediate context demands anything which is given for the purpose of illustrating the general argument. He must remember that every example limps, as the proverb says ; and it is, therefore, especially dangerous for a beginner to press an illustration. Later on he may be able to extend or amend it. Secondly, whenever we speak of " fundamental elements," we mean those which are ultimate from the point of view of empirical science. Whatever philosophy or metaphysics—the transcendental sciences—may have to say further is another matter.

With respect to illustrations it must be remembered that they are not proofs. The justifying evidence of a truth, or principle, must be found in the facts of the case, or they are not likely to be provided in an illustrative example.

Another word of warning may be given to those who take up the study of the science of education after a considerable amount of practical experience in teaching. Such are very often inclined to say : " This may be all very well in theory, but it will not hold in practice." Now, true science is, and can be, nothing more than the fullest expression of our deepest knowledge of things. Such a remark as the above, therefore, implies that the

theory is false; for, if it be true, it must hold in practice, since this is the final and conclusive test of its
validity.

If the objector still persists that he has found that
such-and-such a principle does not hold in practice, or
that its very opposite does, then either the principle is
false, or he has misunderstood the facts to which he
appeals.   Thus a result which he attributes to a certain
condition of things may really have been produced in
spite of it, through his own, or the pupil's, earnestness,
perseverance, and power.

That the principles do, as a matter of fact, hold in
practice is shown by the methods and maxims of the
greatest teachers.   These have arrived at the same conclusions, in a more or less implicit form, from the practical necessities and accidental successes of intelligent
work, that the scientist has from a rational investigation
of the phenomena which they have had to deal with.

Erasmus (1467–1536), whose writings are based on
practical experience as a teacher, says: "We learn with
great willingness from those we love ; there are children
who would be killed sooner than made better by blows:
by mildness and kind admonitions, one may make of
them whatever he will.   Drill in reading and writing is
a little bit tiresome, and the teacher will ingeniously
palliate the tedium by the artifice of an attractive
method; the ancients moulded toothsome dainties into
the forms of letters, and thus, as it were, made children
swallow the alphabet."   All these maxims are based on
the principle of pleasure.

The same writer says : "As the body in infant years

is nourished by little portions distributed at intervals, so should the mind of the child be nurtured by items of knowledge, adapted to its weakness, and distributed little by little" (Compayre, "History of Pedagogy"). Here we have the principle of nourishment stated, and that of stimulation implied.

Ratke's (1571–1635) great rule was : " In everything we should follow the order of nature. There is a certain natural sequence along which the human intelligence moves in acquiring knowledge. This sequence must be studied, and instruction must be based on the knowledge of it " (Quick, " Educational Reformers "). Thus the essentially practical man clearly indicates the principle of inter-relation and inter-dependence.

" Repetitio mater studiorum," said the Jesuits, who had probably the most perfect practical system of teaching of the sixteenth century. Comenius (1592–1671), himself a man of wide experience as a teacher, says : " Repetitio memoriæ pater et mater est." Again and again we find the great teachers insisting upon the principle of repetition.

Quaint old Roger Ascham (1515–1602), when speaking of the order of teaching which the master should pursue in the case of the epistles of Cicero, says : " First, let him teach the childe, cheerfullie and plainlie, the cause and matter of the letter ; then, let him construe it into English, so oft, as the childe maie easilie carrie awaie the understanding of it." So he points out the need of observing the principle of preparation.

Quintillian (35–95 A.D.) says : " The desire of learning depends upon the will, which you are not able to compel." In other words, the only influence which affects the will, and so causes the mind to receive and retain, is a sufficient motive in the individual. So the principle of interest is thus early stated.

"What you think necessary for them to do, settle in them by an indispensable practice, as often as the occasion returns; and, if it be possible, make occasions. This will beget habits in them which, being once established, operate of themselves easily and naturally, without the assistance of memory." Thus Locke, the great philosopher, who was also a practical teacher, indicates the value of the principle of habituation.

Not to omit the moderns, we may quote Dr. Fitch, who urges that "some of the best work of our own lives has taken the form of self-tuition. . . . . Consider, too, how precious and abiding knowledge won by our own efforts always is." Dr. Abbott says: "We remember best . . . . those things which (1) present themselves to us from the first in the most interesting or incisive form, or (2) are impressed by constant repetition." He also advises that, "Before beginning to teach any subject, the teacher should endeavour to excite the pupil's interest by conversations and stories illustrating the utility of it." Canon Daniel insists that "Pleasure accompanies the appropriate exercise of every faculty we possess. . . . . The art of the teacher is to find out appropriate exercises."

Examples of this kind might be easily multiplied, but sufficient have been given to show that experience both leads to and reflects true theory. The value of a study of the history of education is also shown.

CHAPTER IV

THE GENERAL CHARACTERISTICS OF MENTAL
DEVELOPMENT

THE fact of the separate stages of growth and development in the human being is very clearly and definitely recognised in common language. When we speak of babyhood, childhood, youth, and manhood or womanhood, we are marking off the characteristic stages through which the mental and bodily powers pass. There is also a very general agreement as to some of the chief qualities which distinguish these from each other in the ordinary individual. It is as usual as it is true to speak of the helplessness, innocence, guilelessness, and dependence of the baby; the trustfulness, artlessness, inquisitiveness, plasticity, volatility, and receptiveness of the child; and the vigour, rashness, impetuosity, self-assurance, and obstinacy of youth. In the man or woman these qualities are regarded as modified and under the control of an informed and capable judgment, which is taken as the dominating factor in adult life.

Not only are these stages of development recognised as thus broadly marked off from each other, but their dependence and continuity is insisted on in such proverbial sayings as : "The child is father of the man," " As the twig is bent the tree's inclined," "Train up a child in the way he should go, and when he is old he will not depart from it."

Such facts are of the very greatest interest and value to the educationist, for it is this development which he desires to know the nature and laws of. We must, therefore, try to understand the matter from a strictly scientific point of view. This again brings us to psychology as a basis of educational principles.

Since we hold that the mind as a whole can be considered to have three great elements, viz., feeling, knowing, and willing, what we want now to know is whether these develop in any definite and distinct manner, and, if so, how they develop.

Observation has shown that there is an obvious and well-defined line of mental development, both as to the mind as a whole, and with regard to the three mind-elements. We have already pointed out that though the three great mental elements are always present in every act of consciousness, yet they are present in unequal degrees, as a rule. Sometimes one element strongly predominates, sometimes another. It is in these two senses that we speak of an order of mental development, viz., in the sense that, at certain periods in the life of the individual the general character of the mind varies, and also that one of the elements develops at a greater rate, *i.e.*, more extensively and intensely than the others. It is always true that the general and special features are all developing.

One point should be carefully noticed. Although it

is impossible to say at what particular point of time one kind of development actually does, or is likely to, begin, yet we are justified in saying that, as a rule, a certain kind of development will take place about the period within certain years of the ordinary individual's life. Just as in the bodily growth there is a period when the individual is only able to receive and assimilate the nourishment which is prepared for, and administered to, it; then a period in which it is able to do something towards preparing its own food, and to entirely manage the feeding operations; and finally the time when it is able to provide as well as prepare and consume its food: so in the mental life there is progress from dependence to independence.

It is generally agreed that the three chief stages of mental development may, broadly speaking, be regarded as taking place within successive periods of seven years, viz., from birth to the seventh year, from the seventh to the fourteenth year, and from the fourteenth to the twenty-first year. But this view of the matter must be regarded with considerable caution, and only accepted as a more or less trustworthy account of the probable development, under ordinarily favourable conditions, of an individual with the average amount of mental and physical vigour and capacity.

The original powers and peculiarities with which a person begins life, the influences which affect him, and the conditions by which he is surrounded, are so various and so changing that very numerous and considerable differences in the detail of development are inevitable. At the same time the great general characteristics of the human nature and order of development in all individuals will closely resemble each other. Were this not so, any idea of human beings as a class, or scientific knowledge of their nature and laws as a race, would be impossible. A separate science for each individual would have to be made.

The General Nature of Mental Development.—As we have already suggested there is first the period of almost pure receptivity and reproduction, when the mind simply receives and takes account of, in a more or less vague or definite manner, the influences which act upon it, and thus nourishes, strengthens, and, to a limited extent, develops itself. This stage may be called the vegetative stage.

Then follows the stage in which the mental powers begin to take definite shape and form, and the mind appears as an active agent in the general complex of which it is a part. From being an almost wholly passive object, it becomes an active influence in the world of things. But this only in a direct and concrete way, for there are as yet none of the more subtle, profound, and powerful activities of the higher reason. Mind has, so to speak, learnt to run alone. It is now an exploring as well as a receiving organ, and it receives in a much more extensive and appreciative way. It learns to know, in a direct and practical sense, the various objects by which it is surrounded. We may call this the stage of practical knowing.

When practical knowledge has reached to a somewhat considerable degree of fulness and precision, then the mind begins to study itself, through reflecting upon its ideas and experiences, and thus obtains a still higher kind of knowledge. We esteem it an advance in knowledge when we distinguish between our thoughts of things and the things themselves, and afterwards get to know about our thoughts in a similar manner to that in which we know about other objects. It is thus that science and philosophy come into existence. This may be called the stage of rational knowing.

The difference between practical knowing and rational knowing is well illustrated by the difference between the knowledge which the artisan has, who deals with materials according to traditional methods and rule-of-thumb reasons, and the knowledge which the scientist has, who is guided by the nature of the material with which he is dealing, and the general laws which are true of such things.

These three stages of general mental development roughly correspond to the periods of babyhood, childhood (including youth), and manhood. They are as true of the race as of the individual. There is the primitive savage who is almost purely animal in his mode of life, and is in the vegetative stage; then there is the semi-civilised man, who has developed the domestic arts and manufactures to a very considerable extent, and has an extensive store of practical knowledge; and, finally, we have the civilised man, who has developed the sciences and philosophies. Of course these stages more or less overlap, but they are definitely marked off from each other in a broad and general sense.

Plato, long ago, drew attention to this general

movement from the more purely sensuous to the more purely rational. He writes thus : " The soul . . . . is at first without intelligence ; but when the flood of growth and nutriment abates, and the courses of the soul, calming down, go their own way, and become steadier as time goes on, then the several circles return to the natural form . . . . and make the possessor of them to become a rational being " (Dr. Jowett's translation).

Not only does the above apply to the whole life of the individual and the race, but it also applies to each distinct line of development in the race and the individual. For example, in language the race doubtless began by imitating natural sounds and motions, thus making a gesture language consisting of sounds and motions. Thus the sounds "quack, quack," and the motion of the arms like the moving of wings, would mean a flying duck. This is the purely receptive and reproductive stage. Then followed the period in which the practical use of language is largely developed, and in which a written language—at first largely pictorial—was produced. And finally there came the stage when men investigated the origin, nature, and laws of language, as such, and thus arrived at a science and philosophy of language.

Similarly the individual at first simply imitates the words and sentences which are taught to him. Later on he is able to use language freely, and to invent his own combinations for practical purposes. And not till after this is he well prepared for the study of the grammar and philology of a language.

It is important to bear in mind that these stages grow unto each other by a gradual increase in the proportion of the new element and a corresponding proportionate decrease—there is an actual increase—of the dominance of the previously predominant element. Thus, if we take the first seven years of the individual's life as covering the first stage, then during the sixth and seventh year the more purely receptive and reproductive elements are rapidly becoming subordinate, whilst practical mastery and knowledge are rapidly becoming predominant. This kind of movement is always true of stages of development, and unless it is fully recognised serious misconceptions may arise.

There are what we may term the individual elements of general development. The totals which make up the great stages of mental progress are themselves composed of individual items of development. In the case of each separate power of mind there is a more or less constant and steady increase of its extent and strength: of the ease, quickness, accuracy and completeness with which it acts: and of its ability to do more difficult, complex, and profound work. That which is at first slow and laborious, becomes rapid and easy, and later on is done with great skill and finish. When individual powers have so developed they are likely to become habitual. If they do they will require the minimum of attention and effort, and will thus set free energy and skill with which further progress may be made.

We will now consider in detail each of the three great stages in the development of the mind-elements.

For reasons which will appear in the discussions we shall take the view that feeling is the first to predominantly develop, then knowing, and lastly willing. It will be taken for granted that sound and vigorous individuals under favourable conditions are always referred to.

The Development of Feeling.—If it be true that the early part of the life of an individual is chiefly taken up with nutrition and mere growth, then it is clear that its knowing activities will be mainly directed to distinguishing the different pleasurable and painful effects of its experiences. This will, at first, only apply to the elements of pure feeling, for at the very beginning it has nothing to help it to form even very implicitly concrete judgments about anything else. The baby only knows whether its feelings are pleasant or otherwise, and gives immediate expression to this by its cryings or croonings.

Perhaps it would be better to say that the baby practically realises that it feels—although this is not a very happy description—rather than that it knows what it feels. The whole matter is briefly but probably fully expressed from the baby's point of view by simply saying that its mental life consists chiefly of feelings.

Early infancy is almost wholly taken up with the activity and development of the senses. The child realises, to a limited extent, the pleasure-giving powers of its senses, and uses them to an almost unlimited extent. Its restless activity whilst awake is an evidence of its receptive eagerness. Its habit of carrying everything to its mouth and trying to eat it, is doubtless due to its desire for the pleasures of taste, which is the sense whereby it gets most of its very earliest experiences.

This period of receptivity is of the utmost importance for the future life, for now the individual is receiving those elements of experience upon which all later developments are largely dependent. To illustrate this by an extreme example : it is not difficult to realise that if a healthy child were invariably kept in darkness or intense light during the first three years of its life, this would have a very serious if not fatal effect upon the eye, and through it upon the general mental and physical development. The same truth will hold in other matters and degrees. With regard to this point Dr. Höffding speaks of "the predominating importance of the vegetative life."

It is not the case that very great refinement is necessary in the conditions of life during this period, but very great care should be taken to prevent excess or defect in the influences which affect the child. Also it is important that all the most valuable kinds of influences should systematically affect it. Each of the senses should be methodically exercised. This will only require a little care and judgment in arranging the surroundings and playthings of the child.

The infant is all action and growth, and its feeling and senses are peculiarly acute, intense, and susceptible. As Dr. Höffding remarks : " Where adults merely tremble, children fall into convulsions." Hence the child is either all tears or all smiles; it is generally, either crying or laughing. There is in early childhood a very

L

rapid and proportionally great growth of body and mind, and it is this which demands that the life shall be predominantly vegetative and full of feeling. The child that is defective in vital energy is languid and dull, and consequently slow in its growth. The vegetative element must, therefore, be recognised, stimulated, nourished, and carefully exercised.

Feeling is of course, during this early period connected almost wholly with sensations. In other words it is the sensuous feelings which are predominantly developed. The intellectual or æsthetic feelings are only developed to a very limited extent.

All the experiences are, for the most part, direct and concrete at this period of life. There is comparatively little of that reflective activity of consciousness which examines its own experiences and finds more in them than is given by the immediate response of the mind. It is a time when sensations are the chief element in life, and when the mind is most occupied with taking account of them.

These feelings are doubtless, at first, very vague and indefinite, but they soon become more or less sharply marked off from each other. The first experiences of the different feelings are probably somewhat similar in their effect upon the mind to that of a blaze of light upon the eyes. There is a general disturbance, and a keen sense of feeling, but very little else. Later on there would come some notion of the difference between one kind of feeling and another, and some idea of connecting different feelings with different conditions of the surroundings. Thus feelings would be classified, in an elementary way, and in so far as they were associated, however mistakenly, with objects, the objects would also be more or less classified.

In the earliest years of the child's life, its intense susceptibility to feeling is such that its experiences produce emotions and passions rather than feelings proper. This is specially shown in the case of spoilt children who sometimes scream themselves into convulsions if they do not get exactly what they wish. Children, as a rule, perform most of their actions with great vigour and intensity, and often with excessive energy. Doubtless this is due to the ease with which their feelings are excited to a high state of tension.

Bright colours, loud noises, and rapid movements, all seem to greatly delight the young child. Only constant change and variety are able to satisfy its restless activity and its practically unlimited appetite for sense experiences. It is by no means nice or delicate in its mental tastes, but eagerly devours whatever it can obtain. Indeed its mental appetite is like to its bodily: as insatiable as indiscriminate.

The feelings of fear, surprise, joy, disappointment, change, harmony, and so on, are very acute and intense, in so far as as they are practically involved in concrete experiences. There are the beginnings of the higher forms of feelings, *e.g.*, of love in the selfish attachment to what has constantly satisfied the wants: of trust, in the primitive credulity of inexperience and ignorance: and of respect, in the deference which helplessness must pay to strength.

Such are the chief characteristics of the child during

its first three years of existence. During this period it probably receives a greater number of impressions and fresh experiences than during any other three years of its whole life. This may be called the earliest material-collecting time, the great importance of which is due to the fact that, here as elsewhere, first impressions are likely to prove very lasting and leavening.

Feeling has reached a higher stage of development, when the feeling element in an experience is definite and distinct for the mind. It is then the case that the mind grasps the feeling rather than that the feeling takes possession of the mind. When this is so the feeling becomes more significant, for the mind realises something more than the element of pleasure or pain. There is an appreciation of what we may call the feeling-tone : the difference between the feelings of hunger, refreshment, thirst, sweetness, sourness, tiredness, vigour, and so on.

That feelings are thus marked off from each other is, of course, due to the power of knowing. The knowing element helps to still further develop the classifying of feelings by bringing about the association of certain feelings with the conditions and objects which cause them. The power of willing, as exercised in the control of the feelings, is most helpful to the development of feeling, by preventing the loss of significance in the excess of general disturbance.

Above all, progress in the growth and development of feeling is due to the growth and development of the body. As the powers and activities of the sense organs increase, so the mind is supplied more freely and fully with all kinds of sensations; and upon the quality and quantity of this nourishment and exercise depends the mental advance. The health and activity of the body are of the most essential importance in this respect. A feeble or inactive body will mean a more or less undeveloped mind.

There is, however, something more than an extremely powerful and active receptivity in the mental life of the child. Willing is doing its work in the form of simple and direct attention. Similar feelings are aroused by similar experiences, and the mind not only responds in a like manner to like sensations, but it becomes aware that this is the case. In other words, knowing is being developed through the classification of feelings. So also is willing, for the attention gradually becomes more sustained and intense in its working. Thus feelings are classified and known, in an elementary and direct sense.

Knowing may be said to be of a very superficial nature at this stage, and might be compared with the knowledge that an adult has of things through mere signs. A bookseller's assistant may know a great many books, written in languages he is quite ignorant of, by their titles; but, though he would be able to pick them out without hesitation or mistake, they would have no further meaning for him.

The child's knowledge of things through sensation is, at first, of this nature, but after a time it becomes able to relate to one another its various experiences of the same object, and thus begins to form collective ideas of a thing, and of things, in a concrete and practical sense.

It will learn to think of its mother not only as a woman with the attributes of a woman—so far as it knows of them—but as having special relations of practical control, ministration, and guidance, with regard to its own life and the lives of those of the same family. And it may even go so far as to begin to form some general, though vague and very incomplete, idea of what adults understand by motherhood.

Some cautions are necessary here. It is often said that the child has a particularly strong power of imagination, and is, therefore, able to picture to itself all sorts of things and conditions which it has never experienced. Hence its delight in fairy tales, and its habit of attributing human powers and qualities to such objects as dolls and dogs.

Now, if the phrase "power of imagination" is to be understood in the same sense as when applied to adults, the above view is almost certainly mistaken. In the first place, it assumes a power of abstract and reflective thought in the child which there is every evidence to show is absent. Next, if the behaviour of the child be carefully observed, it will be seen that there is real belief behind what is called its imagining. It will cry as seriously about what it thinks to be an injury to its doll, as about its own sufferings. It cannot discriminate at first, between that which superficially resembles a human being and that which is really human. It is serious but utterly wrong judgment based upon profound ignorance, which is mistaken for imagination in children.

. Again, children soon learn to ask if the tales which

are told them are true ; and many develop a great contempt for mere fairy tales whilst retaining all their
liking for stories of real adventure. It is the child's
love of novelty which makes it so eager to hear of
strange things, whilst its complete ignorance, from the
rational and critical point of view, renders it incapable
of making choice of what to accept and what to reject.
It therefore believes everything which affects its mind
in a definite and significant manner. This is what Dr.
Bain calls the primitive credulity of the child.

Such a view is borne out by the history of the race.
What we call the superstitions of the primitive savage
are not, to him, mere imaginings. Unable to decide
between real and apparent coincidence and cause, the
savage mind accepts as positive concrete realities what
we hold to be but the fancies of gross ignorance. It
is hardly likely that anything short of the fullest possible conviction would lead men to suffer such mental
and physical tortures as are involved in most of the
religious systems of uncivilised races.

Some writers also credit children with great readiness in forming general ideas. They say that a child
soon learns to use a name in its wide and general sense,
so that when it knows the word dog it quickly grasps
the notion that it should apply the name to an indefinite
number of animals of a certain kind. Here again
far too much is taken for granted on behalf of the
child. It is indeed one of those mistakes which
the adult is so likely to make when dealing with
the child's mind, viz., reading into the comparative
emptiness and crudeness of the child's mental experi-

ences and activities the fulness and ripeness of the content of his own mental experiences and activities which deal with similar things and conditions. This is a most serious and fatal mistake for the educator to make, and its possibility should always be present to his mind to serve as a caution and a corrective.

To generalise an idea, and, therefore, a name, in any real sense needs either a very extensive practical acquaintance with objects, or a clear and comprehensive rational analysis of, and inductive judgment about, qualities. The child has neither of these qualifications for generalising. Children do apply, and rightly, one name to many objects of the same kind, but in their earliest years the movement of thought is, as a rule, from one object to another, and not from one to many, or even from many to many. Much less is it from one, or a few, to all—except through the ignorant rashness and blindness so characteristic of incompetent beginners, and which often seems more penetrating than the most informed clearness of vision.

Careful observation will show how mistakenly the child proceeds even from one case to another. Thus it will call every man " father," at first, and regards all toys as its own. Its judgments are almost invariably about single facts concerning single objects. It is very positive in its ideas, and, therefore, very much disturbed by contradiction. All this is against anything like a considerable power of generalising ideas. It is rather collective, and multiple, ideas, than general, which children have. They get more or less complex ideas answering to complex wholes, and they learn to apply these to all the individual instances they know of.

Whilst recognising these general limits of early childhood it would be wrong to suppose that there is never anything approaching true generalisation and constructive imagination in the mental life at this period. It may frequently happen in the case of very precocious children, and not infrequently in the case of an average child, that from the third year onwards such developments definitely, but incidentally, appear.

In all children there is a very strong power of reproductive imagination, and imitation, which may easily pass on to constructive imagination. This is well seen in the dramatic way in which they imitatively reproduce the actions and words of their mother or teacher, in playing at being parent or instructor. Children appear to rethink the memories of events as vividly and intensely as they were affected by the original experiences.

The chief point to be remembered is that it is the exception for the higher powers of reason to take definite form in the first three years of life, and that even after this they, for some time, only develop very slowly and subordinately.

Knowing at this stage is of a practical nature. Children obtain what we may call a direct, limited, and descriptive knowledge of things and actions. They understand the qualities and powers of things from the concrete point of view. They know that an apple is large or small, green or red, sweet or sour, hard or soft, a kind of food, the fruit of a tree, and so on; but these facts are rather heaped together than joined together in thought, in relation to the unity of the object.

The use of adjectives instead of abstract nouns, that is, the concrete instead of the abstract term, is a very significant fact in the history of the child and the race. And this is still further emphasised in the use of concrete terms to express abstract ideas, even in the mental sciences.

Observation and imitation are the characteristic activities of children. They are intensely interested in all that surrounds them. Every object and action is a matter to which they give all the attention they can, and from which they often get great pleasure. Everything is new to the child, and has all the charms of novelty, whilst occupying and satisfying its restless energy. So great is the readiness in receiving, and the force in responding to, impressions, that they often result in involuntary imitation of an action, or of a simple series of actions.

In " Practical Education," by Maria and R. L. Edgeworth, there are some very interesting records of children's judgments and ideas, which illustrate much that we have said; but, of course, we cannot draw any general conclusions from them alone. A child who was three years old, on being questioned, said that a watch, fire, horse, and chaise, were live things, but that a tea-urn and book were not. It will thus be noticed that those things which appear to be active in themselves are thought to have life. A boy of five years asked whether a giant had not lived much longer than other men, so as to have time to grow so much more. The same boy, when eight, on being asked what a toothpick case was made of, and being told to look well at it, and feel it, asked if he might smell it. He then felt, looked at, and smelt it, and said : " It is black, and smooth, and strong, and light. What is, let me see, both strong and light, and it will bend— parchment? " An older brother identified the substance, through having used some leather in making a piston for a pump.

Very little need be said of the imitative activities of children. The readiness and thoroughness with which they play at mother and father, shopkeeping, and school-teaching, show not only their powers of copying closely, but also of very exact and searching observation. They are often, in this way, the best of involuntary critics, and give us many a chance of seeing ourselves as others see us.

Similarly willing begins to get more self-dependent and initiative towards the end of the first period. Whilst in the earlier years willing has been more of a passive, spontaneous, automatic, and instinctive nature, it now is somewhat initiative, and is directed to ends fixed upon by the judgment. Self-direction, self-correction, and self-initiation, along the lines of past experiences, begin to appear in a more or less definite form. This is well shown in the school by the child's ability to invent designs in elementary drawing, to set itself sums and to originate little tales out of the mental material it has acquired, even at the very early age of six years.

This kind of development of knowing and willing is likely to take place about the sixth and seventh years. Feeling is still predominant, but much less so than formerly.

The Development of Knowing.—During the second seven years of life there is very great growth and development of knowing. Not only cannot the child fail to mentally receive and appreciate the influences of its surroundings, but it is driven to taking the initiative in obtaining experiences, by the needs of its mental and bodily life. The constant questions as to why and how objects act in certain ways, show the existence of a mental appetite, which is as keen as it is extensive.

By the end of the seventh year most children have formed more or less systematic habits of mental work. They will apply themselves as readily and earnestly to mental activity as to bodily, and, under proper conditions, they obtain nearly, if not quite, as much pleasure from the former as from the latter. Exercise and nourishment of the mind are as necessary and should be as pleasurable to the child as exercise and nourishment of the body.

The practical knowledge of things is very much extended, and made more systematic and complete, so that towards the end of the second period it begins to be definitely scientific, in an elementary sense. The child begins to more definitely realise its power of knowing, and to take delight in exercising it.

This advance is brought about by a closer analysis of experiences, and a more thorough and comprehensive grasp of relations. For example, the parts, powers, and qualities of an object are more clearly recognised to be dependent units which make up the total unity or object. Then again these different details are more carefully compared with each other, and with the details of similar objects, and thus the points of likeness and unlikeness are taken account of in greater fulness. This fuller recognition of similarity and difference is the basis for some of the highest judgments that can be made about things, for they lead on to the discovery of what we call the reasons for things.

Again this closer and more complete analysis of things from the practical point of view, that is, with regard to our actual concrete acquaintance with, and knowledge of, them, enables us to make more definite and satisfactory classifications. Thus a further step is made towards organised knowledge, or science.

The receiving and retaining powers of the child are at their very highest during this period. Indeed, from about the tenth to the fourteenth year memory is stronger than at any other time during the whole life. Hence an enormous store of impressions, facts, and concrete ideas is acquired at this stage. It is, therefore, of vital importance that these should be of the best, most accurate, and most helpful kinds.

Nearly all the materials which are acquired are submitted to the judgment. The judgments which are made about them are still predominantly concrete and direct, but they are more connected and extensive than formerly. This is shown by the ability to give in writing, or orally, a more or less exhaustive account of an object, not only as to its parts and qualities, but also with respect to its powers and its relations with other objects, so far as these are shown by actions and their results.

With this apprehension of the connection between actions and results comes the first form of an idea which later on becomes the most purely rational and highly philosophic of all our ideas—the idea of cause. At first the idea is purely practical and concrete, and consists, as already indicated, in the connecting, in thought, of certain actions with their usual results. But the idea gets fuller and more abstract as time goes on.

We may say that the development of knowing during this stage is shown by the greater definiteness, detail, completeness, accuracy, and unity of practical judgments and ideas. This applies to each separate idea, and to its relation to other ideas, through things. Also these ideas become more and more abstract, that is, they are known to the individual as ideas, apart from the objects and experiences which give rise to them.

Language now begins to be familiar and very helpful. It serves to give clearness, definiteness, and permanence to ideas. Ideas are more readily and thoroughly, surely and easily, controlled. It is much easier to retain and recall an idea through a symbol, than when dealing with the idea itself. Another means of imparting knowledge is also provided by language; and the bridge which carries the individual from the lower to higher kinds of thought is largely built of words.

Where previously there have been groups of judgments about things there will now be series of connected and dependent judgments about them. In other words, the power of reasoning, or connected and dependent judging, appears. Reasoning is at this period predominantly practical, or concrete. It deals mostly with things and events, as a rule, and only with principles and causes, in their purely rational aspects, occasionally and superficially. Mind begins to find in its surroundings a coherence and unity which also belong to its own nature.

That the mental powers take time to reach such a condition of judgment is shown by such facts as the following. In the lowest forms of language abstract terms are entirely wanting. The Tasmanians, when first known, had no general term for a tree, though they had names for each particular kind. Neither could they express qualities such as hard, soft, round, warm, cold, short, and long.

In the North American languages a name sufficiently general to denote an oak-tree is exceptional. The Choctaw language contains names for the black oak, white oak, and red oak, but none for an oak, still less for a tree. The Coroados of Brazil have no conception of the general powers and laws of nature, and therefore cannot express them in words.

All this shows that the mind is, at first, almost entirely taken up with the effort to know single things. It is only gradually that it is able to clearly and definitely take account of groups of things, even with respect to concrete numbers, much less with regard· to their abstract qualities, powers, and principles.

We may illustrate the nature of the knowledge which the average child possesses towards the end of this period, by a description of what we consider would represent his knowledge of an ordinary lamp. In the first place he would have very definite and exact ideas about its function, shape, and parts, and their concrete relations. He would probably be able to give the practical reasons for its having a chimney, and for this being removable: for the need of the perforated arrangement just below the wick: for the use of the weight of the pedestal: the function and action of the wick: and for various other details. Also he would be likely to know the nature of the material of which each part is composed, and the practical relation of this to the special function performed.

This involves a great deal of classification, and, therefore, of judgments based upon previous knowledge. Each detail has to be compared, in thought at least, with previous experiences of things of the same class, and its points of special likeness and difference noted, in relation to the lamp as a particular object. The greater familiarity with, command over, and facility in the use of, language, however, makes this comparatively easy, and ideas, as such, are very readily dealt with through their verbal signs. Through words, a considerable number of ideas can be represented in the mind at the same moment, and comparison and classification are then not so difficult. In a similar way the abstract elements of ideas are more easily developed through the aid of words.

Further, the various details of the lamp will be understood as making up the one whole. There will be the realisation of the fact that the removal of any one separate part changes the previous total more or less seriously; whilst changing the character of an essential part, such as the perforated air-passage, will altogether destroy the former character of the whole. The relation of air to flame will be grasped, from the practical side; and it may be practically demonstrated that it is not the oil itself, but the gas which it gives off, which supports the flame.

Knowledge such as this is just on the borderland of pure science, and will of itself often force the intelligent student to make one or more of those generalised abstractions which go to make up the principles of the different sciences.

Although the child is now less easily deceived than formerly, and more slow to accept first impressions as final truths, yet, when it has new and striking experiences, it is still apt, so to speak, to swallow things whole. Neither its knowledge nor its mental powers enable it to be very cautious or critical.

During this period the bodily powers are growing and developing very considerably. The child is able to influence its surroundings to a very large extent. It finds that it can carry out series of actions which bring about results which are more or less interesting and instructive to it. This leads it to spend its very great physical energy in all kinds of explorations and investigations on its own behalf. Towards the end of the second seven years boys begin to develop the egg-collecting, stamp-collecting, animal-keeping, and other

M

forms of systematic and independent activity.   In their games also they are quite capable of forming and conducting their own little organisations and plans.

Anything which offers the opportunity for the child to bring about results by its own unaided efforts is most eagerly welcomed by it.   To be able to say "I did it all myself," is one of its greatest pleasures. Indeed it is apt to be very intolerant of too much guidance and assistance, however kindly rendered. The bodily vigour enables it to continue constantly active at high pressure, so that the amount of work which it can get through is, comparatively speaking, enormous.   By work is here meant the more or less free, spontaneous, and pleasurable activity of mind and body, in taking appropriate nourishment and exercise.

This parallel progress of bodily power and of knowing, is shown by the appearance of personal tastes, preferences, propensities, and independence of thought and action.   Habits are now being formed, which will later on fix the character of the individual.   Ideas, and even ideals of a simple kind, begin to be the guiding power in life.   Aims and ambitions may take possession of the mind.   In short the higher, or purely rational, mental life is beginning to predominate.

One very important consideration must always be remembered with regard to the development of knowing.   Whilst feeling will be developed very much to the same extent in very different surroundings, the progress of knowing will vary very much according to differences of surroundings.   If, for example, one child is brought up in the home of well-educated and refined parents,

whilst another is reared in the cottage of very poor and
ignorant parents, the former is likely to develop the
purely rational elements of knowing considerably sooner
than the latter. But this consideration must not be
pressed too far. School influences and the struggle for
existence do much to sharpen the wits of the poor.

It is more often the case that the difference is one of
direction rather than degree. The street arab is likely
to be as mentally keen and powerful as the public-
school boy, but with regard to entirely different
matters. Similarly the average country child and the
town child, the agriculturist and the artisan, or the
man of business and the scholar, are likely to have, as
a rule, about the same degree of development of mental
powers, though very different acquirements. A definite
and marked distinction has hitherto existed between
the mental development of the average child in a
primary school and a secondary school; but this now
seems to be largely disappearing.

From what has been said about the advance of knowing at this stage of the child's life, it will be seen that
willing is also making considerable progress. If this
were not so neither thought or action could have those
elements of independence and individuality which have
been suggested.

Now that judgments come freely, the connection of
actions with effect is known, and the possibilities of the
bodily powers are recognised, the mind makes judgments which imitate series of bodily actions. This is
practical willing. The hesitation in taking independent lines of action, and the want of perseverance in

pursuing them when taken, which have characterised the earlier years, now begin to disappear, though they are still frequent and conspicuous.

Children begin to realise their will power, and acquire some control over it. They are no longer so easily moved to action by the mere force of impressions. Involuntary imitative actions become less frequent, and are replaced by voluntarily chosen and designed imitations. The intense volatility of the young child begins to develop into the greater steadiness, power of sustained attention, and regularity, of the youth.

As we have said, plans and series of actions are carried out. This involves the systemising of willing. Thus willing, like knowing, is developing a practical coherence and unity.

Feeling is still very keen, strong, and active, but much more under control. Owing to the progress of knowing and willing the feelings are much more fully and accurately discriminated. Hence they are more significant and less emotional, or passionate. Life has passed from its more purely vegetative to a more purely human character. Feelings become less animal and more humane and sympathetic.

The various feelings, as connected with different experiences, have now far more definiteness and significance than formerly. Both knowing and sense capacity increase the fulness of their meaning and detail. And the feelings in their turn stimulate and promote the desire to know. The sentiments also are taking definite form. Gratitude, affection, respect, sympathy, self-esteem, and many other sentiments, in their more practical and concrete aspects, are possessed by the child.

We shall have much to say about the details of the growth and development of knowing in later chapters on the development of ideas and the growth of knowledge.

The Development of Willing.—In the third seven years of life, willing is predominant in development. But this predominance is, perhaps, hardly so marked as that of feeling and knowing in their respective periods. This is doubtless due to the fact that willing is so very closely connected with knowing, which still develops at a very rapid rate. But there is hardly any question that the advance of willing is the characteristic feature at this stage.

It is generally recognised that youth, and early manhood and womanhood, is the time when individuals begin to assert themselves, to desire their own way, to be impatient of control, to be dogmatic and uncompromising in judgment, and to cling persistently if not obstinately to their opinions and prejudices. At the same time it is a period when great initiativeness, readiness, boldness, perseverance, and power in action are shown.

The average youth is the last to practically admit that "we are all fallible, even the youngest," or to recognise that human powers are, after all, very limited. The sense of power, the feeling of vigorous vitality, the pleasures of action, and the inexperience and ignorance of youth, are all conditions which tend to make the will run riot. What Dr. Bain calls the pleasures of pursuit

are very keenly relished, and there is too much buoy-
ancy in the nature to feel failures very much, even if
they are admitted.

All these characteristics of youth depend upon the
development of willing. Willing as an activity of
mind is now definitely under the general mental control. Involuntary willing is almost entirely superseded
by voluntary willing. What is generally understood
by the will—the power to initiate, and to choose
between, thoughts and actions—now appears. This
fact is realised by the individual, and instead of too
much hesitation and too little steadfastness in willing,
there is often too little hesitation and too much persistence. Youth is apt to be rash and headstrong.

Just as there was an almost limitless desire and
eagerness to know, when the powers and pleasures of
knowing began to be realised, so there is now a constant and eager indulgence in willing for the sake of
the excitement, interest, and satisfaction which the
exercise of the power, and the accompanying actions,
give.

But there is much more than this increase of power
and intensity in willing. The coherence and unity of
the separate activities of the power are developed to a
much higher degree. Series and systems of willings
are carried out, and these are again related to each
other so as to form more comprehensive and complex
unities. Thus the individuality and character are made
to take a much more definite and effective form.

Separate actions, and courses of actions, are now
decided upon according to the individuality of the person.

It is during this period that the individual develops the powers and preferences which are likely, if the matter is left entirely to him, to lead to the choice of a definite kind of life-work. Such a choice, when made after full consideration, and with some realisation of its meaning and consequences, involves one of the most powerful, permanent, and important efforts of will that the individual ever makes. And, if this be so, the fact of such a momentous choice being made is conclusive evidence of the great development of willing.

The chief element of advance in the power of willing is the ability to organise series of actions, mental and physical, which are intended to bring about more or less remote ends. Children have very little, if any, regard to future pleasures or pains. But in later youth and early manhood, or womanhood, when the mind begins to realise more fully its own powers, there is a strong tendency to pay more attention to the future than to the present. The poetry of mental ideals has more attraction than the prose of commonplace realities.

The imagination is now vigorous, but it is neither checked by deep knowledge and critical judgment, nor chastened by the convictions of wide experience and frequent failure. Hence the enthusiasms, Utopian dreams, beliefs in practical perfection, struggles for the realisation of ideals, and living in the future, of young people. Willing is with them such a reality that they fail to distinguish between the reality of a willing and the possibility of its practical realisation. Every one is likely to be more or less of a visionary at this time of life. To conceive ideals is, in youth, to believe in them, and to believe in them is to struggle to realise them. It is in this connection that willing is called upon to initiate and maintain the stimulus to series of actions.

Willing may, therefore, be said to be more concerned with purely intellectual judgments and activities than formerly. Most of the willings necessary for practical affairs have become habitual, and only new departures in ordinary life demand deliberate and self-conscious acts of willing. It is the higher and more purely rational activities which now begin to assert themselves, and which, therefore, need the energising and organising control of the will. Thus willing itself becomes a more purely rational activity, for it is, practically, wholly due to and concerned with the mind, as such. It has become an expression of the intellectual and moral self, or the ego.

In this its highest form willing is chiefly dependent upon knowing. Knowledge is the stimulating influence which is responded to by the higher willings. As we have previously asserted, knowing is a motive for willing.

Since willing is ordinarily, and rightly, associated with acting, we may illustrate its development by a brief account of the development of action. All organised action, with the exception of the instinctive, is at first mainly imitative. Charles Lamb's delight-fully humorous account of the way in which roast pig became such a popular dish really contains many elements of historical truth. Such happy accidents have led men to many, if not most, of their discoveries. Thus it is held that man first learnt to make fire by observing the result of the rubbing together of dried branches when swayed by the wind, or the effect upon dry leaves of falling sparks made by knocking flints together. The history of progress is full of accounts of such stumblings upon discoveries.

Then there is the imitating of the actions involved, and the application of the results to practical affairs. In this way observation and imitation produce many of the highest aids to progress. Much more is it true that imitative action is the means of furthering the more ordinary elements of development. We may say that in such cases willing is acting so as to cause the mental response to impressions to result in re-expression of the original influences—as in the case when a hearer repeats the gestures of one who dramatically tells a story. Such willing is both prompted and guided by presentations.

From these almost compulsory imitations individuals soon learn that it is worth while to look out for helpful examples of causes and effects, and to expend considerable effort in trying to copy them. Thus there comes an element of initiation into imitative action. Willing is prompted and guided by practical experience and knowledge.

Later on, actions, are prompted and guided almost wholly by judgments based upon the knowledge already obtained through observation, action, and previous judgment. Actions of this kind are based upon, and designed to carry out, series of judgments due almost wholly to the purely initiative powers of the mind. Pure rational willing is the cause of such actions. It is the highest form of willing, and the highest results of thought and action in human life are due to it.

As an expression of the individuality of the self, or ego, the will controls the actions which produce habits, and is in time largely controlled by the habits which are formed. Character is an expression of willing, and willing expresses the character. All the powers and possibilities of the individual may be more or less fully realised when willing has reached its highest level of development.

Whilst willing is thus developing up to its highest level, so also is knowing. We have already remarked that knowing begins to be of a strictly scientific character towards the end of the second seven years. During the third seven years, it becomes, under favourable conditions, more completely and generally scientific in character. The learner is no longer satisfied to know things as facts, but he desires to know, and insists upon knowing, in a scientific sense, the causes of things, and the laws and principles which belong to them, so far as this may be possible.

Let us inquire more particularly into what is to be understood by a scientific form of knowing. We have already given the usual definition : science is organised knowledge. To organise knowledge is to set it forth in its proper order of co-ordination and subordination : its inter-relations, inter-dependence, and inter-connection. These therefore must be found out. In other words, we must obtain a knowledge of the elements, laws, principles, causes, and effects of the different kinds or classes of things, and of their nature and actions.

How, then, does the mind obtain this knowledge? As has been previously remarked, the mind at first deals only with individual objects, as concretes. Later on it learns to take account of larger or smaller groups of like things, that is, it forms ideas of classes, in a concrete sense, and makes inclusive judgments about them. But, in the third period of development, it has come, so to speak, face to face with its own mind, and definitely and clearly realises that there is in its knowledge a purely mental element, the application of which is not necessarily confined to one object, or one class of objects.

This fact is not only recognised, but is systematically made use of, and the individual now generalises his judgments in a conscious and purposeful manner. Such a rational use of the judgment is very different from the experience-limited and practical collective judgments of an earlier period. The individual now recognises the fact that there are elements of universal truths in the connection of causes and effects which are discovered in single objects. A very great advance in mental development is involved in this, for knowledge can now be consciously organised, and the existing organisms of knowledge (the sciences)· can be more clearly and comprehensively appreciated from the purely rational or theoretical point of view.

Such a movement of thought from particular instances and judgments of limited application to the recognition of universal truths and the forming of judgments of universal application, is called inductive reasoning. A detailed example of this has already been given in the chapter on the scope and method of education. We will now express the matter in quite general terms.

There is first a particular observation of a certain class of facts, or phenomena, which common experience has shown to have significant points of similarity; then follows a more careful, thorough, complete, and systematic classifying of these facts, according to what is learnt from severely searching observation. This is followed by that higher form of knowledge about the qualities, powers, relations, and nature of the things, which leads to the forming of an opinion as to the reason, or reasons, for the existence of certain general qualities or powers. These general judgments about the reason for such things, are known as theories or hypotheses, and they are, at first, simply supposings, or, as the scientist would say, purely hypothetical theories. They seem, as we say, to offer a satisfactory explanation of matters.

The next thing is to put them to the proof. This is best done by taking two instances of the conditions which constitute the phenomenon which are exactly similar to each other, with the single exception that in one case the condition (or conditions) which is held to be the reason or cause for the phenomenon, is present, whilst in the other it is absent. This must be, so far as we can secure it, absolutely the only difference between the two cases. Then, if, after many experiments and experiences, we always find in the one case that the phenomenon itself is present, whilst in the other it is invariably absent, we may safely conclude that what we have given as reason, cause, or law, is the right one. One other element of proof remains. The theory is regarded as true, and is taken as the basis for reasoning about the phenomena which it represents, and also about other phenomena. If the conclusions of such reasonings prove to be invariably sound when practically applied to concrete cases, then the theory is regarded as finally established.

When principles and laws are arrived at by inductive reasoning, they become centres and sources of numerous other judgments of a more or less general character. As was pointed out in the description of an induction, a universal truth or principle is not finally accepted until it has been frequently tested by practical application to particular cases, and found to be invariably correct. For example, if we hold it to be true that when the worker is interested in his work he produces his best results, then whenever we find particular persons, or groups of persons, really interested in their work, we ought invariably to find that they are doing the best work of which they are capable (at the time).

The reasoning would proceed as follows:—all interested workers do their best work; these persons are interested workers; therefore, these persons do their best work. It will be seen that the first judgment is the result of the investigation which has given the induction, the second is the result of a special and limited investigation as to the character of a class, and the third is the result of a purely rational relation of the two previous ones. The first is a pure universal, that is, it is practically infinite as to its application; the second is general, but definitely limited ; and the third is only as wide as the less comprehensive of the other two.

Instead of referring to a class in the second judgment, we might have referred to an individual only. The third judgment would then refer only to the individual. Such a movement of thought from judgments with a more general to a less general, or individual, application is called deductive reasoning.

It should be noticed that deductions are based, and depend, upon inductions, and that inductions depend upon deductions for their verification. Thus the two processes are inseparably connected with each other, and are really only two phases in the process of establishing rational truth. They directly bring about that interconnection of knowledge which gives it scientific form.

From what has been said of induction and deduction, it will be seen that knowing has what we may call a progressive and a regressive order of development. It first advances from individual experiences and judgments, through close analytic and synthetic investigation, to principles of universal application. When these have become established and familiar, the mind uses them for interpreting and explaining new experiences, and for the more complete understanding of previous knowledge. So there is progress from a knowledge of things to a knowledge of laws, and then from an understanding of laws to an understanding of things, new and old.

Towards the end of this period, and onwards, the mind begins, and continues, to take account of itself in a more or less definite and systematic way. It recognises that judgment, as such, belongs wholly to the mind, and is, as judgment, separate and distinct from experiences which give rise to it. Hence are recognised, in a more or less full and complete sense, the differences between a thing and its attributes, effects and causes, actions and laws, systems and principles. This involves the recognition of the difference between practical and theoretical knowledge, between that which is predominantly sense-given and that which is predominantly reason-given.

Strictly logical reasoning of this kind is very largely dependent upon language. Indeed, with regard to the highest forms, it may be said to practically depend wholly upon the aid which language gives. This is a point with which we shall deal more fully later on. It will be sufficient to say here that language has now reached its highest form of usefulness to thought, and makes possible the most abstract ideas and reasonings.

Let us again refer to the kind of knowledge which may be obtained about a lamp, for the purpose of illustrating what is meant by this higher sort of knowing. From a deeper and more exhaustive study of the parts and functions of a lamp we may arrive at the laws of combustion, as shown by the lamp-flame: conservation of energy, as seen in the products of the burning: cohesion, as exemplified in the different substances of which the parts consist: of capillary attraction, as involved in the function of the wick: and so on.

These would be grasped in a more or less superficial sense at first; and can only be known in some fulness

when studied under special sciences. In the most
advanced stages of such subjects the inter-relation and
inter-dependence of the principles themselves are considered.

Now is understood somewhat of the truth that every
unit is in itself a unity of parts, powers, qualities and
relations, which may be, and generally are, practically
infinite. It has been well said that a fact is an infinity.
And yet these infinite unities are but units in greater
unities, and these of others. Indeed it is only because
of this that we are able to speak of any one thing as
being infinite.

A pen is a simple and commonplace enough article.
And yet what profound truths are involved in the cohesion of the particles which compose it; what a vastly
significant history there is in its development to its
present form; and what a power its work has exerted,
and is exerting, upon the destiny of the world.

If we regard things in such ways, and endeavour to
find the elements of infinite inter-relation and inter-
dependence which they have, then we are making our
views of things tend towards a realisation of what is
believed to be the one grand infinite unity of existence
and knowledge. We may pursue our inquiry still
further, and try to find out what is the nature and
essence of existence or being, as such, both in its
universal (mind and matter) and general (animate and
inanimate things) forms. This is philosophy or metaphysics, and is clearly a purely rational form of
knowing.

How far an individual will go in such a very abstract

form of mental development, must always depend upon his native capacity and vigour of mind and body, educational advantages, and length of life. Every average mind is capable of something in this direction, but not many seem capable of much. Most persons can however appreciate the work of original thinkers.

Both willing and knowing are greatly indebted to the growth and development of the physical powers, in this stage. The extreme energy, vivacity, powers of endurance, delight in action, and desire of conquest, in the ordinarily healthy youth, make the carrying out of willings and the obtaining of knowledge-giving experiences comparatively easy matters. And since exhaustion of the physical energies is very soon recovered from, and the force and fulness of the powers soon re-established, the pursuit of knowledge is constant, and its intensity maintained.

Feeling is still very active and powerful, but is much more subordinate than even in the second seven years. It is now regarded as a sign of weakness to show any marked evidences of the effect of certain feelings, and, indeed, this idea is sometimes taken to such extremes that it is held to be bad form to give emphatic expression to any kind of feelings. But they are still apt to be occasionally violent and excessive, owing to the intensity of willing.

Now the higher and nobler sentiments are greatly developed. Affection, love, admiration, devotion, worship, esteem, sympathy, and the like, assume more purely rational and moral forms. With them are also developed their opposites of dislike, hatred, jealousy,

N

indifference, neglect, contempt, disrespect, and unfeelingness. Also the higher feelings of truth, beauty, goodness, and virtue, take on their fullest and finest characteristics; or are perverted to base and ignoble forms. Feelings of novelty, contrast, surprise, and the like, all have much greater significance, and more direct and remote relations in thought. Fearlessness is more under the purposeful control of willing and knowing; whilst fear is often less frequently shown, and less intense when active. The feeling of power brings with it the feelings of responsibility and obligation.

The development of willing makes it possible to repress the feelings to a very considerable degree. A good illustration of this repression is shown in the amount of physical pain boys will endure rather than admit, either by weeping or appealing for mercy, that they are unable to bear it.

There are, however, higher motives for repressing the feelings. It is soon found that a state of emotion or passion is generally a barrier to accurate and profitable willing and knowing. Hence it is that definite efforts are made to obtain, and maintain, control over the feelings.

On the other hand some of the feelings are deliberately indulged, with a freedom often approaching license, on certain occasions; whilst others are systematically cultivated for pecuniary or personal reasons. It is usually thought right to give very emphatic expressions of feeling on such occasions as: victory in games, exhibitions of power and skill, the appearance of popular or eminent persons, and so forth. One might almost say that it is required of people to show marked signs of distress in connection with certain sad events amongst close relatives or friends. It is clear, therefore, that the feelings must be very much under command.

The systematic cultivation of the feelings takes place in the training of the musician, artist, actor, singer, orator, and the like. All these have need of the power of fully realising in themselves, or to conceive, states of feeling so that they may truthfully express them in their respective arts. We may say that the piano-tuner, the wine-taster, the tea-taster, and others, cultivate the feelings in a more concrete sense.

Ordinary people indulge, and cultivate, their feelings in a more or less systematic way through attendance at dramatic performances, concerts, balls, military and civil pageants, and so forth. Such exercising of the feelings, when under the control of willing and knowing, is helpful to both of these, for there is much in the occasions which conveys knowledge in an attractive and vivid manner, and there is generally a very restful, refreshing, and invigorating change of the activity of willing. The proper indulgence of the feelings is as profitable as it is pleasurable.

The special gratification of the feelings, through sensations, seems likely to receive much more attention in the near future. Already what are called colour-concerts and perfume concerts have been given. In these performances colours and perfumes are made to succeed each other, either singly or in combinations, in a manner resembling solos and harmonies in music.

The sense of taste has been carefully cultivated in all ages through the pleasures of the table.

That the history of the race has many valuable suggestions for the educationist is made evident by even a slight acquaintance with writings on anthropology. Writers on the subject argue from the evidence of historic remains, and the conditions of savage races at the present time, that primitive man was little more than an animal amongst animals. He was a creature of fierce impulses, child-like intellect, and tremendous sense-powers and skill. Constantly fighting for safety and subsistence, he was but a poverty-stricken wanderer without fixed home or interests.

His mental ideas were of the vaguest and most mistaken nature, as is shown by the horrible superstitions which possessed him. And yet he was slowly and painfully learning to know those obvious qualities and differences of things which affected his own life, and which go to make the basis of the science and philosophy of to-day.

Like modern savages his power of sustained attention must have been extremely small, if he could be said to really have any at all; anything in the way of abstract ideas took ages to develop; the idea of a to-morrow was of comparatively late growth; his language consisted almost wholly of gestures and imitative sounds; and his knowledge of number seems not to have exceeded three, or five, for a very long period.

Action was the chief concern of primitive man. It was necessary for him to think in connection with his actions, but not for him to know that he was thinking.

Hence his thought was intuitive, immediate, and practical, in so far as it had to do with his ordinary actions. As these activities grew in number and complexity, and the sphere of their application was increased, so thought and knowledge became fuller and deeper. This is clearly demonstrated by the history of man during the stone age, and the age of metals.

The gradual evolving of the higher products of the thought and action of to-day can be clearly traced from the most primitive thought and action of the earliest races. The present consists chiefly of the remains of the past. Our religious ceremonies, marriage customs, names of days of the week, and many other matters, all contain traces of a very remote past.

A careful study of these things is as necessary as it is helpful to the right understanding of the problem of education. Man has not fundamentally changed his nature, and, indeed, only a fraction of the race seems to have undergone any very considerable change at all, in the way of what we call advance in civilisation. The European nations with their foreign branches, which claim to be the most highly civilised, comprise, at the most, not more than one-third of the total population of the world.

Whatever, therefore, we can know about the past development of the race will, at least, throw very considerable light upon the present nature of human beings. And such a knowledge is one of the first conditions of a grasp of educational principles.

Some General Remarks on Development.—The general order of development as sketched above applies not only to the life as a whole, but also to each particular line of progress and to every considerable unit of advance. And this is true at every stage of life, for the reason that all the elements of mind are always co-active, however much any one of them may predominate.

An adult can often dispense with actual sense experiences in connection with a new form of knowledge, because he may have had a considerable number of similar ones, the details of which he can easily recall to mind. The sense experiences are, so to put it, duplicated. But if he is unable to do this, then the best, and the only certain and really significant, method is to give him the proper sense experiences. As Professor Laurie says: "If ever you have the mind of an undeveloped adult to deal with (a Central African, for example, or a British boor), and desire to teach him anything, you must, even with him, start from the simplest child-elements of it."

There is a point, however, in the history of a well-developed mind when, in consequence of its ripe reason and rich experiences, it is able to make use of what we have termed the order of regressive advance to a very considerable extent. The highest order of scientific mind is able to reason from principles and effects to phenomena. This is best shown in such cases as the discovery of new planets from the actions of known ones, the invention of machinery which exemplifies scientific principles, and the anticipation of concrete discoveries, based upon rational deductions.

But even such very exceptional powers are, in the last resource, obliged to make use of the material obtained from actual experiences, with regard to knowledge about the physical world. In the case of all purely rational knowledge, the mind is, directly and immediately, only indebted to its own activities; but the original source of all that is in the mind as knowledge is the experiences which happen to the senses.

Another point which requires to be clearly understood is that we regard a certain stage of development as reached only when there is a clear consciousness in the individual of the possession of a power, at least in a concrete and practical sense, and a frequent use of it. Incidental powers and results due to the possession of the germs of such powers, must always precede, to a greater or lesser extent, the definite and general development of them.

Still more necessary is it to always bear in mind that our knowledge of the development consists in the realisation of movement rather than steps, of tendencies rather than times, in the life history of a human being. To endeavour to fix the exact times at which exact amounts of development take place is likely to prove even more mischievous than inaccurate. At the same time, our ideas and actions would become chaotic if we fail to recognise and allow for the practically infinite similarities of nature and development amongst individuals of the same kind or class.

Whilst it is impossible to trace in details the different items of development from one stage to another, yet it is quite easy, in most cases, to know that an individual has or has not reached one or other of those important periods which have been mentioned, by the fact that he is able to do certain characteristic mental and physical work. Whilst there is a period when a person seems to be neither quite a girl nor a woman, a boy nor a man, yet this is followed by a period when no one would hesitate to say this person is a woman, or man, and not a girl, or boy.

Perhaps the most important characteristic of true development is the increase of the ability to do more difficult, profound, and complex things. At first only very simple, easy, and obvious things are done. When some measure of facility and accuracy in doing these has been secured, then there is a gradual increase in the power to do greater and higher work. This is true of the general stages of development, and also of every complete particular development and each of its parts.

But there is also the great truth that life includes decay as well as growth. All organisms have a limit of higher organisation, from which, sooner or later, proceed disorganisation, decay, and death. This is true of the whole and of its parts, and the extent to which the whole or separate parts will develop, and the time when they will begin to decay, depend upon the native vigour and capacity of the individual, and the chances and changes of life.

CHAPTER V

FROM our knowledge of the chief phases of mental development come some of the most important of all the educational principles. It will be at once recognised that if we hold that education is the science of human development in so far as this is purposely determined by the systematic imparting of knowledge, then the order of development, and the ordering of instruction so as to best aid and determine it, are the two points with which education has most to do. In fact we may say that all the educational principles directly depend upon, or are related to, this great central consideration. Every principle must either express some aspect of this truth, or be regulated by it. This will appear more and more clearly as we proceed with our discussion.

The Principle of Development.—We have already insisted that it is necessary to have continuity, coherence, system, and unity, in education, so that we may best assist the mind to develop according to its own proper nature. It is just as essential that there should be differences in the matter and manner of the

educating influences, according to the varying character and force of the mental powers at the different
stages of their development.   Hence we have this principle of development.

Rousseau insisted that we ought to "let infancy ripen
in infants."   And Professor Laurie has well said:
"To which we may add 'Let boyhood ripen in boys,
youthhood in youths, and manhood in men.'   Do not
anticipate."   Comenius regarded the period of the complete education of youth as extending from the first to
the twenty-fourth year.   He divides this into four
periods of six years and prescribes a different, but dependent, work for each, according to the powers and
capacities which are developing during each period.

The best way of practically describing development
is to say that every new element in a thing, whether
of quality or quantity, grows out of what was previously present, and grows into that which is afterwards present.   This great truth is popularly expressed
in several generally accepted educational maxims; it
will be convenient, therefore, to discuss the principle in
connection with these.

I. **From the Known to the Unknown.**—This is the
usual form of the rule, but, since we can never fully
know all about a thing, and certainly cannot proceed
straight to the knowledge of the entirely unknown, it
would be better to say: from the more or less known
to the more or less unknown.   The real meaning is
that we must first discover all the known details in a
fresh experience, and use them as means of understanding those which are new.   Since a whole is but a

union and unity of its parts, the more we know of the latter the greater chance there is of understanding the whole.

The same point is involved in the principle of inter-relation and inter-dependence, which is really only a special aspect of the principle of development. The foundation of both is the fact that the meaning of every new experience depends very largely upon the power of interpretation given by past experiences. In other words presentations always involve re-presentations.

A simple illustration of this is seen in the case of a child meeting with a giraffe for the first time. Doubtless, at first, the child would be filled with the most intense astonishment, if not terror. But it will soon recognise that it is a living thing with four legs, a body, a tail, a neck, a head, two eyes, two ears, a nose, and a mouth. This will enable it to class the object as an animal, and a quadruped. It will then be able to give its attention to the chief elements of difference, which are the size and proportion of the well-known details. From this it can be easily led to form some correct ideas of the habitat, and habits, of the giraffe.

Every child is, mentally, full of almost infinite details of elementary knowledge, that is, of mental impressions, left by the experiences which have happened to it. Before ever a human being can definitely affect a child through the properly educative influences, it has been subjected to innumerable influences, which have left important and lasting effects. Were this not so the educator could not do a thousandth part of what is ordinarily done by him. It is only as this inevitable knowledge of the child is clearly recognised and made use of that early education can be as effective or extensive as it might be.

" Jean Paul says of the child, that it learns more in the first three years of its life than an adult in his three years at the university ; that a circumnavigator of the globe is indebted for more notions to his nurse than to all the peoples of the world with whom he has come in contact. It is, in fact, astounding what a ˙relatively immense crowd of ideas a human being gains in the first years. He gets acquainted with a thousand things of home, street, garden, field, wood, the wonders of the heavens, the manifold events of nature, the land and the people of the neighbourhood, and learns to call most of them by name ; he learns to use a great part of the vocabulary of his mother tongue, and its most important forms of word and sentence ; he learns to think in the vernacular " (Dr. Karl Lange).

To directly base formal education upon such facts is most likely to arouse interest in the learner, for it is calculated to make him feel that what he already knows is practically useful and able to bring more knowledge and greater power. The ability to make accurate and ˙ deeper judgments depends upon the readiness and fulness with which we make comparisons, and the kind of standard with which we compare. If we fail to find many connections between the new and the old, it is not possible to make many judgments.

Let it not be forgotten that the most familiar is often the least known. The farm labourer who sees

so much of many kinds of plants and flowers generally knows least about them, in the way of formal
knowledge. At the same time, such a familiarity
with certain objects is the best possible starting point
for scientific knowledge. Nothing becomes known to
us in a full and significant sense unless, and until, we
thoroughly and carefully observe and reflect upon its
parts and powers in their detail and unity.

This rule applies equally to experiences, knowledge,
thoughts, actions, and words. Dr. Bain has well said
that: "If a demonstration proceeds upon principles
not already understood; if a description contains terms
with no meaning to the person addressed; if directions
involve acts that have not been previously performed,
the upshot is a failure."

The following are examples of progress from the
known to the unknown. A little child may be taught
many things about the cat in its own home. Then
other cats of the same kind, in other homes, may be
considered. This will widen its knowledge of the animal
and of homes. Afterwards another species of cat, which
is met with in the same neighbourhood, can be studied
in a similar way. This should be followed by species
met with in England, but not in the child's locality.
Thus some foreign kinds will be introduced. From tame
cats to wild cats may be the next step. Knowledge of
the habitat, and habits, of the latter will prepare the
way for learning about the tiger. So the series can
be extended to any convenient extent; and at any
point there may be a passage from knowledge about
the animal to knowledge about its surroundings, prey,

and foes (animal and human). Hence geography and general natural history may be dealt with.

Also from the same starting point another series may be followed. When some knowledge of a cat has been obtained through observation and talk, this may be used as a basis for getting a knowledge of the signs for spoken words, through a reading lesson. This in turn will serve as a reason for learning about the way of forming the necessary symbols, through lessons in drawing and writing, which give the opportunity for proceeding from the representative (outline of the animal) to the conventional (word) sign. The arrangement of the legs of the animal supply the material for a systematic number lesson. The language material will, later on, serve as the subject-matter for grammar lessons. Similarly all the subjects usually employed may be quite naturally led up to.

The general nature of what will, as a rule, be known by the individual at certain periods of his life has been pointed out in the previous chapter. Knowledge, of the kind appropriate to the different stages, about all the ordinary natural phenomena and common objects, such as: air, light, weather, trees, flowers, fruits, vegetables, household furniture, clothing, and so on, may be taken for granted in every case. Of course there will be differences of detail in knowledge in the cases of town children and country children, and those who live in manufacturing, agricultural, seaside, or mining districts; and there will also be individual differences as to the details of knowledge of those who live in the same district, or even in the same house. The wealth or poverty of parents, and their different occupations, will mean variety in the details of the immediate surroundings of the children.

Nevertheless there is always a substantial and considerable amount of common knowledge which, for all practical purposes, may be taken as possessed by all, in the same sense. House, horse, butter, bread, chair, field, water, and practically innumerable other objects have the same meaning for all, and offer common sources of knowledge-influences in formal education. The elements of individual differences in knowledge must be related to the common items and used as illustrations and examples.

2. **From the Simple to the Complex.**—This again is a rule which directly depends upon the nature of development as such. "Milk for babes and strong meat for men," has been a long-recognised proverbial truth. There is no need to do more than refer to what has been already said about the gradual increase of the mental, and bodily, powers in support of this practical rule.

The only real difficulty in the matter is to decide as to what is simple, and how to proceed so as to solve the complex by the simple additions of simples, in so far as this may be possible.

It is probably true to say that all that is possible for the human mind to know possesses difficulty mainly in so far as it is complex, intricate, and incapable of being presented and grasped in simple separate details. In other words, the greatest of all difficulties is that of complexity. Hence, the function of the educator is to take every means of resolving things into their simplest elements, and to present these in gradually increasing complexity, and in such relations that the total complex is most clearly and fully realised and understood.

But this is always subject to the condition that the whole complex has, in a superficial and elementary sense, first been grasped. It is not possible to understand the nature of a part of a whole unless some general idea of the whole has been formed. Of this we shall have more to say in the chapter on the development of knowledge.

Simplicity and directness are the chief elements of helpfulness to a learner. Each new point must be clear in itself, and in its relation to those other parts which are immediately connected with it. Every fresh item of knowledge must be of a kind that the pupil can apprehend, and must not try his powers beyond their strength. That is to say: both quality and quantity must be suitable.

Comenius puts this point very happily when he says : " Most teachers sow plants instead of seeds ; do not proceed from most simple principles."

Of course the word simple is a purely relative term. What is simple to the philosopher may be extremely complex to the practical man, and conversely. What is simple to the child is complex to the infant. Perhaps the best description of the simple is : that which is well-known, familiar, and under such control that it can, as a rule, be readily and accurately applied either in theory or practice. It is clear that such knowledge will form a safe and sure basis for advance.

The first thing to do, therefore, is to find out what knowledge of such a character the learner has in relation to the knowledge which it is desirable for him to possess, and what power in applying it. The general character of the knowledge possessed at certain stages of development has been described in the previous chapter. The particular items of knowledge will be according to the special experiences and training of the individual.

What we may call the order of greatest simplicity will be best obtained by first taking wholes which are made up of simple units. The whole should be carefully analysed and the relation of each of the parts to the others in the total complex mastered. Then the nature and special qualities of each part should be dealt with. Then we may go on to the analysing of more complex wholes into groups of significant units, and when the general character and relation of these have been mastered, treating these groups in a similar way. In other words we should carefully observe the principle of graduated difficulty.

Probably there is no more severe test of the true educator than his method of demonstrating the complex. A catalogue of the elements involved in a complex is of very little, if any, help to the understanding of the whole. If a clockmaker should begin to instruct an apprentice by telling him the names of every separate part of a clock, he would most likely make confusion worse confounded in the mind of his pupil. The most helpful method would be to proceed in some such way as the following.

Let us suppose that we wish to impart knowledge

O

about a certain complex. We will further assume that this is an object which consists of three principal parts, and that these parts consist of several smaller parts, each of which has three or four units of detail. The first thing is to get a good general idea of the whole, and then of each of the three principal parts. The learner must know in what way these three parts make up the whole, and what are their general characteristics and relations. Much of this will be best learnt by taking the object, or a model of it, and separating the three parts, and then putting them together again.

When so much has been mastered, so that it has become clear and simple to the learner, then the lesser parts should be treated in a similar way. And, after these have been learnt, then their details can be dealt with. Thus the order of simplicity is: from the whole to the chief parts, then to the lesser parts, and finally to the details of these. The relation of each unit, whether a group or an individual, to the whole must always be insisted upon; and each step must be thoroughly known before the next is attempted.

In this way the mind gets knowledge most easily, clearly, and accurately, and acquires a method in its work which greatly economises its energy, and makes possible what would otherwise not be so.

Thus there are two things to be decided, firstly, what are the elements and relations of the knowledge complex, and, secondly, what are the powers and present knowledge of the learner. True knowledge is a growth, not an accumulation; and a child's mind resembles a developing plant, not an empty sack. The mind is an organ which requires to be well and wisely provided with appetising food; but it must do its own eating, digesting, and assimilating.

The educator must always endeavour so to arrange the work of the learner that each component part of a whole, its nature and detail, and its relation to the whole, is most easily observed, understood, and remembered. The movement of thought and knowledge is from wholes to their parts and powers, until the wholes are somewhat fully known. Through such a knowledge of individual wholes all those belonging to the same class or kind are known.

Mr. Herbert Spencer remarks on this maxim: "The mind develops. Like all things that develop it progresses from the homogeneous to the heterogeneous; and a normal training system, being an objective counterpart of this subjective process, must exhibit a like progression. . . . . Not only in its details should education proceed from the simple to the complex, but in its ensemble also."

One of the most valuable practical applications of this rule is found in connecting all the early knowledge lessons with the experiences and objects of the home life. Every home is the world in miniature, just as every person is humanity in the little. Geography can be developed from the home surroundings, natural history from the domestic animals, and so on. The aim must always be to widen the field of knowledge. As Pestalozzi says: "The circle of knowledge commences close round a man and from thence stretches out concentrically."

For all general and practical purposes the simple may be taken to be that which properly belongs to the period of development in which the individual then is, and with which he is actually familiar both with respect to experience and knowledge. The complex will, from this point of view, be that which is unfamiliar to, or in advance of, the present state of development of the individual.

Some most interesting evidence of the development of the power to grasp the simple and the complex is found in the history of the idea of number. One African tribe has been found to have a separate name only for one object, any number of objects more than one being called many. The Bushmen could not count beyond two; other tribes have different words for one and two, but then proceed to combine these thus: two-one, two-two, two-two-one, two-two-two. Many savage races are unable to count the fingers of one hand.

3. **From the Concrete to the Abstract.**—This practical maxim is the most directly expressive of the principle of development. It covers, in a general way, all that has been said about the three great stages of development; and, therefore, has the very highest meaning and authority for the practical educator. Comenius says: "First, the senses should be exercised; then the memory, then the understanding, and lastly, the judgment." Interpreted according to modern psychology, this expression is a good way of stating the matter.

First educate the senses. This is the truth which is insisted upon by this rule. That most ancient of all philosophical and educational truths: "there is nothing in the mind which is not first in the senses," must be recognised and realised from the very first. The abstract can, primarily, come only through, and out of, the concrete. No concrete, no abstract, is the condition.

Rousseau is the great apostle of this truth. But like many great pioneers of scientific thought he has exaggerated the principle, and urged it to the exclusion of others which are equally important. He says: " The first faculties which are formed and perfected in us are the senses. These, then, are the first which should be cultivated."

There is nothing for the mind to exercise its power upon until the senses bring it impressions. Clearly, therefore, the more effective and extensive are the powers of the senses, the wider and deeper are the powers of the mind likely to be. The need and advantages of the cultivation of the senses are obvious when we consider the clumsy and inaccurate manner of their early use, as compared with the delicate and exact work which they can do after careful training.

An adult who had been born blind, but had, after an operation, recovered his sight, thought, at first, that everything was actually touching his eyes. It was some little time before he could visually mark off one thing from another. Like the blind man of old he would "see men as trees, walking." With this may be compared the effects of suddenly waking up in strange surroundings, and the coming out of a railway tunnel into broad daylight, as showing the need of experience and control in the use of the eyes.

So it is with all the senses. Through careful training

the eye gets an almost telescopic range and microscopic power; the ear learns to discriminate minute differences of pitch and tone; the hand decides between delicate shades of texture and temperature; the taste appreciates refinements of flavour; the sense of smell accurately identifies many odours; and the muscular sense estimates very small differences of weight and effort.

Dr. Isambard Owen has suggested in an address to the students of St. George's Hospital Medical School, that school-children should "be trained in numerical perception till forty, let us say, could be as easily distinguished from fifty as four from five, and line, surface, and area estimated with similar exactness."

Whilst the principle involved in this is a very sound and valuable one, the application is probably far too wide for general purposes. It would take too much time and effort to attain to such a power; it would be of comparatively little practical use, and the loss in other directions would be too great a price to pay for it. Some few specialists might find it worth while, but the ordinary man would lose more than he gained. It is a practical necessity, and a constant advantage, for a professional accountant to be able to add up five or six columns of figures simultaneously, but the man in the street has not often to do such work, and cannot afford to acquire such a facility.

Our senses are certainly somewhat neglected from this point of view, but we must beware of the other extreme. Education is as much concerned to avoid total or proportional over-development, as general or relative under-development. The mental power derived from the ability to estimate the number of individuals in a group is hardly of much rational value, and the practical advantage is limited and special. More training is wanted, but not too much, for ordinary purposes.

As Rousseau says : " To call into exercise the senses, is, so to speak, to learn to feel; for we can neither touch, nor see, nor hear, except as we have been taught." It would be better to say that we cannot touch, see, or hear with scientific fulness and accuracy unless we have been well taught and trained. The truth of this will need no demonstration to those who have had a good training in practical science.

According to the correctness and completeness of our sensations will be the precision and depth of our judgments and reasonings about things. The minuteness and comprehensiveness of modern scientific research show most conclusively that those who are well acquainted with details are, as a rule, best qualified to form sound and far-reaching judgments about matters.

It may be said, in general terms, that if one person uses his senses more accurately than another he is likely also to use his judgment and reason more accurately with regard to physical objects. To put the point in another way : one who has good sight will be likely to form more correct judgments about the appearances of things than one who is short-sighted. The same kind of thing is true of the other senses individually, and the truth is still more emphasised in those general judgments about objects which are based upon the materials given by the co-operation of all the senses. The senses both supplement and correct each other, so that the weakness of one is an element of weakness in all the others.

The wonderful precision of sense discrimination which can be obtained by training is well shown in the cases of the blind and deaf mutes. Deaf mutes are, so to speak, taught to hear with their eyes and sense of touch; whilst the blind learn to see with their ears and hands.

Only from correct observations of the forms, materials, actions, and the concrete results of actions, can we form right judgments about the qualities and powers of things. Hence the absolute necessity of first obtaining extensive and exact experiences. To get these we must have powerful and well-trained senses. Thus we are led to take the most careful account of the psychology of the senses, hygiene, and physical training, for purposes of practical education.

Another reason for first dealing with the concrete, in the case of children, is that, as M. Gréard says: "The child is born with the desire to observe and know. The interior life being not yet awakened in him, he belongs entirely to the phenomena of the exterior world. All his senses are on the alert; all the objects that his sight or his hand encounters attract him, interest him, delight him." Thus the principle of interest demands this order.

The foregoing all tends to confirm the opinion that the elements of natural science are the most appropriate and fruitful educative influences in the earliest stages of education. Such influences are always acting upon the child, easy to systemise, and pleasurable in their effects. What the individual consciously and constantly experiences must be known more or less fully and accurately. It is the educator's function to secure the conditions which are favourable to the greatest fulness and accuracy in knowing. Of course such knowledge must be imparted by means of practical observations, experiments, and investigations.

Mr. Herbert Spencer lays down the principle that: "Every study . . . . should have a purely experimental introduction; and only after an ample fund of observations has been accumulated, should reasoning begin."

Whilst, however, this third practical rule is the very corner-stone of educational order, the usual form of expressing it does not suggest all its implications. In the first place, the educator must confine his efforts to imparting knowledge in its concrete or purely practical form during the first stage of development. That is, the first form of the rule should be: from the concrete to the concrete. There must be no attempt to give abstract ideas of the qualities and powers of things, in a definite and explicit manner. Of course the abstract elements must necessarily be involved in the experiences, but they are entirely unrecognised by the individual whilst he is in the first stage of development.

"We should provide for the infant a sufficiency of objects presenting different degrees and kinds of resistance, a sufficiency of objects reflecting different amounts and qualities of light, and a sufficiency of sounds contrasted in their loudness, their pitch, and their timbre. . . . . Moreover, as these simplest elements have to be

mastered, and as the mastery of them whenever
achieved must take time, it becomes an economy of
time to occupy this first stage of childhood, during
which no other intellectual action is possible, in gaining
a complete familiarity with them in all their modifications " (Mr. Herbert Spencer).

Towards the end of the second stage of development
the educator should endeavour to get the pupil to
consciously and clearly recognise the abstract element
of knowledge. What has always been implicit should
now be made explicit. It is to this period, therefore,
that the rule, as ordinarily expressed, most fully
applies.

But when the third stage of development is reached
the learner is in the world of the purely rational, and
should be able to carry out processes of abstract reasonings. The inter-connection and inter-dependence of
truths are now discovered by the activities of pure
thought. So the rule must now read : from the abstract
to the abstract.

This must not, however, be understood as implying
that we can entirely confine ourselves to the world of
the abstract. As Dr. Karl Lange points out : " As the
tree must wither whose cells are not refilled with fresh
sap every spring, so would also our abstract concepts
die away and turn to empty shells, if we did not ever
fill them with material derived from living sense perceptions. In this way the perceptions acquired by the
child in his youth help to master and secure the abstract
ideas. This is shown by still another consideration.

" As is well known, all abstract ideas are denoted by

words that originally applied only to concrete things, to activities and relations of the outer world. Of course this transference did not take place entirely arbitrarily, but words were mostly chosen that referred to a similarity or to certain relations between the concrete and the abstract idea. One that has the concrete ideas in question vividly present, will necessarily unlock the abstract ideas more easily and fully."

This inter-action between the concrete and the abstract must ever be maintained if we wish to obtain the highest value of either. Doubtless, in later life, a man can, so to put it, mentally live upon the stores of previous experience, but if he endeavours to confine himself wholly to these his reasonings will tend to gradually become more and more remote from actualities, and, therefore, less and less accurate and reliable.

Finally, if the mind has sufficient native power and capacity for the work of discovery and invention, then it is able to proceed by what we have paradoxically spoken of as regressive advance. By this we mean the reasoning backwards from abstract principles to concrete facts, as when a scientist reasons out a new theory from the principles of mechanics and then invents machinery to illustrate it. Now, therefore, the form of expression should be: from the abstract to the concrete, or, to put it more exactly: from abstract ideas to their concrete implications.

We may exemplify the above by taking the case of geography used as an educative influence. The first step would be to get the learner to know, in the sense of being acquainted with the general appearance and locality of, the different geographical features in his home surroundings, and to associate with these the right names and verbal descriptions.

Then the same facts should be known in detail. The bed, banks, source, basin, mouth, of the stream or river : the base, summit, slope, height, material, of the hill or mountain : and so on, should be known and described. Practical judgments about these should be made, and communicated. These might be about the practical uses, character, and relations of the different features : the river as a means of irrigation, communication, and propelling force (water-mills); the mountain as a watershed, protection from cold winds, and source of minerals; the relations which exist between mountains and rivers, as to the source, current, direction, and size of the latter. The connection of physical with political and commercial geography should be worked out.

Principles may next be dealt with. The various physical, chemical, mechanical, and other principles which are involved in such phenomena as evaporation, denudation, climate, atmospheric movements, &c., will have to be considered when the mental powers are sufficiently developed to grasp them. Finally, the learner may be invited to use his knowledge and training for the purpose of working out solutions of problems concerning geographical phenomena; as, for example, in an attempt to work out the geographical history of the home locality from its configuration.

The plan of thus working backwards from given conditions to mental conclusions, or practical concrete solutions—as in making a new kind of article according to a given model, or detailed description—should be employed whenever practicable. It is the severest and best test of intelligent apprehension, and gives the most convincing and conclusive evidence of success or failure of mental grasp and practical power. Each stage of progress, and each item in it, will generally admit of some form or other of this kind of work. Very considerable differences of degrees of difficulty can be arranged so that all may be submitted to it.

When the results of such work are consistently satistory in individual cases, it will be safe to assume that right judgment or actions concerning certain matters have been acquired, and, if these have had time to become more or less habitual, the individual is in a fit condition for attempting more advanced work.

The three rules: from the known to the unknown, from the simple to the complex, and from the concrete to the abstract, apply as much to the quality, quantity, and form of educative influences as to the order of the development of the mental powers. We may say that experiences only should first be used, and names for things and actions given; then experiences should be followed by original and suggested judgments, and the understanding of items of information; and, finally, original and suggested reasonings should be gone through. As Herbart puts it, we must proceed from the empirical to the speculative, and thence to the æsthetic, and so make the material arouse those interests which predominate at different periods.

In application the influences will appear in the form of dictation, demonstration, suggestion, and dogma.

That is to say, the first means of imparting knowledge, when a sufficient command of language has been acquired by the pupil, will be by bringing him into relation with objects and actions, telling him what are the names by which they are known, and giving him the simple elements of knowledge connected with them. For example, a child is first taught to play little games with cubes. It is then taught to count with them, and afterwards it is guided in measuring the sides and corners, and then told that all faces of things which have four equal straight sides, and four equal corners, are said to be of a square shape.

Demonstration will consist in so setting forth the parts, connections, and relations of an object, that the right judgments are made by the learners, and so connected with one another as to give the correct idea of the whole. This will belong to the latter part of the first stage of development, and all subsequent periods.

Suggestion involves the giving of such preliminary knowledge, and so much of the new knowledge, as will enable a pupil to complete, more or less fully, the particular whole by his own efforts. Thus, if several species of a certain kind of plants have been fully demonstrated, then a general sketch of past work and a few special hints as to a new species of the same class, ought to enable a pupil to obtain a knowledge of that species by his own investigations. This may be regularly used towards the end of the second stage of development, and subsequently.

Dogma should mean the positive statement and acceptance of principles which have been rationally and practically demonstrated, and which the individual is able to re-demonstrate both theoretically and practically, if the latter be possible. It is only suitable, as a means of education, for those who have reached the stage of regressive advance. General principles are taken as the basis for the construction of deeper and more comprehensive theories, for the criticism of theories, and for guidance in research.

Both dictation and demonstration will be best accomplished by the aid of spoken language; though the former may to some extent, and the latter to a considerable extent, be assisted by written language, so long as this is well within the vocabulary of the learner and exactly reflects the method used in oral exposition. In suggestion the written aids may predominate, whilst in dogma nearly everything can be done through books. The living voice and the personality of the teacher are, as a rule, likely to prove more forcible, attractive, and helpful in special difficulties; whilst the written word is less apt to prejudice the learner: to allow him to shirk his share of the work: to provide for his individual difficulties: or to do too much for him.

The great principle of development applies as much to particular items of development as to general development: to the parts of a subject, as to whole subjects: and to particular periods of an individual's life, as to the whole life.

Educators should always aim at securing a step higher or further; but whenever there is real difficulty in securing progress in a higher stage, according to the proper conditions for that stage, then there must be an appeal to the materials and conditions of a lower stage, and to the lowest if necessary.

Comenius constantly and specially insists upon the principle of development being realised in the details of teaching. In his work entitled "Didactica Magna" he lays down the following principles, amongst others: "Nature does nothing without a foundation or root; nature sends its roots deep; nature produces everything from a root, nothing from any other source; nature, in each of its works, is in perpetual progress, never halts, and never attempts new things, the former things being cast aside, but only continues what has been previously begun, increases it, and perfects it; nature binds together everything by continuous bonds; nature begins all its operations from within outwards" (see Professor Laurie's book on Comenius).

The Principle of Doing.—Much the same ground is covered by this principle as by that of self-activity, but in a different sense. Whilst the latter deals with cultivation of the highest and truest forms, general and particular, of an individual mind, the former is concerned with the general and inevitable activity of the individual which is absolutely essential to full and free reception of any and every educative influence.

If it be true that the beginnings of knowledge are gained through the senses: that these develop through more detailed and systematic practical acquaintance with concretes: and that all the higher forms of knowledge are more or less directly connected with, and dependent on, the lower, then it is clear that the personal activity of the individual is an indispensable condition of acquisition and progress. Exercise is one of the essential conditions of development—nourishment being the other—and regulated activity is the best kind of exercise.

Froebel puts this point very forcibly, in the following words : "The starting-point of all that appears, of all that exists, and therefore of all intellectual conception, is act, action. From the act, from action, must therefore start true human education, the developing education of the man ; in action, in acting, it must be rooted and must spring up " ("The Student's Froebel," W. H. Herford).

Probably the most common and fatal mistake in education is the idea that learners have, for the most part, to sit still and listen, do their best to remember, and afterwards make more or less successful efforts to reproduce the verbal signs for knowledge. Nearly all our knowledge of the physical qualities of things comes through handling and seeing them, and observing the results of their activities. Very little knowledge of things is obtained through tasting and smelling, and only a knowledge of the sounds made by certain things comes through the ear.

The ear is not only one of the least fruitful organs of direct knowledge, but it is the last to be useful in helping us to gain knowledge indirectly, in that the verbal signs of knowledge are of no use to us until we have such a grasp of their application and general meaning, and such a fund of acquired knowledge, that we can readily and rightly reason from the sign to the thing signified.

P

Handling and seeing, if they are to be of any real and considerable use, involve a large amount of physical activity. It is as fatal as it is easy and usual to substitute the teacher's verbal description of what may be seen and felt; but the educative way is for the pupil to handle and look, and describe what he so discovers—when he has sufficient command of words—until he can find out nothing further by himself. Then the educator must suggest and inform; but the pupil must always verify the suggestions and information by his own experiences.

Froebel's kindergarten, and its modern developments, seek to realise the principles of doing as the original and true source of early knowledge. The kindergarten, and its extensions, are not new knowledge-subjects, but new statements of the oldest and best means of obtaining knowledge. They are not educational materials, but educational means and methods. Their keynote is : knowing through doing.

"Learn by doing" was Froebel's great axiom. He insists that "as the perceiving and grasping of a truth, by the way of life and action, is far more unfolding, forming and strengthening, than the mere reception of it in word and idea; so, likewise a forming by and in matter, in life—by doing, connected with thinking and speaking, is far more helpful for a man's development and improvement, than is representation by ideas and by word, without act or deed."

Plato remarks: "The young of all creatures cannot be quiet in their bodies or in their voices; they are always wanting to move and cry out; some leaping and skipping, and overflowing with sportiveness and delight

at something, and others uttering all sorts of cries."
Aristotle says : "Children should have something to
do, and the rattle of Archytas, which people give to
their children in order to amuse them and prevent
them from breaking anything in the house, was a capital
invention, for a young thing cannot be quiet" (Jowett).

Whilst "learn by doing" is a great educational truth,
it is also a much misunderstood and perverted one.
"Throw a boy into the water, if you wish him to know
how to swim," and "give a man the charge of a class,
if he desires to know how to teach," are two typical
examples of the misapplication of the principle. It
is quite true that a boy cannot actually swim without
going into the water, and that a person cannot really
teach without taking charge of a pupil or a class; but
it generally makes all the difference between success
and failure, if the individual has, or has not, had the
best possible preliminary preparation for his task.

Every one can find out some way or other of doing
what is necessary, but the whole point and purpose
of teaching is to impart the best ways of doing things.
There is ordinarily a good deal more in correct style
than elegance and finish; there is precision, effectiveness, control, and resource. Whilst, therefore, we should
insist that the learner must be constantly learning
through doing, we must also insist that he should be
prepared for, and guided in, his actions. To know
exactly what has to be done, and what are the best ways
of doing it, and to have had as much preliminary drill
as possible in the necessary actions—either with or without the actual material—constitute a large part of the
work, and the best guarantees of success.

Hence, the principle of doing involves the systematic and intelligent preparation for, supervision of, and aid in, doing.

Doing is not only a great means of getting knowledge, but it is also one of the best tests of clear apprehension, and one of the greatest aids to the retention, of knowledge. It is a form of expression; and right expression is a proof of correct comprehension. It helps to crystallise thought, and to make it as much a matter of habit as the actions themselves.

In the higher stages of development, doing will take the form of oral work—in occasionally supplying some of the judgments in a reasoning—in solving problems, making abstracts, reproducing arguments, and so on. As Dr. Bain points out: "In the act of learning generally there is a twofold attitude—observing what is to be done, and doing it. In verbal exercises we first listen and then repeat; in handicraft, we look at the model, and then reproduce it. The proportioning of the two attitudes is a matter of economical adjustment." We must regulate the principle of doing by the principle of stimulation.

Physical education, as a means of training the senses is one of the most fruitful and educative forms of doing. The muscles of the body can be trained, by appropriate exercises, to greater precision and susceptibility in estimating effort, and of adaptation in making efforts: the eye in the delicate judging of visual efforts and effects, and in adapting itself for looking, as a basis for judging distance, size, shape, numbers and position: the touch for nice discrimination of roughness, smoothness, temperature, and physical connection or separation: the ear for distinguishing the acoustic differences of sounds: the organ of taste for deciding between flavours: and the organ of smell for responding to differences of odour—which would otherwise be imperceptible to us.

It would be well if this wider meaning of physical education were insisted on as the true one, as against the more narrow, and properly hygienic, limitation of the term to forms of muscular drill. Much might be done through careful instruction and training to make the ordinary powers of the senses more efficient. At present we are, as a rule, content to let the senses blunder into what capacity and accuracy they may according to the force of circumstances and the chapter of accidents.

Systematic training of the ear, as in the ear tests in music, and in piano-tuning: of the eye, as of soldiers in practising the judging of distances: of the hand, as in kindergarten work: of the sense of taste, as in the case of the wine-taster: of the sense of smell, as in the case of chemists: and of the muscular sense, as in gymnastics, games, and arts, if carried out with more definite purpose and extent, and continued in the higher classes of our schools, will do much to further the comprehensiveness and correctness of our sense experiences.

The principles of the education of the deaf, dumb, and blind, have much of guidance and suggestion for the work of general education. If the separate senses can be developed to the extent to which they are in these special cases, it is clear that much must be lost by the absence of any definite training whatsoever. Not that it is either necessary or expedient to train each sense, in ordinary individuals, as though it were deprived of the help of one or more of the other senses.

Physical education, or the proper development and training of all the senses—which really involves the health and vigour of the whole body—is, therefore, another essential condition for the full realisation of the principle of doing.

Doing is not only necessary as a means of receiving and retaining knowledge, and as a condition of life itself, but, as we have previously pointed out, it is also a pleasure, when it is appropriate to the needs and nature of the individual, and not excessive in quantity. Thus the principles of pleasure and interest are realised when the right conditions for action are present.

Mr. Herbert Spencer urges that: " Nature has made the healthful exercise of our faculties both of mind and body pleasurable. . . . . With all faculties lower than these (the highest mental powers), however, the immediate gratification consequent on activity is the normal stimulus, and under good management the only needful stimulus."

Recognising this truth, and also the fact that children are little working machines, which must and will be doing something or other, we cannot escape the conclusion that if we can only find appropriate exercise for their energies, and give them the best conditions, guidance, and help for their work, then we may expect that valuable educational effects will result from satis-fying the desire of children for activity.

Play is the expression of the child's desire for activity. A child must get some kind of knowledge through its play experiences, and there is every reason why its play should be made as fruitful in the mental pleasures of knowledge-getting as in the physical pleasures of sense-exercise. Froebel did much to solve the problem of making play educationally pur-poseful.

The principle of doing applies with just as much force, and in quite as great detail, to mental as to physical work. The mind of the learner must be con-stantly making its own comparisons, judgments, infer-ences, and reasonings. It is the duty of the educator to stimulate, prompt, suggest, challenge, and demand these. Requiring illustrations from personal experi-ence : accounts of analogous instances : oral or written reproductions of subject matter : working of exercises and problems : re-discovery of truths : re-invention of theories and things : and the like, all serve to secure mental activity in the most direct, definite, interesting, and helpful ways.

Of course it is assumed that the educator usually keeps within the limits of the powers and possessions of the learner, though constantly striving to lead him a step beyond these. Reception is the first duty of the learner, and forms the indispensable basis of pro-duction. Imports precede exports in intellectual com-merce.

Dr. Karl Lange states the principle of doing very finely,

both from its mental and physical sides, in the following passage : "It is conceded that all universal historical truths, all geometrical and physical laws, can only be inalienably appropriated when the instruction leads them into the closest connection with living questions and exigencies, and offers examples from the practical life and experience of the child for solution. . . . . For constant, manifold use of the material taught not only intensifies the clearness of it, but it also assimilates it with numerous ranges of thought, so that a fluent reproduction is assured. It brings forward the plain, comprehensible characteristics which the pupil again and again recognises in concrete things. It makes so many concrete fields subject to the universal that the latter is supported as with countless pillars, and is retained in consciousness by a rich treasure of strong sense perceptions. . . . . In this manner it is provided that the newly learned facts shall not remain as dead material in the midst of acquired notions, but shall develop an assured activity and impulsive power. Knowledge now becomes power, and power becomes volition."

Thus the principles of self-activity, inter-relation and inter-dependence, and repetition, are seen to be involved. As Schiller says: "There is no way for the results of thinking to reach the will and the inner life of the child except through self-activity. Nothing but that which has already become a living deed within us, can become such in the outer world."

So Dr. Karl Lange points out that he who has observed children at study under proper educational conditions " knows how far removed their energetic learning is from a simple, passive reception, and that not the teacher, but they themselves have the most to perform. He is convinced that knowledge cannot be transmitted, that the pupil must work it out independently for himself. That is what the poet means when he says : ' What you have inherited from your fathers, you must earn again in order to possess it.' " At least we must earn it by learning how to take possession of it.

The learner is not an empty vessel which has to be filled, nor ought he to be regarded as an automaton which can be made to perform certain processes in a given way. He is an organism which has to be well and wisely supplied with appetising and nourishing food. But it is the organism alone which can, and must, do its own eating, digesting, and assimilating. We cannot give a child knowledge, but only good, or bad, conditions for getting it.

The developing being must be stimulated to desire and seek after knowledge. He must strive till he gets it. There must be definite understanding that the learner has to learn, as well as that the teacher has to teach. No one can do the pupil's work except the pupil, and unless it is done, and well done, there can be little, if any, very high development.

Dr. Goetze, in his handbook on manual training, points out that the inter-dependence of doing and knowing is shown by the history of the race, wherein " work has been the most important means of educating humanity," and by the educational methods used in the most advanced and abstruse parts of knowledge-subjects.

He says : " A celebrated mathematician at the University
of Leipsic had a modelling workshop which adjoined
the lecture-room. He made his pupils model in plaster
the curves and surfaces of the higher order which they
had calculated, so that they might thoroughly understand them whenever drawing on the flat was not an
efficient means of demonstration.

"A well-known member of the medical faculty, a
pathological anatomist, once said to me, that leaving
purely verbal instruction out of the question, even the
knowledge acquired by observation is not sufficient for
the young medical student; he must, through the
methodical dissection of natural objects, train his hand."
And Dr. Goetze himself remarks : "What should we
know about the structure of wood, its density, specific
gravity, sectile properties, combustibility, &c., had we
limited our examination of trees to ocular contempla-
tion? . . . . We wish to educate the child by practical
work exactly as humanity has grown and developed
under the educating influence of work."

A very suggestive statement of the same truth is given
by Dr. Isambard Owen in the address already referred to.
He says : " Training as well as learning is a necessary
part of medical education. . . . . You have to do as well
as to know; and medical doing, like all other doing,
requires a special cultivation of the faculties by which
it must needs be exercised. We have for the most
part to form our judgment from a combination of
observations . . . . of minute changes in the condition of the visible surface, observation of involutions
of the surface by means of optical apparatus, obser-

vations of the results of physical, chemical, and physiological tests, microscopic observations of disrupted fragments, and observations of a series of fine acoustic and tactile phenomena and reactions elicited and appreciated by means of the trained fingers or various artificial appliances." Again : "To neglect laboratory studies is to condemn yourselves to walk in fetters to the end of your days."

Manual training, as a branch of physical education, is an essential condition for full and complete development. As Buffon has said : "The hand, together with reason, is that which makes man a man."

One of the most valuable forms which the principle of doing can take is that of free but purposeful activity. That is, the element of play should be provided for throughout the period of ordinary school education. The educator should see that all kinds of games and sports are properly and systematically made use of ; but beyond initiating, advising, suggesting, co-operating, and preventing abuses, he should have as little as possible to do with the practical control and management. These should be left, as far as possible, entirely in the hands of the pupils.

The relief, refreshment, and invigoration thus obtained are more than can be got from any other source, and of the greatest value in maintaining the maximum of energy and efficiency. Recreation, intervals, half-holidays, and vacations, within reasonable limits, are not matters of indulgence and luxury, but necessities for proper development. They come under the principles of stimulation, nourishment, and pleasure.

And this element of free and purposeful activity can, with very excellent results, be introduced into the ordinary work of school education, under the principle of self-activity. For example, spelling-bees, guessing competitions, class contests after the Jesuit plan, and other exercises in which the pupils themselves conduct the proceedings, under the teacher's guidance, give very great pleasure, and produce permanent and valuable results when wisely managed.

Comenius advises that: "Teaching should be tempered with an agreeable variety, and the playful element admitted. The rivalry and emulation of free games should be encouraged in lessons. And Aristotle says: "The first principle of all action is leisure. Both are required. . . . Amid serious occupations amusement is needed more than at other times (for he who is hard at work has need of relaxation, and amusement gives relaxation, whereas occupation is always accompanied with exertion and effort). At suitable times we should introduce amusements. . . . Leisure of itself gives pleasure and happiness and enjoyment of life, which are experienced not by the busy man, but by those who have leisure."

The Principle of Sympathetic Control.—The first condition of the power to influence any person is to have such a general control as is sufficient to command his co-operation with, or non-resistance to, the influences. It is possible for an individual to resist and resent the efforts made to influence him. Such resistance must always depend upon the power of willing, whatever may be the motive which prompts it. It is necessary, therefore, that we should know how best to secure the co-operation of the individual's will.

Now, since willing is stimulated and largely controlled by the feelings and knowledge, it is through these that we must seek to influence it. And, as feelings and knowledge are powerful to affect the will according as they have interest for the mental life, it is necessary to use the most interesting forms of them.

Also, inasmuch as willing always expresses itself in some form of mental or physical activity, or both, we shall, as a rule, know when we have been successful in our efforts by the fact that work is done by the individual in accordance with our aims.

Those feelings and forms of knowledge will, generally, most interest an individual, which are closest in accord with the general nature of the needs of the particular stage of development which has been reached, and also with the particular inclinations and disposition of the person in question. This applies, in the widest possible sense, to the intellectual, moral, and physical powers. It is, therefore, through securing such conditions as best satisfy the needs of the life and character of individuals that we are likely to obtain the most thorough and complete co-operative control over them.

Our efforts must be as much against bringing about anything like a condition of dependent subjection, as towards the winning of a free and full consent to being guided and rationally governed. The former is fatal to high and vigorous development, whilst the latter is necessary to the success of helpful effort. It is as important that there should be no undue constraint, or restraint, where sound progress is being made, as that authority, wisely used, should if possible, forcibly check unsound and mischievous growths. Force may be no remedy, but it is often an unfortunate necessity for securing an opportunity for remedial efforts to have a chance of taking effect.

In ordinary cases, ordinary means should be both sufficient and efficient. Let us, therefore, accept the principle of sympathetic control as signifying the securing a legitimate influence over the will of an individual by supplying the most appropriate material and conditions, at the proper time, and in the proper proportion and amount, and so helping them to bring about their best effects in the best possible manner.

The highest and truest end of external control being to produce the best form of self-control, there must always be a gradually decreasing amount of the former. Even the securing of good conditions, and the providing of the best material, must, little by little, be undertaken by the individual himself. Indeed, this duty is one of the most satisfactory and pleasant means of securing the desired end. To put responsibility upon a person, by authority, is almost certain to develop self-control and self-dependence in him.

Following the order of development already set forth, we may say that control during the first period should be of the nature of an educative despotism. The utter helplessness of the child, as to directing its own actions so as to further its well-being, makes it necessary that others should take the entire responsibility of ordering its life.

During this period is the only time when the individual should, as a general rule, be entirely subject to the influence and control of the educator. Subject the child must be, either to the unorganised influences of its surroundings, or to these influences definitely organised to aid its development. The absence of physical and mental power places it at the mercy of any and every passing influence, whether this be for its greatest good or harm, unless some educational sponsor guards and guides it.

Herbart declares that : " The child enters the world without a will of its own. . . . . At first, instead of a true will, which renders the child capable of determination, there is only a wild impetuosity, impelling it hither and thither, a principle of disorder, disturbing the plans of the adults, and placing the future personality of the child itself in manifold dangers. This impetuosity must be subdued. . . . . Subjection is brought about by force, and the force must be sufficiently strong, and often enough repeated, to compass this subjection, before any trace of a true will is manifested in the child. The principles of practical philosophy require this."

Hence the need and the justification of this despotic form of educational government. But even so this is only allowable as a means of securing the brief conditions for producing, and until there has been produced, such a development in the individual as enables him to do without it. It must, therefore, be a constantly decreasing power. It is a means, and not an end. As Professor Rein says: "Government, therefore, aims to attain no direct end whatever in the mind of the child, but will only produce order; it aims to be felt as a power that is concerned with nothing further than the enforcement of its measures."

As we have already seen, the highest form of voluntary willing is a development from the involuntary form, in which it is, for all practical purposes, wholly determined by external influences. It is the educator's duty to be the most powerful, purposeful, and helpful, of the influences which are affecting the development of the mind at this early period.

If done in a thoroughly sympathetic manner—with a full knowledge of the needs of the child, and a wise and generous satisfying of them—this kind of control gives the greatest possible pleasure and profit to the little one, and is a bond of union between educator and pupil, which makes for the happiness of both. The egoistic feelings of the child will attach him very closely to one who ministers so fully and constantly to his comfort and well-being.

Inasmuch as the will is very much influenced by the feelings, and the feelings are very stong and active in this stage, they offer a powerful means of controlling the will. It will, therefore, be allowable to gratify the child's love of pleasure, by giving, as rewards for effort and success, such things as sweets, and toys. But great care must be taken that this does not grow into corruption and bribery. It must not be that these things are given so as to get the child to do its work, but merely as generous and occasional recognitions of work well done. Unless this be so the influence will be vicious, and the resulting development undesirable.

To aim at the control of a child merely for the sake of control is as despicable as it is dangerous. It is a mean and petty triumph to subdue a tender and helpless child to one's will, by physical, or other, intimidation; but it is a noble success to exert a reasonable control and guidance over the young, solely with a view to furthering their happiness and progress.

The effects of control, for control's sake, are almost certain to be repression, constraint, helplessness, and a want of originality, initiation, confidence, and self-respect. The results of sympathetic control are likely to be the very opposites of these.

In the second great period of development control should be more of the nature of educative co-operation. The child is beginning to realise, in a practical sense, its own powers and importance; its physical self demands recognition; and it, therefore, no longer requires, enjoys, or profits by, a complete surrender of its individuality to that of another. There is still need of the most thorough and complete guidance and control; but the spirit and form of these must change.

The child has now got beyond the time for spoon-meat, and can feed itself, though it is still unable to provide and prepare its own food. These altered conditions in the powers of the child must be met with altered conditions in the attitude of the educator. It is no longer a case for the imperative, but for the indicative, mood in authority, as the general rule. Not that the imperative suddenly and wholly disappears, but that it is gradually supplanted by the indicative. The educator should be more of the ministering angel

Q

than the master at this stage, though he must still be both.

Sympathetic control now means that " the teacher enters into the feelings of the pupil, and, without permitting it to be noticed, joins in them with tact, or he takes care that the feelings of the pupil can approach his own in some particular way; this is more difficult, but must nevertheless be combined with the other, because only when it is possible for the pupil to unite his activity in some way or other with the teacher's can he contribute force of his own to the relationship between them " (Herbart).

Leading, rather than commanding, must now be the attitude of the educator. The native energy and inquisitiveness of the child renders unnecessary anything more than the control of wise guiding, in most things. Whilst the nature of the individual will compel a general agreement between its own development and that of others, it will not the less require freedom for, and assistance in, the development of personal peculiarities, more or less important and predominant. Anything like a too mechanical or exclusive control is, therefore, likely to prove mischievous and dangerous.

At this stage of development the stronger sentiments of the child must be enlisted on the side of the educator. The child is beginning to know and appreciate the importance of the goodwill and help of others in increasing the amount and fulness of its pleasures and well-being. Its feelings of gratitude and affection are lively and strong, and it is always quick to exercise these towards those who have any real claim upon them.

Whatever actions of the child are due to such feelings will have a very high value as developing influences, for they will be of the nature of self-activity. There is an evident expression of the self in all actions due to feelings of gratitude and affection. The suggestion may, and in early life often must, come from without, but the motive which leads to, and sustains, action will be entirely from within. Hence, to the learner, it will appear that he is working out his desires to please his teacher, not that he is doing something simply because the teacher tells him to do it. The personal character of the educator is, therefore, of the greatest moment. A fondness for, keen sympathy with, and full knowledge of, children are qualifications of the first order in a teacher; for they are direct and powerful agencies of control.

Again, the feelings of respect, admiration, and shame, may all be called forth in the interests of the educating process by the fairness and justice, the learning and capacity, and the sorrow and disgust at wrongdoing, of the educator. That these are by no means fanciful conclusions forced out of psychological truths, is well seen in the almost worship and devotion which boys give to a master who has a great reputation for sports or athletics, or even for deep scholarship. Older boys will render willing service to such, and will insist that their juniors do the like.

Control is never so complete or effective as when it is secured through stimulating and ministering to the proper feelings and desires of persons. The history of the influence of the leaders of great movements in the past gives convincing and conclusive evidence of this. The educator should, therefore, seek to exert every legitimate influence of this kind. It is of little use to urge upon young children that they should be good—which they can only understand in a very concrete sense—because it is so good to be good—which they can hardly understand at all. Even the greatest of moral teachers said : " If ye love me, keep my com-mandments."

Besides making use of the growing sentiments of the child as means of control, the educator may still continue to appeal to its lively sense of pleasure. Rewards, under the restrictions previously suggested, are still lawful means of stimulating the activity of the learner. These should, however, be on a higher plane than formerly. Special private and public expressions of approval ought to be very acceptable, and encouraging, to those whose sense of self is becoming assertive.

Material rewards are also admissible ; but they must satisfy and assist the higher development, by giving opportunities for its exercise. Simple working models of machines, sets of tools, objects of interest—such as a small case of native butterflies—holiday excursions for geographical and historical purposes, social enter-tainments mainly managed by the scholars, and the like, may be made as profitable as pleasurable.

The practical universality of this principle amongst human beings is shown by such proverbial sayings as : "Reward sweetens labour," and "Nothing succeeds like success." The stimulating effect of the concrete results of successful effort, and the demoralising results of failures, are obvious to all. With the child these elements, like many others, need to be more or less artificially emphasised.

Emulation is apt to prove a dangerous instrument at this point, owing to its liability to become purely personal, since the child is unable to sufficiently appreciate the remote and abstract results of competition. Hence it has a tendency to bring about many of the evils which a proper control seeks to avoid, e.g., jealousy, illfeeling, and personal conflict.

Too much care cannot be taken in preventing such exceptional influences from becoming forms of bribery. They ought always to involve more or less of the unexpected and undeserved, in the sense that they are generous additions to the ordinary and sufficient outcomes of activity.

Demonstration is one of the most powerful means of control in the latter part of this period. There is a native desire for a knowledge of the practical reasons for things, which applies as much to educational matters as to others. If the intelligent pupil is led to see that all educational processes are designed for his personal advantage, he will be likely to render a more complete, loyal, and constant, co-operation in the work.

Milton in his "Tractate on Education" most wisely urges that "to season them, and win them early to the love of vertue and true labour, ere any flattering seducement, or vain principle seise them wandering, some easie and delightful book of education would be read to them." Whilst theoretical ideas about education would be better reserved till later, the giving of concrete reasons and rules may very profitably be begun at this stage.

"Assuming that the pupil has already a lively sense of the gain which intellectual guidance brings him, and of the loss which he will suffer from every deprivation, or, indeed, diminution of it, he may then be shown that as a condition of the continuance of this guidance, a perfectly stable relationship is requisite, which can be calculated upon in all instances; and that the teacher must be able to confidently assume there will be instant obedience as soon as he has ground for requiring it. There is now no question at all of mere blind obedience; that is not consistent with any friendly relationship. But everywhere there occur cases in which only one can decide, and the others must follow without opposition. This nevertheless must be followed at the first opportunity by an explanation why that decision was arrived at and no other, so that the pupil's future judgment may meet the command halfway. Conviction of the necessity of subordination must therefore concede what the teacher for himself would not dare to ask" (Herbart).

Now is the time when the processes of education themselves become the best means of control. If anything be true, it must be the fact that when a person is being vigorously developed according to the best model and under the most favourable conditions, his energy is therein fully occupied, his efforts directed to that end, his general needs and desires best satisfied, and his whole being completely harmonised with its surroundings. This is control of the most thorough and ideal kind.

Mr. H. G. Wells has very happily expressed the element of co-operation. He says: " The teacher and the child should agree, as Tennyson says of man and woman, 'like perfect music unto noble words,' and our 'sympathy' means, not coincidence, but the capacity for co-operation."

Putting the matter from the boy's standpoint, Herbart argues that: " Everything must appear to the boy as his work; he must wish to feel he has himself to thank for his improvement. The years from ten to fourteen, when the boy feels intensely he must be educated, are very important. If these are neglected, formation by education is lost: earlier, from the sixth year onward, it is difficult to awake and maintain this spirit in the child."

For the third great stage of development a change of attitude is again necessary. Co-operation, in the somewhat limited sense of guiding and controlling co-operation, must gradually give place to what we may call educative suggestion. Even demonstration must also give place to suggestion, as frequently as may be; for the power of applying knowledge ought to be sufficiently ready and correct to make the need of demonstration much less frequent than formerly; and the growth of the power of willing, and the realisation of the self, are likely to make the individual intolerant of experiencing much that suggests his subjection to guidance and control.

At this point the chief duty of the educator is to supply good material, or to indicate where it can be best obtained. Lectures, text-books, illustrations and the like, will be convenient sources of supply. It is still most important that the material should be supplied in its most educative form, *i.e.*, under favourable conditions, and in a scientifically dependent and connected manner. Educational principles ought to be carefully observed as to the nature and arrangement of the information contained in text-books, lectures, and the like.

Now has come the time when the educator should find the greatest success of his work, in the pupil's ability to look after his own education. The fruition of the educator's efforts is the self-educator. The predominant development of willing, and the strength of a well-informed and vigorous judgment, will need such a self-dependence for their highest and best work, and they will demand it. It will almost certainly be secured in some way or another, and in some one of several forms, legitimate or otherwise.

There are few things more mischievous, and often disastrous, than for the educator, whether of the domestic, religious, or scholastic order, to endeavour to make his own will take the place, and do the duty, of that of the learner. This kind of action is generally the pride and pleasure of the masterful individual who more or less crushes other wills to assert and exalt his own. Not that personal influence should be denied its proper effects, but that it should not be enforced—except at special periods, for right ends, and in a reasonable manner—by any authority or power not derived from its own nature; and even this may be excessive and prejudicial. Forms of slavery, even if benevolent, are likely to produce helpless dependents, parasites, and rebels.

Helpful guidance and co-operation are still indispensable, but they should, in most instances, come in the form of suggestive information and advice. Even the old forms of co-operation and command will be not infrequently necessary, but they must be used with the pupil's free consent, or at his request. There must be a putting away of childish things, and a putting on of the responsibilities and self-dependence of manhood, on the part of the learner.

To subject the will, during this period of special development, to an overwhelming restraint, and a confined sphere of action, is just the way to deprive it of the power and readiness which it will most want when such restraint is no longer possible. Without doubt many characters have been wrecked through an over-solicitude to shield and safeguard them. Crutches assist, and may help to cure, the lame, but they only cumber, and may cripple, the healthy.

As we have before pointed out, the want of sufficient exercise leads to a loss of power and skill, and may finally result in a loss of function. And this is as true of a part as of the whole. To stop short of the conditions necessary for the highest development of the power of willing is to run the risk of losing it, and, certainly, to very much prejudice it.

Reasonable self-dependence is one of the finest attributes of man, and forms one of the foundation-stones of his place in nature. It involves self-command and self-control, and is based upon those habits which have most general influence, and which are themselves the outcome of carefully selected and constantly repeated efforts. There is such a control of the thoughts, feelings, and actions that they can, as a rule, be so organised, and related to systems of ideas and ideals, as to give the very best chance for the realisation of our desires.

Self-activity, in the educational sense, has its origin in this higher stage of willing. The activity based upon self-dependent judgment and willing is the expression of character and individuality. The power and quality of the self-activity of the learner at this period, is generally according to the wisdom and effectiveness of the previous education.

Herbart declares that "in the pupil's seventeenth year education proper is impossible, or at most only possible in those who see what they have missed, and in whom the wish to submit themselves to education is keen. This feeling, however, will not last long, at least not beyond the time that they feel they can carry on their education for themselves."

Now that the mind has the power of appreciating the meaning and value of scientific principles, the will is very greatly influenced by the mental conviction that certain effects can only be obtained through special conditions, if we wish to have them in their best forms, and to get them in the easiest way. Consequently there should now be a direct and explicit appeal to the reason, in the form of critical judgment, as the motive for continuing education, chiefly if not solely, through self-effort—so soon as this appears to be possible. For this there must be sufficient self-dependence, knowledge, skill, and power.

An elementary text-book on the theory of education may be studied by the learner at this stage ; and he ought to derive as much advantage therefrom as an artisan would from an intelligent study of a book on the theory of his trade. In any case very great advantage would be derived from a careful study of the principles of logic—the science of valid thought. There are the same reasons for the self-educator to have this sort of knowledge as for the educator of others to possess it. It will also do something to satisfy that desire to know and understand the self which begins to take form in later youth.

The principal influences by which the will can be affected at this period are those sentiments which are most strongly developed about this time. The higher forms of respect, reverence, affection, love, and pride, are now present in greater or less degree in the learner, and may be stimulated and used as motives for self-education. Ambition, the desire for wealth, the search for happiness, the endeavour to escape the ills of life, and other like motives, will all appeal most strongly in favour of self-education, if the proper thoughts and feelings can be aroused.

Emulation is now allowable, if the value of competition as a stimulus is understood, and the fruits of the struggle are sought in personal progress and increase of knowledge, and not in the mere triumph over another. Self-approval, based on right moral principles, should be a powerful stimulus. " To thine own self be true " is now one of the highest and best motives, so long as the self has been well developed, and has high aims.

Studious youths will generally be found to have some strong motive underlying and sustaining their earnestness and perseverance; such as the hope of securing scholastic success, the desire to please their parents, or the keen personal pleasure derived from the study of a particular subject. In these cases it is clearly the desire to realise one's own idea, or ideal, *i.e.*, some form of the self, which is the all-important element. This attitude toward effort is appropriate to this stage of mental development, desirable in itself, and likely to produce the greatest and best results.

But even in this growth of self-dependence there are the usual stages of gradual increase of self-reliance and self-confidence. Not all at once does the individual order all his actions entirely according to his own judgments and inclinations. There will be many occasions when feelings of helplessness and ignorance will lead to requests for guidance and assistance; when failure will cause a willingness to submit to even despotic control; or when partial success will bring an eagerness to receive co-operative aid.

An extremely interesting illustration of the kind of progress involved is found in a method used for training blind persons in finding their own way about their homes and surroundings. There is first the leading by linking of arms; then the blind person holds the end of a stick; next a piece of string is used; after this the only help obtained is by listening to the footsteps of another; and, finally, the learner is left to himself, and told to fold his left arm across his breast, as some protection in case of a collision, and use the right hand to explore the space just in front of him.

In this system the gradual decrease of external help is very ingeniously contrived, and the result is a growth of confidence and skill in self-dependence. Some such features will be found in the ordinary development of youthful independence ; and, therefore, the educator may become the guide, philosopher, and friend of the self-educator.

Throughout every stage of development, and in all the separate departments of each, there should be a movement appropriate to the imitative, practical, or rational character of the development, from what is, practically, complete dependence on others to a lessening dependence, then a gradual approach to partial self-dependence, which slowly increases until there is complete self-dependence, in the sense which we have set forth.

At the end of each period, and each important department of it, there should be an attempt to obtain from the pupil an expression of his highest powers with regard to the subject in hand. These will be best shown in the ability to invent more or less original designs, exercises, and the like. Thus little children of six years of age sometimes produce extremely effective and clever designs in kindergarten drawing ; some girls and boys in the higher classes of elementary schools for older scholars write excellent fairy stories or other literary compositions; and both girls and boys invent and execute new models in cardboard-work, wood-work, and metal-work. Children of all ages can be educated up to the ability to write, and work, their own exercises in arithmetic.

These efforts show most conclusively that self-activity and self-dependence in their best forms have been secured, and that the learner is in the best possible condition for further progress.

Education should now have accomplished its purpose. Educational development ought now to be supplanted by self-development. Self-activity, self-dependence, self-knowledge, self-control, and self-criticism ought to characterise the life of the individual, who whilst using these powers for securing the fullest possible living of his own life, should, none the less, also regard them as the means of co-ordinating his life with those of his fellows, without whom his own life and powers would be sadly wanting in fulness and richness.

Herbart says: "The young child is not yet capable of valuing the benefit of education. A boy of twelve years, rightly guided from early childhood, prizes it above everything, from his deep sense of the need of guidance. The youth of sixteen begins to take on himself the teacher's work; he has partly appropriated his point of view, he accepts it, and marks out for himself his course accordingly; he manages himself and compares this self-treatment with that which continuously fell to his lot from the teacher. It must be so—for he who knows himself best and looks through himself most directly, will, at times, see with greater clearness, than he who always remains another person. It must be so—for he feels himself unnecessarily constrained, and his obedience transforms itself more and more into forbearance to the benefactor of earlier years. . . . .

"Moreover, it is now of supreme importance that the principles become perfectly formed and purified, which will henceforth rule the life. Instruction, therefore, will still continue, after discipline has almost disappeared. But further, instruction no longer touches a merely receptive mind; the pupil will himself judge. To the end that he may examine, he begins by doubting. That he may be free from his embarrassing confinement within his habitual circle of thought, he enters the sphere of other opposing opinions. Little differences of views, which gradually arise and have hitherto remained unnoticed, acquire voice and growth under the favouring influence of strange impressions, to which the charm of novelty gives force. . . . .

"What will now protect the toilsome work of education? What ought to protect it? What, if not its inner rightness, the truth of convictions, the clearness and breadth of the intellectual gaze, if not the feeling of mastery over men and opinions, and the responsive inward gratitude for that care which has rendered such an ascendency possible?"

Comenius very happily expresses the connection between the principles of stimulation, interest, interrelation, pleasure, sympathetic control, and pain (see next section) in the following passage: "If subjects of study are rightly arranged and taught, they themselves attract and allure all save very exceptional natures; and if they are not rightly taught, the fault is in the teacher, not the pupil. Moreover, if we do not know how to allure by skill, we shall certainly not succeed by the application of mere force. There is no power in stripes and blows to excite a love of literature, but a great power, on the contrary, of generating weariness and disgust. A musician does not dash his instrument against a wall, or give it blows and cuffs, because he cannot draw music from it, but continues to apply his skill till he extracts a melody. So by our skill we have to bring the minds of the young into harmony, and to the love of studies, if we are not to make the careless unwilling and the torpid stolid. A spur and stimulus are often needed, but a sharp word or a public reproof or the praise of others who are doing well, will generally suffice."

The Principle of Pain.—There can hardly be any doubt that pain has a very valuable part to play in the economy of nature. It is, so to speak, the sentinel which nature sets to give the alarm when enemies are beginning to attack our bodily kingdom and endanger our sovereignty. Also it is the adverse criticism of nature upon our methods of dealing with her. Again, it is nature's way of punishing the folly, ignorance, or viciousness of the individual. Not less is it the inevitable outcome of the ordinary conditions of the universe, of which the individual is the unfortunate victim. Certainly nature is by no means sparing in the use of this terribly potent and all too familiar penalty.

From another point of view pain may be regarded as a necessary discipline against itself. Since pain is inevitable man must be prepared to meet it. Often the only possible preventive of severe suffering is a milder form of it. This may be exemplified by the suffering endured through vaccination as a means of resisting, or reducing, the pains to which one is liable in a small-pox epidemic.

Perhaps we may even look upon pain as, up to a certain point, the sauce of life, which adds relish and piquancy to what might otherwise be a dead sea of sweetness. In any case it has taken, and is taking, a large part, whether for good or evil, in the development of the race and the individual.

Whilst, as we have insisted, the conditions referred to under the principle of sympathetic control ought to be sufficient under ordinary conditions, there are, unfortunately, extraordinary conditions which must be taken into account and provided for. The mind is as much subject to disorders, diseases, infections, accidents, incompleteness, malformations, and so on, as the body. There is, therefore, need for preventive and curative agents. The good forms of development have to be strengthened and improved, and the bad forms must be removed or repressed.

Just as in the case of the body it is found advantageous to voluntarily endure considerable suffering with the hope of escaping a very much more serious amount, so it is sometimes expedient to inflict mental pain with a view to prevent the continuing of such lines of thought or action as are morally certain to bring about results which will involve far greater and more permanent forms of mental suffering.

It cannot, however, too often, or too earnestly, be

R

insisted upon that only when all other means have really failed should any kind of pain be purposely employed. And this because it is in itself a mischievous and dangerous influence. It is a destructive force for preventing, if possible, still further destruction; and a corrupting influence used to defeat still more corrupting influences. It may be compared to those poisons which, when skilfully used for medicinal purposes, tend to secure health instead of causing death.

Pain, as such, interferes with and prejudices the general movement of life; blunts, and, maybe, destroys some of the more delicate elements of the mind: represses and checks the development of the self: and disturbs, if it does not destroy, that friendly relation between the teacher and the pupil which is so necessary to the success of the educative processes. All pain does this, to some extent, and how much more is it likely to result from pain inflicted by one who can forbear giving it, and whose kindly intention it is often almost impossible for the victim to appreciate.

Very serious responsibility, therefore, rests upon the person who employs pain as an agent in education. He must be convinced, upon reasonable grounds, that he has rightly estimated the facts of the case : that the result is likely to be the decided advantage of the individual : and that he is making use of the best remedy. Most people will admit that it is not easy to satisfy these requirements. Indeed it is sometimes impossible, and the only thing that can be done is to trust to one's intuition at the moment; but this should only be done in cases of extreme urgency.

Of the means by which the educator can assure himself that it is necessary to use pain as an agent of prevention or reform, we can say little here. This is a matter which comes under the method rather than the theory of education. But we may point out that much psychological knowledge, an extensive acquaintance with and knowledge of the individual, and some acquaintance with the pathology of the mind and body, are required for thoroughly intelligent and scientific action in the matter. Too often it is the case that young people are, through ignorance, subjected to treatment which only aggravates their disorders, or even produces new ones. Supplant rather than suppress, or, suppress by supplanting, is the golden rule.

There is, it is true, a certain amount of traditional and accurate knowledge about the more common conditions which seem to demand the use of pain. As an example we may refer to the fact of the use of corporal punishment often being successful in checking acts of cruelty, when all other means have failed—it is even said to be effective with adult criminals, who have been guilty of robbery with assault.

But in every separate instance of such cases there are generally many special features which need to be taken account of, if we are to treat the case successfully. It is necessary, therefore, that we should, as far as possible, be able to trace the evil to its real source, and to detect all its important special features. Until this is done, very little is possible in the way of remedy.

Having traced an evil to its origin, we then want a knowledge of its ordinary development, if left to itself, and its natural termination. Also we must know what influences most affect the mischievous activities, how they affect them, and what is likely to be the order of events when they are systematically applied. Only when so equipped can we hope to be able to really grapple with the evils.

Speaking generally, we shall expect to find that there will be disorders of willing, knowing, and feeling. In willing there may be that permanent violence of activity which is known as obstinacy, or the occasional excess which we term rashness. Or we may have to deal with the opposite extremes of want of resolution and consistency. The control of thoughts and feelings may be very weak, so that there is chronic inattention, frivolity, and the like. Laziness is often the evidence of a general weakness of will.

Sometimes the power of knowing, in the sense of quickly taking account of experiences and trains of thought, is extremely keen, and apt to be superficial; whilst the thorough assimilation which is necessary for full and clear retention is proportionally weak. On the other hand, the grasp of an idea may be so thorough and fixed, but perverted, that it amounts to a delusion; and this might grow into monomania. Carelessness, inaccuracy, and certain elements of ignorance, involve weaknesses in the powers of knowing and willing.

In the feelings we may find the excesses which lead to the various forms of passion, or the defects which are shown in a lack of enjoyment and relish of those influences usually employed, with success, to stimulate the receiving activities. Hence come violent anger, hysterical enthusiasm, despair, unresponsiveness, indifference, inactivity, and so on. The sentiments may be perverted, and excessive or defective in their action. Thus we get viciousness, idolatry, and absence of sympathetic qualities.

Whenever such defects cannot be remedied by any of the positive and pleasurable forms of educative influences, then it will be necessary to make use of the negative and painful agencies.

Of course we must not expect that the disorders will usually, or even often, be of a simple kind. There will always be elements of disorder of willing, knowing, and feeling in every case of fault; and the only instances of comparative simplicity will be those in which one of the powers is very predominantly at fault, whilst the others are very subordinately so. Often there will be a more or less serious, because more or less unanalysable, complexity in the disorders. Such cases will require very great knowledge, skill, and care in their treatment.

Little need be said about those physical disorders which are the source of, or very much increase, certain mental complaints. It is only necessary that the educator should have a sufficiently intelligent knowledge of them to know which are the more common of them, and when they are probably present; and, therefore, when a medical man should be called in.

The first aim should be to prevent diseases. There should be what we may call a system of mental, as well as physical, hygiene; which would consist in the careful and complete observance of all the principles which secure the best development of an individual. When, in spite of all our efforts to prevent them, diseases arise, as they will arise, our efforts must be directed to removing the causes, and the effects already produced; or, we must endeavour so to influence the diseases as to reduce their ill effects to the lowest possible amount.

As to deciding whether the result will be to the advantage of the patient: this is also a matter in which certain traditional views may be taken as guides, whilst in other cases personal judgment based upon the considerations mentioned above must settle the question, or the opinions of experienced experts may be accepted.

We may classify the pain agencies under three heads: the infliction of specific forms of painful experiences—whether these be artificially imposed, or allowed to arise out of a course of wrong actions—all forms of compulsion, and all kinds of restraint. These may be applied either in the sphere of the reason, the feelings, or the senses. Censure, sarcasm, and tasks to be learnt, are means of causing rational discomfort. Making individuals appear ridiculous, refusing to continue general and pleasant relations, enforcing distasteful duties, and declining to accept usual tributes of affection or esteem, are methods of affecting the feelings and sentiments uncomfortably. Manual impositions, confinement, denying favourite foods, drinks and toys, and beating, are disagreeable sense experiences.

Many of such forms of pain are brought about

through the ordinary actions of the individual. All kinds of physical pains are being constantly inflicted through ignorance or wilfulness in action; feelings are distressed through the loss of the sympathy or esteem of others; and intellectual suffering is caused when conceit and folly produce humiliating failure.

Like Rousseau, Mr. Herbert Spencer, in his book on education, raises the question whether, after all, artificial methods of inflicting pain are necessary, and, therefore, justifiable. He points out that the infliction of pain by one person upon another is sure to produce a feeling of resentment on the part of the victim. After giving detailed illustrations of the "discipline of natural consequences," he urges the following in favour of it:

"First; that it gives that rational knowledge of right and wrong conduct which results from personal experience of their good and bad consequences. Second; that the child, suffering nothing more than the painful effects of its own wrong actions, must recognise more or less clearly the justice of the penalties. Third; that recognising the justice of the penalties, and receiving them through the working of things rather than at the hands of an individual, its temper is less disturbed; while the parent fulfilling the comparatively passive duty of letting the natural penalties be felt, preserves a comparative equanimity. Fourth; that mutual exasperations being thus prevented, a much happier, and a more influential relation, will exist between parent and child."

Now, while it is absolutely essential that the

"discipline of consequences" should be, and must always be from the nature of the case, realised by the individual, yet it is another thing to say that this is the only good method, or the best. If the infliction of pain is regarded only as a penal or a retributive matter, then such a theory might be regarded as satisfactory. But in education we regard pain as a preventive, reformative, and curative agent. From this point of view there is as much reason, and justification, for interfering in mental as in physical irregularities.

It is true that the learner will be corrected, sooner or later, by natural consequences; but it is equally true that he would be generally educated, sooner or later, if left alone. If, therefore, artificial education by the reasoned and systematic application of pleasurable conditions be justifiable, not less is education through pain reasonable, when the necessity for it arises. It is not simply education that is required, but the best education in the shortest time.

Again, it has been very forcibly urged that the necessity for interfering so as to prevent the too serious consequences which would often arise, may easily lead to the child regarding the parent or teacher as one who is setting traps for it, or at least as being adversely neutral. To this may be added the criticism that any very striking natural consequences, especially in certain intellectual faults, are so long in coming that irreparable mischief may have been done before the necessity for reform is realised. Also, the machinery of a system of education creates special conditions which need special remedies. We cannot afford to wait for courses of wrong actions to work themselves out.

But Mr. Herbert Spencer himself allows the necessity for other means. He says : " During infancy a consider-able amount of absolutism is necessary. A three-year-old urchin playing with an open razor, cannot be allowed to learn by this discipline of consequences ; for the consequences may be too serious. But as intelligence increases, the number of peremptory interferences may be, and should be, diminished ; with the view of gradually ending them as maturity is approached."

The discipline of consequences should be employed as often as possible, in its natural form, and should be the model for all artificial methods of inflicting pain for educational purposes. The pain should, as far as possible, be of the same nature as that which would ordinarily arise if there were no personal interference. Also it should be clearly understood that a certain action, or series of actions, will be inevitably followed by a given form of discipline.

When the use of pain is necessary, the mildest, most refined, and what we may call the highest, forms should first be tried. Even these should be employed with hesitation, and the descent to lower forms ought to be undertaken very reluctantly. Only as the last resource of last resources should the infliction of blows upon the body be made use of ; for it is, more or less, brutal in its nature and brutalising in its effects. This should even be the last method employed with the brute beasts ; as, indeed, it seems to be the last way in which they correct each other.

Our aim should always be to gain an educational result with the least possible friction, or disturbance. At the best, the use of pain is a very expensive way of obtaining educational good; it is worse than foolish, therefore, to omit any means, or opportunity, of lessening its amount and frequency.

It is somewhat unfortunate that the term "corporal punishment" has been confined to caning, birching, strapping, or hitting. There are many other forms of bodily punishment, such as: pinching, shaking, posturing, long-continued drilling, and depriving of food. In fact there are comparatively few forms of ordinary punishment which do not involve bodily pains. All such are of the same class; and some of the latter are even more objectionable than the former.

Use pain for the purpose of lessening, if not abolishing, pain, should be the watchword of the educator.

Not only are sarcasm, contempt, bullying, threatening, and punishing, entirely unjustifiable in themselves, under ordinary circumstances, but they defeat their own ends in the long run. They are extreme measures, and to employ them for common events is to waste energy on such, and to deprive the means of the elements of effectiveness—severity and rareness. There are no resources for serious and critical cases if extraordinary measures are employed for ordinary purposes. The chief conditions for success in the control of others are definiteness, decision, and a reasonable persistence in applying the principles of sympathetic control.

Some General Remarks.—It is very necessary to recognise the fact that whilst without a scientific system of education there is very great loss in the extent and fulness in the development of an individual, yet it is possible so to over-elaborate educative processes and conditions that they become a burden, and, therefore, an obstacle to development. There are ways of trying to be helpful which only hinder.

Much in the same way that undiluted milk from the cow cannot be properly assimilated by an infant, and it may practically starve on too rich a diet, so also the infant mind fails to be properly nourished by un-organised experiences. But the other side of the matter also applies. While it is necessary to dilute with water the milk for a child, yet the addition of too much water will lead to starvation ; similarly, the endeavour to make every little detail in education the subject of elaborate application of principles will result in confusion instead of clearness, and hindrance in place of help.

Without pressing the analogy too far, it is probably correct to say that the evil of over-education is as serious as that of under-education, though immeasurably less common. Another good illustration of this truth is seen in the over-training of athletes, which results in weakness instead of strength.

Aristotle, speaking of physical training, remarks : " The evil of excessive training in early years is strikingly proved by the example of Olympic victors ; for not more than two or three of them have gained a prize both as boys and as men ; their early training and severe gymnastic exercises exhausted their constitutions " (Dr. Jowett's translation). He also says : " Men ought not to labour at the same time with their minds and with their bodies; for the two kinds of labour are opposed to one another, the labour of the body impedes the mind, and the labour of the mind the body." Of course more or less severe, continuous, and absorbing work is understood.

There is confusion in too much detail as in too great complexity. An adult would realise this very clearly if a botanist began to explain to him what a plant was by speaking of its molecular organisation. Not too much, but just enough, of detail is what is required. Of course it is difficult to decide what is just enough. But we can fix upon a working average, and begin with this. Then if there is a lack of readiness in grasping the subject, we must go rather less fully into detail, until we find the required facility of understanding. If, on the other hand, there is prompt mastery, then greater detail of knowledge should be presented.

The capacity of children in this respect will be best known through careful observation of their efforts when they are working in their own way and for their own ends. The principles of self-activity and doing, accomplish more than helping development in themselves, they show us also how we can best help it.

Again there should be great caution exercised as to the kind and number of truths which it is attempted to arrive at through one object, or class of objects. Though it is true that as a matter of fact everything involves, more or less remotely, every great principle of knowledge, yet it is neither expedient nor convenient, even if it were possible, to try to get the beginner to realise this, in however concrete or practical a form.

It must be remembered that it is only the person who has obtained knowledge of many principles through much experience of, and thought about, many different classes of things, who is able to realise, in a significant way, that everything is, more or less, in everything.

Jacotot was quite right, philosophically, in insisting that "all is in all"; but he was mistaken, practically, in trying to get complete knowledge of a subject from a very limited amount of its material. The intelligence can, when it has much knowledge, trace the relation of truths to each other in such a way as to find many truths in one fact. But though it is true, in such a sense, to say that all is in each, yet it is not true to say that all comes from each, in so far as the way in which we obtain our knowledge of separate truths is concerned. Some from all, before all in each, is nearer the truth.

As a rule it will be well, at first, to make use of different, though closely related, sets of facts for demonstrating certain truths; and, afterwards, make use of the same material for showing that two—and later on, three—principles are involved. If there be any justification whatever for following the mental evolution of the race, there can be no doubt that this is the right way.

One other suggestion may be indicated. Not every item of truth, or detail of development, is equally important with the others. For example, it is usually better to understand the general law of friction than to know the actual amount of friction in one or two special cases; and it is of greater benefit, in most cases, to develop all the senses to an average level in each case —that of sight and touch being higher than the others —than to specially train one and neglect the others. To endeavour to develop every power to the same extent may result in sacrificing the stronger powers through comparative neglect, and still further weakening the weak powers through overstraining them. Such an harmonious proportion as is likely to be most effective must be striven for.

Where all is emphatic there is no emphasis. To have too much effort given to each point is sometimes not to have enough given to them as a whole. Some rather amusing instances of this are seen in text-books which seek to impress the relative importance of the subject matter upon the reader by the use of six or seven different kinds of type, and three or four arrangements of paragraphs, on the same page; and in the books of those students who underline nearly every word on the pages of their books with differently coloured inks or pencils, and then add short lines for the chiefest of all.

There are truths and beauties which only the whole can give, just as there are those which only the parts possess. We must endeavour, so to speak, neither to lose the forest in a tree, nor the tree in a forest.

The educator must, therefore, carefully observe the actual development of the learner, so that he may the better understand the problem, and make use of the development itself as a means of furthering its own progress.

But in so doing, except in the case of individual education, he must beware of being misled by the exceptionally capable or deficient. For purposes of collective education it is the average individual who must be the standard. Whilst a musical genius may in childhood play like an angel and compose like a god, the ordinary person, after much training and effort, may only be able to play like a barrel-organ and compose like a machine, when an adult.

It should be observed that each general principle of education is itself a subject to which the other principles are to be applied. Thus the principle of doing ought to be worked out according to the general principle of development, and the principles of interest, preparation, repetition, pleasure, and pain (if necessary). Of course the two incompatible principles of pleasure and pain cannot be applied to each other, but the former should supplement, and supplant, the latter as much as possible.

Aristotle pointed out the need of following the order of development in these words: "As the body is prior in order of generation to the soul, so the irrational is prior to the rational. The proof is that anger and will and desire are implanted in children from their very birth, but reason and understanding are developed as they grow older. Wherefore the care of the body ought to precede that of the soul, and the training of the appetitive part should follow; none the less our care of it must be for the sake of the reason, and

our care of the body for the sake of the soul." Again
he says : " Now it is clear that in education habit must
go before reason, and the body before the mind."

The testimony of great teachers in support of the
educational maxims discussed in this chapter is simply
overwhelming; in fact, the history of education is
largely a record of the discovery and re-discovery,
assertion and re-assertion, of them repeated over and
over again. Thus Jacotot (1770–1840) in his famous
paradox " all is in all " endeavours to proceed from the
most simple and superficial knowledge about a given
subject, step by step, to a most complete and exhaustive
knowledge of the thing itself, and of all that is related
to it, by means of analyses of ever-increasing fulness
and depth.

Basedow (1723–1790) over-elaborated the progress
from the concrete to the abstract by ill-chosen and too
detailed representations and imitations of scenes and
actions. Everything was to begin with intuition or
teaching by sight. He says : " A boy whose acutest
faculties are his senses, and who has no perception of
anything abstract must first of all be made acquainted
with the world as it presents itself to the senses. Let
this be shown him in nature herself, or, where this
is impossible, in faithful drawings or models."

Samuel Wilderspin, speaking of his early experiences
and difficulties with infants, exclaims : " It was now
evident that the senses of the children must be
engaged, that the great secret of training them was to
descend to their level, and become a child ; and that
the error had been to expect in infancy what is only the

product of after years" (Leitch, "Practical Educationists"). Thus he arrives at the rule: From the simple to the complex. Comenius lays down as principles of guidance the assertions that: "Nature proceeds from the more easy to the more difficult;" "Nature does not overweight itself, but is content with few things at a time;" and, "Nature does all things uniformly" (Laurie).

From among the more recent writers on practical education, we may quote Mr. Arthur Sidgwick and the late Mr. W. H. Widgery, in reference to the principle of doing. The former in his lecture on "Stimulus" says: "Another potent stimulus to thought and interest is supplied by getting the pupils, wherever it is possible, in however humble a department of knowledge, to share in anything like original research; the boy may be set to find instances of a point of style or grammar for himself; or if there is a mistake in his notes he may be made to correct it; or, still more delightful, he may confute his master."

Mr. Widgery writes: "I managed to get some algebra into the class this morning by making boys do a large number of examples in books, saving the answers, and then making them get the factors backward. They seemed to feel under a moral obligation to do what they knew had only just passed through their hands" ("Life of W. H. Widgery," by W. K. Hill).

A good example of the working of the principle of sympathetic control is also given by Mr. Widgery. He writes: "I gave my boys plenty of rope to-day and let them ask me as many questions as they liked.

S

And wasn't I tired ? " His biographer says : " Once he made every boy in the class write down individually, (1) What had been his chief difficulty in learning Euclid's geometry ; and (2) How he would like to be taught the propositions it contained."

Dr. Welldon has said : " If a boy did not know the nature of the sentence upon which he was engaged, there was little or no probability of his being able to convert it into correct Latin." Thus he recognises the maxim : from the known to the unknown. Professor L. C. Miall asserts that " Children, young people, and most men and women are more easily interested in what is actual and concrete than in what is theoretical and abstract." The same writer contends that " Sarcasm becomes base and cowardly when the power of retort is taken away . . . . the teacher must not use biting words." Mr. Thring says : " Force and presumptuous superiority must be discarded for ever from the kingdom of life, and the learner's world. Education requires that the right object shall be pursued, and pursued in the right way. . . . . The most complete definition of the right way is, the winning love by love." Dr. Abbott affirms that : " It is a pleasure to healthy children to move and to act; and it must be the trainer's object not to suppress action but to regulate it with a view to producing good habits."

Canon Daniel has well said : " It is as unwise to withhold the rod in all cases as to prescribe it in all cases. Children sometimes grow so vicious through neglect, that they will not respond to the motives that actuate well-trained children, and in such cases severity becomes indispensable until higher influences gradually render it unnecessary."

CHAPTER VI

THE consideration of the principal features of general mental development has prepared the way for dealing with one of the special elements which is particularly concerned with education. Since we regard the systematic imparting of knowledge as the essential element for educational development, it is necessary that we should examine very closely into its nature, so as to be able to. clearly understand how best to secure the highest and greatest results from it.

By knowledge we generally understand those groups of related judgments which make up the mental whole which corresponds to a physical whole. Knowledge, therefore, consists of more or less organised judgments about things. Our idea of an orange is made up of the judgments that it is a round, yellow, soft, sweet, odorous, rined, pulped, thing. Our knowledge of an orange will involve further judgments about the above points, and the relating of them in a botanical sense ; also of judgments about the value of the fruit as a food, and for commercial purposes. But, as we shall see later on, some ideas are simple in that they consist of only one judgment.

Thus we see that knowledge is built up from judgments. Now, a judgment is neither more nor less, in its simplest form, than the exercising of the power of knowing : the mental marking off of likeness and difference. This may be a direct and immediate result necessarily involved in the reaction of mind, as when we mark off light from darkness ; or it may be the outcome of a number of such results, which have themselves been related by a higher exercise of judgment, as when we judge that, since colours are the results of certain rates of vibration of light waves, if a disc on which different coloured bands have been painted is made to revolve at a sufficient rate the result will be an approach to the appearance of white colour.

Knowing, in a lower or higher form, is an element in every state of consciousness, from the very beginning to the end of life. It is regarded as the highest attribute of man, because in him it incomparably exceeds that of any other animal ; whilst there is no reason for supposing that in feeling and willing, except in so far as they are influenced by the higher knowing, man is superior to the beasts of the field. Indeed, he is obviously inferior to some of them in so far as the feelings depend upon the senses, for their senses are much more acute than his. But in man thought, in a systematic, scientific, and philosophic form, is the outcome of sense experiences.

What we have now to do is to trace the general development of ideas, as such, and to discover what are the elements of which they are composed. From the results thus obtained we shall be able to throw some further light on educational principles.

General Development of Ideas.—We have already dealt with this topic in connection with the general mental development, and it only remains to briefly point out the special elements with which we are now concerned. It is the development of knowing, from a particular point of view, that we have to consider.

The beginnings of ideas have necessarily the same starting-point as those of knowing, viz., the earliest experiences of life. Sensations and feelings are the first sources of knowledge, and, therefore, from them come the first elements and forms of ideas.

That there is a marking off, or knowing, of one sensation from another, even by the infant, is shown by its crowing and crying. Similar evidence is given of its realisation of degrees of quantity in its pleasures and pains. Later on it learns to distinguish one kind of sensation from another, and uses its eyes, hands, ears, or mouth; subsequently it shows a preference for certain kinds, according to the feelings produced.

This taking account of the quality, quantity, and kind of sensations and feelings is the first element of ideas, and upon it is based all the after-development. It can hardly be said to be an idea, except in an implicit sense, at this stage, for the predominant feature in the experience is the feeling element.

After a sufficient number of experiences have occurred, the mind not only takes account of its own general condition of pleasure or pain, but it begins to

give an outer reference to the inner conditions.　For
example, the child who is pleased with the colour of a
toy learns to associate the feeling with the object, and
finds a way of demanding the presence of the toy ; or,
if it is pained by too hot food, it connects the pain with
the substance with which it is being fed, and thrusts it
away from its mouth.

This assumes that the marking off of things in space,
through their colour outlines and the touch experiences
connected with them, has already taken place.　The
beginning of such a marking off is doubtless due almost
wholly to colour differences, but the hands soon join
with the eyes in giving greater definiteness and precision
to the process; and the other senses stimulate their
activity.　If a sweet is put into the mouth of a child,
without its having seen it, it will be likely to take it
out and look at it.

From this starting-point of a higher stage of knowing,
and nearer approach to ideas, the mind goes on to the
association of many different sensations and kinds of
sensations — and　feelings — with　the　same　physical
object.　The object is then thought of as a whole with
many details.　Its parts, powers, actions, and functions,
are all included, in a practical and concrete sense, as
time goes on.　The whole world of the child's immediate
surroundings is thus dealt with, and so divided up into
a multitude of distinct and significant objects.

Since each of these details implies a judgment, it
would appear that we now have a group of related judgments, which make an idea.　But we have not yet
arrived at the highest kind of ideas, inasmuch as we

limit this term to a purely rational complex. In the above, the sensations and judgments occur together, and the latter are never absent from the former. Hence the object itself must always be present, in the sense of acting upon the senses, so as to cause the judgments to come together in the mind. For this reason we say that we have only, as yet, arrived at practical ideas.

When a physical object is fairly familiar to us we are able to call up in the mind a purely mental picture of it, even after the thing itself has ceased to exist. These images are, like the percepts which they represent, individual things at first. But whilst percepts always remain individual so far as they themselves are concerned, images become general, in the course of time.

This is brought about by the association of like images in such a way that, so to put it, a minimum amount of necessary detail is left for the purpose of suggesting the right kind of object. It is as though an artist were to make fairly full sketches of particular dogs, and then, as he came to compare them with one another and with sketches of other individual dogs, to erase all that was peculiar to each of them, until he had left only those quite general details of form—the element of exact size, being neglected—which were necessary to show that they were sketches of dogs, and not of cats, or other animals.

An image of this kind, when once formed, is perfectly general in its reference, and is, therefore, called a generic image. It constitutes a most significant advance in mental life, for it bridges over the movement of thought from particular things to general ideas. Percepts, however numerous, never in themselves make the general elements in things obvious.

A word or two is necessary as to the scientific and popular use of the word imagine. In the strictly psychological sense, we can only imagine, *i.e.*, produce, or reproduce, a mental image of some physical object of which we have had a percept, or percepts. Whilst in popular language the word is used in this scientific sense, it is also use as meaning suppose, believe, and conceive, as in the sentences: Imagine such a thing happening; I cannot imagine that it is true; Can you imagine the reality of it?

Images are reproduced, or re-presented like other remembered mental results. They are also associated and combined into new and unexperienced complexes. Thus it is quite easy for us to imagine what a man would look like whose head grew under one of his arms, or to imagine the appearance of a satyr from a written description. Similarly, mental pictures of landscapes, of the concrete details of incidents, and the like, can be constructed by the mind itself, so far as it has had the necessary elements supplied by previous experiences. This is called constructive imagination.

After a somewhat extensive knowledge of the mental impressions which objects and their details produce has been obtained, the mind comes to think of the mental effects of these impressions apart from their connection with such-and-such objects, that is, solely as mental wholes, and, therefore, things in themselves. They are then regarded as things which are possessed by certain objects, and which could be possessed by an unlimited number of objects. Thus, instead of thinking of individual things as being strong, large, hard, thick, sweet, heavy, and so on, we think of them as having strength, largeness, hardness, thickness, sweetness, and heaviness. We say that they have these qualities, and we think about qualities as though they were distinct things possessed by an object, whereas they are nothing more than the mental results produced by the different influences which objects exert upon us.

Thus we think of apples as having redness, brownness, greenness, hardness, thickness, flavour, sweetness, usefulness, and wholesomeness. And all these thoughts can be together in the mind without any of the sensations upon which they are based actually taking place at the same time. Now, therefore, we have a purely rational complex which represents our experience, but which is otherwise independent of it ; for we regard it in a way in which we cannot regard the apple itself— we should not have an apple, if we separated its sweetness, hardness, and so on from each other—and we can deal with it wholly from the mental point of view, for we can compare the mental details with each other, and the whole to other wholes, without reference to the physical objects. This, therefore, is the purely abstract, or highest kind of, idea.

Out of abstract ideas arise all our sciences and philosophies. From the pure thought elements of experience we derive other and higher thoughts, and build these into systems of thought. These are the highest, and purely rational, values of our experiences, and can only

come directly from that which is itself wholly mental.
Ideas are themselves the most general elements of
knowledge, for they have an infinite applicability. An
infinite number of things have size, shape, weight, and
so on. Sciences and philosophies involve the most
generalised forms of ideas.

We may illustrate these stages by taking an instance
in which the same phenomenon is presented to different
classes of individuals. Let us take an audience which
is listening to a lecture on psychology. If some children
in arms have the misfortune to be present, the lecture
can be nothing more than an experience of the noise
made by the speaker's voice, and possibly by other
voices: of the effects of the lights, if it be in the
evening: of the comfortable, or otherwise, feelings
produced by the temperature of the room : and some
vague impressions of the general surroundings.

Girls and boys, and uneducated adults, who were
present, would attach clear and definite meanings to
such experiences ; and would, besides, understand many
of the words, and, possibly, some of the sentences used
by the lecturer, in so far as they applied to concrete
things. They would understand something of the significance of the speaker's gesture, and recognise, more
or less clearly, their effects upon the listeners. Any
practical illustrations or amusing anecdotes would be
relished by them. But, otherwise, the lecture would
have very little, if any, significance for them.

To the minds capable of scientific thought, the lecture
would mean the setting forth of ideas which form a part
of an organised body of knowledge. And, though the

sensations experienced by the previous classes would be necessary as means of communication between them and the lecturer, these would be almost entirely forgotten in the mental activity aroused by the ideas as such. If they were really following the lecture they would be likely to think of very few concrete things at all, but would, under the guidance of the speaker, be engaged in observing, analysing, and synthesising ideas about ideas.

Similarly, to take another example, a concrete object, such as a windmill, has different meanings for different capacities. To the little child it is, from the outside, simply something which is marked off in the general colour world, and which has a peculiar effect upon the sight if the sails are moving. From the inside, it will mean a particular kind of rumbling noise, and the effects of unequal distribution of light and air.

For older children and uneducated adults, who are allowed to become familiar with the windmill, the above impressions will have definite significance, and will very distinctly mark off the object as a whole from other objects. They will be able to decide at once, and without mistake as a rule, whether a given object is or is not a windmill. Then they will give definite meanings in a practical sense to the various parts, powers, and actions of the mill; and will be able to mark off the different details from each other, in a similar manner to that in which they mark off the whole from other wholes. This kind of knowledge will be made much more complete and clear if a dissectible model can be made use of. But everything so known is directly sense-given, for it is only as the learner sees, feels, hears, and judges, in direct connection with each concrete detail, that such knowledge is obtained.

In the case of those whose minds have reached the stage of pure ideas, there will be all the previously mentioned details, but with a higher significance. The ideas of unity, purpose, design, power, effectiveness, usefulness, dependence (on man and wind), destructibility, finiteness, function, and so on, will be connected with the mill, and it will possibly be more often thought of in such relations than merely as a physical machinery. Again, the relation of the various parts to each other, with regard to support and motion, will lead to some of those ideas which, when built up into a system, we call the principles of mechanics.

The Elements of Ideas.—From the above we see that there are three characteristic conditions, or stages, in the ordinary development of an idea. First there must be that which can, and does, affect the senses, and is taken account of by the mind. This is known as a presentation—which has been already discussed in the second chapter.

As we shall see later on, ideas themselves give rise to other ideas, without any special action of the senses at the time; but the original source of all ideas is the activities of the senses. The receiving and consciously realising of sensations is the beginning of mental life, and the origin of the most purely rational elements of the highest intellectual life.

Next there is the giving of a definite mental meaning, and an external reference to separate presentations, or groups of presentations, in addition to simply realising them. The mental-with-physical result of this is termed a percept.

Finally, we have the stage when only the purely rational results of the foregoing are taken account of, for the time being. When we are able thus to look into the mind itself for our knowledge of what a thing means to us, we say that we have a purely rational conception of it. Hence we name such a rational complex a concept.

We will now consider each of these elements in greater detail. In doing this it will be necessary to bear in mind that, as in all mental phenomena, each of them involves the others to a greater or lesser degree. The presentation contains the substance of the percept and the germs of the concept ; the percept is an extension of the presentation and supplies the materials for the concept ; and the concept is derived from the percept and presentation. Also, that all three elements are constantly developing simultaneously, though in different proportions. It is the explicit recognition, and making conscious use of the different elements which form the principal features of progress.

1. **Presentations.**—A clearer idea of what a presentation involves may be obtained from the analysis of the details involved. This has been dealt with in the second chapter.

So far as a presentation, as such, is concerned, there need not, and in the first instance cannot, be anything more than a vague realisation of something having happened to the mental life as a whole. There is a kind of general estimate as to whether this is a comfortable or uncomfortable matter, but no further discrimination of its particular character and meaning in reference to the self and other things. When these occur a percept is formed.

It is necessary that what is technically known as the impression should be of a certain intensity, or no presentation will result from it. The truth of this will be recognised when one reflects that if every stimulus which is acting upon the whole body had to be definitely responded to by the mind there would be mental chaos; for there are doubtless millions of stimuli acting upon an individual at any given moment.

Again, this intensity must vary according to the general condition of mind and body at the time. In cases of certain bodily disorders a very slight stimulus may cause very violent disturbance, or a very violent stimulus may cause very slight response. Similarly with the mind: if the attention is already fixed and absorbed, by another matter, a very strong impression will meet with little, if any, response; whilst, on the other hand, if the attention is lively and vigorous, but not pre-occupied, the slightest and most trivial impression may receive very full response.

The intensity which is necessary to bring an impression into full consciousness is technically known as the liminal intensity. This not only varies with the particular condition of the individual at the moment, but also with regard to different periods and for different classes of impressions. Thus, the child, as a rule, requires much less to take its attention, but more to keep it, than an adult or even a youth. Again, the same person is affected more by stimuli of one kind than of another, *e.g.*, a botanist would very definitely notice a variation in a flower, when the ordinary man would very likely not notice the flower at all. A botanist, thus easily and strongly affected by a plant, might be wholly unsusceptible to the ordinary influences of the phenomena of physics, in a scientific sense. A shepherd can recognise his sheep by their faces as readily as he can his personal friends.

If a stimulus be too intense there is no proper discrimination of it, but only a painfully violent disturbance and a sense of shock. The mind is unable to adjust itself to the proper reception of the impression, and a state of strain and friction is set up; much in the same way as when the wind is blowing hard into our open mouth we have the feelings of choking, through inability to adjust our breathing organs to such an excessive supply.

Similarly, when we try very hard to take account of impressions which have not a liminal intensity, there is a painful sense of mental strain and failure. This may be compared to the results of trying to discern points of detail which the eye is really incapable of seeing. In both cases it is the inability of the organism to adjust itself to the stimulus which causes the effort to produce the disturbance and pain.

Both over-intensity and under-intensity may produce permanently mischievous, and even disastrous, results. This is seen in cases where children are made permanently fearful, or even driven into imbecility, by having the emotion of fear over-excited by, to them, horrible stories about the bogey-man. On the other hand, an individual may develop a cold and unsympathetic character, through not having had his feelings of gratitude and affection sufficiently aroused in early life.

Another very important feature in presentations is the relation between the intensity of the sensation and the stimulus. It is found by experiments that when a certain sensation is being experienced it is necessary for the stimulus to be doubled before there is a definite consciousness of an increase in the intensity of the sensation. If, for example, a pound weight is resting upon the hand, and more and more weight is gradually added, it is not until the total amounts to two pounds that there is a clear consciousness of an increase of sensation. Of course, this assumes that the eye and ear are prevented from helping the judgment. To get still another conscious recognition of an increase of sensation the weight must be increased to four pounds.

This fact is generally expressed by saying that: to increase the sensation in arithmetical progression, we must increase the stimulus in geometrical progression. That is, if the progress of sensation is to be as 1, 2, 3, 4, 5, the progress of stimulus must be as 1, 2, 4, 8, 16. This is known as Weber's, or Fechner's law, because its recognition was chiefly due to the investigations of Weber, and Fechner. But it is an analogy rather than a law, for it is hardly true to say that the sensation increases in arithmetical progression. The mind is conscious of "more," not of "one unit more," sensation.

A presentation may be simple or complex. It may be simple, in that it is a single impression conveyed through one of the senses, *e.g.*, a single colour or a single sound, or a succession of such. A complex presentation may arise from several impressions coming through the same sense, or through different senses, at one time, as when a combination of colours is seen, or when we see the performers in an orchestra, hear the music, and feel the vibrations caused by the double-bass.

We may define a presentation as: anything which is attended to by the mind. This definition is designedly wider than much of the foregoing discussion suggests. We must make it thus wide, because when the mind has reached a reflective stage, and is, therefore, able to think about its own thoughts, these become matters which are dealt with in a manner similar to that in which we deal with sense-presentations. Were it not for the fact that we are able to do this, we could not have such a science as psychology. Purely mental presentations imply that introspective, reflective, self-consciousness which makes the knowledge of the mind possible.

The whole universe of mind and matter may be looked upon as one vast presentation, made up of a series of related presentations, which the mind, in its growth and development, partly creates, absorbs, and reflects. In a more restricted sense, the world of experience is our presentation universe. This has been termed the presentation continuum by Dr. James Ward, because of its continuity and unity. From it smaller

T

systems, or continua, such as the visual, aural, tactual, ideational, emotional, and so on, are evolved as life goes on; but these are always inter-dependent upon, and inter-related with, the great unity of life and thought.

2. **Percepts.**—From what has already been said it will be seen that percepts involve what we have spoken of as the knowledge of the concrete and practical elements of things, and of their parts, powers, and actions. To put the matter in general terms, we may say that the percept involves the mental realisation of the fact that certain complexes of impressions express the existence and nature of particular things, or physical objects, as we usually name them.

We will proceed to investigate more closely the nature of a percept. It will be necessary throughout the following discussions to guard ourselves against confusing the psychological use of the word percept with some of the ordinary uses of the word perceive. In ordinary speech we meet with such a sentence as: You will perceive the truth of the argument. Now, there can be no psychological percept referred to in such a sentence, for there is no concrete object involved. Truth and argument are both abstract ideas. The word perceive has here the meaning of understand, apprehend, or grasp. But in such a sentence as: You did not, perhaps, perceive the man place his hand under the cloth, the word is used in a strictly psychological sense, and means: You did not, perhaps, have a percept of the man placing his hand under the cloth.

We have already pointed out that in the percept there

is a definite significance given to sense-impressions. There is the recognising that certain colour sensations are like to each other, but unlike others which are also like to each other. Thus a certain colour will appear to the mind as such-and-such an one, that is, when language is known, we say that it is white, black, red, or blue. And, similarly, all other sensations will have a definite character or meaning.

This recognising and classifying of sense-presentations is known as the element of assimilation in percepts. Assimilation here, as always, involves its correlative—discrimination—for wherever there is a marking out as to likeness, there must be a marking off as to unlikeness. This applies equally to ideational, emotional, and other presentations.

Assimilation implies the retention and re-presentation of mental effects, for there could be no re-cognition unless previous cognitions, however vague, are represented along with the presentation. If we assume that this takes place automatically, from the nature of mind itself, and that it is followed by what Dr. Bain calls the "shock of agreement," and "flash of identity in diversity," then assimilation and discrimination are accounted for.

From the standpoint of later knowledge, we may say that assimilation is the result of the spontaneous activity of memory and association. As has been frequently insisted, the meaning of a presentation is largely due to the representative elements, which the mind itself supplies for purposes of interpretation and assimilation.

Besides this internal mental assimilation of the sense-presentation, there is the giving it an external reference. Probably the first element in this external reference is the clear recognition that the impression, or impressions, come through a certain sense. The young child doubtless learns that colour sensations come through the eyes, because of what happens when it closes its eyes, and because of the local disturbance, which causes blinking and shutting of the eyes, when there is a dazzling light.

" It is by the daily renewed conjunctions of simple sense-experiences, and more particularly those of sight and touch, that the little learner comes to refer its impressions to objects. By continually looking at the objects handled, the usual perception of direction becomes perfected, as also that of distance within certain limits. . . . . A child known to the present writer was first seen to stretch out his hand to an object when two and a half months old. The hand misses the exact point at first, passing beside it, but practice gives precision to the movement. The same child at six months knew when an object was within reach. If a biscuit or other object was held out of his reach, he made no movement, but as soon as it was brought within his reach he instantly put out his hand to take it." (Sully.)

Then a still more remote external reference is given to sensations. Thus colours are regarded as spread over a certain amount of space, sounds as coming from a certain direction, tastes as being connected with certain objects, and so on.

Such references of impressions to that which is external to the mind itself is termed the element of localisation in percepts.

Localisation involves the idea of space, the origin of which we cannot go into now. We may say in general terms that, to obtain correct space elements in a percept, we must have explored an object by means of the sense of touch combined with movements. The tactual sensations must be continuous until the limits of the object are reached, whether the movement is forwards or backwards. Also the usual sensations must be unbroken during the sweep of the eye over the object.

Both of these series must be simultaneously presented to the mind, and there must be a sense of more or less of what we may call bigness or massiveness about the total—in the sense that the sight of a huge elephant impresses one in a different sense from that of a minature model of it, though the extent of the retinal impression may be the same in each case. This is technically known as the extensity of the sensation.

But this localisation of a percept involves much more than vague references to that which is not mind. There is a definite recognition of a something underlying the sensation, or sense-impression, itself, and which is the original source from whence it arises. This we call concrete substance; and we regard it as having different forms, each having distinct and separate units, and classes of such units, with their sub-classes. In other words, there are organic and inorganic forms of matter, with all their divisions and sub-divisions of forms.

Each distinct and separate unit we call a thing; and this element of the realisation of a special and separate source of the activities which gives rise to sense-impressions we call the intuition of things.

Since each part of a percept is the outcome of the re-action of the mind, according to its own fundamental nature, to the action of external influences, we can only point out the conditions and details involved. We cannot give any other reason for the nature of the result than to say that it appears to be the necessary effect of the re-action of such an organism as mind to the special influences which act upon it.

The grouping of the details of a percept, through the recognition of their concrete relations to each other, involves a series of practical judgments, and is, therefore, in this respect, a mediate, and not an immediate product. The full meaning of this will appear as we proceed.

The intuition of things involves several essential elements. First and foremost is the realisation of the actuality or reality of what we call the thing. This consists in the inevitable conviction, under normal conditions, that there is that of which the senses are taking account, and which they cannot escape taking account of, unless prevented by something which interferes with the ordinary relation between their own activities and those of an external object.

There is that which is recognised as a fundamental difference between a sense-presentation and a mental representation. The latter is, more or less, under the control of the will, both as to time and form, while the form can, more or less, compel the will as to these. Thus we can think of a being, half man and half horse, when we will, but we are compelled to have the proper percept of a horse, if such an animal is before us, under normal conditions. It is the mind which takes account of qualities, but there is some concrete thing which possesses that which gives rise to the ideas.

Next there is the element of resistibility in a concrete or physical thing. Experience teaches us that there is what we call free space, in which our limbs can move without hindrance ; but where there is what we know as a physical object, there our movements are more or less retarded, or entirely stopped. This leads us to the idea that there is something which is a thing in itself, or entity, in the same sense that our body is known to us as a kind of physical self.

Then there is also the element of unity and complexity. As has been pointed out, certain sounds, sights, smells, tastes, and muscular sensations, are all referred to one objective centre, as in the case of an orange. The object, as a whole, is regarded as made up of those constituents which respectively give rise to the different sense-impressions. Moreover, such a complex is, as a rule, regarded as a separate and self-contained whole, whatever may be its relations to other wholes. Its extent, as determined by the limits of its special form of resistibility, has limits in space, and it is thus physically marked off as a unit.

Another element is that of permanence or temporal continuity. The unit has such a unity that it can, as a

rule, change its position without being otherwise
materially altered, or, at any rate, not so changed as to
spoil its identity, or prevent its recognition as such-
and-such a specimen of a certain class. It has a physical individuality which is, as a whole, maintained in
spite of many changes of detail. It is not as though
each man were simply something more of man as a
race; but he is a thing in itself, which has its own
permanent individuality, though belonging to a special
class of objects.

Finally, there is the element of substantiality in the
intuition of things. This really sums up, in a sort of
final expression, all the elements. It more especially
suggests the space-occupying attribute. This is a more
or less monopolising and exclusive element. Where
the actual substance is, there, so far as we know,
nothing else can be. No substance is known to be
absolutely solid, but all seem to have more or less
extensive interstices between the final units of which
they are composed. Pieces of solid steel and sponge
are suggestive of the more or less monopolising of space
by substance. This it is which forms the basis of our
idea of a physical object.

Of course each of these elements does not come to us
consecutively, or even separately; and they are, in the
end, inseparably united in the total percept. Such a
separation as here made is a purely rational analysis
of the meaning and significance of a percept. The
separate elements of the percept, as such, are direct
and immediate forms of cognition. The whole
becomes more and more full of content as experience

and knowledge widen and deepen ; but at any given moment it is a distinct and definite whole.

A percept, or concrete idea, may be defined as an intelligible synthesis of impressions. The word intelligible must here be understood to mean : by the intelligence, for the intelligence. It should be carefully noted that a percept is not defined as a synthesis of presentations, for this would include purely intellectual presentations, which are beyond the sphere of percepts.

Great care must be taken not to confuse actual percepts with those judgments which previous experiences and judgments cause us to instinctively base upon the percepts. For example, we do not perceive, in the strictly psychological sense, the distance of an object from us. There is nothing in a ray of light itself to tell us whether it has been reflected from an object an inch away or a million of miles away.

What really happens is this : because of the muscular sensations which are involved in a certain visual experience, we judge—after mentally comparing the present sensations with past ones which are associated with the experiences attending a walk to the object seen—that if we were to walk to the object the time and energy required would be such-and-such, and we, therefore, say that the object seen is far away or near.

The same kind of criticism applies to some judgments based upon aural, tactual, and muscular experiences. We cannot perceive that a tune is melodious, bright, or bold, by looking at the score : that an object is heavy, hard, or damp, by seeing it : or that an apple is ripe, sweet, soft, or juicy, from a sight of it.

As an illustration of the elements in a percept we may take the case of a book. The impressions which a book gives rise to are recognised, when re-acted upon by consciousness, as such-and-such sensations, which we afterwards learn to call visual, tactual, and muscular sensations. This is assimilation, and justifies us in saying that a certain object is a book, and not a box, or a leather bag. If challenged, we should assert that certain of these sensations come through the eye, others through the skin, and muscles ; and also that they were due to a certain something which occupied a certain definitely limited space area. This is localisation, and is implied in saying : the object in such-and-such a position is a book.

Then there is the conviction that no person, in a normal state, could fail to be aware of this object, under proper conditions, because it is such that it necessarily affects the senses in various ways, and has a permanent individuality. This is the intuition of the thing, and implies that we regard the book as a kind of physical self, more or less of the nature of our own body-self. It has a separate existence, and is, therefore an entity or thing in itself.

From what has been said, it will be seen that all percepts are practical judgments, and that many of them are very complex judgments. But all the judgments about the parts, as such, are, direct and immediate, or intuitive judgments. If they were not so, judgment in a higher sense could not exist, for it would have no starting-point, nor material to deal with. These concrete judgments are related to each other in systematic, practical forms—hence the arts—and the mental processes involved constitute what is called practical reason. Of the activities involved we shall treat more fully in dealing with concepts. It is this relating of the parts and wholes to each other which constitutes the immediate, or more or less explicitly connected, character of percepts.

This may well be called the practical reason. Its most striking form is seen in those inventions connected with mechanical details which are so often made by artisans, and are said to have done almost as much for the development of machinery as the original designs. Almost every intelligent worker is constantly finding out little ways in which concrete materials are more easily and effectively controlled. Workmen have what we call " knacks " in doing their work.

All such involve what we may term perceptual reasoning. Direct judgments are made about things, whilst, and because, persons are handling them. There is no explicit thinking out of matters by, say, a bricklayer, as is the case, for example, with an architect in his office, but a kind of almost instinctive realising that such and such materials, in a certain concrete relation, will lead to given practical results.

Of course all the elements of experience-given knowledge, and mental ideas, and their relations are implicit, and may later on become explicit. But, at the time, the individual himself regards the whole matter as one of doing, and not of thinking. It is thus that the arts precede the sciences. And in this way the race has done great things in the way of action, whilst the power of abstract thinking has been small.

These remarks on perceptual reasoning should be carefully compared with what was said about the development of practical knowing, when we were dealing with the development of feeling and knowing in the fourth chapter.

3. **Concepts.**—The movement from the wholly individual and particular elements of thought, as found in percepts, to the perfectly general elements which are found in the concept, or abstract idea, is a very momentous one. It is the basis of that higher self-consciousness, and reflective reason, which distinguish man from the lower animals. If this step were not taken, man would always remain in the sphere of the empirical and the particular. Instinct would be the only organising activity of thought, and life would be limited to a cycle of more or less advanced, and perhaps advancing, habits.

At a certain point in his development the human being comes, so to say, face to face with his own mind. No higher progress is possible unless he recognises the fact that a fundamental element in his experiences is supplied by a special capacity belonging to himself. He must grasp the truth that certain elements which he has hitherto regarded as part and parcel of things themselves exist, in a sense, only in his own mind. In other words, it is necessary that he should realise that what we call the qualities of things have separate existence only in so far as they are purely mental wholes.

Now, the abstract, as such, is known as different from the concrete. This makes possible the existence of knowledge, as knowledge, *i.e.*, a mental store of truths, known as truths. Of course this is realised, at first, only in a very simple and direct sense, and not in any scientific or philosophic manner. The individual has simply learnt to distinguish between his impressions, as such, and his judgments about them. He can separate the latter from the former, and, to some extent, can still further investigate the nature and meaning of them. From this starting-point there stretches out before him infinite possibilities of rational progress. Infinite, for him, because he has to deal with a universe of infinite detail and complexity with finite powers and a limited amount of time.

Already there has been an organising of knowledge and actions into systems for practical purposes—the arts. Now this is followed by that deeper insight into the inner unity of things, which results in the ideas of general relations, principles, and laws; the organising of these into those systems of knowledge which we term sciences; and the attempt to organise these into that still higher unity of knowledge which we name philosophy.

Let us, therefore, examine more closely into the nature and details of concepts, with regard to their origin, constitution, and activities. We have already asserted that they are derived from percepts, and presentations generally; and it only remains to say how they are evolved.

Some details have previously been given of the way in which concepts are developed. The foundation of the whole process is the recognition of the distinction between an experience and our judgment, or judgments, about it ; and the keeping of these distinct for mental purposes. This is done, spontaneously at first, and designedly afterwards, both with regard to experiences as a whole and to each detail of them.

Thus one of the processes in the development of the concept is the separation of the more purely mental elements from the more purely material. This is the result of a process of analysis, and is usually spoken of as the element of abstraction in the concept.

But this analysis involves more than the mere separation, in thought, of the mental from the other elements in an experience. These mental elements, or qualities, are themselves separated from each other by their similarities and differences, and are classified and grouped. Thus different shades of blueness are classified, and the classes grouped under the general system of colour ideas. So also classes of abstract ideas are separated from each other, but, again, all grouped under a general system. Abstract ideas derived from visual experiences are kept distinct from those obtained through the sense of touch; but both are grouped, with others, under the system of those derived from sense experiences generally.

Such a process of classification involves very careful and close comparison of abstract ideas with one another; and, therefore, the result is commonly called the element of comparison in the concept. Like abstraction, it is primarily due to an analytic process, but it also obviously involves a process of synthesis.

But there is a further process of synthesis in the formation of a concept. All those ideas of qualities which are derived through experiences connected with one and the same thing are synthesised into a mental whole, which retains a permanent distinctness and individuality of its own in the mental world. We may illustrate this by pointing out that the percept of a square is expressed by saying that it is a straight-sided, four-sided, equal-sided, right-angled, figure; whilst the concept of it—which is the concept of squareness—is expressed by saying it is an idea which involves the ideas of rectilinealness, quadrilateralness, equilateralness, and equiangularity.

Such concepts as those of rectilinealness, blueness, length, and the like, are those to which we have previously referred as simple ideas. They involve in themselves, so far as we know, only one single element of thought and experience.

The concept definition shows at once the elements of abstraction, in the four ideational units : of comparison, as implied in the different names : and of synthesis, as involved in their grouping as the expression of one total idea.

It would be clearer and more exact to speak of the elements of analysis and synthesis in the concept, rather than of those of abstraction and comparison; for abstraction and comparison are neither so clear in themselves, nor do they so clearly express the facts of the case.

In addition to the elements of abstraction and comparison, or analysis and synthesis, there is another very important element in the concept. When once the more purely mental elements or qualities have been separated from an experience, there is no reason why they should be looked upon as belonging to any particular presentation ; although particular presentations must always be thought of as involving particular concepts. Hence, concepts, whether of complexes or individual elements, are regarded as perfectly general in their significance, and application to experience. Thus one's concept of squareness does not belong to this, that, or the other square, but to any and every square that now exists, or ever may exist. Similarly, the concept of equiangularity is also generalised.

The element in the concept which is thus added is known as the element of generalisation. The application, extension, and expansion of this element plays the most essential and fruitful part in the higher rational development.

We may sum up the foregoing by defining a concept, or abstract idea, as : an intelligible synthesis of attributes. The word intelligible must be understood in the same sense as in the definition of a percept.

Since it is merely the distinct conscious separation, in thought, of the mental from the other elements in experience which gives the rationally separate existence to the concept, it is clear that the concept is implicit in every experience, and that it may be made explicit under favourable conditions.

Concepts, like all mental elements, have certain forms

of activity by which they become related to the members of their own and other classes. Hence concepts are associated with one another in classes, and these classes are united into systems.

As well as being thus associated with each other, concepts are consciously related to each other, as to their general or particular agreement or difference. For example, the judgments : all truthfulness is virtue ; some success is moral; force is no remedy; some criminals are not vicious ; involve relations of concepts as to their general or particular agreement or difference. Such relatings of concepts to one another constitute judgments in pure reason.

But there is, under the stimulus and guidance of the mind as a whole, a higher kind of activity amongst concepts than is involved in judgments. This consists in such an inter-relating of judgments that other concepts result from them. From this source come purely rational judgments, and trains of rational judgments, or reasonings.

Reasonings may be of two kinds. We may take two or more judgments dealing with one and the same common subject matter and so relate these to each other as to build up a new judgment. Thus, if we have the two judgments : all knowledge is helpful ; and, the science of education is knowledge; then we can hardly help recognising that the judgment : the science of education is helpful, is involved in them. This is clearly a synthetic process. It is called deductive reasoning, or deduction. The activity is a systematic extension of the synthetic processes involved in the

U

formation of a concept, which are themselves higher forms of the fundamental activities of assimilation and discrimination.

The other kind of reasoning consists in analysing a single judgment, or a series of similar judgments, and finding that a universal judgment is involved. When Newton saw the apple fall to the ground he would, implicitly at least, make a judgment to that effect. But he also proceeded to analyse this judgment, and others like it, until he became convinced that he was justified in making the judgment: The reason why bodies sometimes fall is, because all physical bodies attract each other.

Such universal judgments, we say, express principles, or laws. The process of thought is obviously analytic, except as to the summing up of results in the final judgment. The whole is called inductive reasoning or induction. A detailed example of inductive reasoning is given in the second chapter, and discussed in the fourth. The process is a systematic expansion of the analytic activities involved in the formation of a concept, which are themselves higher forms of the fundamental activities of assimilation and discrimination.

A great deal might be said in connection with reasoning and its educational bearings, for these are very numerous and important. But the subject is much too wide to be dealt with now. It could only be properly considered in a book on logic and its relations to education.

The above form what we may call the unit elements

of knowledge. These are unified by the general activity of mind, both by direct and indirect means. The direct means is the organising effects of attention, and the indirect means is the use of a symbolic machinery which mind invents, and which we term language. It will be necessary to consider these.

Ideas and Attention. Apperception.—Attention constitutes, or rather expresses, both the receiving and the responding activities of the mind. Sensations, percepts, and concepts, that is, all kinds of presentations, must stimulate the attention if they are to have any definite effect upon consciousness. When they do have a definite effect, they are not only dealt with as individual presentations, but their relations to other like experiences are taken account of.

So much is necessary before a presentation can have definite significance for us. But a great deal more than this takes place, either implicitly or explicitly. The activity of attention continues the work of assimilation and discrimination, to a greater or lesser extent, into the higher regions of thought. The implicit and explicit features in such a mental pursuit are illustrated by such incidents as the following.

A schoolboy is discovered in what strikes the teacher as a particularly bad act of copying. The teacher is so impressed with the gravity of the offence that he begins to carefully think the matter over, to see if it may not be the result of ignorance and thoughtlessness on the boy's part. But no sooner does he begin to attend vigorously to his line of thought than all sorts of things come crowding in upon his mind. The boy has been in ill odour with his fellows through some mysterious disappearances of private stores from their boxes; he shirks games; his preparation-work has been suspiciously superior to his class-work; many of his actions which have been regarded as not too refined are seen to have a sinister connection with each other; and so on, till the teacher is somewhat astounded at the result, and at the fact that he has not noticed these things before.

As a matter of fact, much of the result was already prepared in the mind, through the implicit organising effects of attention, and it only required the more definite act of special attention to make them, and others, explicit. The final issue might be to remove the act from the class of individual slips in conduct to a striking manifestation of vicious disposition and character. This will have involved the highest processes of assimilation and discrimination, or analytic and synthetic thought, viz., inductive and deductive reasonings.

From an examination of the separate judgments about details of conduct, the general, though limited, inductive judgment: all these actions are vicious, would be made. Then the following deductive reasoning would occur, either implicitly or explicitly: all boys who systematically do vicious acts are of vicious disposition and character; this boy is a boy who systematically does vicious acts; therefore, this boy is of a vicious disposition and character.

From such an example it will be seen that attention carries on the work of assimilation and discrimination, from its lowest to its highest forms, through an organic and complete system of processes. This involves the relating of a presentation to a class of like presentations, the relating of it through this class to allied classes in a system of such presentations, and the inter-relating of it, through this system, more or less fully, directly, and explicitly, with the whole mind.

Such a more or less completely systematic inter-relation of a presentation with representative elements is known as apperception. Professor J. M. Baldwin has well defined apperception as: "The synthesis in consciousness by which mental data of any kind (sensations, percepts, concepts) are constructed into higher forms of relation, and the perception of things which are related becomes the perception [*i.e.*, rational realisation] of the relation of things."

He also says: "This use of the word apperception to express the broadest act of mental relation is of great importance and value. The treatment of the very distinct and familiar act of mind in attention, of grasping details and relating them to one another in a new mental product, has heretofore been confined to its special operations—as perception, conception, judgment—to each of which a different name was given. The term apperception singles out that act of mind which is common to them all—the relating activity of consciousness—and thus, by its general application, emphasises the unity of the intellectual function as a whole."

Through this process ideas become systemised into the highest forms of thought. The concentration of

the energy of attention results in the thorough organisation of presentations in relation to the whole mental
structure.

Whilst association of ideas is determined by the order
of experiences, the apperception of ideas is determined
by their own nature, and the general constitution and
condition of mind at the moment. We may regard
each of the ideas possessed by the mind as eagerly
striving to obtain from a presentation whatever is of
like nature to itself. When, therefore, the mind has
acquired skill in this complete assimilation of the
different mental elements in a presentation, there is no
longer a process of "swallowing things whole" and
reproducing them with literal accuracy as in youth;
but, in place of this, the items of the presentation
seem to disappear and leave few, if any, traces of their
original forms.

Because of this, adults often think they have lost
their powers of memory when, as a matter of fact, these
are most active, powerful, and fruitful. But they act
more through assimilative, than through mechanical,
retention. The mind reads, marks, learns, and inwardly
digests the significance, instead of retaining merely the
direct effects of experiences.

A group of ideas which absorbs an idea from a
presentation is called an apperceiving group; the
idea is said to be apperceived; and the total of ideas,
then and subsequently, make up an apperceptive group.

The association of ideas as determined by the order
of experiences is an important point in connection with
the building up of systems of ideas, for the right order of

dependence and inter-relation may be largely indicated by the order in which they are remembered.

If we experiment on ourselves, we shall find that the order of association corresponds to the order of presentation in a series. Thus, if the words geranium, catapult, dog, cake, book, be read through twice, the reader will probably be able to repeat them from memory. But if he immediately try, without any kind of preparation, to say them backwards, he will undoubtedly fail. It is only by arranging them in a backward order, and so making a new series of them, that they can be so associated.

The arrangement of ideas which are to form a system should, therefore, be carefully systemised in experience, so far as this may be possible.

Persons are very apt to be too much dominated by a particular apperceptive group. Almost every person is necessarily influenced most by some one apperceptive group, from the fact that he is most concerned with some special interest in life—such as his business, profession, or hobby—and, therefore, develops the ideas connected therewith very extensively. But, if this be allowed to become too absorbing, the general mental life will become narrow and stereotyped, with the result that the specially developed apperceptive group is likely to be much less strong and sound than it might otherwise be.

Because of the general inter-relation and interdependence of every part of mind, no one power can be both exclusively, and soundly, developed; for the weakness of one, or more, of the other powers will inevitably tend to weaken the predominant one. The other chief powers should therefore be maintained at an average state, at least, of power and skill. Otherwise, there will be a danger of developing mischievous forms of enthusiasm, faddism, monomania, and the like.

Ideas and Language.—Doubtless the beginnings of speech are to be found in the cries and movements with which primitive man expressed his emotions. These would be likely to repeat themselves, and thus to be so impressed upon the person using them that the emotion would suggest the usual signs of expression. These would become general, and practically traditional, through the imitativeness of children. Hence primitive man would, on hearing certain cries, or seeing certain actions, immediately think that certain emotions, and other experiences, were being undergone.

Besides this, the necessity and desire of communicating his experiences to his fellows would lead to the imitation of the cries and actions of animate things, and the shapes and movements of, and the sounds made by, inanimate things. Thus a very crude form of vocal language, and a somewhat complex form of gesture language, would be evolved.

Soon, however, as the necessity and convenience of signs as a means of communication became more fully recognised, the limitations of gestures for this purpose would be felt. The great ease with which vocal signs can be formed ; the delicate shades of expression which they admit of ; the distances at which they are effective ; their independence of visual aid, so that they are equally useful during day and night ; and the possibility of increasing them to a practically unlimited extent, would all force themselves upon those who most desired to communicate with others.

Hence vocal signs would get more and more coherent and systematic, until articulate speech was developed. When this step had been taken, language, in the form that we know it, would begin to take definite shape. But a long period would elapse before anything like an extensive or systematically arranged language would appear. Very much later still would it be before speech was reduced to writing—first of a pictorial and then of a conventional character.

We have spoken of the necessity as well as the convenience of language. Now this necessity is a mental as well as a practical one. Only through a means of communication could man procure much aid or helpful companionship from his fellow man ; and only through the aid of signs can the mind carry on its highest processes. For example, it is found that though the deaf and dumb can express, with great freedom and accuracy, their percepts and practical experiences, through gestures and imitations—either with or without the deaf and dumb alphabet—yet they seem incapable of forming many, or very complex, general ideas, because they cannot express them.

Doubtless this is due to the difficulty, which becomes an impossibility in some instances, of retaining in full consciousness all the elements of an abstract idea, or indeed of a complex percept. To give an extreme example of this, the total idea of man includes all the ideas involved in those attributes, powers, and activities which are treated of in psychology, logic, ethics, human physiology, and human anatomy, as well as a great many others treated of in the various sciences. It is clearly impossible to have all these, or even a very small fraction of them, in clear consciousness at any one moment.

If this be true of a single concept, much more is it true of two concepts and the processes of relating them, as involved in a judgment. And still more urgent becomes the necessity of symbols for thinking out series of judgments, or reasonings. It is because of this that the place and function of language in development is of such essential importance.

Mind has, therefore, invented for itself a kind of mental algebra, which we call language. Just as in algebra we say let the sign " x " stand for such-and-such things, so in thought we say let the symbol "man" (spoken and written) stand for whatever of our total concept of man is being dealt with. In both systems we must always be prepared to translate the sign into the thing signified, whenever occasion demands it.

Thought is originally a spontaneous development of mind, and is necessarily existent before there can be any need of language for its further progress. As Dr. J. Ward says: "While it is possible for thought to begin without language, just as arts may begin without tools, yet language enables us to carry the same process enormously farther. . . . . But thought as a permanent activity may be fairly said to originate in, and even to depend upon, the acquisition of speech."

In thinking proper there is always the exercise of

voluntary willing upon ideas. In other words, all thinking is a voluntary effort. There is also an inevitable element of design as to the line of thought, and some prevision, however slight, of what the end will be. We never think, so to speak, entirely in the dark. It is necessary that we should know what end we are trying to reach, or we can never achieve any intelligible thought at all, for there is no centre to which ideas are directed. To this extent the result of our thought is always more or less pre-determined.

Some element of interest is, therefore, required. This will be supplied by our judgment as to the relation of the results to our feelings of pleasure and pain; whether through intellectual effects, both as to the processes and products of the train of thought, or as to the actions which we may propose to take on the final judgments arrived at. As a rule, trains of thought will be prompted by some definite desire on the part of the thinker.

In all such thought processes and conditions, the percept is itself its own symbol of the purely mental elements which it involves, and which are always implicitly active, so long as the percept is before the mind presentatively, or representatively—through the mental image. But for purely rational thought, through explicit abstract ideas, or concepts, no such natural symbol is possible, and, therefore, its place is taken by the artificial word sign.

Just as the percept, or its image, as a symbol, is an inseparable part of practical thought, so, when once an abstract idea has been definitely associated with a word sign, the word and the concept—the sign and its significance—are inseparably connected in thought processes. The word is, so to put it, not merely a deputy, but a deputy with full powers to act for the central authority. This must be so, if what we have said about the dependence of thought on language be true, for, in that case, to endeavour to get rid of the word-signs in a train of reasoning would be to render the reasoning impossible.

Words represent the content of concepts in their most abbreviated and condensed forms. They fix most clearly and permanently in mind the expression of the ends, processes, and products of thought; and they tend to make ideas more vivid and definite. Written language is a means of perpetuating the achievements of experience and reason, and so prevents loss, and much useless repetition of effort.

At the same time, however, words often prove a very serious stumbling-block to thought and communication. Since it would be practically impossible to have an entirely different word for every different concept, much less for all the various shades of difference in each of our concepts—for this would prove too great a burden for the memory—we have to use the same sign for several ideas, or things. Thus the word box has many meanings, as is seen in the terms: clothes' box, box seat, shooting-box, boxer, horse-box, in the wrong box, and so on. Similarly the word tenderness varies in meaning according as it relates to personal affection, softness of material, sensibility of a wound, and delicate handling.

Great practical advantage is derived from this economy of language, but there is great danger of confusion and error if the inevitable ambiguity is not provided for. It is often expedient in ordinary speech, and always necessary in cases where precision and accuracy are important, to make quite clear the particular sense in which we are using a word. Even when a word has only one meaning and reference, as in the case of oxygen, it is still possible to use it in a restricted sense —e.g., with regard to its combustion supporting power —and in so doing to mislead a beginner.

Another very frequent and often serious source of mischief in the use of words is when one person, who has a very full content of meaning for certain words, uses them in his sense to another who has a very small content of meaning. Hence the adult often confuses the child, and is himself misled by words used by children. So, also, learned and ignorant persons misunderstand each other.

As Dr. Sully remarks: "The fact that the child is hearing a highly developed language spoken about him, which embodies the finer distinctions of mature intelligence, must tend to bewilder his mind at first. He finds it hard to distinguish between closely related and overlapping words, 'healthy' and 'strong,' 'sensible' and 'clever,' and so forth."

It is necessary, therefore, to constantly bear in mind these liabilities to error, and to take care to demand the exact significance of the sign where error is likely to arise through such causes as the above. But this must not be pressed too far, for the effort to be over-precise is apt to be as confusing as the lack of precision. Popularly accepted meanings, scientific assumptions, trade usages, personal implications, and contexts, all play their part in indicating the precise meaning of terms. A good practical rule is : when in doubt challenge the meaning.

The necessity of taking account of these things is seen when we reflect that, after all, it is the ideas which we wish to develop or communicate. The words are in themselves simply the machinery, not the material, of thought and communication.

Some General Remarks.—From the above it is clear that the general movement of ideational development is from sensuous elements to perceptual apprehension, and thence to conceptual abstractions. The higher, or conceptual, development we find to be dependent upon the use of language. Hence we may now see in greater fulness of detail what is implied in the three great stages of the general development of feeling, knowing, and willing.

We may put the same point in other ways by saying that the line of progress is from experiences to ideas, and from ideas to language; or, that the growth of ideas is from individual and particular ideas to general ideas. By particular ideas we mean groups of similar individual ideas, as to which the elements of generality are not consciously or fully realised.

The inter-dependence of these cannot be too strongly insisted upon in view of the unity of the mental life as a whole. The percept involves an implicit concept, for its element of meaning is purely mental. The concept implies the percept, for it is only possible to abstract a mental meaning from that which has it. Both concept and percept depend upon sensations, for without these the existence of mental life, as we know it, would be impossible.

Dr. Sully puts this very clearly in the following passage : " The powers of comparison and of abstraction in its wide sense are developed in connection with the process of perception itself, in carrying out those detailed operations of examining objects of sense on all sides which are involved in the formation of clear percepts.

" Again, the power of seizing similarity in the midst of diversity, which is the essential process in building up notions of classes and the qualities of things, manifests itself in a lower form in the first year of life. To recognise the mother's voice, for example, as one and the same through all the changes of loudness and softness, and all the variations of pitch, or her figure, through all the changes of light, distance, and position, clearly implies a certain rudimentary power of comparing unlike impressions and detecting likeness amid this unlikeness."

So also individual and particular ideas involve general ideas, for it is the recognition of a universal element in particular ideas which constitutes the general idea. The direct dependence of general ideas on individual ones is thus obvious. The inter-dependence is seen in detail in the consideration of inductive and deductive reasoning.

Another point which needs special emphasis is the

dependence of language on experience and thought. Language cannot exist without thought, or thought without experience; and language only exists, in a significant sense for the individual, in so far as it is directly connected, through his concepts and percepts, with some content of purely mental or general experience. To read a paragraph of English on psychology, with plenty of technical terms in it, is, for all practical purposes, almost as meaningless to children—and, experience shows, to intelligent but uninstructed adults—as to read to them a passage of Chinese.

Liebnitz says: "For the most part, especially in longer analyses, we do not behold at a glance the whole nature of the thing, but employ signs instead of things. We commonly omit, for the sake of expedition, any explication of these signs in present thought, knowing or believing that we have such explication in our power. Thus, when I think of a chiliagon, or a polygon of a thousand equal sides, I do not always expressly consider the nature of a side, of equality, and of a thousand (or cube of ten); but I employ these words—whose meaning is only obscurely and imperfectly perceived by the mind at once" (T. S. Baynes).

There must, therefore, either through direct experience, or through the interpretative power of thought as based upon experience, always be a real content of meaning put into a word by the individual himself—this includes the acceptance, after intelligent apprehension, of what is offered as meaning by another—before it can have any proper significance for him.

As has been previously pointed out, it is possible,

when a very advanced stage of mental power and skill has been reached, to, in some degree, work backwards from the sign to the thing signified; but this is only possible where there is already a rich content of significance for all ordinary signs. Perhaps a good example, in a special form, of this is the skill which some few persons have shown in working out the meaning of private systems of mnemonics and shorthand, to which no direct key of any kind existed, so far as they knew.

As a merely suggestive indication of the relation between the special development of ideas and the general order of development, the following statement may be submitted. In the first period, and in order of predominant importance, we have: sense presentations, a gradual growth of percepts, increase of the fulness and definiteness of more or less implicit ideas, and a limited command of language. In the second period there will be: sense and percept presentations, an increasing thoroughness and systemisation of percepts, practical reasoning, elementary but progressive abstract ideas and reasoning, and a good command of language. During the third period the chief features will be: percept, sense, and concept presentations, great progress in thoroughness and systemisation of abstract ideas and reasonings, higher relatings of perceptual and sensuous elements, and a more or less complete familiarity with, and facility in the use of, language. These will vary at the beginning of the period, and in later years, according to the individuality and surroundings of a person.

x

WE shall now be able to obtain a still fuller and more detailed idea of what is involved in the general "principle of development" in education; and also to deal with some other principles. The fuller inquiry into a special element in the general development of an individual has given us a more complete insight into the precise order of progress; and has also shown us the place and function of other important influences and conditions, viz., language and apperception, and the ways in which they affect development.

The Principle of Development.—Following the previous method of treatment, we will discuss this principle under the various practical maxims which are generally accepted as guiding principles in practical teaching. As before, we shall find that they are in certain respects incomplete, and often somewhat misleading in their general suggestions; but they will serve very well as texts through which the more precise truth can be interpreted.

1. **From the Concrete to the Abstract.**—This will now be understood to mean: from presentations to percepts,

and from percepts to concepts, in the building up of each item of knowledge development. But it must still be borne in mind that the different stages of development require that we should proceed from presentation to presentation, next from percept to percept, then from percept to concept, afterwards from concept to concept, and finally, at least in the case of the more capable, from a constructive concept to the realisation of what certain possible percepts would mean for us, in mental effects.

By the term "constructive concept" is meant a concept which is built up by the mind itself, apart from any single actual experience, direct from the concept elements given by various experiences. Those concepts which are directly formed from, and answer to, given percepts may be called "reproductive concepts," since they only involve the separate reproduction of the purely mental effects of experience. We shall discuss this matter more fully when dealing with the principle of analysis and synthesis.

Dr. Karl Lange, speaking of the child's gradual development, says: "As the compass of its outward experiences arrives at a certain completion only after the work of years, so also does the breadth of its consciousness, the power to grasp and retain ideas as a whole, increase but gradually. The epoch of development in which the child is able to think only in pictures is followed by another in which it really gives him pleasure to lift himself in the abstract above the confusing variety of individual objects up to the universal law, that is, to rule and concept." This points

out the movement of development through presentations, percepts, images, and concepts.

As Pestalozzi says : " No matter what a teacher may
attempt, he can at best do no more than assist the
child's nature in the efforts it makes to unfold itself.
To so manage that the instruction given to a child shall
keep exact pace with the unfolding of his mind is one
grand secret of education." In so far as the development of ideas is concerned, this will mean : first from
percepts to perceptual reasonings, and then from concepts to conceptual reasonings. It may be said that
the former will very largely look after themselves, but
the latter—and both, for their highest forms—need
careful cultivation.

The educator must, therefore, provide the proper
presentative and perceptive experiences, in the best
order, for producing full and exact ideas in the mind.
When something like a considerable store of ideas has
thus been acquired, the mind itself may be called upon
to do much of the work for itself, by filling in the
details of ideas, through its power of representing and
recombining images and ideas. That is, there will be
an advance from reproductive to constructive ideas,
both practical and purely rational.

To lead up to the formation of concepts, there will
have to be a good deal in the way of simple experiment and verbal explanation. For example, if it be
desired to get a pupil to form a full and accurate
concept of squareness we must proceed somewhat after
the following manner. All the necessary concrete experiences, or presentative elements, involved in ex-

ploring a square object by the hands and eyes, and measuring by a ruler and a set square, must be first employed, until they have produced permanently clear and distinct ideas. Thus the percept is secured.

Then the verbal expression for a square should be deduced, or supplied. We will suppose that the following simple form is used : a square is a straight-lined, four-sided figure, with all its sides equal, and all its angles right angles. It is now required to get the mind to think only of the mental effects made by the concrete facts, and in so doing to entirely ignore, for the time being, the actual sense experiences involved.

Assuming that the learner's mind is unfamiliar with the process of forming explicit concepts, we must carefully lead up to the mental abstraction involved. In the first place we must vary the square shaped concrete material as much as possible, so as to, so to speak, loosen the connection between the mental effects and the sense experiences. If we have first dealt with the square face of a wooden cube, we might next take a very thin piece of wood which is square. Afterwards other materials should be used, such as iron, tin, copper, cloth, and paper; and the square should be of many sizes. Each of these should be as thin as possible. A square piece might be cut out of a very thin piece of shaving. This is to lead up to and suggest the fact that the minimum of material has all the conditions for being a square. Next cut out as much as possible of the material of the square, leaving only a very thin edging of it. This forms a still nearer approach to the idea of mere outline, shape, or form, which is the basis of the concept.

Practically all that is possible has now been done in fining down the elements of concrete experience as involved in the idea. The next step is, therefore, an important one. We want to get from the material the something which it involves, but which can be separated from it. Happily the physical world itself gives us the necessary conditions. Let the last, and least, physical form of a square be held in front of a looking-glass.

No very great difficulty is likely to be met with in getting the learner to grasp the fact that whilst there is none of the material of the actual square in the looking-glass, yet there is all of that which makes it a square for our minds, viz., its shape. There are the four straight and equal sides, and the four right angles, reflected in the glass; and this reflection gives all that the mind requires for the idea of a square. It can now be pointed out that the idea of square has only to do with the shape, or form, of a thing.

Finally, it remains to secure the mental realisation of the possible separateness of the idea from the experience. The first approach to this is to require the learner to shut his eyes and try to see a picture of the square in his mind, in other words, to will the imaging of a square. He will doubtless be able to do this easily enough. Let him then be carefully questioned about it. He will probably describe it as like to the looking-glass reflection. He should then be asked if there were four sides; if they appeared to be straight and equal sides; and if the angles seemed to be right angles.

Now language may be properly brought in to assist pure thought. The learner can be told that a square thing is said to have squareness. He should then be questioned as to whether he thinks that the squareness of a thing can be seen by itself, as the thing is so seen. He ought not to have much difficulty, if the previous work has been thorough and successful, in grasping the fact that one can by seeing a thing judge that it is square, but cannot see its squareness, as such. Where then is the squareness, is the next point. Here again the learner ought now to be able to realise that it is simply the idea in the mind which expresses the mental effects produced by square objects. We cannot see, touch, hear, taste, or smell, squareness, we can only think it.

Further, the total idea of squareness involves all the separate effects produced by the details of a square. That is, squareness implies straight-sidedness, four-sidedness, equal-sidedness, and right-angledness; or, to use the technical terms of geometry, rectilinealness, quadrilateralness, equilateralness, and rectangularity. Each of these elements represents a mental abstraction, by which the mental effects of the distinct details of a complex experience are regarded as things in themselves, though parts of a total mental whole.

This may appear a long and laborious method by which to arrive at a single concept. But it must be remembered that not only is a concept thus most easily, fully, clearly, and accurately formed; but the discipline in method derived from thus carefully forming one or two concepts is likely to give such facility, power, and skill, in the forming of explicit concepts, that the final results will be incomparably more extensive and intensive in product, and more rapid and accurate in process, than any haphazard blundering into success, through force of circumstances, and severe struggles. It is not success in doing one thing that is primarily aimed at by the educator, but the finally obtaining power to do many things successfully.

It should be noticed that, in the above example, the conceptual elements are always based upon, and derived from, the perceptual. The young thinker must always have a foundation in experience, wherever possible.

Canon Daniel has well said: "Children are not sufficiently required to use their senses. They are allowed to observe by deputy. They look at nature through the spectacles of books, and through the eyes of the teacher, but do not observe for themselves . . . . [Teachers] have taught as though their pupils had eyes that saw not, and ears that heard not, and noses that smelled not, and palates that tasted not, and skins that felt not, and muscles that would not work. They have insisted on taking the words out of nature's mouth and speaking for her. They have thought it derogatory to play a subordinate part to the object itself."

2. **From the Particular to the General.**—A presentation, or a percept, must always refer directly, and only, to just this or that object. It is this or that impression which is actually influencing the mind at the moment. Hence it is impossible for it, in itself, to refer to, imply, or involve, anything except itself. To put the point in another way, a percept of this page or this book is just

itself and nothing else; nor does it, or can it, directly involve any other percept or percepts. It is true that the effects of other experiences are involved in the interpreting of the present one, but this element of interpretation is an essential part of the percept, so that neither interpretation nor percept exists apart from each other.

Because of this we say that a presentation or a percept is an individual thing. In so far as, from the point of view of later knowledge, it is one of a large class of like presentations or percepts it is said to be particular, because it is a part only of a general or common class of things.

From the idea of a single concrete whole, we gradually arrive, through repeated and extended experiences, at what we have called the collective idea of a group of similar concrete wholes. Not that such wholes need actually be seen in a group, but that the mind can think of the repeated percepts as though they occurred together. This may be called a concrete general idea.

When the idea, and its elements, as such, are separated from the impressions which give rise to them, and come to exist as those distinct mental wholes which we term concepts, then the idea, as such, is entirely and purely general, for it stands for a possible infinity of like things, so far as certain mental effects produced by them are concerned.

Thus there is a movement from the particular to the general. This is true not only of ideas but also of judgments, when an inductive judgment is being formed, and, therefore, of reasonings. Also, the general movement consists of several stages. First, we have the progress from the particular to the particular, then from particulars to generals, next from generals to other generals—wider, in induction ; or in deduction as wide, or less wide, but not wider—or to particulars.

We may illustrate the maxim by the following. A child gets a clear idea of an oak-tree, through frequent experiences connected with one near its home. As it grows able to run about more it sees other oak-trees, and its idea becomes more full and distinct. In time it will have a satisfactorily distinct idea of an oak-tree, and will, as a rule, be able to identify one without hesitation or mistake. This movement from the particular to the particular makes the individual idea clear and distinct.

As time goes on the idea will take on a collective significance, that is, it will stand for all the oak-trees the individual has actually seen or heard about. That is, the child now has what we have called the concrete general idea. Later on the essential characteristics and qualities of an oak-tree will be known, and the learner will be able to make the judgment: all trees which have such-and-such qualities are oak-trees. Now the true general idea is formed, and the learner realises what a class is, in the scientific sense of the term. The movement from the particular to the general, in its fullest sense, has now been made.

Next we may suppose that the individual notices that the order of events in the life of a tree results in the production of seeds every year, and, so far as he understands the nature of the tree's life, he judges that this result must inevitably occur under normal conditions. He, therefore, asserts that all oak-trees produce seed. It will be seen that this is a higher kind of generalisation than the former; for that was but a formal or classifying judgment, whilst this is judgment about cause and effect, and gives us what we may call constructive knowledge about all oak-trees.

From this last-mentioned judgment the scientific observer, investigator, and thinker, is able to hazard, and finally establish, the wider inductive judgment that: all living organisms reproduce themselves. Thus from a limited generalisation comes an absolutely universal one. Again from this we may reason backwards thus : all organisms are reproductive ; all trees are organisms ; therefore, all trees are reproductive. So we get deductively from a wider to a less wide general judgment. And, finally, we may reason down to the particular, thus : all trees are reproductive ; a mulberry is a tree ; therefore, a mulberry is reproductive.

Such a procedure is by far the easiest, surest, and most fruitful, method by which the beginner can acquire knowledge. As Mr. Herbert Spencer points out : " General formulas which men have devised to express groups of detail, and which have severally simplified their conceptions by uniting many facts into one fact, they have supposed must simplify the conceptions of a child also. They have forgotten that a generalisation is simple only in comparison with the whole mass of particular truths it comprehends—that it is more complex than any one of these truths taken singly—that only after many of these single truths have been acquired, does the generalisation ease the memory and help the reason—and that to a mind not possessing these single truths it is necessarily a mystery. Thus confounding two kinds of simplification, teachers have constantly erred by setting out with ‘first principles’: a proceeding essentially, though not apparently, at variance with the primary rule, which implies that the mind should be introduced to principles through the medium of examples, and so should be led from the particular to the general.”

The whole process is really one of systematic apperception. An apperceptive group is formed, and all further and deeper knowledge about the same kind of things is apperceived by it. The more closely the educator can cause the influences to correspond with the proper order of mental development, the more easily, completely, and accurately, will the apperceptive group develop. In other words, the teacher should, as a rule, not begin with a definition, law, or formula, but end with it.

Dr. De Garmo says: “Education must make it a special business to teach the child to pass easily from the individual to the general, because the generalisations of children, savages, and uneducated or poorly educated persons are very elementary and incomplete. They do not contain all the characteristics common to a given class, nor do they exclude all characteristics which were only in certain individuals. The untrained thinker is content with types chosen from among individuals; so that, even in the formation of general conceptions regarding things, the mind must be trained to distinguish the essential from the non-essential. But if this be true of things, how much more must it be true in regard to . . . . the necessary relation of things" (Essentials of Method).

A word or two is necessary here as to what characteristics shall be regarded as essential, in the sense of constituting the general idea, or class concept. In the first place they must, of course, be common to every member of the class. Next they must be causal and not casual, that is, they must have some definite connection with the very existence of the individuals composing the class, and not be mere accidental features. Thus, the fact of being able to breathe when in and under water, and unable to breathe when out of it, and not the fact of spending its life in the water marks off the real fish kind from such animals as the whale. Finally, the attributes should be as few as possible, so long as they clearly and unmistakably mark off, and mark out, one class from another. Only scientific experts can settle such points authoritatively.

Whilst it is hardly possible to attach too much importance to this order of progress from the particular to the general, yet here, as elsewhere in the mental life, the two elements are developing simultaneously, though in very different proportions. It is again a case of proportional waning and waxing (in predominance only), respectively, of the two elements. This must be recognised ; and there should always be provision for, and encouragement of, that which is at first subordinate.

Language is always an implicit helper in this matter,

and should be made an explicit one, so far as the educator is concerned. Thus, in teaching the child to call a certain animal a dog, and then other animals which are like it, on the whole, but unlike it as to details, by the same name, we are, either implicitly or explicitly, helping them to develop the general and the particular elements of ideas at the same time. The more this is attended to by the educator, the greater will be the progress towards accurate general ideas on the part of the learner.

But this should be, so to say, concealed from the child, that is, no effort should be made to make the general elements of ideas explicit, until there is a full and facile command of the elements of explicit individual and particular ideas. Nothing should be done which is likely to hinder the latter development, or, in the long run, the former will be even more hindered in consequence.

The practical progress of the general idea can be very much helped through a system of word combinations. Thus the animal in the house which is known as a dog will also doubtless be known by another name, say, Carlo. This fact may be made use of by sometimes requiring the child to say Carlo-dog. When its experience of dogs extend, then it may be taught to say: dog, not Carlo-dog. Later on will come: dog, little-dog, poodle-dog, little-poodle-dog, big-white-poodle-dog, and so on.

Such word combinations should, however, not be used too frequently, or they may prove puzzling, and hinder more than help. Their only purpose is to get the learner to express something of the connection of the ideas by a connection of words, which will always suggest somewhat of the inner truth, and, finally, should directly indicate it. This kind of term building is seen in its most scientific and suggestive form in the technical terms of botany and chemistry.

A basis of such verbal help is already provided in the child's own efforts, assisted by the mother or nurse, at connecting imitative gesture language with the purely conventional in such combinations as "moo-cow," and "bow-wow-dog." The effect of a purposeful organisation of words on such lines is to provide a strong mechanical momentum towards general ideas. The common name in all the combinations represents the class, or general element, and the varying words represent the different sub-classes or individuals, and, therefore, the particular or individual elements.

At the proper time in the general development all these points will be made explicit, and then there will be no further need of such complex terms, for mental association will do far more than word combinations can possibly accomplish. The mind will fill the verbal form with content, without much detailed suggestion from the word itself.

The highest educational success is to obtain such a mastery, by the individual, of the processes involved in the development from the particular to the general, that either a progressive or regressive advance has become comparatively easy and reliable.

The Principle of Analysis and Synthesis.—As we have before stated, all progress in thought involves higher and deeper forms of the fundamental processes of the mental powers of assimilation and discrimination. We have seen that the highest forms of these are inductive and deductive reasoning, and that they are, respectively, essentially analytic and synthetic in their nature. Hence the principle of analysis and synthesis is one of the most fundamental, general, and significant, of all the educational principles.

It is through a scientifically logical arrangement of the elements dealt with in analysing and synthesising that we obtain the order of greatest simplicity in dealing with a complex whole, and are thus able to lead the learner from the more known to the less known by gradual, consecutive, coherent, and systematic steps and stages. In fact, it is hardly too much to say that, from the point of view of practical work in educating, this principle must always take the first place as the controlling element in the organisation of method.

The ability to discriminate or realise differences between two or more experiences is necessary for the mere possibility of knowledge; for, an absolute similarity of mental effect from all impressions would mean an unknown, and unknowable, world. Similarly, the power to recognise, or assimilate, that is, to realise similarity or likeness, is absolutely essential to the actual building up of knowledge; for, meaning and significance come from the relating of the new to the old, the presentative to the re-presentative. Thus, difference is, logically, most important for the beginnings of knowledge, and assimilation for the actual forming and developing of it. The same kind of thing is true, in a physical sense, in the case of all forms of organic life : there must be a proper power of selection and assimilation.

A special capacity for particular kinds of assimilation and discrimination is the active element in the development of individuality. Dr. Bain says : "This is the deepest foundation of disparity of intellectual character, as well as of variety in likings and pursuits. If, from the beginning, one man can interpolate five shades of discrimination of colour where another can feel but one transition, the careers of the two men are foreshadowed and will be widely apart." But this view must not be pressed too far, for some of the highest powers are the latest in significant development. As a rule, we should have a sufficiently general survey of a more or less fully developed individual before making anything like final judgments on such matters.

Two of the most essential conditions for impressing differences are juxtaposition, and intensity of stimulus. Unlike things placed side by side cannot but compel attention to the fact of unlikeness, if the elements involved are sufficiently powerful as stimuli to command the attention. At the same time, however, the intensity of the stimuli must not be too great, or the effects of contrast will be lost in the state of surprise, or wonder.

The condition of co-presentation is of great importance, because representative elements are seldom so full and vivid as presentative ones, and the points of contrast are, therefore, much less sharply defined if there is any considerable interval between the presentations of the things compared.

As a rule, the intensity of the stimuli involved should

Y

be of an average degree, and only when there is some difficulty in getting the learner to grasp the differences should extreme or exaggerated forms be made use of. If there is great facility and accuracy in discrimination, then the intensity of the stimuli may be somewhat below the average, for the purpose of calling forth an even keener exercise of the power.

Dr. Bain thus illustrates the use of juxtaposition: "We compare two notes by sounding them in close succession; two shades of colour by placing them side by side; two weights by holding them in the two hands, and attending to the two feelings by turns. . . . . For mere length we lay the two things alongside; so for an angle. For number we can place two groups in contiguous rows—three by the side of four or five—and observe the surplus. . . . . Sometimes there is a strong and overpowering similarity, with a small and unconspicuous difference, as in our cyphers (compare 3 and 5), and in the letters of our alphabet (C and G), and still more in the Hebrew alphabet. For such comparisons, the difference, such as it is, needs to be very clearly drawn or even exaggerated. Another method is to have models of the same size to lay over one another."

But beside juxtaposition and intensity there are two other conditions which greatly assist in making discrimination complete and permanent. These are repetition, and multiplication, of instances. Such are in fact nothing more than the application of the principle of repetition.

Each of the above four conditions applies with equal force to the impressing of points of similarity upon the mind; in addition to which the laws of association also apply. Further, the principle of preparation is of very great assistance.

Discrimination is a form of analysis, for it separates the different elements of experience from each other; and assimilation is a form of synthesis, for it combines in thought those experiences which, as a whole, are like each other. When both activities are applied to the parts and details of one and the same object, the separating and combining processes are more clearly seen. Hence, wherever there is discrimination and assimilation there is analysis and synthesis: and wherever there is analysis and synthesis there is discrimination and assimilation.

· Throughout the whole range of thought, therefore, the principle of analysis and synthesis is always active. But, whilst analysis can never do more than clearly realise each separate element of a whole, though this involves great advance in power with regard to the more complex, and the purely rational, wholes, synthesis progresses from the recombining of the details of a given whole, as given by analysis, to the selecting of certain elements given in various experiences, and the combining of these into wholes which have never before been met with in the individual's own experiences.

Synthesis is, therefore, said to be reproductive or constructive. The former is inevitable; but there must first be a familiarity with, and power and skill in, reproductive synthesis, before constructive synthesis is likely to be either possible or sound. Also, a store of material gained by previous efforts must have been acquired.

No constructive effort is possible unless there be something to construct from.

It is this power of constructive synthesis which characterises the most capable and original minds. In the higher regions of thought, we speak of it as the power of inventiveness, discovery, original investigation and research, ability, talent, or genius. As a matter of fact, these powers are shown very early in an individual's life, in very modest ways. Quite young children can invent and discover, so far as their own knowledge is concerned. In other words, if they have obtained an intelligent mastery of reproductive synthesis, they should be able, in however humble a way, to do something in the way of constructive synthesis.

At every stage in the child's career he should pass from the imitative to the initiative mastery of a subject, or part of a subject. This is the most valuable evidence of intelligent self-activity, and shows that the educative processes have been entirely successful. It is, therefore, most desirable that the educator should encourage and stimulate such synthetic efforts on the part of the learner. They should be looked upon as the crowning point of each step and stage of development, and proper provision for securing good results in them should be made.

Dr. Sully says: "Children find out many new combinations of movements for themselves. The mere pleasure of doing a thing, and of overcoming a difficulty, is an ample reward for many an effort in practical construction. Such activity is, moreover, closely connected with the impulse of curiosity, the desire to find out about things, their structure and less obvious qualities. In this way practical invention assists in the discovery of facts and truths. A considerable part of a boy's knowledge of things is thus gained experimentally, that is to say, by means of actively dividing, joining together, and otherwise manipulating objects."

Children show an inventive activity very early in life. Darwin says that one of his children, when he was just a year old, invented the word "mum" as a name for all kinds of food. He further invented additional sounds for particular kinds of food, calling sugar "shu-mum." All teachers know how all too apt children are to invent such verbal forms as "go-ed," "come-d," and the like.

There should, however, be nothing like asking the pupils to make bricks without straw. They should have been previously well furnished with the raw material, and such simple suggestions and indications as will make the first trials fairly easy, and likely to be successful. Discouragement in little things should be avoided as far as possible, or encouragement for bigger efforts will be hard to provide.

Some such method as the following might be used. When certain kinds of exercises are quite familiar to the learner, let him be required to reproduce two or more of them, selected by the educator with a view to the further treatment of them. Then, after being given what suggestions and help, if any, are thought to be necessary, the pupil should be asked to combine the two exercises into an intelligible and consistent whole. Thus two anecdotes might be worked up into one; two designs in drawing made into a single design ; or two sums combined in one problem ; the materials in each case being given by the reproduced exercises. Next, the pupil should try to frame other such combinations, being guided by the model already worked out. This will involve his selecting his own material, and making the combination by himself. Finally, he should be invited to attempt something involving quite different sorts of materials, and another kind of combination —" all out of his own head," as children say.

Very surprising results are sometimes obtained by giving school children the opportunity to do this kind of work, although absolutely no previous specific preparation for, or effort in, it has been made. Most difficult arithmetical problems, in the various rules they have been taught, are invented and worked by small boys. Excellent original stories are written by young scholars, and very happy designs in colour and geometrical outlines are made by them. Some very meritorious and instructive examples of such are published in the " School Field Magazine," 1890–94 (Longmans), which gives specimens of the actual work done by children in an experimental school organised by Mr. Sargeant.

Such products are of the highest possible educational value, for they represent the development of the mind up to creative ability, and they express the individuality of the learner. They may be small and simple things in themselves, but, if obtained at the appropriate periods, they are great results, and full of possibilities for the future.

A German writer, named Lazarus, has well said :

" Neither discoveries nor inventions are made in the school; neither are discoveries or inventions brought to maturity there, but the pupils should be so trained as to discover what has already been discovered, to investigate what has been investigated, to seek for what has been found." Obviously the first part of this is only true from the point of view of the adult, for to the child there is a real discovery; but the central truth, that children must realise and master the methods of discovery and investigation, is the important point. Only so can they fully and intelligently realise and appreciate the work of original investigators and discoverers. That is what the poet means when he says : " What you have inherited from your fathers, you must earn again in order to possess it " (Lange).

Moreover this effort after constructive command is a native tendency of the child, which gives it very much, and great, pleasure. The late Professor Tyndall, speaking of his experiences as a teacher, says : " It was often my custom to give the boys their choice of pursuing their propositions in the book, or of trying their strength at others not to be found there. Never in a single instance have I known the book to be chosen. I was ever ready to assist when I deemed help needful, but my offers of assistance were habitually declined. The boys had tasted the sweets of intellectual conquest and demanded victories of their own . . . . . Some of the most delightful hours of my existence have been spent in marking the vigorous and cheerful expansion of mental power, when appealed to in the manner I have described."

Mr. Page, an American writer, says of a class of boys about fourteen years of age : " A difficult problem in algebra had been before the class for a day or two, when I suggested giving them some assistance. ' Not yet, sir,' was the exclamation of nearly all. Nor shall I forget the expression that beamed from the face of one, when—forgetting in his elation the school pro-prieties—he cried out ' I've got it ! I've got it ! ' It was a proud moment for him. He felt his own power as he had never done before. Nor was I less gratified to find that his fellows were still unwilling to be told the method of his solution. Next day a large proportion brought the example correctly solved, the working giving evidence of originality."

The special value of such self-development is thus described by Mr. Herbert Spencer : " In the first place, it guarantees a vividness and permanency of impression which the usual methods can never produce. Any piece of knowledge which the pupil has himself acquired—any problem which he has himself solved, becomes, by virtue of the conquest, much more thoroughly his than it could else be. The preliminary activity of mind which his success implies, the concen-tration of thought necessary to it, and the excitement consequent on his triumph, conspire to register the facts in his memory in a way that no mere information heard from a teacher, or read in a school-book, can be registered.

" Even if he fails, the tension to which his faculties have been wound up, insures his remembrance of the solution when given to him, better than half-a-dozen repetitions would. Observe, again, that this discipline necessitates a continuous organisation of the knowledge he acquires. It is in the very nature of facts and inferences assimilated in this normal manner, that they successively become the premises of further conclusions —the means of solving further questions. The solution of yesterday's problem helps the pupil in mastering to-day's."

Dr. Bain speaks of "a tenfold power in the feeling of organisation . . . . . Now, it is one of the delicate arts of an accomplished instructor, to lay before the pupils a set of facts pointing to a conclusion, and to leave them to draw the conclusion for themselves. Exactly to hit the mean between a leap too small to have any merit, and one too wide for the ordinary pupil, is a fine adjustment and a great success."

As Froebel says : " A child between one and three years old, playing alone, will first examine shape and colour of an object which it can lay hold of and handle ; will try its solidity ; will then endeavour to take it to pieces, at least to alter its form so as to detect new qualities in it, and put it to new uses. This done, it is seen trying either to reunite the parts or to arrange them into a fresh whole." There is probably some exaggeration here in the suggestion of a definite design to make a new whole ; but there is certainly much more of implicit purpose in what is too often ignorantly called the mischievous destructiveness of a child, than the ordinary observer is likely to detect.

Childish activities thus illustrate what we must always insist upon : the fact that analysis and synthesis are but complementary parts, or phases, of one complete process of thought, whether the thought be superficial or profound. In every implicit complex percept or concept, and much more, therefore, in all that are explicit, both analysis and synthesis have taken place. The former has realised and discriminated the separate parts and details, and the latter has combined them into a self-consistent whole. In every judgment the concepts involved are first thought of analytically, for they are regarded as at least separate and distinct, however much they may resemble each other; and are then synthesised into the intelligible mental whole which we call a judgment. The same conditions hold as to the connecting of judgments in reasonings.

This truth must not be educationally abused. Whilst it is necessary that the learner should form ideas, judgments, and reasonings, through an explicit and detailed use of analysis and synthesis, so as to obtain the necessary power, skill, and facility, for doing this whenever it is desirable; yet there is no need whatever for always proceeding in such a precise way. On the contrary, we must learn to economise mental strength and energy, by making every legitimate short cut in thought, so long as such are based upon explicit experiences and knowledge, and we have the power of making the process explicit if required.

The application of the principle of analysis and synthesis in the region of pure thought, or reasoning, may be shown by considering a first lesson on grammar. This should be about the simple sentence, for that is the known unit from which the unknown technical details are best derived. The force of the educational principle is specially well shown here, because we realise it in grammatical analysis. By asking the pupils to mention topics to be talked about, a column of subjects can easily be obtained. Then they should be requested to say something about each of these subjects. Thus the predicates are provided, and complete sentences formed. Not only has grammatical analysis thus been performed, under the guidance of the teacher, but it has been done by way of synthesis, and the learners will easily express the full synthesis of the details thus arrived at in some such descriptive definition as : a sentence consists of two parts, something which is spoken of, and that which is said about it.

It is always thus. The very fact that we are, as a rule, dealing with a whole which must always remain a whole, makes it necessary that analysis and synthesis should proceed concurrently. A unit becomes a unity, or a unity becomes a more detailed and complex one, through the further activity of thought upon mental wholes.

This principle is involved in the maxims : from the known to the unknown : from the simple to the complex : from the concrete to the abstract : and, from the general to the particular. Professor Laurie expresses it in the following practical rules : "Teach all that is complex analytico-synthetically, *i.e.*, reduce an object to its elements, and then build it up again ; practise pupils in the analysis of complex things and the synthesis of many particulars in one whole, in order to train to exactness of conception ; teach generalisations as generalisations, *i.e.*, advance from the particular to the general, from the concrete to the abstract; teach reasonings as reasonings, *i.e.*, get the pupil to make explicit all implicit reasonings."

An example of causal analysis and synthesis will show the highest application of the principle. Let us take the case in which we wish to lead up to the inductive judgment : water must always seek its own level. This is to be arrived at through observation, experiment, analysis (physical and mental), and judgment.

Take a piece of wood, a handful of wool, and a glass of water. Let the wool and wood be dropped, and the water poured on the ground. Then questions should obtain answers which express the fact that little, if any, change of shape has taken place in the first two, but a very great deal in the last. Now let them be put into a vessel with holes in it, smaller that either the size of the wood or wool. The wool can be pushed and pulled through, but not the wood, whilst the water pushes itself through. Skilful questioning should now obtain the judgment that water moves about very freely, because its parts do not hold together like those of the wood and wool. This gives the element of difference, in the sense of the logical "method of difference," for discovering causes.

Next let the water be poured into a small hollow india-rubber ball. Then, if a pin is thrust through it in various places all round, the water will be seen to come out. Here, again, therefore, the water is found to be pushing itself, so to speak. But it is now further seen that it pushes itself in all directions.

Now take a glass vessel of the shape of a watering-pot, with a telescopic spout. Let the spout be full out at first, and the pot gradually filled with water. It will be seen that some of the water is pushed up the spout until it is level with that in the pot. Pauses should be made to show this. When the pot is full, then let the telescopic spout be gradually lowered beyond the level of the top of the pot. Then sufficient water will be pushed out, through the shortened spout, to establish a new level. And so the movement will go on with each lowering of the spout.

From this it will be seen that the level is always determined by the limits of that which resists the pressure which the water is exerting upon itself; in other words, the water will keep on moving itself till something stops it, and this will only be when the water, as a body, has a level surface. Therefore, it is clear, from what is thus seen of the nature of water, that it must always seek its own level. Of course the liquid condition is taken for granted.

Thus, though our idea of water has remained throughout as a mental unit, it has been filled in with detail, and has become a complex unity, through further analysis and re-synthesis. From what is discovered of its practical nature, we are able to say that water, in a liquid state, must always and everywhere, under ordinary conditions, seek its own level. This is a judgment as to cause and effect, and represents the highest form of rational generalisation, viz., causal induction. It has been arrived at through concurrent perceptual and conceptual reasonings.

Many interesting problems can be submitted to the learner concerning this principle, as to the water supply of a town, the working of canal locks, and the making of fountains. He might be invited to invent a toy fountain, if he has obtained the necessary technical knowledge and manual skill, through manual instruction classes, or otherwise.

Few would deny that such a form of education is likely to be attractive and stimulating to the individual, and to prove effective and sound in drawing out, strengthening, sharpening, and polishing the mental powers.

The very highest value of the principle of analysis and synthesis is that it is the best possible training for self-education, in that it gives the learner right methods of work, and the power and facility in applying them.

Mr. Herbert Spencer urges that a principle "which cannot be too strongly insisted upon, is, that in education the process of self-development should be encouraged to the uttermost. Children should be led to make their own investigations, and to draw their own inferences. They should be told as little as possible, and induced to discover as much as possible. Humanity has progressed solely by self-instruction; and that to achieve the best results, each mind must progress somewhat after the same fashion, is continually proved by the marked success of self-made men."

In further support of this he points out that: "the all-important knowledge of surrounding objects which a child gets in its early years, it got without help . . . .

the child is self-taught in the use of its mother tongue;" and, that there is a large "amount of that experience of life, that out-of-school wisdom which every boy gathers for himself." He reminds his readers of "the unusual intelligence of the uncared-for London gamin, as shown in whatever direction his faculties have been tasked," and of the fact that "many minds have struggled up unaided, not only through the mysteries of our irrationally-planned curriculum, but through hosts of other obstacles besides." Therefore, he says, it is "a not unreasonable conclusion, that if the subjects be put before him in right order and right form, any pupil of ordinary capacity will surmount his successive difficulties with but little assistance."

Rousseau is not less emphatic than is his wont about the same truth. He contends that : "Educated in the spirit of our principles, accustomed to look for resources within himself, and to have recourse to others only when he finds himself really helpless, he will examine every new object for a long time without saying a word. He is thoughtful, and not disposed to ask questions. Be satisfied, therefore, with presenting objects at appropriate times and in appropriate ways." (Emile. Miss Worthington's translation).

The Principle of Symbolism.—A good deal has been said about the necessity of symbols for the higher developments of thought. Besides this fundamental place of language in the progress of the purely rational powers, we have to take into consideration the fact that language is the great channel through which we bring most of the educative influences to bear upon the mind.

The way in which thought is carried on through verbal signs—whether spoken, written, or only thought—is, perhaps, best shown in the learning of a new language. First there is the very laborious and troublesome work of getting a ready and accurate association between the right words and the right ideas. The ease with which a person goes wrong in this is often painfully apparent when we hear a foreigner, who is just beginning to learn our own language, try to speak it, but very hard to realise when we begin to speak a foreign language. Genders and cases are apt to prove especially provoking in this respect.

Another point worthy of notice is the way in which we very slowly, and with great difficulty, make out the meaning, in English, of a foreign language, even from printed matter. Much more difficult is it when the words are spoken. We find ourselves slowly saying or thinking the words, one by one, and searching for the right English equivalents. Later on this is done more readily, but still we find that we have to explicitly think out the exact meaning. If we wish to speak in the new language, the details of the process are still more obvious. We think in English, and slowly translate the thought mentally—probably with grave anxiety as to the words and their right order—and then try to speak it.

But, finally, there arrives the happy time when, as we say, we are able to think in the language. Now the word counters are all-sufficient, for their separate

and combined values are so familiar and well understood that they literally go without saying. The full
meaning is conveyed to the mind by a mere hurried
sight, or hearing, of the thought symbols. Now we
can realise more fully the value of words for thought.

All this is of the greatest possible significance to
the educator, for to the child, what we call his own
language is not his until he has acquired it in the
above sense. If we wish to convince ourselves of this,
we can easily do so by reading a piece of Carlyle to a
small child, or by getting some friend to talk to us in
a highly technical form of language, which we have no
previous knowledge of, and observing how unmeaning
it all is. It is not very helpful to most persons to
inform them—in fact they are not so informed—that
a physiological being is a unit and unity of systematic
anatomical articulation.

It is very amusing to hear an Englishman trying to
make a foreigner, ignorant of English, understand what
he is saying to him in English, by shouting it at the
top of his voice, under the impression that if he only
hears it plainly he must understand it. And it would
be equally amusing were the consequences involved
not much more serious, to hear a teacher doing exactly
the same kind of thing with his pupils.

We may safely say that there is more need of educational system and gradation in the development of the
acquiring and using of language, than even in
knowledge-subjects proper; for the sign is much more
likely to be misleading in communication, than the
thing signified in experience. Very careful attention

z

must, therefore, be given to this subject by the educator.

Rousseau says, in his characteristically trenchant
way: "I do not disapprove of a nurse's amusing the
child with songs, and with blithe and varied tones. But
I disapprove of her perpetually deafening him with a
multitude of useless words, of which he understands
only the tone she gives them.

"I would like the first articulate sounds he must
hear to be few in number, easy, distinct, often repeated.
The words they form should represent only material
objects which can be shown him.   Our unfortunate
readiness to content ourselves with words that have
no meaning to us whatever, begins earlier than we
suppose. . . . .

"Children who are too much urged to speak have not
time sufficient for learning either to pronounce carefully
or to understand thoroughly what they are made to say.
If, instead, they are left to themselves, they first
practise using the syllables they can most readily utter;
and gradually attaching to these some meaning that
can be gathered from their gestures, they give you
their own words before acquiring yours.   Thus they
receive yours only after they understand them.   Not
being urged to use them, they notice carefully what
meaning you give them; and when they are sure of
this, they adopt it as their own."

Let us, then, first briefly review the development of
language in the race, to see what it has to teach us
concerning the forms which have been found most
suggestive and convenient. We have already treated

somewhat fully of the general nature and history of language, in the discussion on the connection between ideas and language. It may be helpful, however, to add a few words about the development of written language.

Written language is, like vocal language, purely imitative in its earliest forms. Picture-writing is the first kind of written language. Crude outlines of animals are found among the historical survivals of the stone age. These in time, probably later than the stony age, developed into a connected series showing the details of the chase. The Esquimaux of to-day covers his weapons with outline drawings of animals and hunting scenes. The Red Indian developed the art of picture writing to very great precision and fulness. But this represents great progress in general, as well as special, development. Some aborigines of Australia were found to be unable even to identify any drawing except a most exaggerated outline of a man, in which the head was drawn very much too large, proportionally.

Following this form would come, in order of logical development, such forms as the Egyptian hieroglyphics, in which pictures are used to represent syllables or letters, and not merely the objects which they outline. Whether or no these preceded the simple picture writing, historically, seems to be an open question. In any case, it is generally agreed that alphabetic writing is derived from hieroglyphics. Thus from the purely imitative comes the semi-conventional, and from the semi-conventional the purely conventional, or wholly arbitrary, system of signs.

It is very instructive to notice that the progress which the actual history of the language suggests is on exactly similar lines to the best forms, and order, actually employed by intelligent practical teachers to-day. Thus the language has, broadly, followed this order : from real objects to as full an imitation as possible—by gesture and sounds—then an outline imitation, next a more or less conventional sign, and, finally, entirely conventional signs. So the practical teacher says, first use the real object, if possible, in teaching, or use a model of it—as close an imitation as may be—if not a model, then a full or an outline picture, and, finally, talk about these in words.

So we find, for example, that the following way of giving first lessons in reading is strongly, and rightly, favoured by good teachers. Let a model, and a picture, of a man be shown to the learner. Then ask him to name them. Draw an outline figure of a man on the black-board. The child will doubtless recognise, and name it. Then write the word man beside this picture on the black-board. Get the child to recognise either of the three symbols in any order, and to grasp the fact that the word is to do duty for the pictures in suggesting the idea of man to the mind.

Next, clean the black-board, and ask the child to speak the name for man. Then write it again on the black-board. An endeavour should be made to get the learner to tell that, previously, the teacher wrote, and he spoke, this sign as a name for the object man. Further exercises in associating the written sign and the idea may easily be invented. Next let a real pan be shown

—a miniature one, which should not be regarded as a model. The same process of obtaining the association of the word sign with the thing signified should be gone through ; but it ought to be possible to do it more quickly and briefly.

Then little sentences can be made; such as: This is a man ; here is a pan ; a man and a pan ; and so on. All that need be done with regard to the smaller words, at present, is to insist upon their correct association with the spoken words. Later on such sentences may be expanded by setting up various concrete relations between the model man and the miniature pan. Let the man be put in the pan, and then form such sentences as: The man is in the pan. Is the man in the pan ? Yes, the man is in the pan. Is the pan in the man ? No, the pan is not in the man. Of course a good deal of talk between the teacher and the pupil should lead up to, and involve, the construction of the sentences. And there is no reason why they should not be more or less amusing.

The verb "can" should next be introduced, for the purpose of giving variety to the sentences, and also because it carries on the series of similar words : man, pan, can; thereby exercising visual discrimination as well as mental assimilation. And so a truly scientific system of word-building is realised, and can be carried on indefinitely.

Let it be carefully observed that the above is here used as an illustration of the educational manner of acquiring language, and not an example of a first reading lesson, though it happens that the two coincide, for all reading lessons must be, to a greater or lesser extent, language lessons. It is to show the realisation of the evolutional progress from experience to expression, through ideas. This is the great truth for the educator to realise, that words have, and can have, no meaning except as our experiences and thought give us a content of meaning which we associate with them. It is not very likely to prove helpful, therefore, to give words to beginners unless we first give them the experiences and create, or arouse, in them the ideas which are to be associated with the verbal symbols.

A practically simultaneous development of ideas and words should, as a rule, take place ; that is, they should keep pace with each other, or the community may incur loss with regard to the individual who has valuable ideas, but is unable to express them ; and it may also suffer much from the man who has many expressions and few ideas.

In connection with this concurrent development of thought and language, in their relation to each other, there are two practical dangers to be avoided, viz., the giving too little or too much ideational content to words. The former is by far the most common fault, but the latter is hardly less mischievous, in many respects, when it occurs.

Since words are an inseparable part of the knowledge of adults, it is too often taken for granted by them that those who can acquire the words have acquired the knowledge they represent. The absurdity of this is apparent when it is critically considered, but, unfortunately, it is just this consideration which is ordinarily omitted. A very little child would as readily learn texts of scripture in the original Hebrew or Greek, as in English. And a passage from the Revelations would be equally unmeaning to it, in either language.

In the beginnings of the use of language the learner should need a word before it is supplied. That is, there should be a content of experience, before a name is given to it. As Madame Necker points out: "When the want of a word has preceded the possession of it, the child can apply it naturally and justly." Later on the use of language will, by enabling the individual to more clearly analyse his ideas, also help him to render them clearer, and more easy to relate to others. Herein lies the true basis of what is called word-building.

The acquisition of a large number of terms, expressions, verbal formulæ, and the like, which express knowledge, without the full and systematic acquiring of the perceptual and conceptual experiences which constitute it, we call "cram." We may define cram, therefore, as: the acquiring of the maximum of the verbal expressions of knowledge, with the minimum of intelligent content.

Popular ideas about what is called cram are, as a rule, very vague and confused. If we accept the above definition, we shall not regard rapid learning as necessarily being cram. So long as the knowledge material is fully presented, received, and assimilated, true educational results will follow. Of course the more quickly this is attempted the more danger there is of the processes and products being incomplete, and, therefore, of using words as substitutes for ideas, *i.e.*, cram.

Again, to learn off certain lists of words is not necessarily cram. All proper names are, in themselves, nothing more than verbal labels, and, therefore, must be known as such. But, of course, they should always be intelligently and suggestively associated with things. Also there is a beauty of the verbal forms in which thoughts are expressed, as in poetry, and to learn the words, as such, for the sake of the form, is not cram. But, here, again, the proper associations must be secured, for form without matter is barren.

The danger of overloading a word with ideas, although not a very common, is a very real one. Mr. Quick rightly points out that: "after all, though we may and should bring the young in connection with the objects of thought and not with words merely, we must not forget that the scholastic aspect of things will differ from the practical. When brought into the schoolroom the thing must be divested of details and surroundings, and used to give a conception of one of a class. The fir tree of the schoolboy cannot be the fir tree of the woodcutter."

Jacotot's mistake largely consisted in trying to get too many ideas into too few words. We cannot know everything in one thing, and much less can we express it in one word, or sentence. As there are shades of difference of meanings in otherwise similar experiences, so we need slight differences of verbal signs which apply to the same kind of wholes. There are significant differences involved in describing a person as clever, talented, able, though they all imply a similar general capacity of mind.

When a good foundation of related experience, knowledge, and language, has been secured, then, as in other subjects, we may proceed by the method of regressive progress. Terms, and phrases, may be given, which have certain limitations imposed by their contexts, and the learner required to find the proper content of full meaning. A good example of this kind of work is seen in the interpretation of a particular passage in a chapter, play, or treatise, by other passages, and the general purpose and meaning of the whole.

Only by carefully determining the function and powers of language with regard to such points, can we hope to make it as helpful an instrument of development as the nature of the case will allow. The primary educational purpose of language is to aid in developing power, not in storing up information. The latter comes later.

By such combinations as were suggested in the discussion of the principle of analysis and synthesis, the child's language should be made as fully expressive and self-interpretative as possible. They are the most explicit form of verbal signs. Thus, if we take one individual from a group, we say that the group is then less one, that is, without one which was previously there. So we say a man is armless, senseless, homeless, and so on, when he is without arms, sense, or home. In this way word combinations can be given a practically real content of meaning, from the beginning, and many such combinations can be temporarily made use of to assist in the easier formation of exact ideas.

Our language is very sadly unsystematic, and, therefore, much less helpful than it might be, in many respects. Writers on logic have discussed this topic and have suggested certain rules for the formation of a more philosophical form of language, whilst scientists have actually carried out precise systems of word-building, in framing the technical names for their sciences.

Gesture language has by no means wholly disappeared. A Frenchman, for example, uses a good deal of delicate and refined gesture language, and even the phlegmatic Englishman indulges in his "nods and becks and wreathed smiles," as means of expressing his thoughts and feelings. Frowns, shrugs, manual threats, facial movements, and the like, are often economical, and very expressive, ways of indicating our ideas about things. It is, therefore, essentially educational that little children should, to a limited extent, be taught to express facts and feelings through gestures, as they do in kindergarten songs and games. What is possible in this direction is well shown by clever actors, who can bring tears and smiles from an audience, whilst confining themselves wholly to gesture language, or dumbshow as it is called.

Ordinary thought symbols—that is, words in the sense in which we have been speaking of them, are often themselves symbolised, as in the use of such a form as H_2O, which is equivalent to the phrase: a compound of hydrogen and oxygen, in the proportion of two parts of hydrogen to one of oxygen. Also the usual form of words in a sentence is often taken to imply many other sentences, as in the analogy: A man with a mind like an inflated balloon; which may mean a mind which is full of airy nothings: is empty of solid sense: is light and frivolous: is very little under control: and so on.

Now, such forms and uses of language are both necessary and helpful, because they are economical, and often specially vivid, unmistakable, and full, in meaning. As Dr. Karl Lange says: "We see how a striking figure, a fitting comparison, often transmits understanding of a point to the mind like lightning, and lends to concepts a distinctness that could not be reached without the help of concrete ideas." But they can, as a rule, only be really helpful to those who have great familiarity with, and command over, the use of language. They ought, therefore, to come late—at least, if used to any considerable amount—for educational purposes.

No greater mistake in education can be made than to take it for granted that if vivid, attractive, and accurate verbal descriptions of things are given to learners, then there will inevitably, or even generally, be formed in them the ideas, feelings, and knowledge which are possessed by the speaker. If this were so, then the manufacture of phonographs might become the greatest educational agency of this century. But it is not so. Ideas can be put before the mind, but they cannot be put into the mind, except as the mind takes them in. Words only express knowledge-giving experience; they neither make it nor give it.

More will be said about the principle of symbolism

in the next chapter but one, after we have considered more fully the function of language in imparting knowledge.

Some General Remarks.—There are connected with this chapter, as with the others, many points which it is not convenient to discuss at length, owing to the great increase of the size of the book which would result. For example, systems of mnemonics and of scientific nomenclature and terminology, might have been briefly discussed in connection with the principle of symbolism; though the two last belong more properly to the treatment of education from the point of view of logic. But such points, and many others, may be regarded as problems to be worked out by the student himself.

The inter-relation of the principles set forth in this chapter with those previously described should be carefully considered. The connection between the principle of symbolism and that of pleasure has been suggested in reference to the beauty of verbal forms. A more ordinary instance of it is seen in the keen enjoyment which children show in listening to graphic and attractive verbal descriptions, well-told stories, and the like.

Let us again quote the testimony of practical teachers in support of the principles just discussed. Plato, when speaking of the education of youths for citizenship, says: "And when they have made a good beginning in play, and by the help of music have gained the habit of good order, then this habit of order, in a manner how unlike the lawless play of others! will accompany them in all their actions and be a principle of growth to them, and if there be any fallen places in the state will raise them up again. Thus educated, they will invent for themselves any lesser rules which their predecessors have altogether neglected." He thus clearly recognises inventiveness as the crown of educational development.

Mr. H. G. Wells, in a lecture on science teaching, says: "Instruction in physics and chemistry should finally take the form of lessons in explanation of an experiment or group of related experiments, and exercises upon the lessons. The full importance of these experiments should be elucidated by questions. The pupils should draw the apparatus and describe the experiment orally, and should set down precisely what has been seen and what is to be inferred. They should also perform experimental work, involving measurements and computation, and further illustrating the principles evolved, and should be called upon to imagine and describe the laws they had already become familiar with under new conditions." Herein is contained a clear and complete application of the principle of analysis and synthesis.

Professor L. C. Miall in an article on "Finding out and being told," says: "When the children have been cutting out paper, or putting sticks together, the teacher will not say: 'That side is too long or too short.' He will point out that there is something wrong, and encourage the child to discover what it is. When a model is to be drawn, he will not begin by prescribing the size of the drawing, but will inquire, together with the child, whether the first attempt is convenient in point of size."

Again, the Hon. Rev. E. Lyttleton, in his contribution to "Thirteen Essays on Education," remarks, respecting the teaching of Latin syntax : "Surely it would not be impossible for boys to be given carefully graduated examples of certain constructions, and led to discover the rules exemplified, and to put them first into his own words, then, for convenience, into the technical phraseology."

Of the need for a mental content being joined to all verbal forms, as the principle of symbolism requires, Mr. Quick speaks in very definite terms. He says : "Boys' minds are frequently dwarfed, and their interest in intellectual pursuits blighted, by the practice of employing the first years of their school-life in learning by heart things which it is quite impossible for them to understand or care for. Teachers set out by assuming that little boys cannot understand anything, and that all we can do with them is to keep them quiet and cram them with forms which will come in useful at a later stage.

"When the boys have been taught on this system for two or three years, their teacher complains that they are stupid and inattentive, and that so long as they can say a thing by heart they never trouble themselves to understand it. In other words, the teacher grumbles at them for doing precisely what they have been taught to do, for repeating words without any thought of their meaning."

Mr. Thring forcibly indicates the after effects of a

non-observance of the principle in the following passage :
" As long as the great majority of educated people do
not know the precise meaning of their own language,
when they use it, the confusion and muddle in public
and private life must be as great as it is. A man who
knows the real meaning of his own words will not use
them ambiguously unless he is a knave ; and if he is
a knave, an audience accustomed to study thought in its
process of taking shape in words will detect his knavery.
At present words have absurd power because they
are swallowed whole." (Theory and Practice of
Teaching.)

CHAPTER VIII

THE DEVELOPMENT OF KNOWLEDGE

WE have already said that knowledge consists of more or less organised judgments, or a store of truths known as truths. We now seek to make more explicit the nature and growth of knowledge.

Sources of Knowledge.—Herbart says: "Knowledge imitates what lies before it in idea. . . . . In knowledge there is an antithesis between the thing and the idea. . . . . [Knowledge] is always at its beginning. Receptivity is as becoming in the man as in the boy." Herein is implied the inner and outer elements of knowledge; the subjective and objective elements, or the physical and mental, as they are often called. Also there is a definite recognition of the fact, which we have so often insisted upon, viz., that the same principles of education, though in somewhat different proportions, are applicable to all individuals, whatever be the age of the learner. "Knowledge, in the wider sense, comprehends both cognition, which rests on perception (and on the evidence transmitting perceptions of which we are ignorant), and also . . . . [that] which is attained by thinking" (Ueberweg). This passage recognises the element of direct intuition as a source of knowledge, and also that of reflective thought. Both of these have been constantly referred to in previous discussions.

Besides these two original sources of knowledge, there is what we may call a fundamental channel of knowledge arising out of the existence of language, viz., communication. This also has been already referred to.

It may be said, therefore, that knowledge comes to us in three ways, viz., through intuition, reflection, and communication; the ultimate basis of all three being experience. We will discuss each of these in some detail.

1. **Intuition.**—Much has already been said as to the nature of intuition. In referring to the fundamental nature of the simplest forms of knowing, we have really dealt, in general terms, with the fact of intuition. We have said that a living mind is bound to react to stimuli which act upon it, in some definite and significant manner, because of its nature as mind. For example, the general meaning and value for the mind of each sensation, as to whether it is pleasurable or painful—*i.e.*, agreeable or disagreeable—must be realised in the case of the very earliest sensations; or there is no reason why the millionth should be so realised.

Similarly we must know, in however vague and indefinite a way, the general value and significance of a great many other experiences, on the first occasion of their happening to us in definite form, or we shall never

2 A

know them. There can be no reference to and comparison with, even in an implicit sense, the results of previous experiences, in the very beginning of life.

It is these first cognitions which are included under intuition. Intuition may, therefore, be defined as : the direct or immediate mental realisation of the essential value of an experience. By "direct or immediate" we mean without reference to previous experience or knowledge. Of course the word intuition is now used in its very widest sense, so as to apply to all kinds of experiences. The intuition of things—or of thingness, as it might be put—as dealt with in treating of percepts, is only one form of intuition.

This original apprehension of the significance of an experience does not in the least include, or exclude, that fuller content of meaning which is given to the same kind of experience, when knowledge and thought have developed. We must be able to distinguish between light and darkness at the first; but light cannot, to begin with, mean what it will mean when we have a good knowledge of the science of optics.

Since all our experiences are included under the mainly sensuous or the mainly rational kind, we may likewise divide intuitions into two classes, viz., sense intuitions and rational intuitions. As we have said, all the primary elements of knowledge of the physical details which are involved in a percept, and which are due to the sensations, as such, are immediate or direct, i.e., they are sense intuitions. Thus the eyes must enable the mind to judge at once whether an object is white or black ; the muscles of the hands must indicate whether it be hard or soft; the sense of touch must guide the mind as to whether it is rough or smooth; and so on. All these are matters of sense intuition.

" The sense-perceptions work together to assist us to a knowledge of the outer world, of which lights and colours, noises and musical sounds, smells and tastes, degrees of warmth, hardness, and roughness, are to be regarded as the elements. Our perceptions of the same external thing, gained through the different senses, come together in our consciousness into a whole, or total perception, of which the sight-perception takes its central place, hence the name intuition.

"Thus, in the sense-perception (intuition) of common salt, for example, are included the whitish colour, the hexahedral form, the peculiar taste, the rough, hygroscopic feeling, and the peculiar crackling when pressed together." (Lindner, Empirical Psychology.)

All such intuitions necessarily involve a purely intellectual element—that of meaning or significance—but in so far as this is inseparably bound up with the total complex we may regard it as included in the term sense intuition. But there are cases in which it is as necessary for this element to act separately, in an intuitive manner. If the higher self-conscious, reflective, mental life is to exist at all there must be a spontaneous beginning of it.

We find that, as a matter of fact, such purely mental intuitions are made. The mind intuits, or directly cognises, the fact that it has existence, feelings, knowings, willings, desires, ideas, and the like. Again, all axiomatic truths such as : the whole is greater than any one of its parts ; if equals be added to equals the wholes are equal ; and others, in their abstract forms, are direct and immediate rational judgments. The element of universal truth· in them is grasped by a normal mind at the very first occasion on which the relation involved is definitely presented to it.

If this were not so, it is impossible to see how such judgments could arise. An unlimited number of similar presentations—of course it is understood that the presentation, as such, is thoroughly complete and sound in every detail—can add nothing new in the way of explanation or suggestion. It is, as in the case of physical sight, necessary that we realise at once, when all the conditions, including the capacity to realise, are normal ; or there is no possibility of our ever realising. Intuitions which have to do with the purely mental elements of experience are called rational intuitions.

Care must be taken in forming a concept of intuition not to press the element of immediateness too far. It can never mean anything like absolute independence of the ordinary rational elements, for these are always finally inter-dependent and inter-related. The very fact of speaking of the direct grasp of "the meaning and value of an experience" shows that this inter-relation is implicitly involved. Perhaps the best way of expressing the difference between an intuition and other units of knowledge, is to say that in an intuition the implicitness is, from the practical point of view, absolute, in the first instance.

All physical wholes, as wholes, are directly known through intuition, as are also all parts as separate units, or smaller wholes, in so far as knowledge of them comes through direct experience, *i.e.*, as percepts. Images and concepts of physical wholes may be formed through the constructive powers of thought alone.

Accepting intuitions in this sense, it is clear that they are the foundation elements of all knowledge. It is from them, and in relation to them, that all other details of knowledge have their significance and value. All the highest rational products must be based upon, and conform with, these fundamental elements, in the same way that the most profound and complex geometrical theorem is, in the last analysis, founded upon and in accord with the simplest geometrical axioms.

Of the truth of intuitions we can offer no further justification than that they always impress themselves upon us with the same inevitable and unvarying significance ; and that when we accurately relate other experiences and judgments to them, we find that all actions based upon such are in harmony with the general order of nature, so far as we are able to apprehend by the resulting effects upon ourselves and other objects.   They, therefore, are to us the fundamental, or ultimate, elements of knowledge, beyond which we cannot go, and without which we should be unable to relate our experiences so as to form any systems of knowledge.

" The sum of our perceptions [intuitions] forms the circle of our sense experience, and at the same time the material which conditions all the higher activities of the soul.   The greatest extension of this circle is seen in the first years of life, and in the following periods of childhood and youth, and it also experiences constant extension during middle life" (Lindner).

2. **Reflection.**—Of the ways in which knowledge comes to us by reflection, we have been treating throughout all our discussions hitherto. The knowledge which comes to us through simple assimilation and discrimination, association, relation, and reason, in connection with all and every kind and item of experience, is reflection-given. All that comes to us immediately, or through the implicit or explicit mental connection of one thing with another is included under this head.

3. **Communication.**—Very limited indeed would be the total amount of knowledge that any one person could acquire in a lifetime, if he had only his own experiences to depend upon; and infinitely more restricted, comparatively speaking, would be that of the race, were it not for the almost boundless supplies of knowledge-giving information which can be communicated through written and spoken language.

As we have seen, a large part of the meaning which mind gets from a presentation is due to the representative elements which interpret and apperceive it. These representative elements must necessarily act through their associated symbols, for it would be manifestly impossible to have all the details of all the representations in clear consciousness, together with the details of the presentation, and also to carry on the necessary mental processes.

In the same way as mind thus works with the

symbols for its own mental units, so also it can make use of the symbols with which others supply it, so long as it has more or less of the appropriate contents of meanings which must be given to the signs. The modifications and adaptations of one's own knowledge, as gained from experience, can be made effective through judgment, in accordance with the suggestions or demands of that which is communicated. On this point we have already had a good deal to say.

There are, however, certain conditions and precautions which should always be insisted upon either by, or on behalf of, the learner, before accepting the description of the nature, effects, and meanings of the experiences of others, for the same purposes, and in the same sense, as they themselves receive and make use of the symbols which represent their own experiences and knowledge. Of course we assume that, as a rule, individuals secure sound knowledge, and, therefore, that it is only the symbols of correct ideas that they use in obtaining further knowledge. One must make certain that he has every reasonable guarantee that the symbols which he gets from others are quite trustworthy.

Probably the most important points to insist upon are the following. Firstly, there must be no rational contradictions, or contradictions between parts, in any series or systems of facts and ideas communicated through language. It may seem that the first condition is a little far-fetched in character. But when it is remembered how many systems of so-called religion, science, philosophy, and medicine, are based upon pretensions of having solved mysteries, made the complex absolutely simple, apprehended the inexpressible, or discovered universal and infallible remedies, it will be recognised that the condition is not superfluous.

The latter part of the requirement is not necessarily a vital one, for a sound theory may be incompletely apprehended as to some of its details. At the same time, however, we must beware of hastily accepting every detail of constitution or application of what we have every reason to believe to be sound as a whole. And it may be that some essential parts of a whole hopelessly conflict with each other. Such a contradiction is fatal.

Secondly, we must assure ourselves that there are no contradictions of generally accepted principles, unless the assertions which involve them are conclusively proved, and the orthodox views convincingly disproved. When such an issue is involved there should be what the logician calls an "experimentum crucis," or test case. Such an experiment must be devised as will at once show that one theory is true and the other false.

Dr. Fowler gives the following example of a crucial experiment in his "Inductive Logic." "It has been determined, from theoretical considerations, that, on the assumption of the undulatory theory, the velocity of light must be less in the more highly refracting medium, while, according to the emission theory, it ought to be greater. When M. Foucault had invented his apparatus for determining the velocity of light, it became possible to submit the question to direct experiment; and it was established by M. Fizeau that the velocity of light is less in water (the more highly refracting medium) than in air, in the inverse proportion of the refractive indices. The result is, therefore, decisive in favour of the undulatory, or at least, against the emission theory."

Thirdly, we should be convinced, on completely satisfactory grounds, that the communicator is thoroughly reliable as to his statement of facts, and as to the soundness of the more direct inferences which he draws from them. This is a matter which is by no means involved in the former conditions. A person may put on record a most plausible account of observations, and deductions from them, which he himself most sincerely and conscientiously believes, but which are nevertheless seriously misleading, or radically unsound.

It often requires a very wise and skilful person to see what he sees, in a scientific sense. We all have eyes that see not, and ears that hear not, with regard to certain elements of experience. If medical men were to trust wholly to what their patients, or relatives, could tell them of the symptoms and effects of their disorders, the results would be likely to be disastrous to the sick ones. Again, it requires a psychologist, and an unprejudiced one, to rightly observe the signs and stages of mental development in children.

Hence, we ought to regard the proper qualifications of the communicator as one of the essential guarantees of the trustworthiness of the communication. A commonplace example of the necessity of such a safeguard is afforded by the way in which witnesses of alleged furious driving estimate the rate of travelling at all sorts of degrees, varying from five to twenty miles an hour.

Fourthly, we should be reasonably certain that we are rightly interpreting, at least approximately, the symbols used. What has been said about the ambiguity of terms applies equally to phrases, sentences, and even trains of reasoning. An amusing example of an ambiguous sentence is the invitation, said to have been given by a travelling Irishman to an acquaintance: "If ever you are within a mile of my house, I hope you will stay there the night." The ambiguity of arguments is shown by a case in which one might say: which proves that A stole the cheque, or that B told lies.

Where, therefore, there is no explicit statement of a communicator's purposes or views, and the context does not obviously and conclusively demand and allow of one, and only one, interpretation, then the learner should definitely recognise that he is in the region of conjecture, uncertainty, and, it may be, intellectual danger. Under such conditions there can be no definite communication of final knowledge-giving information, as to conclusions on any special points at issue.

The history of schools of thought, controversies, schisms, factions, parties, persecutions, and the like, all show how much turns upon a determination to fill in, rather than accept only that which is obviously given out by, verbal forms. The world of knowledge is full of the evidence of foolish perversity in this

matter, as witness the volumes of various interpreta-
tions of great writers. How often might weary readers
exclaim in righteous wrath : "One might understand
this passage, if it were not for the commentators!"

When the above conditions are reasonably satisfied,
there is hardly any more likelihood of rational error
arising from mentally working with the symbols of
other people's thoughts and experiences, than with
those of one's own.

Of course the above remarks only apply, in their
fullest sense, to advanced youths and adults; but
exactly the same matters, as to principle, occasionally
occur in connection with the verbal element in the
education of young children. These should be dealt
with, in a very simple manner, as far as possible on the
lines suggested.

To take a simple illustration, let us suppose that a
child is reading about a small boy's first ride in a railway carriage, and comes to the sentence, "Oh, mother,
do look at the houses all running by!" Without letting the little reader go on to the correction which will
doubtless be found in the following lines, the educator
can make this an opportunity for asking such questions as: Have you ever seen houses run? Do you
think they can run? Why not? Thus the element
of inaccuracy in the judgment is made obvious, for the
words express something which is opposed to known
truths.

Then the unfitness of the observer for giving a sound
and accurate judgment about what was happening
might be brought out, by such questions as, "Do little

boys know very much ? Do they understand all that happens around them (as, how the engine can draw the carriages) ? Do older people sometimes make mistakes ? Does it look as though the houses moved ? What does move ?

Stages of Development in Knowledge.—That knowledge does not come to us in an absolutely clear, full, and final form in the first instance, none would be likely to dispute. Even intuitions, though they can never be said to alter their essential characters, become more clear and definite after repeated experiences. It is this progress in clearness, definiteness, and fulness, of ideas with which we are concerned in tracing the stages in the development of knowledge ; for as ideas become more precise in form, and more rich in content, so also will judgments, reasonings, and the whole of organised knowledge.

Dr. Lindner says: "Not clearness, therefore, but obscurity is the original form of consciousness, as is the case with the new born child, the majority of animals, and with the adult in the condition of sleep." So also Dr. Höffding remarks : " Distinctness and individuality are relative conceptions, and our ideas may in this respect pass through a whole scale. The ideas of children and of primitive men have often a certain abstract, vague, and general character, because they do not distinctly apprehend and hold fast the individual shades and differences. At the first, only particular sides of the object are apprehended and preserved."

The same fact is insisted upon by Dr. Ward, who indicates the character of infantile presentations thus :

" In place of the many things which we can now see and hear, not merely would there then be a confused presentation of the whole field of vision and of a mass of undistinguished sounds, but even the difference between sights and sounds themselves would be without its present distinctness."

An infant, or any person suddenly called upon to deal with what we should ordinarily call utterly unknown experiences, may be described as looking out upon the vague and vast unknown ; except that there would be the recognition, with what we have termed absolute implicitness by the infant, but with more or less explicitness by an adult, of a something which it may be possible to know.

The first necessity for knowledge in such a case is to be able to make out some element of difference in the general presentation. This will probably consist of suggestions of limits or boundaries, of some kind or other. These will then gradually become more and more clear and definite until the whole is more or less completely marked off into areas. The content and significance of these areas will doubtless remain as vague as ever for some considerable time. But a beginning has been made. This may be regarded as the first stage in the development of knowledge.

When so much has been accomplished, the marking off of concrete differences, more or less superficial, is likely to go on to a very considerable extent. In this way each of the areas, or smaller wholes, into which the original presentation was divided, will themselves be known as consisting of distinguishable details or parts.

Also the knowledge of these parts will become clearer and more definite through repeated experiences. To again quote Dr. Ward : "Because things are so often a world within themselves, their several parts or members not only having distinguishing qualities but moving and changing with more or less independence of the rest, it comes about that what is from one point of view one thing becomes from another point of view several, like a tree with its separable branches and fruits, for example." Such a marking off of the first recognised wholes into their smaller wholes or constituent parts, is the second stage of knowledge.

There then remains, in general terms, only the knowledge of the relations, qualities, laws, and principles, which are involved the great total, the constituent wholes, and their details, to be acquired. To know these exhaustively it will be necessary to have a complete knowledge of the minutest details of each of the parts. Herein lies the third stage of knowledge, which is obviously a very wide, and practically unlimited, region.

Leibnitz has called these three stages of knowledge the clear, the distinct, and the adequate. Knowledge is clear when we are able to mark off wholes from each other, in the first division of the total presentation. It is distinct when we know each separate and distinct part of a whole. To know in these stages means to have such clear and definite percepts that we can, as a rule, without hesitation or mistake, recognise or identify a whole, or part, as such-and-such. Knowledge is adequate when, if ever, we know all about all the parts of a whole.

These stages may be illustrated by the following example. We have clear knowledge of an oak tree when we are able to clearly mark it off from anything that is not a tree, and also from other trees, so that we are almost invariably right, under ordinary conditions, when we say : this is an oak tree. When we can, in a similar manner, distinguish between the trunk, branches, roots, leaves, blossoms, seeds, and all the essential botanical parts of a tree, we have distinct knowledge of the tree. If we are able to attain to a knowledge of every constituent element and of every principle concerning the nature, development, and life of the tree, and its direct relations to other wholes, we might approximate to an adequate knowledge of it, as a whole.

The way in which knowledge gradually grows in the mind has been very aptly compared to experiences on a foggy morning. A person walking along and looking straight ahead sees nothing but a boundless misty vagueness before him. Presently there looms before him a kind of intensified and limited vagueness, making in the general vagueness a suggestion of a something definite within, or behind it. Further progress makes the suggestiveness more definite, and it may be that a guess is hazarded as to its being some animal, a man, or a house. Soon after there is no longer any doubt as between these, for the outline has become so definite that it is clearly that of a house. This is the point when knowledge is clear.

As he gets nearer to the house he sees that it is a cottage built of bricks, with a thatched roof, and four windows at the front. Next he comes up to the building and sees all the external details. If we suppose him to enter the house, go into each room, and carefully take account of every concrete detail, he could thus gain a distinct knowledge of it.

Now the fog may be assumed to have disappeared, and the full sunlight to be shining upon the house and its surroundings. There is no further obstacle to a complete knowledge of all the concrete constituents of the object. Not all at once, however, are all the details seen and known. Much practical effort and concrete analysis must be gone through before completely distinct knowledge is gained.

From this point there is only the purely rational obscurity which has to be explored. The progress in this is very similar to the previous advance. Of course at the present time, when the opportunities for getting knowledge are so numerous, and aids so plentiful and efficient, it is not easy to realise, so fully and in such detail, all the mental difficulties. But if we consider how the race has advanced through what we should call the absurdest superstitions about material things to exact scientific knowledge of them, we shall understand more of what is actually involved in rational progress.

If, then, the traveller pursues his inquiries until he understands all about all the details of the house, in the light of all that each of the physical sciences has to tell or suggest about them, then he is in the way of obtaining adequate knowledge about the object as a whole.

A few words of detail about each of the stages may help to make matters still clearer.

1. **Clear Knowledge.**—Doubtless it will have been noticed that clear knowledge involves the intuition of a thing as a distinct whole. This wholeness is the first element of what we have called thingness. There is no suggestion of parts or contents involved in it, much less any apprehension, however vague, of them. Hence, clear knowledge may be said to include all primary intuitions, and percepts, of things. But the complex and immediate percept, known as such, is wholly excluded.

Knowledge which falls short of the definiteness and accuracy required for clear knowledge, in the sense that one is frequently, say, mistaking an oak tree for an elm tree, and otherwise confusing wholes with one another, is said to be obscure.

Liebnitz says: "A notion is obscure when it is not sufficient to enable us to recognise the thing which it represents; when, for example, I remember some flower or animal which I have formerly seen, but this remembrance is not sufficient to enable me to recognise its image, or to discriminate it from others which resemble it. When, again, I think of some term . . . . which has never been sufficiently explained, such for example as the . . . . term cause . . . . the proposition is obscure into which such a notion enters." (A. S. Baynes' translation.)

The element of indefiniteness in ordinary thought is well pointed out by Dr. Isambard Owen, in the following passage : " Or take the evidence of language (it is

2 B

a practical point), and mark how vagueness of arithmetic conception [perception] reflects and even exaggerates itself in vagueness of arithmetic diction. Our grammars contain an ample list of numerals; the State supplies a set of standard measures; but in speech and writing, even the most careful, numerals and terms of measurement have to give place to a host of words, such as 'many,' 'few,' 'large,' 'small,' 'often,' 'seldom,' to which it is difficult to attach any definite meaning. We are fain, however, to use them, not precisely because our conceptions [perceptions] are equally vague, but because they are still not definite enough to find arithmetical expression."

Although it is not usual to re-apply the names clear, distinct, and adequate, to stages of development in what is termed purely rational knowledge, yet there would seem to be much to recommend such a course. Those who have studied the pure sciences, and, more especially those who have studied the mental sciences, will know that there is the same kind of development in the power to clearly apprehend the purely rational. We shall, therefore, briefly point out how the terms do so apply.

In the realm of what is known as pure reason, clear knowledge will embrace all rational intuitions, and simple primary forms of conceptual judgment. The accurate marking off of presentations from percepts, percepts from concepts, pleasures from pains, desires from willings, feeling from knowing, and the like, will be included under clear knowledge. All knowledge which fails to rightly and habitually mark these off from each other will be obscure.

It is interesting to notice how the individual is constantly repeating this cycle of progress in knowledge, throughout his life. If a man who had lived in a city all his life, and knew next to nothing of practical affairs beyond the limits of a business office, were required to distinguish one dog from another in a pack of hounds, he would, probably, very keenly realise the fact that he had eyes which had not yet learnt to see in this particular sphere.

Much in the same way men who have had a long training in practical affairs, or even in the physical sciences, are at first wholly at a loss in attempting the mental sciences; and are very apt to consider such subjects as little better than elaborate verbal frauds. Their mental eyes are not yet opened to mental objects. But none such need despair, for they have eyes which may be opened.

2. **Distinct Knowledge.**—This corresponds to and includes all complex percepts. There will be, so far as the concrete is concerned, no concept element, known as different from the percept, in it. It is simply the application of the conditions of clear knowledge to each and every distinct part of a concrete whole.

If there be so much indefiniteness or incompleteness in such knowledge that one part is more or less frequently taken for another, then the knowledge is, from this point of view, said to be confused.

With regard to the application of the term in the sphere of the purely rational, our knowledge will be distinct when we can distinguish definitely between the constituent elements in a complete concept, *e.g.*, the concepts of animality and rationality as composing the concept of humanity. When there is failure in this respect the knowledge is confused.

As Dr. Sully says: "A boy has a distinct idea of coal when he clearly distinguishes and grasps together as a whole its several qualities, as its black colour, its frangibility, combustibility, &c. On the other hand, an idea is indistinct, hazy, or ill-defined, when the constituent qualities of the objects are not thus distinctly represented. . . . . A concept is indistinct when it is apt to be confused with a kindred concept. Thus a boy studying history has confused notions when he does not discriminate an aggressive from a defensive war, a limited from an absolute monarchy, and so forth."

One can hardly help being struck with the tremendous difficulty, often amounting to practical impossibility, of really knowing every distinct part of some very complex wholes. And this becomes more and more true as knowledge advances, for definite differences of structure, nature, and function of details, which were previously thought to be non-distinctive parts of a part, are being constantly discovered. Anatomy and chemistry give good examples of this.

It, therefore, becomes a question as to how far knowledge must go before it can be said to be really distinct. For practical purposes it is sufficient to have a knowledge of the more important and obviously distinguishable, parts. But it is, perhaps, well to take an ideal standard of knowledge, and to admit that there are comparatively few things, if any, of which we can really have exhaustively distinct knowledge.

Liebnitz thus distinguishes between confused and distinct knowledge : " It is confused when we are not able to enumerate marks sufficient to discriminate the thing from others, although it may, in reality, have such marks and requisites into which its notion may be resolved.   Thus. . . . painters and other artists discern well enough what is well or ill done ; but often are not able to give a reason for their judgment, and reply to those who inquire what it is that displeases them in the work, that there is something, they know not what, wanting.

" But a distinct notion is such as the assayers have concerning gold, by marks and tests which are sufficient to distinguish it from all other similar bodies. . . . A distinct knowledge of an indefinable notion is . . . . possible when it is primitive or self-evident—that is, when it is ultimate."   In other words, intuitions are included in distinct notions.

3. **Adequate Knowledge.**—From what has already been said it will have been gathered that adequate knowledge must mean perfectly exhaustive and correct knowledge about an object.   Strictly understood, it implies that condition of knowledge in which it is clearly seen that all is in all, as Jacotot says.   But this is omniscience.

In this strict sense we cannot be said to have adequate knowledge of any one thing, for to do so we must know everything about everything.   For example, can we claim to know everything about our own alphabet ? We can certainly have a completely distinct knowledge of it, for it is easily analysed into its geometrical elements of outline.   But when we go beyond this we have to regard it, as a system of thought-symbol elements. This brings us to a consideration of the functions and principles of language, and at once we are in a boundless region of fact and philosophy.

Adequate knowledge may, indeed, be regarded as wholly impossible for us. We can only hope to more and more approximate to it as our knowledge and powers increase. Leibnitz said that adequate knowledge is intuitive and perfect. For all knowledge to be intuitive would mean that there would be no knowledge in our present sense of the term. An omniscient individual does not learn, relate, compare, and so on ; he simply cognises in an absolutely immediate and complete sense. He cannot be said to analyse or synthesise, for everything must come to him already analysed and synthesised, as universal and perfect intuition.

Both the concrete and the purely rational elements of knowledge are included in adequate knowledge. There is, therefore, no need to speak of the latter separately. All knowledge that falls short of being adequate is described as inadequate, or imperfect.

We may illustrate the application of the stages of knowledge, in the case of a judgment, by the following. The judgment " all dogs are quadrupeds " is clear, in a perceptual sense, when the concrete ideas of dog and quadruped, and the significance of including both in the same group, are clear. It is clear, in a conceptual sense, when the concepts of dog and quadruped, and the significance of the relation between them, are clear. The judgment is distinct when all the elements of the percepts, or of the concepts, are distinct. It will

approximate to the adequate, when more or less of all
the perceptual and conceptual elements of fact, signi-
fication, implication, and universal inter-relation and
dependence, are known. We must know the concrete
and rational details involved in the arriving at the
judgment inductively, and their deductive implications.

Of adequate knowledge Liebnitz says : " When everything which enters into a distinct notion is distinctly
known, or when the last analysis is known, the knowledge is adequate, of which I scarcely know whether
a perfect example can be offered ; the knowledge of
numbers, however, approaches near to it."

So does the greatest of all human possessions come to
man. There are the first frightened peeps into
the great unknown : then the timid gaze : the shy
reaching forth of the hand : the hesitating grasping of
things : and the doubting appropriation of the facts of
life and thought. Then follow : the earnest strivings
to know truly : the realisation of the infinity of knowledge : the thrilling and sometimes lasting joys of
conquest : and the strength of the humility of knowing
one's ignorance.

CHAPTER IX

AGAIN we have to deal with the general "principle of development" in education, from the point of view of greater detail with regard to a particular aspect of it. It will be well to remind ourselves that when we speak of the educational principle of development, we mean the manner in which the educator should use certain kinds of educative influences so as to bring about the greatest possible harmony and co-operation between the developing mind and the educating processes.

The Principle of Development.—Whereas we were treating of the elements of knowledge, and the educational principles connected therewith, under the title of the development of ideas, we have now to speak of the educational principles derived from a consideration of the nature and development of what we may call the units of knowledge. A unit of knowledge may be said to be the apprehension, however vague and superficial at first, of any whole of experience. Obviously this will take us to sensations as the first units of knowledge; after which will follow the realisation of physical wholes, when the sense organs begin to do their work more definitely.

1. **From the Concrete to the Abstract.**—It will be seen that further light is thrown upon this maxim, by what has been said about the development of knowledge from the clear to the distinct, and then to the adequate. But it is not necessary to do more than draw attention to the fact that we thereby learn that there is a progress in the clearness, as well as the fulness, of ideas. We must not expect that first ideas will, ordinarily, be quite clear and definite, any more than that they will be full and accurate.

2. **From the Known to the Unknown.**—We now see that what is first known is very imperfectly known to begin with, and that we have to proceed from a very vague, indefinite, and incomplete knowledge of a thing, to a more clear, distinct, and approximately adequate knowledge of it. Also we find that large unknown wholes are first divided into smaller unknown wholes, at least in many cases; and, although the large whole is the better known in that we have still further analysed it, yet the new units will probably be almost, if not quite, as unknown as the inclusive unit was at first.

Thus we have what we may call the reciprocal truth of the converse of this maxim. That is to say, whilst it is true that we are proceeding from what we first know to what at first was not known, we are also advancing from a slight knowledge of a whole to a much fuller mastery of it. From the latter point of view we are progressing from the less known to the more known, with respect to the same inclusive unit of experience and knowledge. This truth must be recognised and remembered by the educator, or he will be likely to take wrong attitudes towards the maxim.

Let it be carefully noted that both points of view apply to the same unit of knowledge. For example, when an individual learns about levers, he should first be called upon to tell how he has gained help in moving and lifting heavy bodies from simple mechanical aids, or has seen others do so. A boy may have noticed the large and heavy piles of luggage which a porter is able to raise and move by means of his specially-constructed barrow. He will also know how very greatly a claw-hammer helps in drawing out a nail from a piece of wood, and a poker in loosening the fire. These items of general, and more or less superficial, knowledge are brought together to prepare for, and assist in, the discovery of more exact practical knowledge about levers. He is, therefore, proceeding from the more known to the more or less unknown.

But, on the other hand, in so far as his previous knowledge was really knowledge about levers which it is now proposed to extend and make more exact, he is progressing from the less known to the more known, in his knowledge of levers. This is, after all, only two ways of stating the same truth, but the putting of the point explicitly may prevent possible confusion.

The gradual development of knowledge, from the latter point of view, also deserves attention. There is first the progress from one thing that is slightly known to another which is also slightly known; then there is the advance from slight knowledge to a fuller knowledge of the same inclusive, or separate, unit of knowledge; and, finally, we have the growth from a comparatively fuller knowledge of a thing to a more and more full, scientific, and profound knowledge of it. These stages move consecutively with regard to the same unit of knowledge, but concurrently as to different units.

Having regard to any fresh step in knowledge, simply as a fresh step, then the statement of the maxim: from the more known to the less known, must be held to have an invariable and universal application. In other words, we must always provide for interpreting the presentative by the representative: for understanding the new by means of the old: and for growing out of what we are into that which we are becoming.

3. **From the Simple to the Complex.**—Again we get further, and valuable, knowledge of the significance of this maxim. We have previously described the simple, for educational purposes, as that which is well known, familiar, and under such control that it can, as a rule, be readily and accurately applied either in theory or practice. But it is necessary that we should have some idea as to what are to be regarded as the first forms of the simple, in the development of knowledge in the individual. It is most important that we should know this, because such things will constitute the best, and the only really trustworthy, points of departure for imparting knowledge.

There can hardly be any question as to the truth of

the fact that every first unit of knowledge must come from within the limits of the individual's own experience. What we want to know, therefore, is : what are the first ideas which the individual is likely to derive from his experiences of his surroundings, with regard to any given knowledge-subject which the educator usually employs.

Fortunately there is very general agreement as to what are the first units of knowledge in some subjects, and these will at least form a basis for obtaining some support from practical thought for what we shall urge as the truly scientific view. Thus in geography most educationists would agree that the proper matter to start with is the child's knowledge of his own surroundings, and that this should be so organised as to lead on to all the ordinary forms of geographical knowledge.

Again, the view that grammar should begin with the sentence, because it is, either in a full or elliptical form, the first unit of language knowledge which the child acquires, is usually accepted as the right one. That writing should be introduced by drawing, and that formal and symbolic reckoning (arithmetic) ought to be preceded by concrete grouping and mental exercises, are generally recognised educational truths.

Now the scientific justification for such views is the fact that in each case the foundations of the educational exercises are laid within the sphere of the child's own actual experience and present knowledge; though the latter is more or less implicit, in so far as the formal organisation of it is concerned. This point must be emphatically insisted upon, and constantly borne in mind. It is the whole within the beginner's knowledge and experience which must be made use of, and not a more perfect and comprehensive one which is quite familiar and easy to the ordinary adult, or to the educator.

Much less should it be a whole which represents, not the primal, but the present knowledge possession of the race. And yet many have advocated this last named whole, and some even still use it. Geography was formerly, and in some cases is still, begun with an outline account of the geography of the world. To begin with the whole of one's native land is equally bad, for it is quite as much an unknown world to the child.

The teaching of history, strangely enough, is still in the stage of practical blundering, except in the case of a few scientific thinkers, notwithstanding the recognition of its intimate connection with geography. It is thought that beginning with vivid biographical accounts of some of the most striking or important personages of former times is a sufficient simplification of the subject matter; whilst a good many hold that a short outline sketch of a brief period of the earliest history of the fatherland, with plenty of illustrations, will do all that is required. Others, again, still hold to the "good old way, the ancient plan" of beginning with the creation of the world, and working down through a very brief sketch of all the history of all the nations.

But surely history should begin, like geography, with the knowledge of the home life. If the child realises anything at all, it must know something about the changes connected with its own life. The change from the home life to the school life, from the school for younger to that for older scholars, from a day school to a boarding school: the significant change from the dress of childhood to that of youth: the difference between the dress of a grandmother and grandfather and that of a grown-up sister and brother: the comparison of the organisation and government of the home with those of the school: old houses, and local customs, institutions, and traditions: the disused canal beside the busy railway: and the like, all form starting points for biographical, social, local, political, commercial, and national history.

Reading is another subject which is not yet generally, or completely, delivered from the bondage of educational ignorance. A more widespread recognition of the fact that the combined aural and visual whole should, as in the case of the vocal and aural whole, be a sentence is required. This does not exclude the giving of single words as a preliminary to short sentences; for such a proceeding is quite in accord with the development of language. The first efforts in language consist of single word sentences, that is, exclamations. To exclaim "Man!" and to point with the finger, is a combination of vocal and gesture language, and has some such meaning as: that is a man; here is a man; or, I see a man there.

We have discussed this point is some detail, because we are of opinion that much hindrance arises, and great mischief is often caused, in relation to the earliest stage of education, owing to misconceptions about it, or the want of a clear and definite realisation of the truth. It is of the greatest moment that we should understand, and endeavour always to realise in practice, those words of Pestalozzi: " The circle of knowledge commences close round a man, and from thence stretches out concentrically."

Such are the conditions which will provide the order of greatest simplicity. And this will be still more effectively secured if careful consideration be given to the gradual progress from clear to distinct, and from distinct to adequate, ideas, in each separate item of knowledge. At first a brief outline of the whole should be considered, until its general nature and significance, from the practical standpoint, are made reasonably clear and permanent. Then may come the fuller and fuller detail, until all the important parts of the whole are also made clear, and so the idea of the whole becomes distinct. Later on still higher and deeper knowledge of the powers, relations, and laws of the matter should be attempted.

This maxim, like all the others, should be understood in its detailed meaning. It should be stated thus: from simple to simple, from simple to complex, from complex to more complex, from complex to simple.

4. **From the Particular to the General.**—We find, in the foregoing chapter, a very definite confirmation of what had previously been laid down about this maxim. There is the same progress from the one to the many, and from the knowledge of facts to a knowledge of the reasons for them. But that knowledge of the one which suggests, and enables us finally to work out, the higher knowledge of the many, is now seen to be itself a matter

of gradual and systematic growth, which needs time and care for its successful cultivation.

Another point also is impressed upon us. There is a second way in which we can be said to move from the general to the particular. The first way is through the purely rational process of deductive reasoning. But from the practical point of view the greater wholes, which contain smaller wholes, are often in themselves a unity representing a class. Thus, to look out upon a forest is, in a very implicitly practical sense, to begin with an impression of a class. In such cases it is clear that the movement of analysis is from the general to the particular.

But all this is quite implicit from the point of view of the beginner; and is only worthy of notice, because it involves the conditions through which the educator can encourage the concurrent development of the ideas of the general and the particular. We previously drew attention to the fact of such a simultaneous development being inevitable; and we now see how it can be assisted, by arranging that the beginner shall have as many helpful experiences of the above kind as can be conveniently provided.

The full statement of this principle will be : From the particular to the particular, from particulars to the general, from the general to the more general, and from the general to the particular.

Pestalozzi says : " It is a chief business of education to pass from distinctly perceived individual notions to clear general notions " (De Garmo). The other point of view is expressed by Comenius in his maxims. He says : "Nature begins all its formation from generals, and thence proceeds to specialise . . . . A painter in painting a portrait does not draw first the nose, then the ears, etc., but outlines the whole man on canvas roughly with chalk, and then proceeds to fill in. So with instruction, the outline should first be given." "Everything should be so taught as to show how it is and becomes—*i.e.*, per causas. Priora should come first, and posteriora next; and, therefore, whatever is presented as an object of knowledge, should be presented first generally, and thereafter in its parts. All the parts of a thing should be known, even the more minute, none being omitted : also its order, situation, and connection with other things " (Laurie).

Dr. C. A. McMurry remarks that " Perfect vigour of thought which we aim at in education, is marked by strength along three lines—the vigour of the individual ideas; the extent and variety of ideas under control; and the connection and harmony of ideas."

5. **From the Indefinite to the Definite.**—This is a maxim with which we have not hitherto dealt. It is peculiarly appropriate to the development of knowledge, from the educational standpoint. To get clear, distinct, and approximately adequate ideas, we must pass, more or less slowly, through the obscure, confused, and very inadequate, stages of such ideas.

Mr. Herbert Spencer has put this matter very clearly and convincingly. He says : "The first perceptions and thoughts are extremely vague. As from a rudimentary eye, discerning only the difference between light and darkness, the progress is to an eye that distinguishes

kinds and gradations of colour, and details of form, with
the greatest exactness; so, the intellect as a whole and in
each faculty, beginning with the rudest discriminations
among objects and actions, advances towards discriminations of increasing nicety and distinctness. . . . It
is not practicable, nor would it be desirable if practicable, to put precise ideas into the undeveloped mind.

"Only as the multiplication of experiences gives
material for definite conceptions—only as observation
year by year discloses the less conspicuous attributes
which distinguish things and processes previously
confounded together—only as each class of co-existences
and sequences become familiar through the recurrences
of cases coming under it—only as the various classes of
relations get accurately marked off from each other by
mutual limitation; can the exact definitions of advanced
knowledge become truly comprehensible.

"Thus in education we must be content to set out
with crude notions. These we must aim to make
gradually clearer by facilitating the acquisition of
experiences such as will correct, first their greatest
errors, and afterwards their successively less marked
errors. And the scientific formulæ must be given only
as fast as the conceptions are perfected."

The same point is emphasised by Plato in what
appears to be the contradictory assertion that the child
must be taught the false before he can learn the true.
But this must not be taken to mean that the educator
is to deliberately misrepresent things to the learner,
and get him to learn that which is known to be false.
On the contrary, this is just what the educator must

above all things avoid. His chief function is to help the beginner to learn truth through truth to the greatest possible extent. It is because only vague and superficial notions of things can at first be given to the learner, and that these can only be more or less dimly understood, that misleading and false ideas are sure to arise in the ignorant mind.

Even the most learned scientist is, at first, in just such a condition, when engaged in trying to work out new lines of thought and action. And those who have had experience in teaching older pupils, and adults, well know how difficult it is to get them to form first ideas about new knowledge-subjects, and how that it is still more difficult to correct the misleading suggestions which the misconceptions of these first notions involve.

Great caution ought, therefore, to be exercised as to the use of fairy tales. By all means let the first presentations of knowledge be as vivid, graphic, and striking as possible; but in education, as elsewhere, it is the case that truth is stranger than fiction, and certainly it is vastly more helpful. To carefully build up in the child's mind, when it is in its most receptive, responsive, and retentive stage, just what we know we shall have to endeavour to pull down again because it is unsound, and prejudicial to that which is accurate and valuable, is, to say the least of it, not very wise or economical. As stories of " bogies " are often permanently disastrous to the moral nature, so are others likely to be to the intellectual powers.

Children love not fairy tales because they are false,

but by reason of their wonderfulness. Equally wonderful to the child are the stories of real adventure in unknown lands, amongst strange surroundings, with ferocious animals and savage men. The facts of science may be made equally surprising and attractive to them, if they are carefully presented with verbal picturesqueness and allowable literary art.

A grave misconception as to the educational significance of the history of the race seems to us to underlie the ordinary advocacy of the use of ancient fairy tales and traditional folk-lore. Now, we ought not to repeat even the manner of the racial development in so far as we have reason to hold that it has been mischievous or undesirable. Much less ought we to repeat the material; for this would be to go back to primitive savagery, both mentally and morally. Again, the proportion of the lengths of the different stages of development in the race are more or less inversely related in the development of the individual of to-day. Primitive man was, for nearly the whole of his life, in that stage of development which children of to-day should pass through, and in many respects beyond, in their first seven years.

Just in the same way an adult of the present time will, as a rule, pass through the perceptual stage of a new knowledge-subject in a fraction of the time in which a child would do so; and, in many cases, the adult will be able, practically, to begin with the conceptual elements of a fresh subject.

If these contentions be allowed, it is clear that there are several conditions which we should insist upon before making use of the suggestions of racial development. Much more will these apply to the ancient products of racial development. First, then, we ought to satisfy ourselves that the influence involved in the telling of fairy tales is a desirable one. There can be but little, if any, doubt that it is an entirely effective, and, from that point of view, a desirable one. The excited interest, vigorous, and even absorbed, attention which stories arouse, are the most valuable and effective agents in early development. We may therefore accept thrilling stories as having an educational place and function in early life.

Next we must consider to what end, and, therefore, for what period, such an influence should be used. Without discussing this point in detail, we will take it as generally allowed that the purpose of such stories is to introduce a more exact and serious knowledge about things. If this be admitted, it will probably also be granted that their systematic use ought to be discontinued so soon as the powers of attention and work become somewhat steady and vigorous. We should suggest that this is the case by the seventh year at the latest.

Again, it is necessary to very carefully examine the question of the wisdom of employing very old material for our purposes. It must be remembered that traditional folk-lore represents, to a considerable extent, the real beliefs of our forefathers, due to what we consider to be their gross ignorance and consequent superstitiousness. If this be so, to invite children to receive and retain such material is to subject them to a lower form of development, instead of introducing them to a higher.

One other very serious objection to the use of tales which are in direct opposition to the truths of nature and knowledge is that their use violates the maxims: from the known to the unknown : and, from the simple to the complex. Ordinary fairy tales and folk-lore are not only beyond a child's experience, but outside experience altogether. And inasmuch as they encourage the personifying tendency of the little learner, they directly lead to error, and make the path to truth very much harder to travel.

If it be urged that such stories give special pleasure to children, it may be replied that experience shows that equally attractive stories based upon actual facts give just as much present pleasure, and provide an abiding source of further enjoyment, instead of future difficulties. All who have observed little children will know how hardly they part from their beliefs in the personality of some of their toys, especially if they have been encouraged in what is supposed to be their very clever imaginings, but which are but the mistakes of profound ignorance.

That period in the history of the race in which life, personality, and intelligent design—as in the human being—are attributed to each of the separate powers of nature, as then known (which anthropologists technically speak of as animism), is doubtless an inevitable feature in human development ; but these errors should be corrected by the better knowledge which we possess, and not fostered by repeating that which expresses original ignorance.

The chief value of the old fairy tales, traditions, and

folk-lore, is to serve as models to the educator as to the form in which he may expect verbal communication to be most effective, in very early years. As Dr. Karl Lange points out, the fairy tale involves no definite limitations of time or space. It is simply " once upon a time," " long, long ago," as to when things happened; and there is, as a rule, no definite place, or scene of action; whilst fairies can transport themselves to the uttermost ends of the earth in the twinkling of an eye. These features are not originally due to a profound and luxurious power of constructive imagination, but to ignorance, and want of power to realise the details and relations of space, time, energy, and the like.

Here 'then are the elements through which we may make the very earliest communications most attractive and effective : strangeness, wonderfulness, and magical-ness, in the sense that the details of the real relations of time, space, power, process, and sequence, are more or less ignored. After all, therefore, we see that it is the element of indefiniteness which is the essential feature. And this is so because of its appropriateness to the child's powers and experiences, and its consequent in-ability to grasp either detail or dependence. It is the manner, and not the matter, which is of real value.

Surely, therefore, the proper thing to do is to subject children to the fairy tale material of our own times and knowledge. The fairy tales and wonders of science, history, travel, adventure, and the like, will, we hold, satisfy, in the best form, every possible requirement of the case. If this be so, then the period during which we seek to get progress through proceeding from the

indefinite to the indefinite, and so gradually to the
definite, will be very much shortened. The old method
is quite off the line of approach to the definite, and,
therefore, tends to prolong the period of indefinite
ideas.

Plato has the following on this point : " Shall we just
carelessly allow children to hear any casual tales which
may be devised by casual persons, and to receive into
their minds ideas for the most part the very opposite of
those which we should wish them to have when they
are grown up ? . . . Then the first thing will be to
establish a censorship of the works of fiction, and let
the censors receive any tale of fiction which is good,
and reject the bad ; and we will desire mothers and
nurses to tell their children the authorised ones only.
Let them fashion the mind with such tales, even more
fondly than they mould the body with their hands ;
but most of those which are now in use must be discarded " (Dr. Jowett).

Broadly speaking, we should say that the maxim :
from the indefinite to the definite, requires that the
educator should first endeavour to impart general
ideas about the more obvious and superficial features of
an object. This should be done by an outline sketch
of the whole. Not that this is to be supplied wholly
by him. The learner must tell all he knows, and discover as much more as possible, under wise guidance,
before communicated information is made use of. This
involves the mastery of most of the more or less indefinite elements of knowledge connected with any given
unit.

Next we must make a closer analysis of each of the main features, or constituent wholes, and so gain a fuller and clearer idea of them and of the unit whole. When we have thus arrived at a practically complete knowledge of the chief characteristics of each of the main features, or constituent wholes, and their concrete relations to each other and the total, we may consider that we possess definite ideas about the matter. Thus we have progressed from the indefinite to the definite in its simpler and less profound form.

Finally we go on making further and further analyses till almost every practicable particle, or feature, of the whole is known to us. For arriving at such a result, the previous, or first, form of definite ideas is a necessary condition. In this way we proceed from the definite to the still more definite.

We have made reference only to concrete ideas, or percepts, in describing the three stages, but the same order of progress applies to the formation of purely rational ideas. It will be seen, therefore, that the maxim applies separately, to the concrete or perceptual form of knowledge, and likewise to the abstract or conceptual form. This is because the stages of development are definitely repeated with regard to these; as they are also repeated, in different proportions as to the length and intensity of each stage, in all markedly new departures in knowledge during later life.

The Principle of Information.—The opinion that the chief, if not sole, end of so-called education is the imparting of as much information as possible in a given time, was formerly, and in many cases is still, held.

But this is in direct conflict with the views of education which we have contended for. Yet the view that
as much information as possible should be given, is
by no means entirely excluded from having a proper
place and function in a scientific system of educative
development. For we can only educate through
information, experiential and verbal, and the more
knowledge we can impart the better. Whenever information is really imparted more or less educational
development must result, whether this be designed and
systematic, or incidental and unmethodical. Hence
the greater the amount of information imparted, within
reasonable limits, the larger will be the resulting
development.

Herbart expresses the connection between education
and information thus : " I have no conception of education without instruction, just as, conversely, in this
book at least, I do not acknowledge any instruction
which does not educate. Whatever arts and acquirements a young man may learn from a teacher for the
mere sake of profit, are as indifferent to the educator as
the colour he chooses for his coat. But how his circle
of thought is being formed is everything to the teacher,
for out of thoughts come feelings, and from them principles and modes of action.

" To think out in relation to this chain of development each and everything that can be offered to the
pupil and find a place in his mind, to inquire how each
is connected with the whole, how one part must follow
another, and again become a link to that which succeeds
—this, applied to the treatment of individual objects,

affords an infinite number of problems to the teacher, and also unlimited material, by the help of which he can ceaselessly think over and criticise all the knowledge and works accessible, as well as all the principal occupations and exercises he must carry on."

The great difference between the educationist and the informationist is that the former regards the imparting of information, in the first place, as only a means of education, though finally as an end; whilst the latter always regards it as an end, and looks upon education as being merely the giving of information, or rather offering the individual an opportunity of appropriating it, if he can. The educationist asks : How can I so impart information that it shall draw out, exercise, develop, and improve the mental powers, and thus make the learner able to acquire knowledge in the most easy and effective way; but the informationist only concerns himself with the endeavour to thrust upon the individual as much information as it seems advisable for him to have. The educationist is ever striving to secure development by his work; but the mere informationist is only educative in so far as he cannot avoid it, and is driven to make use of educational processes by the inevitable necessities of the case.

We may, therefore, say that education proper prepares for the adequate reception of information, as such; and that appropriate information, as such, should, as a rule, be given only when the powers and processes necessary for its most effective appropriation have been satisfactorily developed. In other words,

the time to give information, at least to any considerable extent, otherwise than as directly necessary to
illustrate the details in educative processes, is when
the learner has acquired, through systematic educational
influences, the power to apply knowledge obtained to
the solution of problems, the interpretation of the experiences of others, and the invention of more or less
simple forms.

When the learner is thus able to deal with information, as such, the more he is provided with the better,
so long as it does not injuriously interrupt a proper
rate of progress. For in this way the mind is richly
stored with material which is always helpful to the
fuller and freer interpretation of both old and new
forms of knowledge, as well as being a pleasurable and
profitable possession in other directions. Also the
novelty thus provided is demanded by the principle
of interest as a constant stimulus to, and reward for,
vigorous attention and reproductive and constructive
effort.

Further, this is necessary to the proper progress of
knowledge. A wearisome repetition of the same small
circle of knowledge as based upon experience, is likely,
in the long run, to prove comparatively barren and
unsatisfactory with respect to the total development.
Whilst it is absolutely essential that education must
begin within the sphere of present experience and
knowledge, it is not less important that it should
gradually extend to knowledge more and more remote
from the actual environment and personal experience.
Information is an important and valuable means of

securing this extension; and rational inference is the only other means of so doing.

Information which is thus given, should, to a large extent, be of the greatest possible practical utility. As was pointed out in the discussion on the element of the "utility value" of educative forms of knowledge, practical life is, in many respects, the starting-point and goal of knowledge. It is as necessary, therefore, as it is pleasurable and profitable, to relate our knowledge as closely and extensively as possible with our lives. We cannot escape doing this, to a very considerable extent; and it is allowable and advisable that we should seek to do it in every reasonable way.

Dr. Bain says, of the ordinary facts of knowledge: " In so far as they are devoid of connection and system, they are information solely. In so far as they can be embodied in an orderly scheme—a descriptive method, which facilitates both the recollection and the understanding of them, they rise to some sort of training. They require the pupils to master the scheme, and so give them possession of it, as an art that they may themselves employ in dealing with similar detail." It is this power which comes from drilling in the art of systemising which makes the learning of Latin so valuable a mental training.

" All those facts that relate to useful operation in the arts of life, that serve to guide artificers in their work, and to instruct every one how to obtain desirable ends, constitute a vast body of useful information. The recipes of cookery, the arts of industry and of manufacture, the cure of disease, the procedure in courts of law, are most valuable as information ; but they are not regarded as giving us any form of discipline. . . .

"Nevertheless, it is not a low order of intelligence that has taken in, remembered, and is able to apply an extensive stock of maxims of practice and utility in various departments. There may not be anything amounting to high discipline, but there is an expenditure of good intellectual force. The higher the character of the work, the more scope is there for fine discrimination or accurate perception, in order to suit means to the end . . . . and when we touch the higher degrees, we come upon something that involves the best faculties or forces of the mind.

"The truth is, that for the higher professions the extent of practical knowledge is such that it cannot be comprehended, held together, or rendered sufficiently precise, unless we have a certain amount of science and scientific method, such as would probably come within the scope of discipline."

The high mental value, and great practical importance of information, as such, must not be lost sight of in education. But it should be remembered that the mind which has not had its powers and skill first developed is either lumbered or crushed with a mass of material. Not information but power to use it is the first aim of education. As Locke puts it : "The business of education is not, as I think, to make the young perfect in any one of the sciences, but so to open and dispose their minds as may best make them capable of any when they shall apply themselves to it."

The great danger to be avoided is what has been

called encyclopædism, or, as old writers on education termed it, pansophism. Strangely enough, Comenius, great thinker though he was, believed in pansophism. "Let all the arts and sciences," he said, " be taught in their elements in all schools, and more fully at each successive stage of the pupil's progress. It is by knowledge that we are what we are, and the necessary conclusion from this must be, ' Let all things be taught to all' " (Laurie).

Professor Laurie remarks on this passage : "The mind stored with facts, even if these be ordered facts, will not necessarily be much raised in the scale of humanity as an intelligence. The natural powers may be simply overweighted by the process, and the natural channels of spontaneous reason choked."

Speaking of the curriculum of the American schools of to-day, Dr. C. A. McMurry says : " Children have too much to learn. They become pack-horses, instead of free spirits walking in the fields of knowledge. . . . . The cultivation therefore, of a many-sided interest ceases to be a blessing as encyclopædic knowledge becomes its aim." He adds that we must not identify " many-sided interest with encyclopædic knowledge, but [with] such a detailed study of typical forms in each case as will give insight into that branch without any pretension to exhaustive knowledge."

But culture value in information must not be neglected, for this makes life richer and more delightful to the individual, and to the community. This should, therefore, be freely supplied through appropriate subjects. The giving of such through appropriate subjects is a very. important condition ; for, we submit, to use some of the choicest extracts of the great literary classics for the purpose of grammatical analysis, parsing, and, above all, of paraphrase, is much more likely to prevent the possibility of getting any culture influence from them than to obtain even a suggestion of it. It is not by mechanically pulling artistic wholes to pieces that we realise their æsthetic beauties. Literature should be presented as literature, and not as grammar, composition, etymology, archæology, or history.

So also the culture elements in history and geography must be kept quite clear from the more technical aspects, if they are to have their proper culture effect. Similarly, with respect to music and colour-work, there must be definite efforts to secure the realisation of the purely asthetic values of a song or a picture, apart from the technical details which are necessary for the production of the actual results. It is true that the more fully the practical details are understood the deeper and truer the purely artistic appreciation is likely to be; but the two things are distinct, as is shown by the fact that persons with really no technical knowledge often have the keenest possible appreciation of art, whilst there are those who have learnt to produce the mechanical effects of art but are quite without real artistic feeling.

We can now estimate more accurately the exact place and functions of institutions for students who are about eighteen years of age, and upwards. If such students have been subjected to an ordinarily full course of scientific education during their childhood and youth, they are no longer either in need of, or suitable for, the usual processes of education as carried on by a formal educator. The individual ought to have arrived, fully equipped, at the stage of self-education. All that is necessary, therefore, should be the supplying of appropriate, accurate, and advanced information.

Hence one of the chief functions of such institutions as universities, university colleges, technical colleges, and all places of learning of these kinds, is to provide the most complete and profound forms of information. We may say that all such as these should be places whose function is informational rather than educational. Nevertheless, it is as necessary in them, as elsewhere, that information should be presented in a scientifically educational way, if the student is to derive the greatest and highest good from it.

But the very highest function of such institutions is to encourage, provide for, and assist the student in that self-education which seeks to develop the productive and inventive ability to its best form. Hence research, investigation, experiment, scientific theorisation, invention, and constructive and destructive criticism, should be well provided for at such centres.

The Principle of Symbolism.—From the point of view of progress in knowledge, language is something upon which we must constantly exercise severe and searching criticism. But it is also, in its relation to logic, an instrument of criticism, for in so far as words—whose content of meaning is for the time being a known and fixed quantity—will fit into certain verbal forms, and fulfil the proper logical laws, they thereby prove them-

2 D

selves to be worthy of rational credence, or otherwise, with respect to definite inferences and implications.

In so far as the self-consistency of the verbal expression of judgments is concerned, we can test this by the laws of deductive logic. For example: if a writer argued that all boys are mischievous, later on mentioned that all boys are scholars, and finally concluded by asserting that it followed from what he had said that all scholars are mischievous, logic would show that the very words which are used do not allow of such a conclusion. In the first two judgments there is no implication of all scholars, and, therefore, there is in them no justification for making any judgment about all scholars.

The educator must demonstrate such principles as these in simple and concrete cases, so that the learner may be able to guard himself from the dangers of language. Since, in his early years, the learner is unable to grasp logical principles, as such, he should be drilled in what we may call concrete logic, of a simple and practically useful kind. For example, that great type of all syllogistic, or deductive, reasoning, which is involved in the following : all money is useful; all farthings are money; therefore, all farthings are useful; should be concretely demonstrated. Let there be provided four convenient boxes labelled, " all money," " useful," " all farthings," and " money."

Then the boxes may be placed near to each other, and connected by pieces of cardboard on which the predicate word is written. Thus could be arranged a concrete form of the first two sentences. Next the learner should be led to see that since the farthings are said to be money there is no reason why they should not be put in the box in the first line. So also with regard to the box labelled "money" in the second line. But this is only possible in that the box on the first line is said to represent "all money." If it had been "some money" the case would be different. This point could be worked out more fully afterwards, and thus other forms of syllogisms would be demonstrated.

When things have been arranged as just suggested, it will be quite clear that all farthings may be said to be useful. It is true that this kind of demonstration gives an almost purely quantitative, or class meaning, to syllogistic reasoning; but there is no real objection to this, since it is certainly the only way in which it can be intelligently understood in the percept period; and such a form of it leads up to the conceptual usage.

If it be agreed that such a process is likely to prove helpful to the learner, by forming habits of scientifically critical thought, then it ought to be regularly provided for, at least in the finishing exercises of each important stage of development. Much more ought the principles of logic to be a conscious possession and power in the case of the self-educator.

Some practical knowledge of the inductive canons of criticism should also be given. Especially should this be the case if we accept the conclusion that some form of natural science knowledge ought to be the first to be imparted to the young mind. Nothing is more necessary, or likely to be more helpful, than to get the youthful thinker to recognise, in however simple and

practical a form, that there may often be, and generally is, a plurality of causes for a given effect; and,
therefore, the real problem is to satisfy ourselves that,
in a particular instance, it is, and can be, only such-
and-such a cause which is actually present. This
involves an application of the logical "method of difference."

To give a very simple example: an inkstand may
have been left on a table in the schoolroom at the end
of morning school, and at the beginning of the afternoon
work it may be found lying on the floor, near the table,
and broken to pieces. An inquiry may be undertaken
as to how this came about. Even very young children
would be able to suggest several possible causes, such
as: someone purposely threw it down; it was acci-
dentally knocked down by a pupil when passing the
table; it was pushed down when some books were put
on the table; the table has been moved, and it was
shaken off; there has been a heavy storm of wind,
and it was blown off when the school door was opened;
and so on. So much will be quite sufficient to impress
the fact of the plurality of causes, and the need of
sufficient reasons for asserting that it was such-and-such
a cause which has led to the given effect.

Next as to which is to be considered the active cause
in this case. Let us suppose that it can be shown that
the inkstand was seen to be quite safe and sound on
the table five minutes before the beginning of afternoon
school, and that no one entered the room during that
five minutes. Further, that when the door was opened
there occurred a very violent gust of wind, which swept

through the room. Clearly, then, the only element of difference which can account for the change in the position and state of the inkstand is the force of the gust of wind. And it is known, from actual experience and experiment, that the wind is able to do such things. Therefore we conclude without hesitation, and with full rational certainty, that the wind was the cause of the fall of the inkstand.

Thus we demonstrate, in a very simple and commonplace way, the logical " method of difference," as involved in a practical form of inductive reasoning. Later on in the child's development more technical applications of the rule can be made, in its studies of the phenomena of natural science.

In this way language has become an instrument of scientific criticism of thought, through its inseparable connection with it, and through the original activities of thought criticism which it expresses and records, and which, expressed in technical forms, serve as mechanical means of testing the accuracy and reliability of a particular reasoning. More and more of the logical principles, in concrete applications, could be given as the powers of the pupil develop, and as occasion offers ; until he is finally introduced to the study of logic, as such.

Language has reached its highest uses when it thus becomes a means by which thought consciously checks and corrects itself. This function of symbolism should be made use of at the very earliest moment, and its full and explicit employment gradually and systematically developed. The full significance and value of this can only be shown by a complete discussion of the relations between logic and education.

One of the most important points to be observed in the use of language is that of proper gradation. Words which are quite familiar to the hearer, and which are used in a sense equally familiar to him, are the only suitable ones for imparting full and significant knowledge. Very great care and art, are, therefore, necessary in introducing new words, or groupings of words, which involve new significations. Very full material and opportunity for associating the sign and its significance must be provided.

Gradation in language means, of course, gradation in the thought which it symbolises. It is seldom that the form of a word, as such, is difficult to remember, but the content of meaning is very often so. Dr. Abbott remarks : " The ' In Memoriam ' is written mainly in monosyllables ; yet there is in it little which a child could thoroughly understand. . . . . But give a boy a piece of description, narrative, or stirring incident, and you will find that long words will create little difficulty." Mr. Welldon insists on the same truth in arguing that boys are allowed to begin the study of Shakespeare at too early an age. He says that, in his own case, he attributes the small pleasure he derived from his first reading of " Hamlet," as compared with the intense delight which he obtained from his first reading of " Faust," to the fact that he was too young when he read the former.

In connection with the above we may discuss the place of books in educational work. The right use of books in education is by no means a simple or easy matter to decide. Perhaps the most essential point to be considered is the fact that books are, primarily, records. They are, in themselves, dead voices, and, except under very favourable conditions of interpretation by the living voice of an expert, they are liable to all the misconstructions which the ambiguity of language, the literary style of the author, and the ignorance of readers can conjointly perpetrate.

There is no possibility of making the book say exactly what it means by such-and-such statements : of obtaining from it more detailed exposition, or fuller demonstration : or of securing from it a reply to individual objections to the assertions it contains. It simply contains so much matter, of which the reader is left to make the best, or worst, use that he can. All this must always be true of every book, except in so far as the reader has been carefully and wisely prepared for rightly using and understanding a particular book. That is, the principle of preparation is an essential condition to the best use of books for educational purposes.

Books, as educational agencies, should primarily represent the best forms of summaries and records of knowledge, gained in the usual way. To this end the first books should be the direct outcome of lessons, and the student's own efforts. In other words, the learner must make and use his own books before he is allowed to—or, indeed, can profitably—make use of those made by others. This must be true, if what we have previously said about the use of words be correct.

Let us illustrate this by an example. The earliest

formal and systematic lesson on a natural object—in the later stages of kindergarten work—will necessarily be a language lesson as well as a thought and information lesson. The new words introduced should be written on the blackboard; the sentences in which they are properly used should also be so recorded; and these sentences ought to be combined so as to form a simple narrative. Thus the blackboard is the earliest form of the book, for formal educational purposes. In this way we proceed from experiences to ideas, from ideas to expressions, and from expressions to records.

When the purpose and significance of books have thus become real and familiar, they may be used as substitutes. for the learner's own records, to expand them, and, finally, to supplant them; and even to introduce a new subject, when the stage of regressive advance has been reached. We may say, therefore, that, except in the very latest stage of ordinary school education, the text-book should invariably be used as a convenient record and summary of the results of concrete demonstrations and oral instruction. Its proper use is to serve for purposes of revision, and not of introduction, much less as a substitute for experience and demonstration. As Mr. H. G. Wells insists, in his lecture on science teaching: "Above all, except in the upper forms, there would be no text-book. Each pupil would build up his own in his note-book as he proceeded."

The chief function of books, in education, is to be an aid to self-education. Mr. Wells urges that: "The ideal school should have a good library . . . . and therein would be all the big science text-books . . . . and to these the boy or girl in the higher forms would go for facts and discussions, guided at first by references provided by the teacher. In this way the ability to use books intelligently, and to work alone, would be acquired."

It may be remarked here that the purely literary reading-book should—except as the records of stories told orally, in prose or verse—follow the properly descriptive and informational reading-book, at each stage of development. And this because its effective use can only thus be properly provided for; and, also, because the æsthetic powers to which it ministers are later in their development.

We must remember that want of exactness in the use of words will tend to bring about inaccuracy in thought. Dr. Sully emphasises this fact, and urges that the learner " Should be well practised from the first in explaining the words he employs. It is of great importance to see that a child never employs any word without attaching some intelligible meaning to it. He should be questioned as to his meaning, and prove himself able to give concrete instances or examples of the notion, and (where possible) to define his term, roughly at least."

The Principle of Gradation.—A truth which has been forced upon us with special emphasis during the previous discussions is : that development is very gradual both in quality, quantity, and kind. Again and again, we have had to urge the need of the most careful consideration being given to the securing of the right order, amount, and time, for the various developing influences.

Educators might well have as their mottoes: " Make haste slowly "; and " Precept upon precept, precept upon precept; line upon line, line upon line; here a little, and there a little." There is no principle in the whole range of the science of education which is of greater importance than this. Too much, or too little, of stimulation, nourishment, and exercise: too rapid, or too slow, a rate of advance: or too spasmodic, and too violent, bursts of development, must mean a warped, or dwarfed, development.

Rousseau has the following passages in his " Emile." " May I venture to state here the greatest, the most important, the most useful rule in all education? It is not to gain time but to lose it. Forgive the paradox, O my ordinary reader! It must be uttered by any one who reflects, and whatever you may say, I prefer paradoxes to prejudices. . . . . Listen to a little fellow who has just been under instruction. Let him prattle, question, blunder, just as he pleases, and you will be surprised at the turn your reasonings have taken in his mind. He confounds one thing with another; he reverses everything; he tires you, sometimes worries you, by unexpected objections. He forces you to hold your peace, or to make him hold his."

Very much, therefore, depends upon the clear and complete understanding of what is involved in this principle, and we can hardly spend too much time or effort in the endeavour to thoroughly grasp its nature and implications. A great deal has already been said about it, since it is but a special aspect of the general principle of development. That is, the principle seeks to secure in the educative influences a development coinciding as nearly as possible, and co-operating, with what we believe to be the proper development of mind.

We will briefly recall what has been previously said about this principle. When dealing with the principle of stimulation, we urged that the quantity, proportion, and duration of influences and re-actions, must be properly regulated. Similarly, the quality and quantity of nourishment must be appropriate. The principle of preparation may be regarded as a specially systemised effort in gradation, in that it involves a deliberate and thorough provision for the easy and right reception and appreciation of experiences.

The great central and fundamental principle of development may be described as a principle of gradation. It enforces and emphasises the great truth of the necessity of proceeding in certain definite orders. Gradation is the burden of the maxims : from the concrete to the concrete : from the concrete to the abstract : from the abstract to the concrete. So also with the other practical rules, and the educational meaning which they possess ; they all insist upon the need of gradation.

But the most explicit and emphatic statement of the essential feature of the principle is contained in what has been said about the maxim : from the simple to the complex. In the several discussions of this maxim, we have constantly insisted upon the necessity of observing the order of greatest simplicity, because complexity is the chief element of difficulty to both mind and body. Professor L. C. Miall remarks : " Whatever subject you handle, go for simplicity of impression. If you bring in many details, make them help one another."

So, again, the principles of doing, sympathetic control, analysis and synthesis, and symbolism, all involve, imply, and explicate, the idea of gradual increase in kind and degree of the processes and produces of development. All the concrete examples and illustrations of these principles which have been given show in detail how the elements of gradation have to be provided for.

We may sum up the significance of these, by saying that the principle of gradation must provide for the careful observance of the following features in any system of developing influences. First, they must, at each stage, correspond, as exactly as possible, with the nature and vigour of the actual developing powers, so that, whilst providing for, and encouraging those powers which may be expected to immediately follow, they may not prevent or pervert those which are explicitly developing.

Secondly, they must change in their kind and degree according to the significant changes in the development of the individual. This is a very wide condition, and embraces all that is implied in the progress from the known to the unknown, the simple to the complex, the concrete to the abstract, childhood to manhood, ignorance to knowledge, weakness to strength, inability and awkwardness to capacity and facility, and so on.

Besides these there are other points about which it will be well to say a few words. We have before dwelt upon the need of clearness in overcoming the difficulty presented by a complex. But this point is deserving of further notice. Dr. De Garmo deals with it under the term "the law of successive clearness." He speaks of the need of a certain amount of time for presentations to be properly apperceived, and then says : " Upon the fact that certain easily distinguishable amounts of time are required for this reception and apprehension of individual notions, and the interaction between individual and general conceptions, is based the law of successive clearness.

"This law was first announced by Ratich [Ratke], and was afterwards developed and applied by Herbart and Ziller. According to this idea, the matter of instruction must not be presented in the mass, but in small, logically connected sections, to each of which, in succession, the pupil should give his undivided attention. In this way, one by one, individual notions are clearly perceived. . . . . After the mind has given its concentrated attention to each of the successive sections of the lesson in turn, these subdivisions must be brought into close relation and connection, i.e., . . . into a unity in consciousness."

Now this method of procedure clearly involves the existence of a series. As Dr. De Garmo goes on to say : " It is a prime duty of the teacher to see that the elements of what is presented are arranged in natural series, so that intimate and lasting associations can be formed." This applies not only to the details within the same unit, but also to items of knowledge which do not appear to have any obvious organic connection, c.g., arithmetical tables, declensions, conjugations, formation of genders, geographical names, historical dates, and the like. Herein lies the value of any reasonable system of mnemonics.

Another very important feature in the principle of gradation is that of regularity. The cumulation of effect, which comes from a constant and uninterrupted addition of suitable amounts, is of the very greatest value. Both substance and power are thus secured. Dr. Abbott insists that: " Second-rate regular teaching is better for the very young than first-rate teaching, if the latter be very irregular." This applies as much to the details of a sound system as to the system itself. By regularity, progress is made more easy, consistent, and permanent.

A gradual increase in the rapidity with which processes are carried through should also be provided for. Facility in action is as much a matter of development as power in action. Only when the details of an action, or a series of actions, are thoroughly familiar, and when the pupil can accurately perform them—taking as much time as he finds necessary for this—should there be any endeavour to cultivate speed for its own sake. When, however, this stage has been reached then rapidity should be striven for.

Then there is what we may call the element of grasp. A beginner is only able to take account of small and single things. Later on he can manage larger things, and a few at a time. This applies both to mental and physical matters. The educator must, therefore, carefully graduate the size and number of the items dealt with. Here, as elsewhere, we must expect that, as a rule, success will come through failure, and accuracy through inaccuracy.

Both in perceptual and conceptual development we must observe each and all of these conditions of gradations. More particularly, the practical educator should take note that he will have to begin over again, so to speak, when he comes to deal with explicit conceptual development, after the perceptual has been brought to a comparatively high level. Dr. Bain remarks : " All the difficulties of the higher knowledge have reference to the generalising process—the seeing of one in many. The arts of the teacher and the expositor are supremely requisite in sweetening the toil of this operation."

Always, and in everything, the principle of inter-relation and inter-dependence must be combined with that of gradation. Step by step we must pass out of the old into the new, from the near to the remote. There ought not to be any attempts at making jumps in education. However briefly and lightly we may be able to deal with certain elements in a given case, we must always assure ourselves that the power is there, and that it is able to fully discharge its proper duties.

Very careful attention needs to be given to the actual physical powers and capacities, and their progressive development. The vigour, acuteness, and capacity of the sense organs, and of the whole muscular system, have an essential bearing upon the ordering of the educating influences. The great differences which have to be made because of such considerations are best shown in the case of exceptionally bright or dull children. In Germany they have special schools for such. In these schools the dull child is allowed to take an hour for what would take an ordinary child about ten minutes; whilst the very susceptible pupil is promptly sent off to play—or to bed—directly it begins to get over-excited by its work.

From an easy task to one somewhat less easy, the learner should be led on, step by step, to more and more difficult work. Each step, in the earlier stages, must be well within his grasp and power; but it should increase in difficulty, both as to quality and quantity, according to his growing capacities and knowledge. It is often the beginnings of things which are most difficult.

This does not mean that the pupil is never to have any task in which there is a serious difficulty for him to overcome. Occasionally such tasks should be designedly given, so that he may realise the element of difficulty, and learn to appreciate the real value of his previous training, and the power of the method of gradual attack and progressive mastery. The judicious use of problems just in advance of the pupil's power and knowledge is one of the most stimulating influences. But such ought always to be, more or less directly, based upon work actually done, and powers known to be possessed. Easy new adaptations, and applications of old knowledge, are all that ought to be expected from beginners.

Dr. Abbott says: "Sometimes we must set easy tasks so as to generate a habit of reasonable self-reliance, and prevent the pupil from becoming dispirited by continual failures. Sometimes we must set more difficult tasks, such as involve some wholesome strain of the powers, so as to lead the child up to a higher standard of exertion, and prevent him from becoming too easily contented with himself."

As with other principles, so with this, the fuller reading of it must be borne in mind. From the easy to the easy: from the easy to the difficult: from the difficult to the difficult: and from the difficult to the easy, make up the fuller reading. The secret of success for the practical educator is the rule: Gradation; again gradation; and always gradation.

Some General Remarks.—A few quotations from writers on the practice of education will be sufficient to show that the principles discussed in this chapter have forced themselves upon practical workers. Professor Huxley insists on the principle of information in the following passage: "The business of education is, in the first place, to provide the young with the means and the habit of observation; and, secondly, to supply the subject-matter of knowledge, either in the shape of science or of art, or of both combined."

Dr. Fitch puts the value of this principle very forcibly in these words: "We must not, in our zeal for those parts of instruction which are specially educative, lose sight of the value of even empirical instruction about these things. To impart facts is not a teacher's highest business, but it is a substantial part of his business. . . . . The best reasons for seeking to give your pupils a good basis of facts are that the possession of them is very useful; that all future scientific generalisation pre-supposes them; that they furnish pabulum

2 E

for the thought and the imagination ; and generally that life is rich and interesting in proportion to the number of things we know and care about."

The principle of symbolism is recognised in the following opinion of the late Professor Freeman, the historian : " The difference between good and bad teaching mainly consists in this, whether the words used are really clothed with a meaning or not." Mr. Thring points out the great value of words as an aid to thought, and says : " The schoolboy who will not study words had better follow the plough, for he will never be a thinker of thoughts. . . . . New words mean new powers of thought." This same truth is thus expressed by Dr. De Garmo : " Language reflects thought as the mirror reflects the image of him who stands before it. For this reason the study of language is often the most direct road to an understanding of the various elements of thought."

David Stow bases his " Training System " almost wholly on what he calls " picturing out in words," which, he argues, " enables the pupils to draw the lesson or deduction [*i.e.*, 'the inference which every complete sentence or paragraph is intended to convey '] in their own language, the master acting throughout the whole process as the trainer or conductor, and only furnishing facts which he ascertains that the children do not know, and, therefore, for the sake of advancement, must be told." He adds : " We cannot picture out or express objects with which we are not acquainted."

He also wisely remarks : " Any word used by a speaker

or teacher, and not clearly apprehended by his pupils, is without meaning; by the person speaking it may be perfectly understood, but to those addressed, he in reality speaks in a foreign tongue. . . . . A reverend divine, on being requested to examine the Sabbath-school children of a friend, commenced by putting the following question : ' Children, in the work of regeneration, can you tell me whether the spirit operates causally or instrumentally ?' If these children could have answered this question, they might certainly have been transplanted, we think, to the Divinity Hall of the University."

Dr. De Garmo sets forth the principle of gradation from the practical side, thus : "The matter of instruction must, therefore, be presented in natural subdivisions, thus giving resting-places which allow the mind to recover from its absorption, and to fortify itself against distraction by bringing its knowledge into wholes. How minute the subdivisions of the lessons should be, must be determined by the age and mental strength of the pupils. . . . . If the steps of reasoning in a problem are not separated and mastered one by one, there is instant danger of confusion, though the amount which a pupil can master at one impulse grows with advancing mental ability. The same law holds, also, in all other branches."

A good example of the practical use of this principle is given by Dr. Abbott. He advises teachers to adopt the following method in teaching a book of Cæsar. " Select from the book to be studied, fifteen or twenty of the most difficult of the long sentences, exhibiting most

prominently the ordinary complications that perplex
boys—abundant conjunctions, the idioms of oratio
obliqua, sentences subordinate to others which are themselves in turn subordinate, ambiguous pronouns, and
the like. Do not show these sentences to your pupils
as yet; but take them to pieces and show them the
pieces separately. Then, by degrees, put the pieces together, and make the boys help you in building up the
complete sentence."

From the two preceding quotations it will be seen
how the principles of gradation and analysis and synthesis are practically combined. Such combinations
are found in many of the illustrations.

The application of the various maxims, and several of
the general principles, to the higher branches of study
is well shown in Dr. R. Wormell's book " Plotting or
Graphic Mathematics." In the introduction, the author
says : " Although the educational methods which are
associated with the name of Froebel have been brought
very near to perfection in the kindergarten, they are to
a great extent suspended when the pupil passes from
the infant school. They reappear, however, in the
schools and colleges for technical and experimental
science. The graphical and synthetical methods of comparing results and tracing laws, which have been extensively developed in these colleges, are but an
advanced application of Froebellian methods. . . . .

" The charm of the method, as in the kindergarten,
is inherent in its nature. It gives something to be done
by the hand and followed by the eye—keeping pace
with the course of thought and reasoning. The proof

of a rule or law often lies entirely in the process by which the rule or law is graphically illustrated, and the consequence is that the pupil, while following the course, is constantly on a voyage of discovery, and has all the pleasure and stimulus of an original investigator."

Rousseau says : "Whatever the study may be, without the idea of the things represented the signs representing them go for nothing" (Quick). Comenius writes : "Let words always be conjoined with things. Thereby we shall learn about realities" (Laurie). Montaigne argues that : "For learning to judge well and speak well, whatever presents itself to our eyes serves as a sufficient book" (Compayré).

A good instance of the application of the principle of information is given by Comenius, when he urges that : "The child may receive elementary notions even of politics, in observing that certain persons assemble at the city hall, and that they are called councillors ; and that among these persons there is one called mayor, &c." (Compayré).

The principle of gradation has been put very clearly, in its philosophic form, by Descartes (1596–1650), as follows : "The first precept is never to receive anything for true that I do not know, upon evidence, to be such . . . . and to comprise no more within my judgments than what is presented so clearly and distinctly to my mind that I have no occasion to call it in question" (Compayré).

CHAPTER X

DETERMINANTS OF MENTAL GROWTH AND DEVELOPMENT

General Determinants.—That which is alive is always in a state of greater or lesser activity, and this activity necessarily involves more or less waste. It is absolutely necessary for such waste to be repaired if life is to continue. This means that nourishment must be supplied to, and assimilated by, all living organisms. It must follow from this that according to the kind of nourishment and the results of the assimilation of it will be the general condition of the organism.

Now the assimilation of nourishment will be according to the nature of that which assimilates and that which is assimilated. We must, therefore, take into consideration, in connection with this matter, the proper nature of mind and of that which nourishes it. Both of these have been somewhat fully dealt with in the preceding chapters, and it only remains to notice some special elements of relation between them.

The general relation is one of action and reaction.

Organism and nourishment interact upon each other. Neither is an absolute principal at any moment, and, therefore, neither is an absolute subordinate.   There are always elements of initiative and of passive reaction in each.   But, at the same time, there is a general predominance of the human organism, both as to initiative and control, in the processes involved.   This is of consequence because it implies, at least in a practical sense, that the element of responsibility rests largely upon the human being with regard to the particular character of actual development.

But it is not implied that this practical responsibility rests wholly, or even chiefly, upon the individual. Up to a certain point it is laid upon those who have charge of him, such as parents, guardians, and teachers. Sooner or later, however, the individual must himself be responsible, although this responsibility must always be shared in, to some extent, by the society in which he lives, in so far as it in any way limits or controls his life.

The original nature of the individual is, therefore, of essential importance in determining the general and particular nature of his development. The element of mere growth is chiefly dependent upon the kind and amount of nourishment, and the possession of the ordinary powers of assimilation.   Hence these are the two fundamental determinants.

Since the mental powers are always engaged in receiving, interpreting, relating, recording, and organising into higher relations, the significations of experience, we may regard experiences, in the very widest sense, as constituting the whole and sole nourishment for mind. We shall, therefore, deal with the subject-matter of this chapter under two heads : the original character of the human being, and experiences.

In both of these there are constant, irregular, and accidental elements. Those elements are constant which exert a regular power or influence for considerable periods, or during the whole of life. In the original character of an individual they will be such qualities as impulsiveness, optimism, pessimism, reserve, timidity, sulkiness, and so on. Amongst influences there will be : food, exercise, light and darkness, social life, and others.

Irregular elements will be those which occur more or less frequently, but at uncertain and often lengthy intervals. In the individuality of a person there may be involved elements which cause occasional periods of intense dulness or gaiety, hope or despondency, and the like. Among the experiences there are : occasional spells of foreign travel, indulgence in special pleasures, sickness, notable success, disheartening failure, and so on.

Accidental elements are those which seem never to repeat themselves, or, at most, to do so after exceptionally long intervals. Such are : slips into violent impatience of those who have exceptional patience as a rule, great excitement at some critical moment in a characteristically phlegmatic person, and the like, with regard to individuality ; and, a very serious accident, a complete loss of fortune, the death of a particularly dear friend, and the like, amongst experiences.

All the above exert special influences, either favourable or adverse, upon the development of an individual. The constant and irregular have varying but considerable effect because of their repetition. The accidental frequently bring about very definite results, on account of their impressiveness and rareness.

Every single power and experience has, of course, its share, however small, in determining the general line of development. But very many are so slight in themselves and so sub-conscious in their effects that we can practically afford to neglect them. As a matter of fact, however, they are important in that they form a kind of background which throws into more striking relief the definitely significant elements.

Another point which demands attention is the fact that only at certain periods of life is the individual directly determined to any considerable extent by general influences. After a certain time he is only indirectly determined by these, the direct and most powerful influence being that of the more or less developed self. It is during infancy that most is directly done by external influences. These gradually have less and less direct effect, and more and more indirect effect, through the reason.

Determinants may be classified also as formative and directive. Those determinants are formative which supply nourishment to the self. They may be either external or internal. All kinds of physical materials, sensations, percepts, and general experiences, which go to supply the elements of the bodily, mental, and moral powers, make up the external group. The internal will include what may be spoken of as all the purely self-given elements. Just as the body, though dependent upon the nourishment which it receives from outside itself, may be rightly said to give to such material much of its final nutritive value, so the mind puts into its nourishment (in new forms) much of the goodness of it.

Directive determinants include those elements of influence which result from the methods, whether implicit or explicit, involved in the efforts to secure development. If, for example, logical and scientific methods are uniformly involved in the organising of the influences brought to bear upon an individual, they will, in course of time, produce similar methods in the activities of the developing organism. These will in time become habits, and in such form they will have a permanent and powerful influence in determining the nature of the development. The want of good methods will certainly be more or less unfavourable to the best form of development.

Good directive determinants add skill, and, therefore, power to the activities of the self. They make easier and more effective the necessary self-efforts of the individual. Whilst not in themselves directly adding to the substance, so to speak, of mind, they indirectly assist in its growth, by perfecting the effectiveness of the activities concerned in it. There should, therefore, be constant effort to secure them.

From another point of view all determinants may be divided into involuntary and voluntary. The involuntary are those which are due to what we may call the inevitable minimum of organic activity necessary to the

being and existence of an organism, as such. This is
due to an inexplicable element—an unknown quantity
—which we term vital force. So far, therefore, as the
inevitable activities of organisms other than the self
must inevitably affect the self, in so far we look upon
such determination as involuntary. There are the com-
pelling influences of what we call the force of circumstances, over which, we say, we have no control.

But when the equally inexplicable individuality of
the human being has taken definite form, and begins
to assert itself, then we have voluntary determinants.
By voluntary determinants then we mean the self-
determination of the self. The individual develops a
power of initiation, and becomes aggressive, in respect
to his own development. A man, as we say, seeks his
own good in his own way. More will be said of this a
few pages on.

In organising the conditions for making certain
determinants most effective in their form and function
care must be taken that there is plenty of time for the
complete reception, assimilation, and organisation of the
elements which are to constitute the determinant.
For example, if it is desired that truthfulness should
control the speech and thought of an individual, it
must not be expected that one or two exhortations or
corrections will be sufficient to establish such a determinant.

There must be the careful and repeated demonstration of what truthfulness and untruthfulness involve in
themselves and their effects, from the practical point of
view at first. Then there must follow proper opportu-

nities for practising truthfulness under reasonable tests.
This should continue until truthfulness is a habit.
Then there may be an exposition of the higher nature
of the virtue and its place and function in an ethical
system. Thus it may be developed to its highest
powers as a determinant.

Original Character of the Human Being.—In this there
are obviously two elements : the racial and the individual. Both of these require to be intelligently understood and definitely provided for in all the essential
educational processes. To be too much taken up with
either the one element or the other, to the practical
neglect or omission of either, must involve more or less
mischievous results.

Were it not the case that every human being
possesses substantial and permanent general resemblances, we could not even know the human being as a
type, genus, or class. On the other hand, if there were
not also substantial and permanent individual differences
we could not know one species, or smaller class, of men
from others, or one individual from another in the same
species. The fact that we do know them in the senses
suggested is sufficient evidence that there exist such
invariable common qualities, and such varying individual ones.

White men, black men, yellow men, and red men,
are all animals, however much or little this element
may be restrained and refined in them, and they are all
rational, no matter to what extent, large or small, this
quality has been developed. Civilisation is a matter of
degree and not of fundamental difference. It has been

forcibly said that one has but to scratch a civilised person to find the savage in him.

Racial Elements.—Man from the racial point of view is a rational animal. His rationality and animality are, so far as we know, absolutely inseparable, but the nature of each is perfectly distinct and characteristic. This difference is summed up in the distinction between mind and matter—a philosophical and profound question into which we have no need to go since we are only concerned with the empirical aspects of scientific knowledge.

Each of these factors—mind and body—have their own special and characteristic place and functions in the general problem. Each brings a certain total of practically invariable powers and processes to take part in the general working of the human being as an organism. The mind, through its powers of intellectual assimilation and discrimination, and their various forms, not only interprets the world for the individual as a whole, but, in so doing, also enables the body to secure the most favourable conditions for itself. The body by its powers of physical assimilation of different kinds, brings the mind into communication with the outer world, and so makes it possible for the mind to obtain the best conditions for its growth and development. It does this chiefly through its powers of receiving all kinds of sense-impressions, and also through its power of locomotion.

At any one period in the history of a race it may be said to have certain general characteristics which are the results of its previous history. This will not involve very much with regard to the race as a whole, because of the very numerous and important variations in the rate of civilisation of the different branches of the human family. For example, so far as is known, every branch of the race has employed, to a greater or lesser extent, fire as a means of cooking food. Man might, therefore, be clearly distinguished from other animals by being termed a food-cooking animal.

With respect to certain sections of mankind, especially the more civilised peoples, there are many common qualities possessed by the individuals composing them. For example, we may mention : forms of government, systems of industry and trade, social forms and ceremonies and the like. All such have had very considerable effects in moulding individuals to a common type, within certain limits.

A given group of human beings may, therefore, be regarded as having common resemblances very much in excess of what the whole race has. So that whilst a system of developing conditions could be devised which would be suitable for all mankind up to a certain point, any attempt to go further with such a scheme would break down because of the common resemblances ceasing there.

But a scheme could be formed which would go very much further with all the nations of Western Europe, but only up to the point where common characteristics prevailed. Again a common plan would hold up to a still higher point for each separate nation ; and even to a more advanced one for distinct groups within a nation—as to special subjects and purposes. Wherever similarities of characteristics prevail there, obviously, common conditions for development are favourable, with regard to such like qualities and up to, at least, an average development of them.

In all ordinary matters, all ordinary human beings can attain to an average standard of power and skill. The great majority of people are always approximating to such a level. There are comparatively few who either very much exceed, or fall short of, this. Not only are we all very human, but we are most of us very averagely human. Fortunately this average is not a fixed quantity, as the progress of a race from savagery to civilisation shows.

To put the matter briefly: every class of objects has its inevitable and permanent minimum of characteristics common to its members and marking them off from every other class. It is only thus that we can know classes, and it is as futile to ignore this as it would be to neglect the individual differences. The essential resemblances of violins to one another are as constant and as characteristic as their more or less superficial differences of material, form, and tone, from those of cornets, are unmistakable.

In living organisms there has been a perpetual transmission from individual to individual of these common resemblances of nature and form, through all the ages. Not that either has remained absolutely constant, but the essential elements have never fundamentally changed. Heredity has not only thus continued the type, but has also continued those important differences which mark off the various races and distinct groups of men.

All that has been said with regard to the human being as a whole is peculiarly true of the mental activities of man. As Mr. Herbert Spencer remarks: "Some of the best illustrations of functional heredity are furnished by the mental characteristics of the human race."

One interesting and important fact connected with heredity deserves special notice. Though heredity, as a rule, tends to hand on the general elements of progress, yet it sometimes, so to put it, turns backward the stream of resemblance, and an individual comes into existence who is very closely alike to those of the same class in past times. This is known as a reversion to ancestral type.

Individual Elements.—We have previously remarked that there are, practically, infinite differences as well as infinite similarities amongst what we term classes of things, and throughout the universe. For us the similarities are of primary importance for they mean coherence, significance, system and knowledge; whilst the infinite differences could, by themselves, only cause chaos in the mental world. Of course absolutely infinite similarity could mean nothing more than "a something" to us, for the element of relativity would be absent. Similarity and difference are absolutely necessary to each other so far as the constitution of our knowledge of the world is concerned.

It is doubtless true to say, even from the practical point of view, that no two things have ever been, or are likely to be, found absolutely and entirely similar. It might be thought that two straight lines of equal length and thickness would satisfy the conditions. But a microscope would show that the inevitable irregularity of the sides of such lines would not exactly coincide. If this be true of form how much more likely is it to be so of content.

We may take it, therefore, that every distinct and separate member of a class is, from the very beginning of its existence, more or less different from every other member. It starts, so to say, with an element of bias, which will cause it to deviate, to a greater or lesser extent, from the common course, whilst generally conforming therewith. A totality so infinitely complex as a human being is more liable to such variations than almost any other whole in the universe. This is the source and substance of individuality ; which may be said to consist in special forms, or combinations, of ordinary attributes.

A good illustration of what is here meant is afforded by the making of violins. Two violins may be made from a single piece of wood which seems in all respects to be uniform throughout. The same person makes both, and takes every pains and means to produce every detail in both instruments as exactly similar to each other as he possibly can. And yet the invariable result would be that a difference of tone, often a very great one, will be found between the two.

Such a fact is really a mystery to us. We can only say that it appears to be inevitable. Dr. Höffding says : " The inner unity, to which all elements refer, and by virtue of which the individuality is a psychical individuality, remains for us an eternal riddle." But

2 F

though in itself it is unexplainable, yet we can point out ways in which it is emphasised and developed.

Heredity appears to affect individuality as well as type. If a parent has well marked peculiarities, whether physical or mental, or both, there is almost sure to be a predisposition in an offspring to develop similar peculiarities. It was formerly thought that such attributes were inevitably handed on, as positive possessions, to the next generation. But this theory is now regarded as untenable, and it is held that there is nothing more than a tendency to develop such qualities. If the conditions of life are favourable to their growth they will definitely appear; but under other circumstances they may never take positive form.

The great developing influence of individuality is, however, the reaction of the general organism itself to the influences which affect it. Just as with the two violins referred to above, though the same bow may be drawn across the strings by the same hand in a practically identical manner, yet the responding tones are very different in special character though generally alike; so influences which are practically identical produce reactions in the human being, which though on the whole of a like character have elements of special difference.

For example: a lecture, which to one person is interesting and instructive, is to another also inspiring; and whilst it gives to both knowledge, it may arouse in only one of them an effort of self-endeavour, because of the element of difference in the total complex of the self. Herbart says: "The entire life, the whole observation of mankind, proves that every one makes out of his experience and intercourse something answering to himself—that he here works out the ideas and feelings he has brought with him."

When hereditary tendencies are developed by favouring circumstances they emphasise individuality, and cause experiences to have a special effect, in addition to the ordinary results. This becomes cumulative, and in course of time it may even become the predominant feature in the influence of experiences. This is seen in the case of persons who are said to be eccentric. Their individuality has become so pronounced that it prejudices the ordinary effects of experiences.

Thus the original germ of individuality, if we may so call it, is in itself a means of furthering its own development. But with this, as with all other elements, there is an ordinary amount of development in the average person. As a rule each person has just enough individuality to mark him off clearly and distinctly from his fellows. Only comparatively few have such striking personalities as to stand out like solitary mountains in an otherwise gently undulating area. And, again, not very many are so wanting in special characteristics as to seem colourless.

So far as it is valuable or expedient, to develop any or all of a person's peculiarities, as constituting his individuality, it is quite clear that there must be special influences brought to bear upon him, and special conditions favourable to his nature provided. Systems for furthering development which suit another, therein fail to be suitable for him, so far as his individuality is concerned.

It is, however, a first condition for the best development of individuality that all the ordinary common characteristics of the individual shall have been developed to, at least, an average extent. There can be no more fatal mistake than to assume that any one power of mind, or body, can be brought to its most powerful and fullest state of development by receiving exclusive attention. This is impossible from the very nature of mind itself. To impoverish the many powers will finally result in destroying the support of the one, and will always more or less prejudice its soundness and thoroughness.

Experiences.—Mind builds itself up from experiences, and these are, of course, provided by the surroundings. According as the individual is more or less limited to a definite environment, and this environment itself is of a more or less constant character, so will the effects of the surroundings upon the individual be more marked and definite. This is well seen in the cases of a typical rustic and a typical cockney, or in those of the book-worm and the man of affairs.

From what has been said about individuality it will be seen that the same environment will have different, as well as similar, effects upon various individuals. We must, therefore, consider not only the nature and influence of the environment as a whole, but also the special classes of stimuli which are found in it, and their influences upon individuals. We will proceed, therefore, to discuss the subject under the heads of environment and stimuli.

1. **Environment.**—The general surroundings of man

may be divided into the physical, social, and purely rational. The physical will include all those concretes which we usually call natural objects, and all those activities which we call physical. In the social environment will be all those influences which arise out of the family life, companionship, national life, local and central government, sports and pastimes, and the like, in a practical sense. Purely rational environment will embrace all those influences which act through the intelligence only, such as general and scientific literature, periodicals, systems of what is called higher education, and all study of the pure sciences, philosophy, and metaphysics.

Physical environment acts most directly and predominantly through climatic and other such physical influences. Upon these depend to a large extent the more general modifications of the physiological powers and parts. Thus the inhabitant of Central Africa is more fitted to resist those effects of heat which would probably prove very disastrous to an Esquimaux; whilst the Esquimaux can endure extremes of cold which would doubtless prove fatal to the Central African.

Then again, the body has acquired special power in assimilating those foods which are best suited to the climatic conditions of a locality. The dweller in the Arctic regions lives largely on blubber, and regards a tallow candle as a perfect luxury in diet, whilst the inhabitant of tropical countries can be perfectly happy on an almost exclusively rice diet, with ripe fruit as a relish. Thus the former is best fitted to survive rigorous cold, and the latter intense heat.

EDUCATION

All such circumstances have a very direct and general effect upon the mind. Their results are general, specific, and individual. The fact that men have to meet and provide against the undesirable effects of climate, brings out the powers of the mind in devising more or less ingenious and complex ways of doing so. Habitations, dress, diet, and so on, are adapted to meet the necessities of the cases. So far similar kinds, but not details, of effects are produced universally.

Specific effects are produced in the special lines of thought and action which have to be taken in dealing with the particular kinds of climatic and other geographical conditions. Because of this, the modes of thought of a Mexican would differ very considerably, as to the practical point of view, from that of a Patagonian. The local colour, so to speak, would be very marked. The individual effects would be due to the fact that each person would respond to the influences in a manner more or less different from that of his fellows, according to the strength of his individuality, in the sense already discussed.

To put the matter in another way, all mankind will be alike in that they have to adapt themselves to their environment. All Europeans will be alike in so far as they have to meet generally similar conditions of surroundings, but different from Asiatics so far as the conditions are different. All the individuals of a European country will be alike, inasmuch as the general environment is common, and different from those of all other countries as far as these differ. Similarly, each person in distinct groups of individuals in a country will agree with each other, and differ from those of other groups. Individuals will vary from each other according to the foregoing, and, in so far as they react differently upon the influences which affect them, because of their individuality.

Hygienic conditions, as involved in the physical environment, are of the very highest importance. Good hygienic conditions represent the most perfect practical forms of natural surroundings. They are, therefore, of very great and direct physiological value, and of equally considerable and indirect psychological worth.

Of the actual way in which the physical environment acts upon the body, and therefore upon the mind, the different physical and mental sciences give us more or less complete information. It is only as we know these that we are able to most effectively organise the action of physical influences.

Dr. Karl Lange says: " It is not a matter of indifference whether we passed our youth in a quiet, retired forest-village, or in a dark, damp dwelling in the turmoil of the metropolis. It is not the same whether we played before the door of a lonely hut on the heath, or whether mighty mountain giants looked in at us through the window early and late. . . . . Different in many respects are the thoughts and feelings of the child from the metropolis and the child from the village or country town."

The social environment acts in a similar way to the physical, and, therefore, we need only point out the principal elements of it. It affects both the physical and rational sides of man's nature, in a practical and direct manner. The necessities of social life considerably modify both the physical and rational life. Manners and customs very largely control our modes of action, dress, and thought.

Though manners and customs had, in most cases, an original appropriateness for the actual conditions of life, they often survive their fitness and become obstacles and hindrances to development, if not positively mischievous and destructive. It is, therefore, very needful that the individual should resist such as cause too great friction, or the sacrifice of other and more valuable forms of activity.

So far, however, as social environment practically expresses the collective life, thought, tastes, and general development of a community, its influence upon the individual is most advantageous, in that it is a ready and generally pleasant means of raising him to the general level. From this point of view the social surroundings have very considerable and valuable effects in promoting development. It constitutes the general effect of the social environment.

The specific results are seen in those social characteristics which distinguish one nation from another, and different national groups from each other. There is no difficulty in distinguishing the typical Frenchman, Italian, German, American, and Englishman, from each other, so far as their social qualities are concerned. Again, those who live lives of leisure, professional work, business, or manual labour, are easily known from each other by the effects which their various social surroundings have upon them.

In the same way those who move constantly in academic, artistic, literary, or musical circles, have well-marked characteristics of thought and action. Children of educated and refined parents are easily distinguished from those of the uneducated and unrefined. All social groups in fact, exert a special influence upon their members, and this is shown in characteristic traits. These are the specific effects of the social environment.

The elements of special difference between such groups is shown by the ways in which a legal matter appeals to the lawyer and the man in the street ; or the attitudes of mind of the clergyman, the lawyer, and the layman, towards church affairs. These differences depend upon what we have called " the mental local colour " which results from particular and constant influences in an environment.

Individual effects are of a similar nature, and proceed from causes similar to those which result from the physical environment.

Theories of politics, government, law, crime, and the sciences of ethics and economics, all throw, indirectly, some light upon the nature and principles of social life and relations ; and it is to these that we must go for guidance in attempting to organise social influences as means of furthering development. Mr. Herbert Spencer has treated all social phenomena as constituting a department of knowledge in his book on sociology.

Of the action of the rational environment but little remains to be said. It includes all the mental results which arise from the study, only, of works on pure

science, and general literary works. The general effect
is to give what may be called intellectual tone. This
may be illustrated by comparing, what would be likely
to be, the intellectual tone of those who constantly read
the writings of Shakespeare, Addison, and the other great
English writers, with that of those who read little else
than police court news and "penny dreadful" novelettes.
Or, we may compare the effects of hearing ordinary
music-hall songs with that produced by listening to
able renderings of Beethoven's sonatas.

The specific effects will be seen in those who confine
themselves to a purely scientific, or a purely literary,
course of study : to natural, mental, or mathematical
science : to poetry or prose : to classics or modern
languages : to history or theology : and so on. The
individual effects would be on lines similar to those in
the other cases.

In the highest sense, it is the rational self which is
the great determinant of self in all its forms ; for the
ideals which the reason itself sets up mould and govern
all the thoughts and actions to definite purposes. So
far as there is a fixed and dominating ideal, which an
individual consistently strives after, this must obviously
determine what manner of man he will be, at least within
the possibilities of later life.

We may say, therefore, that mind makes its own
immediate rational environment in later life ; and that
it has, therefore, the most definite and extensive influence upon itself. The nearest approach to this is the
influence of other minds upon an individual, as shown
by the effects of close companionship. One of the most

definite and powerful of these influences should be that of the educator.

But such an influence of the higher self upon the whole self assumes a permanent and powerful form of the rational self. Such a form is the outcome of the original powers of the individual and of the formation of mental and physical habits. As we have seen, habits represent the positive and permanent achievements in development, and are the corner-stones of further progress. Habits, therefore, may be regarded as the chief factors in the self-determination of development; for the chief element of fixedness and power in the self is that supplied by habits.

Self-determination of the self is also the most constant of all determinants when once the rational self has taken definite form. It is, as a rule, only interrupted, or thrown off its balance, by those passing and infrequent intense states of tonic excitement or depression which come to most people some time or other in their lives.

2. **Stimuli.**—These are simply the definite activities into which the environment and the self can be analysed. So far as we are here practically concerned with them, they must be such as have sufficient intensity to command definite attention from the individual as a whole. All that has gone before has dealt, more or less directly, with the nature and effects of the various forms of stimuli. Only one or two points need, therefore, be noticed here.

Owing to the reflective powers of mind it is able to stimulate itself, and is, indeed, its own most potent stimulator. Mental stimuli consist in the activities of willing due to knowledge and designed to further it. The will stimulates the mind, and causes concepts, judgments, and reasonings to be represented, and still further analysed and synthesised. Since such stimuli are purely rational they have a kind of concentrated effect upon mind; for the purely mental has most significance and value for, and, on that account, the most effect on, mind.

Next to such direct influence of a mind upon itself is the indirect influence of other minds upon it through spoken, written, or gesture language. The last of these is meant to include actions generally, which, as we say, sometimes speak more than words. Practically all actions of others convey some meaning to the individual who attends to them.

According to the powers and skill of the individual, and the appropriateness and the fulness of the stimuli, will be the actual benefit that is obtained from the latter; and this will largely decide whether or not certain stimuli will become real mental determinants.

CHAPTER XI

SOME very valuable principles, both from the theoretical and practical points of view, follow from what has been said in the last chapter. It is there pointed out, that men are, practically, infinitely like to, and different from, each other. The element of difference is at its minimum with regard to the most fundamental elements of human nature, and at its maximum in that which makes up the individuality of a person. The likeness is at its greatest with respect to those elements of form and function, which mark off the great natural orders from each other. It gets less, though still the predominant feature, in each sub-order and species, in proportion as these are more or less narrow.

Thus the great elemental attributes which distinguish man, as man, from other beings are, practically, absolutely the same throughout creation. In other words, animality and rationality are in their ultimate meaning invariable. In this sense there is no difference between man and man, whether they be white, yellow, or black.

But these three types of men have each their own

common and invariable elements of likeness amongst their own members, and differences from the members of other types. Thus the white (including the dark or swarthy) or wavy-haired type is distinguished by its colour, oval-shaped face, and the fact that a section of the hair is elliptical. The yellow or straight-haired type has its own colour, and a section of the hair is circular. The black or woolly-haired type is marked off by colour, hair, lips, and elongated skulls. Besides these quite distinctive general likenesses and unlikenesses, there are many more characteristic similarities and dissimilarities between them.

Again, there are many nations within each of these great groups, which have certain general resemblances and otherwise, as groups and as individuals. And so through all smaller groups such as tribes, highlanders, lowlanders, country-folk, town-folk, soldiers, sailors, teachers, pupils, schools, families and the like, elements of likeness and difference will be found ; the former decreasing, and the latter increasing, as the groups get smaller. When we come to individuals, as such, the elements of difference are, in rare cases, so numerous and pronounced as to seem to almost cut them off from their fellows. Some eccentric geniuses are good examples of this. But they always have all the common attributes, however strangely presented, of animality and rationality.

Obviously such significant elements as these must be carefully provided for in any system for securing proper development. Hence we must carefully consider what we shall term the principles of collectivism and individualism in education. The former takes account of the common points of likeness in a group, however large or small, and the latter is concerned with elements of difference amongst individuals.

The Principle of Collectivism.—It is well to remind ourselves that the common points of likeness among things are, at least in the first instance, of most importance for us. It is the realisation of these which makes knowledge possible. When we have secured a good basis of knowledge about similarities, then a grasp of the elements of difference is vital to progress and profoundness. Of course, the element of difference is always implicit from the first; but it is likeness which is most significant at the beginnings of knowledge. This is true of the beginning of life, and more or less, of all beginnings in new departments of knowledge. M. Perez, speaking of children, "from the age of fifteen months, and especially between twenty months and two years," says that: "They are very little on the look-out for differences, although they are very much struck by them when they see them; but everywhere they are on the look-out for resemblances."

The great truth involved in the above is this: not only can we, but we ought, and, indeed must, if we desire to secure the best development, submit each individual of a group to exactly similar influences, up to a certain point. This point is the limit to which we hold that the common attributes of the group extend, and the level to which the average individual can be developed in them. To neglect this truth must tend to break up the unity and community of social life, and to produce ill-balanced and exaggerated forms of mental development. To carry it too far would be likely to hinder progress by repressing individuality, and so to produce a tendency to stagnation and deterioration.

The system of dealing with groups for educational purposes will, so long as the common likenesses in the groups are exhaustively dealt with, serve to maintain the elements of diversity between different groups, and so have a considerable effect in preserving a general kind of individuality, if the term may be allowed—in the sense that Scotchmen, as a race, may be said to have a racial individuality.

Hence the element of nationality in a system of education is not only legitimate but necessary. Not that there should be any endeavour to crystallise national traits, but that unless the qualities which are expressed in the national character are cultivated to a reasonable extent, an important part of the individual will be neglected. The aim should be so to develop such national traits that the individual may be able to rise superior to them. A reasonable cosmopolitanism represents a wider, deeper, and truer development of social ideas than nationalism. But the latter is most valuable as a stepping-stone to the former.

This point is well put by Dr. Karl Lange. He urges that: "First of all, it is indeed clear that the matter to be taught must on the whole lie close to the child's experience. Since the latter has its root in the home soil, the material of the studies must be taken from the national treasures of knowledge, or at least stand in close relation to national interests, sentiments

and ideas. It must, to be sure, be subject-matter that
apparently transfers the child into unknown regions,
but yet in reality leads it back to the realm of its most
familiar ideas, its daily needs and experiences. Such a
choice of subject-matter presupposes a thorough analysis
of the sphere of national thought, an exact knowledge
of the lasting and permanently valuable possessions of
the national culture."

But we must supplement, extend, interpret, correct
and intensify, such elements through some knowledge
of, and by intelligent comparison with, the culture of
other nations. Just as we should, also, expand the
experiences of rural life by a knowledge of those of town
life, and conversely.

So far, therefore, as education is held to be an
essential part of the national life, a system of schools
under the authority of the central government and
subject to a similar minimum, not maximum, course of
education, would appear to be a national necessity. One
of the most important subjects of instruction, from this
point of view, is that of what is commonly called
citizenship. Dr. Rein says: "The schools should preserve and impart the inherited blessings of civilisation,
those priceless treasures upon which thousands of years
have laboured. They should strive to develop efficient
members of society, that the people may never be
lacking in national power."

Again Dr. Rein urges that: "The state .... has the
right to demand that education and instruction shall not
be neglected, that the schools shall pursue no course
hostile to its interests, and that they shall attain certain

results which are essential to its task.   As regards the latter it should fix upon certain minimum aims to be attained by the various kinds of schools." This involves the question of the limits of state interference, but, if these be taken for granted, all would probably agree that Dr. Rein's views are correct.

The above is, however, a political question, from the practical side, and is here used as an illustration and not as an argument. The general educational idea underlying it is that which is expressed in the term "the principle of collectivism." Seek to develop the greatest aggregate of powers as well the highest maximum in each, is the conclusion which is forced upon us by theory and practice; and it is a particular application of this truth which we have been dealing with.

An interesting point arises here in connection with the question whether girls and boys should receive the same course of education. So far as the foregoing is accepted as sound, the conclusion is obvious. To the extent to which girls and boys can rightly be regarded as forming but one group with regard to certain common qualities, to that extent both should undergo an exactly similar course of education. And this should be continued so long as the conditions hold.

But whenever, and in whatever respect, the difference of sex requires educational conditions which conflict with one another, then, and therefore, girls must form one group, and boys another, for educational purposes. It is a case in which what we may term the class-individuality must receive its proper attention.

Whether or no there ever really is such a ground of educational division between girls and boys during that part of their lives which is ordinarily given up to school work, is a question which lies outside our present province. One point may, however, be submitted for consideration. So far as education proper is concerned, the specific training of girls for domestic work is as much a matter for technical instruction, as against pure education, as teaching boys those trades which will fit them to be bread-winners. From the point of view of physical, and also mental, education, however, the general principles of both kinds of work can be advantageously made use of in ordinary education.

Let us consider a few of the ways in which the details of principle of collectivism in education are forced upon us by circumstances, and demanded by the conditions of life.

In the first place, so far as the life of the present day is concerned, the social organisation more or less compels many elements of collectivism. One of the first and chiefest of practical necessities is the fitting in of the individual life with the common whole. This can be harmoniously and thoroughly done only when there is a general bond of likeness between the one and the many.

The social life as a whole may be regarded as not only demanding so much uniformity from the individual as is necessary for reasonable union, but actually enforcing it. Habits, customs, and laws which society has formed and observes have their inevitable effect in moulding the individual more or less perfectly to the common type. Dr. C. A. McMurry has well said that: "No narrow, one-sided culture will ever equip a child to act a just part in the complex social, political, and industrial society of our time" (General Method).

Again the actually existing stores of accessible knowledge, and the general level of acquirement, in the community, will largely determine the nature and extent of the system, and its details, adopted for educational purposes. Since even pure education must at least take account of the need of so developing a person that he will be able to readily adapt himself to his surroundings, it must always use the materials which practical life offers, and so use them that a reasonable mastery is obtained. Progress from the more known to the less known must always involve very great dependence on the concrete and rational surroundings.

Before and beyond all, from a practical point of view, in its insistence upon collective education, is the element of economy. It is absolutely impossible to provide a separate teacher for every separate pupil. The preparation of teachers, in any general organised system of teaching, also demands the same kind of economy. But it may be remarked, in passing, that if this idea of economy is carried too far it soon results in mischievous waste. A teacher with too many scholars means many scholars with too little teaching.

Then there are the inevitable effects which those influences which are exactly similar, for all practical purposes, must have upon minds which are, as mental organisms, likewise similar. For example, a rose and a

daisy have, respectively, exactly similar effects upon, and
are distinguished from each other in the same general
sense by, every rational being who properly uses his senses
and judgments with regard to them. This is essential;
for, were it not so, it would be impossible for us to communicate with each other about these two flowers in any
intelligible manner. Thus the uniformity of the actions
and influences of things upon mind, and the uniformity
of the reactions of minds to similar stimuli compel a
like constitution and development of minds, with the
same general environment, to a certain extent.

Next we may see in what ways the principle of
collectivism is realised in education. In the first place
there is the fact that a single educator can deal with a
group of individuals. How large this group may be
will depend upon a great many practical elements, and
can only be decided by the results of a good deal of
experience. It is a question which belongs to the art
of education. From the theoretical side it is necessary
that the group should be composed of individuals with
as many general resemblances as possible; and, in fact,
with respect to the subjects used for educational purposes, and the extent to which they are taught, the
members of the group should be very closely similar
to each other.

It follows also that a common curriculum may, and
should, be used up to the extent that the average
capacity of the group is found, or judged, to be equal
to. How high this level is to be must be decided by
the educator according to his knowledge and estimate
of the powers of the individuals in the group. This is

a matter which demands very full knowledge, wide experience, and ripe judgment. There is of course a certain universal minimum for the averagely normal individual and the extent of this is pretty generally agreed upon. But any given group needs to be dealt with on its own merits, for its average may possibly be considerably above or below this, as in the case, say, of a class consisting of those who have won, and are trying for other, special scholarships, and a class of the most backward and dull boys in a school. The standard of judgment will always be the general minimum for the averagely normal individual.

The number of subjects included in a common curriculum will be such as are held to be necessary to influence the development of all the well-marked common mental characteristics. Speaking generally they will be those which affect the feeling, knowing, and willing powers, in all their definitely distinct manifestations. Music, art, sports, and games to develop the feelings; history, tales of adventures, biographies, travels, novels, morals, and religion, to influence the sentiments; geography, the arts, and the applied sciences to minister to the growth of practical knowing; the pure and mental sciences to develop the purely rational; and rules, duties,. occupations, systematic work, and conditions involving general independence, to secure the advance of willing. These are the kinds of arrangements which have to be carefully worked out in detail, according to the other educational principles.

Still another way in which this principle is realised

is in collective, or class, demonstration. On the assumption that the same illustrations, experiments, opportunities of observation, words, and the like, will appeal in similar ways to similar minds, the educator feels justified in conducting class demonstrations. In the same way, and on like grounds, it is held that a uniform series of mental and physical exercises will produce substantially similar effects upon the minds and bodies of a properly selected group of individuals.

Finally, we will mention some of the effects of the principle of collectivism in education. Perhaps one of the most beneficial results is the development of the social sympathies. The influences which the many exert upon the one, and each upon all, are the very foundation elements of mutual consideration, compromise, disciplined co-operation, public opinion, toleration, common interests, the sense of corporate life, and the like, which form the links which bind together a community. Hence we may regard these results as not only involving a very great development of the higher sentiments, but as also including the very best training for the wider social life of the whole community.

This applies as much to the purely intellectual feelings as to the ethical. The love of knowledge for its own sake, the sense of the community of knowledge, intellectual tolerance, rational co-operation and subordination, and so on, are all fostered by common mental experiences, aims, and acquirements.

There is, too, a strong element of encouragement in collective education. The feeling that so many are all striving together for a like result is apt to give a sense of power, as though a mental difficulty which would defeat an individual cannot possibly resist the united efforts of a group. It is somewhat of an inspiration, which comes from the force of numbers. After the same manner a man, who is by himself a coward in the face of difficulty or danger, may be capable of facing serious risks as one of a group inspired by a common purpose.

Emulation is aroused amongst the individuals in a group engaged on similar work. Up to a certain point this is undoubtedly an inevitable and wholesome feature; but beyond this it is distinctly mischievous, and may become a serious mental, physical, and moral danger. It may lead to too long and violent effort, resulting in a serious mental and physical breakdown through overwork; and it is likely to give rise to personal jealousy, ill-feeling, enmity and conflict. More especially are these things likely to arise if the element of emulation is unwisely stimulated by artificial rewards.

Unless groups are carefully selected, and even when they are, nervous and timid individuals may suffer a good deal through being required to take a more or less public part in the common work. Such should be allowed some time to get used to their surroundings, and should be excused as much as possible of the more public elements.

The very great extra force, and the specific advantages, which collective work may put into the developing influences are well seen in the mental vigour, robustness, self-dependence, tolerance, and general tone of the average public schoolboy, as compared with the more quiet, refined, dependent, and often dogmatic, condition of mind of the ordinary boy when taught at home by a private tutor. Each doubtless gains much that the other loses, but the collective elements are certainly valuable and necessary.

Collectivism in education, therefore, means much greater force, and new features, in many of the developing influences, though less in others, whether these are, in themselves, either for good or evil.

To whatever point, with respect to any given group, it is held that collective education can be profitably carried, for general purposes, in so far specialisation of any kind is excluded. Every individual has more or less of every ordinary human power, and this justifies us in insisting that a certain amount of quite general education is an indispensable preliminary to special education.

In most respects each person has an average amount of power and capacity, and may be said to be normal. In other instances every one is more or less below or above the average. Collectivism in education is therefore the universal rule. It seeks to realise, in all, what Herbart calls the many-sidedness of interest, but it does not exclude individuality. For, as Herbart himself points out: "There are many individualities; the idea of many-sidedness is but one. The former is contained in the latter collectively as the part in the whole. And the part can be measured by the whole; it can also be enlarged to the whole."

Specialisation must not be mistaken for individualisation. The former has reference to the fact that every one is likely to take up some special kind of mental or physical work, whatever his characteristics may be, and will, therefore, need more or less special preparation for it; whilst the latter refers to the cultivation of a person's special powers quite apart from any particular work in which he may afterwards engage. When the two coincide, then the maximum result may be expected.

The Average and the Normal.—A few words as to the difference between these two ideas may help to prevent confusion with regard to the principle of collectivism in education, in which both ideas are involved.

The normal may be looked upon as a universal ideal average. As we have said, every ordinary individual, as a whole, approaches more or less closely to this, but not one actually coincides with it in any one respect, and much less in all points. Hence it is that whilst every ordinary individual can acquire a certain minimum of power and skill in all common human capacities, yet it is necessary to form separate groups for different capacities so as to get the maximum of actual general development.

Such groups must be dealt with not according to what is normal, but what is actual. In other words a practical average must be adopted. Average will then have its ordinary meaning, viz., that which is about half-way between the extremes. This assumes that we make a sort of quantitative estimate of the value of qualities.

The idea of an average as a standard for educational

purposes will be very misleading and mischievous, if it be not carefully remembered that the more widely the extremes are separated from each other, the less will such a standard be suitable for each individual in a group. It is from this point of view that it is urged that all the members of a group for educational processes should be as nearly as possible equal to each other in the power, or powers, needed for the educative influences which it is proposed to apply.

Not less important is it that this standard should not in any way be regarded as a fixed one, so far as it concerns a given group. Very great care and skill will be required to determine what it should be at first, when a new group is formed ; and it will be quite as difficult to keep it in accord with the growing knowledge and capacity of the average individual of the group.

The great difference between the universal ideal normal, and the average of a group, is, of course, best seen in the case of two groups, one of which is made up of very dull pupils and the other of exceptionally bright ones. Both groups are considerably removed from the normal, and each has its own average.

The Principle of Individualism.—To generally neglect the element of individuality in persons would be in effect to very much limit and repress the general progress of the race. For it is chiefly to the new lines of thought and action which have been taken by persons of strong and well-developed individuality that many of the greatest steps of progress are due. Great leaders, thinkers, statesmen, scientists, and workers, have been

men whose personalities have been exceptional, it may
be to the extent of eccentricity, or even monomania.

Nothing is so likely to be unprogressive as a thoroughly homogeneous group. Although the conditions
which result from the successful carrying out of the
principle of collectivism in education are indispensable
for sound progress, both general and individual ; yet,
in itself, the effort to secure uniformity is obviously
opposed to very much progress, because the advance
will have to be limited to the capacity of the average.
On the other hand, if the ablest members of a group
are aided and encouraged in developing their strong
points to the greatest advantage, the final result may
be a considerable intensifying and enriching of the
general rational environment of the whole group.

Whilst the sacrificing of the general welfare to a
particular development is, finally, bad for even the
special power, it is equally true that the reasonable
furthering of individual powers tends to enrich the
whole, both directly and indirectly. Directly because
the extra nourishment and exercise must affect the
whole mind to some extent ; and indirectly because of
the reflective nature of mind. If great shrewdness is
developed in a person with regard to a certain line of
thought or action, it means that certain habits have
been acquired which are sure to affect the whole mind,
to a greater or lesser degree.

If the development of a man's individuality be
ignored, his greatest force and value is likely to be
sacrificed. So long as the individuality is not vicious,
it involves the greatest good that either its possessor

himself or the community can obtain from his life. The whole world is out of joint to one who finds his keenest and most constant desires almost invariably neglected or repressed. The history of the struggle of those great men who, possessed of overwhelming desires to gratify the inclinations of their genius, have been compelled to engage in work entirely opposed to their nature supplies plenty of evidence of this.

Every individual should be able, in the fullest and truest sense, to "live his own life," as we express it. This does not exclude, but depends upon, a reasonable conformity with the common life. The idea of absolute independence would probably mean, when logically applied, a more or less rapid movement to savagery and the extinction of the race; for each person would have to be able to supply all his own wants, and this would necessitate that they should be of the most primitive kind. Even if we assume that we could start by appropriating all the present possessions of the race, purely individual effort could no more maintain them than it could have produced them.

Again, the most elementary forms of the conjugal and domestic states involve the common life, and the sacrifice of these would certainly involve the extinction of the race. In any case it is obvious that whatever evils may arise from the collective life, the advantages of it are very extensive and definite. It is by united efforts that mankind has made the greatest progress. The most primitive as well as the most highly developed forms of humanity have the collective element in them. The greatest individualities have been the outcomes of

the most civilised forms of collective life.   It is worth
while to emphasise and insist upon this mutual inter-
dependence of the individual and the collective life, for
there are many dangers attending the ignoring of it.

How, then, can we secure the best conditions for
developing the individuality of each person.   Clearly
the very first thing required, and the most difficult to
acquire, is some knowledge of its nature in any
given case.   The difficulty lies in the fact that individuality usually consists in a special intensity or
tendency of ordinary mental powers, possessed by a
particular person.   There is no reason whatever to
suppose that any person has got a power which is absolutely and fundamentally different from what is possessed by others.   Such a thing would imply a different
kind of human being from those we know.

To know the individuality of a person is, therefore,
to know which of his particular mental powers have a
special intensity or tendency (bias), and how these
interact on each other and the whole mind.   The body
of a person has also individuality, as : in the appearance
of the face : the gait : great swiftness of movement :
delicacy of touch : capacity for particular games, sports
and pastimes : and so on.   These also involve special
details of intensity and tendency, of certain features,
and the resulting variety in the total complex.

But such a knowledge can be gained only by well-
informed, carefully trained, skilful scientific observers ;
for a full recognition of all the psychological and physiological elements and details involved is necessary, before
the particular differences can be discriminated.   This

is no case in which scientifically ignorant persons should rush in where wise men walk warily.

All the conditions which were laid down as guarantees for accuracy in obtaining knowledge through communication should be rigorously enforced. Not only is the problem a very difficult and delicate one with regard to the interests of the individual, but the elements are very complex and intricate. It requires great skill to be able to note what is in one's own mind, and very much more to judge by systematic observation of his actions and words of what is in another's.

A very suggestive illustration of what is at issue is afforded by the relation of a doctor to his patient. The patient himself can give only a limited, and often very inaccurate, account of what his condition is. He judges wrongly of his own experiences, and often when he judges rightly he expresses himself wrongly, as every one does in dealing with what is technical and unfamiliar.

As a rule a trained nurse can give a far more exact and extensive account of the physical condition of a patient, at least in so far as scientific precision is concerned, than the patient himself. But the nurse has usually a comparatively limited knowledge ; and is far from discriminating all the common elements in the general condition, much less the peculiar and exceptional.

Perhaps the worst observer, for strictly scientific purposes, is a relative or friend who has no special knowledge and is much concerned about the patient. With keen attention such an one notices all that appeals to him. But through ignorance and interest he will be likely to exaggerate what he supposes to be favourable symptoms, and minimise the unfavourable or otherwise. Again, those which he thus notes will probably be only superficial after all; for the deeper and more significant symptoms usually require the skilled and instructed attention.

Ordinary persons who only see the patient occasionally and for brief periods would, as a rule, be entirely useless so far as obtaining any trustworthy evidence from them is concerned.

It is only the well-informed, thoroughly trained, experienced, skilful, scientific observation of the doctor himself that is able to discriminate the elements involved. His judgment and power of rightly relating what he observes can alone give a satisfactory basis for scientific treatment. And his observation is aided by all the mechanical appliances which knowledge and skill have discovered for giving precision, detail, and completeness of information. Not that he disregards the evidence which other persons can supply; on the contrary he is glad to receive much of it; but he treats it as that which, for the most part, can at best be only suggestive, and confirmatory of his own observation. Of course there are certain obvious symptoms, which any intelligent person can take account of, and some mechanical observations which they can make.

Similarly with mental matters, it is only the technical expert who is really qualified to make scientifically trustworthy observations, to appreciate the significance of the knowledge thus gained, and to prescribe a suitable course of technical treatment. In other words, it is the educationist who is the only fit and proper person to deal authoritatively with the question of individuality for educational purposes. By an educationist we mean one who has been trained in the practical knowledge of, and taught in the rational study of, the phenomena and laws which are dealt with in the science of education.

The teacher can give valuable information up to a certain point as to the evidences which he has observed. By a teacher is meant one who is able to intelligently carry out the practical processes involved in an educative course, but has not, necessarily, the deeper knowledge of the educationist.

Parents and others may have more or less observed children, and the results of their observations may be of greater or lesser value; but they must always be received with the very greatest caution, and only accepted, except as suggestive of courses of inquiry and experiment, after the severest scientific criticism. But it is always worth while to collect as much of such evidence as possible for purposes of scientific investigations.

There are several special dangers attending the study of individuals, more especially children, with respect to their individuality, which it may be helpful to mention. Forgetting the great basis of similarity which prevails, there may be a very one-sided and exaggerated view taken of what is involved in the total difference. If the attention is fixed too much on a particular element of difference, this may be thought to

2 H

affect every part of the whole. We may, so to put it, miss seeing the mountain through looking too closely at the mole-hill.

The vagueness and indefiniteness of early ideas may easily appear as profundity and universality. An adult observer is very liable to read into certain thought forms of the child his own content of thought. If once a person gets the idea that there is a great deal behind the beginner's thought, he will very soon discover, at least to his own satisfaction, greater mysteries in the attempts at thought of the child, than in the most profound explicit reasonings of the philosopher.

We ought not to expect to find wonders in the child's thoughts, but rather wonder that we find so much of ordinary content. The child is doubtless much more puzzled, and filled with what wonder it is capable of, by the want of clear meaning in its own thoughts, than the observer is by what he may suppose to be their fulness of meaning. If there be in the child's mind anything like what some enthusiastic seekers after the wonderful would have us believe, it must get surprisingly ignorant as it gets older.

Language as used by beginners is often entirely misleading. Of course children are often unable to express their thoughts through want of a sufficient command of language; but more often it is because the ideas themselves are vague, half-formed, or incoherent. Adults with a practically perfect command of language, often cannot express what first comes to them in a new department of knowledge, for similar reasons. Again, children often repeat words and phrases in unusual combinations simply because they have, for some reason or other, associated and remembered odds and ends of sentences.

Finally, it should be remembered that there is much of the child in the adult, and, therefore, the more fully we can know an adult, the better we shall be able to guide and check our observations of children. Much suggestion and guidance can also be obtained from the study of the most interesting history of primitive races ; for therein we see the childhood of mankind, which is one of the best introductions to a knowledge of the childhood of the individual.

When we have obtained, through careful and considerable observation, experiment, and thought, what we believe to be a sound view of that which mainly constitutes the individuality of the learner, we shall have the fullest possible guide to the points of special treatment which will be required in his particular case. If a pupil be exceptionally phlegmatic or lively, imaginative or unimaginative, optimistic or pessimistic, prosaic or poetic, reflective or active, generous or selfish, scientific or artistic, and the like, we shall have to make use of the different educational principles, or different features of them, with varying fulness and force.

An exact knowledge of the individuality of a person will enable the educator to use the various principles to the greatest effect. He will know how best to appeal to the individuality through the principle of interest, and will so obtain the further advantage of the maximum of self-activity. That which gives the greatest pleasure, because it is most in harmony with the personality, can be wisely made use of, and thus the greatest amount of co-operation secured, through the principle of sympathetic control. It will be seen whether the concrete elements of knowledge must be specially insisted upon, to correct a tendency to hasty imagination, as in filling in the details of a percept by mental pictures; or, on the other hand, if the imagination needs particular attention, so as to get the learner to see behind and beyond his own little world, as in picturing objects and scenes outside the range of actual experience.

And so all the elements of various individualities can be related to the different educational principles. But it must always be understood that the general, or collective, elements in the individuality have been provided for by the ordinary collective applications of these principles. It is only an extended and special application of them that we are now considering.

By such a special adaptation of principles to persons we may hope to obtain the very highest values of individual development, and, through these, the greatest possible progress of the race. Not only, therefore, is the individual directly advantaged by this, but also the race; and thus other individuals are indirectly advantaged. Progress is cumulative for one and all. Each is for all, and all for each.

Such a knowledge of the individual as is required for the above cannot possibly be obtained from observations confined to the schoolroom, where both the conduct of the child and the environment are so largely artificial. The educator must observe the child during its free and unconstrained play, in social intercourse, and under as many varying conditions as possible. He must also obtain as much reliable information as he can about the child from its parents, and others.

Something must now be said as to the way in which this principle affects any general scheme of education. Its function is to secure the full and final value of the individual, and the way in which this may be realised must be indicated.

However predominantly the individuality of a person may appear to belong to only one or two particular powers, it will be found, on careful observation and analysis, that it affects all; and it is doubtless made up of a combination of details proceeding from all the powers, though manifesting itself chiefly through one or two. Hence a certain amount of individuality will probably have to be provided for, in every separate item of development.

This will mean that whilst by far the greater part of all early education is collective, a small part will have to be individualistic. In other words, each individual in a group must receive some small amount of personal help even with respect to the processes and products of collective education. This will be necessary throughout the collective course. Hence, class-demonstrations will be followed, as far as possible, by individual testing and such additional personal help as is shown to be required. Class exercises will give many opportunities for individual attention.

It will be seen that the above has a very important

bearing upon the actual size of a group for educational work. It should never be so large that a reasonable amount of individual teaching is impossible; for, if it be, there must result a very large sacrifice of individual and general progress.

But by far the most important point connected with the principle of individualism is that of specialisation. The element of individuality demands specialisation. Because of a person's special characteristics he is most fitted for certain lines of development, and very unfitted for others. If, therefore, he is to fulfil his greatest possibilities these particular powers must receive special attention.

Dr. Hertel has drawn attention to a very essential consideration in the following passage: "It is hardly fair, on the part of school teachers, to claim of the child an exclusive right to his time. There is much which he ought to learn beyond what the school imposes on him; if he has any special talent or tastes—music or drawing, for example—he should have time at his own disposal in which to cultivate them. He should be able to pursue privately any of his school studies which specially attract or interest him, and altogether have more opportunities of independent growth allowed him. . . . .

"Are there not many students who have so little knowledge of themselves, their own powers, tastes and inclinations, that it is a mere matter of chance what course of study they take up when they go to the university? For this reason many a young man, after having wasted a year or two, often makes a complete change and begins upon a totally different career. Those wasted years might often have been saved had he had opportunities, while at school, of studying a little by himself, and thus of judging in what direction his talents and predilections lay" (Overpressure in Schools).

The chief thing to decide with regard to this matter is the period at which the special attention should be given. Happily this may be regarded as practically determined by the individual himself. When the individuality of a person is definite and aggressive, then it should be attended to by the educator, or it will look after itself, and almost certainly prejudice, if not pervert, its development.

Ordinarily, the individuality begins to assert itself about the middle of the third great stage of general development, when willing becomes predominant, and the individual becomes a law unto himself. We may say that, roughly, this is about the sixteenth or seventeenth years. This, therefore, will as a rule be the time when it should begin to receive definite attention. That is to say, this is the period when specialisation should be considered; but not, necessarily, begun, for something like a settled preference on the part of the individual should first be allowed to form itself.

There should, by this time, be such a general development of mental powers and possessions that no danger of warping the individual is incurred. Herbart points out this danger. He says: "The individual grasps rightly what is natural to him, but the more he exclusively cultivates himself in this direction the more certainly does he falsify through his habitual frame of mind every other impression." Individuality ought, as a rule, to be so developed that it will be true to say of the person : he is good in most things, but specially strong in such-and-such. Thus the ideal in learning is to know something of everything, through types, and, so far as is possible, everything of something, through details.

In those cases, however, where, as with precocious geniuses, the individuality is definitely and decidedly developed at a very early age, it should always receive proper attention. But very great care will be needed to guard against sacrificing the best development of the special power, through neglecting the general powers. A certain amount of restraint will, therefore, be necessary ; but this should never take the form of direct and positive repression, or the whole nature will suffer.

Too much attention may easily be given to the element of individuality. It should be remembered that this is the strongest as well as the most active element in an individual. It, therefore, needs the least intensity of stimulus. Also it is always more or less active and insists upon being ministered to, for all ordinary experiences are received in such a way that they influence it, and it influences them.

Dr. Karl Lange remarks: "We admit that very strong natures, which are distinguished by unusual inner activity, are accustomed to supply without the aid of others those apperceiving ideas which make possible the comprehension of a new object of study, since it is a fact that a genius even with bad instruction, by his own powers, finds the right road to development."

When education has secured a good basis for the special development of individuality and has helped it forward on the road to its fullest, most vigorous, and best form, the individual must do the rest. The education that has put the individual in possession of his best and truest self has, indeed, done its perfect work.

The Principle of Proportion.—What has just been said about the principles of collectivism and individualism in education emphasises an element which has been more or less explicit throughout the whole of the discussions concerning the science, viz., that of the proportion of intensity, extensity, duration, frequency, and the like which should exist between various principles, so as to secure the most effective and desirable application of them.

We must say, at once, that this is a most difficult and very far-reaching inquiry ; and the most we can do now is to suggest some of the considerations which will have to be taken into account. Not until our knowledge of the human being generally, and of the mental sciences in particular, is much more extensive and precise than it is at present, can we hope to be able to lay down anything approaching definite conclusions on the matter.

At the same time, however, we can, from our present knowledge, learn how to avoid very exaggerated and mischievous forms of disproportion in the application of educational principles. What has been said about the order of development, the relative waxing and waning of predominance of the developing elements, and the periods during which these may be expected ordinarily to take place, ought to save us from serious errors, in this respect.

One of the very first points to be considered will be the order and proportion in which we shall attempt to realise the discipline, culture, and utility values of educational material. At the very beginning of things it is certainly the utility value which must be predominantly acquired, for the law of self-preservation is then imperative. But very soon this must give way to the discipline value, for, if we are to have progress, we must have power and skill.

Hardly less obvious is it that the culture value must come last in order of predominant development. If we accept Matthew Arnold's dictum that to have culture: "is to know the best that has been thought and said in the world;" or Professor Huxley's statement, that: "It is the criticism of life contained in literature;" then it is clear that not only does it demand the highest mental powers, but that some amount of leisure is also required for its fuller acquisition.

Professor Huxley has well said that: "No man ever understood Shakespeare until he is old, though the youngest may admire him; the reason being that he satisfies the artistic instinct of the youngest, and harmonises with the ripest and richest experience of the oldest." This also suggests the truth so often insisted upon, viz., that there is always a concurrent as well as a predominant development of the different elements.

Such considerations obviously go far to solve the problem of the place and the function of realism and humanism in education, or, to put it in concrete form, of practical science and literature in school work.

Another point which soon forces itself upon the attention of the practical educator is, how much of the various knowledge-subjects should he attempt to impart. Rousseau has well said : " Human intelligence has its limits. We can neither know everything, nor be thoroughly acquainted with the little that other men know. . . . . The question is, not what may be known, but what will be of most use when it is known. From these few we must again deduct such as require ripeness of understanding and a knowledge of human relations which a child cannot possibly acquire."

Understanding that the phrase " of most use," in the above passage, refers to both educational and practical utility, we may say that as much as can be received and retained, should be, so long as the vigour and freshness of the powers are not prejudiced. This brings us to the consideration of the relation between work and play.

Professor Huxley insists on the great importance of mental relaxation, in the following words : "I have no compassion for sloth, but youth has more need for intellectual rest than age ; and the cheerfulness, the tenacity of purpose, and power of work which make many a successful man what he is, must often be placed to the credit not of his hours of industry, but to that of his hours of idleness, in boyhood. Even the hardest worker of us all, if he has to deal with anything above mere details, will do well, now and again, to let his brain lie fallow for a space. The next crop of thought will certainly be all the fuller in the ear and the weeds fewer."

Again, he remarks: "Above all things, let my imaginary pupil have preserved the freshness and vigour of youth in his mind as well as his body. The educational abomination of desolation of the present day is the stimulation of young people to work at high pressure by incessant competitive examinations."

To the same effect, Dr. Abbott observes that: "The intellect is like the body in requiring the alternation between wholesome strain and wholesome relaxation, if it is to become healthy and robust." Dr. Hertel, in his book on "Overpressure in Schools," says: "We must not lose sight of the fact that one long spell of work is far more exhausting to the child than the same number of hours would be if split up by a considerable interval."

In connection with this point it is instructive to notice that in Germany, lectures at the universities are for forty-five minutes, and there is an interval of fifteen minutes between all lectures. At Oxford and Cambridge it is the rule to give the whole of every afternoon to sports. The greater the amount of controlled educational activity, the larger should be the amount of free recreative activity. Dr. Hertel informs us that when some of the Swedish High Schools applied for permission to extend the limits of continuous instruction, for the five youngest classes in the schools, from two to three hours, the Government referred the question to the Medical Society for an opinion. The following is a summary of their views : "Three hours' consecutive work is permissible if an interval of ten minutes be allowed for every hour, and one hour of the three set apart for easy work, such as singing, writing, or the like. After that there must be two hours' complete rest."

As we have before urged, this is a question which demands very serious attention. The issues at stake are of the gravest kind. Health, happiness, and usefulness in life may all be sacrificed by making a mistake in this matter. Nothing is so dangerous as an uninformed zeal for what is popularly supposed to be education, viz., encyclopædic instruction in words and formulæ.

Sir J. Crichton-Browne points out that: "There is no better preparation for a stormy life than a tranquil and happy childhood, and sound policy should guide us to postpone as long as possible the entrance of our children on that struggle in which so much is to be required of them. . . . . Education without pressure—education in which hereditary restrictions, the laws of growth, the constitution of the organism, the vivifying power of happiness, and the paralysing effects of fear and rivalry are held constantly in view—may . . . brace and strengthen them to encounter without risk the trials that are in store for them " (Introduction to Dr. Hertel's book).

Of the proportion which should exist between the principles of collectivism and individualism a good deal has been said. Herbart has the following remarks on this matter : " Some steps must . . . . be taken to adjust individuality to character and many-sidedness . . . . . The more individuality is blended with many-sidedness, the more easily will the character assert its sway over the individual."

He points out the danger of undue attention to individual traits in these words : " By no means, however, should the presence of incidental prominent tendencies in the years of cultivation be regarded as a sign that they are to be further strengthened by education. This practice, which shelters disproportion, is devised by love of arbitrariness, and recommended by bad taste. Doubtless the lover of the bizarre and of caricature would rejoice to see, instead of many fully and proportionately developed men fit to move in rank and file, a crowd of humpbacks and cripples of all kinds, tumbling wildly over each other. But this is what happens where society is composed of men of widely different modes of thought; each brags of his own individuality, and no one understands his fellows."

To push the principle of individualism too far would not only imply the necessity of a special science of education for each human being—which is in itself sufficiently absurd—but also that each human being would form a different science of education for any one given individual—which is surely a " reductio ad absurdum." Equally unscientific is it to regard human beings as being as like to each other as though they were cast in a mechanical mould.

The practical educator must avoid being too precise,

or nice, about matters. The useful should come before the ornamental, and necessities before luxuries. Mr. Thring urges that: " A teacher must be content to omit much, and not be concerned about the glossiness of his work. The mind of a working, vigorous little boy is much like his clothes, very untidy, but very serviceable, entirely regardless of everything but the object at the moment. No doubt order and tidiness are part of the training ; but dress boots won't do for turnip fields, or mountains. Strength is needed first. Strong ideas are wanted, put forth by an unseen plan." But mountain boots should be of good material and specially well made.

It is not the educator's duty to insist that every detail of development which has been mentioned shall be carefully elaborated in the case of every child. Each child will be likely to linger over some points through want of average ability in that particular, and will skip lightly over others because it has special power for such work. But the educator must be able to recognise where help is needed, and know how to give it in the best form.

To put the principle in quite general terms, we may say that the principle of stimulation ought to procure energising without violence ; nourishment should produce keenness and vigour, but never surfeit ; pleasure ought to satisfy but not corrupt ; pain should compel without cowing ; interest should concentrate energy, not dissipate it ; habituation ought to secure regularity without automatism ; self-activity must bring about the progress of the ego without egotism ; collectivism should cultivate humanity but not neglect the man; individualism should provide for the man but not neglect the race; development must attend to the details without omitting the whole; gradation should secure simplicity but not make matters too easy; symbolism should give expression and facility to thought without verbalism; repetition ought to secure frequency whilst avoiding weariness; sympathetic control must win without weakness or indulgence; preparation should bring about adaptation without actual anticipation; inter-relation and inter-dependence ought to unify but not make too much of the linking; analysis and synthesis must give the units and unity of detail, but not overwhelm with them; doing should secure precision and facility in action but avoid the mechanical; and proportion must guide in all these.

We want to help without creating dependence; to increase refinement but preserve vigour; to get delicacy and charm, but retain energy, force, and stamina; to adorn the edifice with the highest and most graceful pinnacles, whilst keeping broad and sure the foundations; and to secure the unity of the whole without uniformity in each.

The Principle of Pleasure.—Something more may now be said about this principle. In so far as pleasure is the outcome of normal conditions acting upon a normal being, whenever we are able to secure the fullest and best realisation of educational principles we shall bring about a state of pleasure for the individual who is being educated. Hence, as we have constantly insisted, the surest and soundest way of securing the interested co-operation of the learner is to provide the most perfect conditions for learning.

If the kind, quality, and quantity, of the developing influence be appropriate to the powers and possessions of the pupil, then it will be as pleasurable for him to receive an educative lesson as to eat a well-prepared meal when he is hungry. The former does for the mind what the latter does for the body, it supplies a natural want in the most agreeable and healthy manner.

This condition of things is, probably, best realised through the observance of the educational maxim : from the known to the unknown. The quite ecstatic delight shown by the little people in kindergarten classes, when some familiar objects, such as tea-sets, are made use of— with as near an approach as possible to the actual conditions of ordinary life—for educational purposes, is really striking, and very pleasurable to see.

Similarly older children take the greatest possible interest and delight in bringing small curiosities from their own homes when they are to be used as subjects for a lesson. There is little difficulty, and immense advantage, in getting boys to make simple apparatus, or to collect natural specimens, for science lessons.

Again, the element of explicit co-operation in the educating process can be made both effective and interesting. To occasionally allow the pupils in the higher classes to put questions to each other, and to the teacher, about the subject matter of a lesson which has just been given is a means of realising this. Or, better still, to require—without undue pressure—that the more advanced children shall, in turn, prepare and impart to the class some information about a given topic, which is well within their powers, will do much to develop both self-dependence and a truly pleasurable interest in the work of the school.

One of the most fruitful sources of pleasure in education should arise from the realising of the culture value of knowledge subjects. If what we have said about the highest type of mind being the most cultured be true, then in endeavouring to get the pupils to realise the culture elements of knowledge, we are helping them to obtain the highest, and, therefore, the most delightful mental values of things.

In every department of school work, therefore, there should be an attempt to reach such a standard of excellence as will bring out, clearly and effectively, the æsthetic elements. In reading there should be such a standard of elocution and dramatic feeling—where fitting—as will give real pleasure to the hearers. Writing ought to have grace and proportion sufficient to definitely gratify the eye. Singing should be so well done that one half of a class could get real enjoyment from hearing the other half sing. Drawing and colouring ought to result in work that will adorn the school walls. Not that many will do such work, or much of it, but at least some should be obtained, and, what is still more important, a true appreciation of its merits and beauties by the scholars must be aroused. If this appreciation is secured, so also is the most happy and helpful stimulus to further production.

In every branch of school work this pleasure-giving

level of proficiency should be obtained, for the sake of its educational value as a stimulus and a satisfaction. Every pupil ought to be regarded as a possible little artist, in a very elementary way, with respect to the work he does. Not only is it one of the greatest of pleasures to give pleasure, but it is also one of the most stimulating results of work. The true artist probably appreciates and enjoys the processes of good work even more than others delight in the products.

But, of course, beginners must not be left entirely to the results of their own efforts for their supply of the pleasures which the æsthetic features of work can give. They should be enlightened and encouraged by models of design and finish; and these should be systematically used to form their tastes, and to arouse their ambition. From this point of view, the furnishing of a schoolroom is as much a matter for the expert judgment of a scientific educationist as the formulating of a course of educative lessons. And a place should always be found for works of pure art, which, whilst appealing to youthful sympathies and powers, yet, because of their intrinsic beauty are silent voices that speak of higher things, and best tell their own tales.

The principles of development and gradation are, when properly observed, very powerful agents of pleasure. They must be so applied that they make possible a sure and solid progress. If they do this, they will provide a constant source of pleasure to the learner. Nothing is more gratifying to old and young than the feeling of conquest and mastery. In education, as in other things, nothing succeeds like success.

Again, the principles of self-activity and doing are full of possibilities as pleasure-giving agents. Boys can, under capable tuition, be trained to be as active, purposeful, and skilful, in mental gymnastics as in physical. And they can derive as much pleasure from the one as from the other. To this end, pupils should play audience as little as possible in educational work. They should rather resemble a team of football players fighting under a skilful captain, and sharing both the work of conquest and the glory of victory.

Learners should seldom be mere listeners, during the period of education proper. They ought more often to be in a state rather of aggressiveness than receptiveness : telling than being told : discovering than hearing of discoveries : experimenting than seeing experiments : describing than defining, or listening to descriptions, and so on. And this if only because it is more agreeable to the nature of the child to be active rather than passive.

But, besides all this, there should be in education, and for educational purposes, a supply of what we may call free pleasure, just as there should be periods of free recreation and play, though all educative work should be more or less recreative and playful. For, after all, the predominance of the serious side of true education can never be wholly ignored, and ought always to be clearly recognised and enforced. Work must not become play, any more than play should be made a task.

Free pleasure in education can be provided by making the school a centre of social life for the pupils. It may be made a type of human life in the little—a microcosm of humanity. This can be brought about in one direction, through the systematic organisation of games. Cricket, football, tennis, and other games' clubs, at schools, have a direct and definite function in the general educational scheme. They develop many of the best ethical and social qualities, as well as arouse the interest and pride of the scholars in their school. " Floreat Etona " must mean "flourish my Eton," if it is to be really significant and sincere.

There must also be an internal as well as an external social school-life. The school community should have its own little social functions. Receptions, at-homes, musical parties, dances, and the like, should be given by, and to, the members of the school, and, if convenient, in the schoolroom itself. What this means to the school life as a whole, will be best appreciated by those who, as adults, have been taught at institutions where the social life has been well cared for. It imparts a vitality and meaning of an entirely new kind to the whole machinery. Not only the interests but the affections are enlisted on behalf of the institution as a whole. A fuller and more significant life is realised in the process of work, and the feeling of " esprit de corps " is as inevitable as it is stimulative. School life becomes a member rather than a misfortune of the whole life.

It is probably true to say that, in the interests of pure education, far too little is done to systematically develop the social graces in young people. Whilst " deportment " was formerly almost the only subject which received any considerable attention, in many schools, there now seems some danger that it is soon likely to be the only one which is entirely neglected.

Let it not be forgotten that youth is the springtime
of life, when showers do but minister to sunshine, and
sunshine to showers. The early years should be full of
the buds and blossoms of pleasure, and the joy of living.
Is it not an outrage upon young humanity if the morbid-
ness, disappointment, and pessimistic sourness of unhappy or unfortunate adults, be allowed to affect the few
brief, bright years of innocent happiness which ought to
be the privileged possession of the child?

If so, no one who feels life a burden, or thinks happiness a mistake, is fit to be an educator of the young.
Hardly anything can be more adverse to a vigorous and
healthy development in young children than the absence
of brightness, cheerfulness, and even gaiety. The inevitable suffering and sadness of life are more than enough
as discipline for the little ones. The sunshine of cheerfulness is as necessary for the development of the
mental and moral powers, as are light and warmth for
that of the physical nature. The educator must be the
pupil's sun.

Complete harmony between the self and the surroundings, i.e., pleasure, must bring about the greatest and
best development. A writer has put the matter very
happily in the following passage, urging teachers to
" fill their rooms with perpetual sunshine. First, that
outward sunshine which includes abundance of light
and air, cheerful surroundings, tastefully decorated
walls, and a generally attractive appearance. Then,
more important still, the inward sunshine of their own
good temper and happy, hopeful disposition; of their
habit of always looking on the bright side of everything

and saying the kindest thing possible of every one. These may seem small things, but they will not prove so to the young child. He will find joy in the genial atmosphere of his school, and grow rapidly in all graces of mind and soul under the influence of its light and warmth" (Elementary Education, Kilburn Series).

Those who have realised the spirit of kindergarten teaching know the truth of this ; and those who know it not, do not understand the kindergarten.

Any means which makes for pleasure in the educational system as a whole, or in any particular part of it, should be highly esteemed, as a means of vivifying and furthering the work of education ; and every effort should be made to practically realise the advantages of such powerful influences.

The Principle of Inter-relation and Inter-dependence.— The very great and fundamental importance of this principle demands that something more should be said about it, now that we have reviewed the general outlines of the science, and have thus obtained a better opportunity for understanding the conditions which it must fulfil. We have constantly found it necessary to draw attention to the need of dependently relating the different educational influences, and principles, both as units and with respect to their details. Some further applications of this will now be dealt with, in some detail.

As we have previously pointed out, the great aim should always be to secure such a continuity, coherence, system, and unity, amongst the educating influences as will best develop these elements in the mind itself.

Another purpose, which has also been referred to, is the relating of knowledge subjects in such a way that a special interest in any particular subject shall act as a motive for, and stimulus in, the study of others. As Dr. De Garmo points out: "every child is sure to be interested in something, so that if he can see that other things are related to his favourite ones, life at once broadens before him." And, as appears from what was said about apperception, this inter-connection is the most ready, and only true, means of mentally interpreting our experiences in the most significant way.

Again, since all knowledge inevitably becomes more or less directly and definitely related to conduct, the systematic organisation of it will have a very determining influence upon the moral nature. Dr. Rein says: "Without such concentration of mental forces no moral character is conceivable," and Dr. De Garmo urges that: "If knowledge lies in isolated tracts, it has in the first place little cumulative effect upon the motives of the child; and in the second place, even if each separate tract should give rise to its own little round of interests and motives, there is small probability that the resulting acts of will would of themselves drop into a co-ordinated line of consistent actions."

Another important aim arises in connection with the principle of proportion. There must be a limit to the number and the extent of the knowledge subjects which are used for educational purposes, or the pupil "not having time to digest any subject thoroughly, soon becomes a mere taster in all learning" (Dr. De Garmo). The more zealous we are for the highest success of practical education, the more necessary is it that we should take account of this. As Dr. De Garmo remarks : " Nothing appears more essential to our further advance, than a rigid examination of the curriculum, that indispensable parts may be properly related, and needless ones eliminated."

The question as to what should be the great central subject from which all the others should be derived, and to which they should be referred, has already been discussed ; and reasons were given for holding that the beginnings of physical science form the true original germ of our earliest knowledge, and, therefore, must be this central subject. Dr. Rein, however, following Ziller, the original exponent of the principle, takes a different view, and regards literature as the true central subject.

He therefore develops education on humanistic lines, *i.e.*, from the point of view of literary culture. The following are the considerations (as given by Dr. De Garmo) on which he bases his selection :—

" 1. By following the order of the national culture, and presenting it in the light of ethical judgment, we shall call forth permanent interest in the developing child ; hence, chronological progress from older and simpler, to newer and more complicated stages and conditions.

" 2. As a basis for this material we must use child-like classical, religious, literary and historical matter. ' Periods which no master has described, whose spirit no poet has breathed, are of small value for education ' (Herbart). Only classical presentations invite the pupil to constant and profitable repetitions; they alone furnish nourishment for the interests and aspirations of children. Only through these does the past speak in full tones to the present.

"3. Only large, connected unities of subject-matter are able to arouse and keep alive the deep sympathy of the youthful mind, thereby contributing to the development of character. 'Great moral energy is the effect of entire scenes and unbroken thought masses'" (Herbart).

On this theory Dr. Rein has worked out a truly admirable scheme of educational work for the first eight years of school life. The following—from Dr. De Garmo's book on "Herbart"—is the scheme for the first year:

"Studies $\begin{cases} 1. \text{ Core of concentration} \\ 2. \text{ Nature-study} \end{cases}$ Drawing, singing, number, reading, and writing.

"1. Ethical core of concentration; Grimm's Fairy Tales. These form the centre, or core, of instruction. The other branches are concentrated about them; and by them the remaining topics are largely determined.

"2. Nature study. All the subjects that are suggested by the fairy tales, receiving a special illumination from them and thereby awakening an intensified interest, are first chosen for treatment. School life and individual experience furnish much supplementary matter. (See list of object lessons below.)

"3. Drawing. For this purpose the objects mentioned in the fairy tales, and in the nature-study are used.

"4. Singing. The choice of songs is determined by the moods developed by instruction and by school life. The various songs must express emotion at fitting times.

"5. Number work. This is connected closely with the things that are considered in the various culture and nature subjects.

"6. Reading and writing. The material is chosen from the topics treated during instruction in fairy tales and nature-study."

The object lessons referred to include thirty-two topics, of which brief outlines are given, as follows :

"1. Room. Four walls (names), ceiling, and floor. Protects from rain, wind, and cold.

"2. Bed. We lie in bed when tired, sick. Soft and warm in bed. We will not be sluggards.

"3. Clothing. Names of parts of clothing. We wear clothing, (1) that we may not freeze, (2) that we need not be ashamed, (3) for adornment, (4) for carrying things.

"4. Food. (1) There is much that we can eat. (2) We eat many things raw, many boiled, roasted, baked. (3) There are foods from flour, flesh, milk, fruits, leaves, roots."

So the list goes on, and includes all the most familiar objects of the garden, field, wood, heavens, schoolhouse, and the home surroundings.

We urge that instead of the fancied and impossible experiences suggested by fairy tales, the real experiences of child life, expanded and crystallised by educational means, should be used. Our objections to the use of fairy tales have been set forth, and we need only add, that we hold that they should nowadays be looked upon, historically, as a kind of anthropological poetry; or, from the literary standpoint, as delightful examples of poetic licence, but as the last and most obscure, because fanciful, expressions of knowledge.

There is another most valuable application of the principle, which seeks to co-ordinate the different grades of studies—primary, secondary, and higher—with each other. An extremely interesting and suggestive scheme of this character, by Dr. Otto Frick, in also given in Dr. De Garmo's book on "Herbart."

The general order of subjects is: geography, natural history, history, German (the mother tongue), Latin, religion. This is a sequence which very largely corresponds to the views we have contended for.

We will quote the scheme in so far as it deals with geography, natural history, and German (the centre of the whole).

" A.—Primary Studies. Two Years. Age, 10 to 12.

First Year.

" 1. Geography (first semester). The typical geographical concepts illustrated by the home environment. Introduction to understanding of relief, and the reading of a map. General lessons upon the globe.

"(Second semester.) Division of the earth into land and water. General descriptive view of all the continents.

" 2. Natural History. First introduction into sys-

tematic observation of plant and animal life, according
to chief types found in the child's environment. (Biological home studies.) In summer the plants, in winter
the animals, are brought to the front.

" Enlivening of the geography heretofore presented.

" Opening up of the home environment. The awakening and cultivation of the feeling for nature and home
surroundings.

" 3. German. A national reading book, part I. (with
an appendix of the local or home environment), for
extending and deepening the impression and concepts
obtained in local geography and natural history. Pictures illustrating local traditions."

SECOND YEAR.

" 1. Geography. Lands. More minute descriptions
(with an emphasis of geographical types).

" (First semester.) Home province, and state, and the
whole of Germany.

" (Second semester.) The remainder of Europe.

" 2. Natural History. Extension of observation to
neighbouring regions in order to enlarge the observation of plant and animal life according to important
types. Extension of study to foreign lands.

" In summer and winter as in first year.

" 3. German. A national reading book, part II.,
corresponding to part I., but with stronger emphasis
upon national history, legends, and historical poems
from ancient and mediæval German history. Charac-
terisations of great historical personalities therein contained."

B.—Secondary Studies. Four Years. Age, 12 to 16.

Third Year.

" 1. Geography. Land divisions. Extended description (with emphasis of types) of non-European countries. Especial study of German Colonies.

" 2. Natural Science. Elementary and general.

"(First semester.) Physical geography.

"(Second semester.) Geology (according to the scope and treatment of the subject in the books of Geikie-Schmidt).

" 3 German. The Franco-Prussian war of 1870–1 in a form prepared for schools. A few of the most important war poems; then furnished with material from Grecian history and culture, e.g., Geibel, Schiller, (Ring des Polykr, Krainche des Ibycus)."

The subjects are extended each year. In the fourth year Greek is added, in the fifth year physics is introduced, and in the sixth year geography becomes "not a subject to be taught, but a principle to be observed at every opportunity," whilst in German the following books are taken: Goethe's "Hermann und Dorothea;" Schiller's "Wilhelm Tell," "Jungfrau von Orleans," and "Maria Stuart."

C.—Higher Studies. Age 16–19.

Seventh Year.

" 1 Geography. Not a subject to be taught, but a principle to be observed at every opportunity.

"2 Natural Science. (First semester). Elements of chemistry.

"(Second semester). Physics.

"3 German. (First semester.) Niebelungen Lied (und Gudrun).

"(Second semester). Heliand, Walter von der Vogel-weide (selections—natural feeling, knightly service, Kaiser songs, God's service)."

In the eighth year the outlines of mathematical geography are introduced under natural science, and "view of the inner development of German literature," under German. The ninth and last year includes a study of the "conception and nature of the cosmos" ('nature as a whole moved and quickened by an inner power')," as a natural science subject, and an "impressive gathering up of the important fundamental ideas presented in the instruction in 'German," as a literary subject.

If what we have said about the principle of development be sound, it would appear that the application of the principle of inter-relation and inter-independence must be mainly regulated by two great truths, viz., that activity is necessary for experience, experience for ideas, and ideas for expressions, and also that there must, primarily at least, be progress from the concrete to the abstract.

Our general scheme must therefore so order the educative influences and knowledge subjects, that the active powers are first engaged in such a way as to provide the fullest and most appropriate experiences for producing the required ideas. Next the ideas, as such, must be developed, and crystallised in verbal forms. This must apply to the scheme as a whole and to each part, as also must the movement from the concrete to the abstract.

A mode of applying the principle on these lines may be illustrated by an example. Taking the home as the concrete centre from which knowledge is to be primarily derived, because it is the practical centre of our life and interests, we should proceed as follows.

1. Kindergarten.—First the child's receptivity and imitativeness must be made use of. The outlines of a model of a house can be imitated by stick-laying, and the whole structure reproduced in wooden bricks. What we may call its cubical outlines should be copied in cork and pea work. Weaving and paper-folding can be employed for making copies of household articles and ornaments.

All these will, if properly used, cultivate the child's powers of observation, and its capacity for reproductive imitation. Ideas about the house, as such, must also be obtained, e.g., the necessity for protection from the weather, and how it is secured; the functions of the roof, windows, chimney, etc.; the special uses of the separate rooms, and their appropriate positions and furnishing; and some very simple notions about the draining, ventilation, and cleaning of the house. This will be informational rather than inferential, and according to interest and familiarity, rather than interconnection and sequence.

2. Geography.—Next there must be an endeavour to introduce systematic information, as a preparation for

systematic thought, *i.e.*, science. We can now begin to pass over from the material to the symbolic, in a simple and obvious way. A clay model of a house, with its roof off, should be made, and from this the idea of the plan must be deduced, and then drawn. A suggestive way of getting the concrete idea of the meaning of the plan would be to have a wooden model of the "shell" of a house, and to rub the bottom parts with ink, and then press it on a piece of white paper.

When the plan of the house has been developed then its surroundings should be similarly treated, the plan (or map) being coloured so as to distinguish the chief features. The points of the compass should be associated with the sun's movements, and marked on the map.

A further study of that which has been thus dealt with will introduce physical geography. Commercial and political geography can be approached through the local industries and institutions, the local habitations of which should be indicated on the model and map.

3. Science.—The flowers and trees which are in the garden, or near the home; the domestic animals; and the warming and lighting of the house; will serve as starting points for elementary ideas about botany, natural history, and physics, in the form of simple object lessons. Indeed, all the sciences can be thus approached from the objects and experiences met with in or about the home.

4. Art.—Art in the wider sense of systematic work,

or in the narrower sense of systematic expressions of
the beautiful, is directly connected with the home life.
The different trades which have to do with the domestic
life, such as those of the butcher, baker, bricklayer, shoemaker, tailor, and grocer, and the industries which they
in turn depend upon, may all be dealt with.　The beauty
of the surrounding scenery at the various seasons of
the year, and of pictures representing it; the beauties
of form in ornaments and articles of furniture; and
the grace and harmony of rhythmic movement and
sound, are not difficult to bring into prominence, and
so to arouse purposeful thought.

　5. Reading, Writing, and Arithmetic.—These, as
formal systems, should not be taken as subjects till
after the foregoing, since, as systems of symbols, they
have no real meaning, and can have no significant
existence for the individual until the experience, ideas,
and knowledge which they express are actually possessed
by him.　It is true that vocal and visual signs have
been freely used, and must be so used, in the imparting
of knowledge.　But to use words as convenient marks
of things and experiences, ideas, and knowledge, is
very different from using them as a word system, i.e.,
as a series of signs which the learner must know how
to spell, write, and connect according to recognised
forms.

　Reading in the lower classes can be connected with
the new words introduced by the kindergarten and
object lessons; indeed, the first reading lessons ought
to be built up on the blackboard from the verbal
material used in these.　This will not only serve to

impress the new ideas more clearly and firmly upon the memory, but it will make the reading lesson have a reality and purpose for the child which nothing else can give it.

Foreign languages are best learnt by thus directly associating words with things, and by using the mother tongue as a model and a means of transition.

In the higher classes reading can be used to extend the information already gained about particular objects and processes. But this does not mean that reading, as a form of elocution and a means of culture, should be cultivated through such subject matter. These must be obtained through the best literature, which ought to be made to stimulate, nourish, and form, the literary tastes.

The verbal accounts of lessons which are produced in the way suggested above, might very well be given as composition lessons, either reproductively through memory or dictation, or constructively, from a more or less full outline sketch. If these are preserved in special exercise books, they will form a self-made text-book— the very best of text-books for the beginner.

Arithmetic can be very usefully associated with the object lessons. If the teacher gets some accurate information as to the number of slates to a square yard of roofing, the number of bricks to a square yard of wall, the cost of materials, and the like, a great many exercises in arithmetic could be devised. There is every reason for thus making arithmetic the channel of a great deal of correct information. The higher branches of mathematics, such as mensuration, geometry, and trigonometry, can be developed in connection with the measurements of a house and its surroundings.

6. Grammar.—This must come after reading and writing are somewhat advanced, inasmuch as it has to do with the science and art of verbal forms. Dealing with grammar in connection with its concrete basis—experiences and thoughts, the expressions for which it systematically and technically expounds, and regulates according to established usage—the educator can give grammar lessons implicitly by careful blackboard arrangements of subject and predicate, etc. These he can afterwards explicitly expound from the grammatical point of view. Such a method has the very great advantage of demonstrating and emphasing the relation between the symbol and the thing signified, whilst, at the same time, it lends itself most helpfully to distinguishing between the study of words and the study of the things which they stand for.

7. History.—Old houses, and old pictures of old buildings, people, and costumes, will serve as points of departure for history lessons. All survivals of former times invite comparison with their modern rivals. Old-fashioned customs and observances both stimulate and partly satisfy the curiosity of the intelligent observer.

The government of the home, as compared with that of the school, and any form of scholars' club or society, will introduce the elements of constitutional history. The study of the forms of local government should be the transition step to the wider field of national political institutions. The study of forms of government which affect large areas will lead to a fuller treatment of political geography.

Of course all this must, in the early stages, be of a very concrete character—that is, it must consist chiefly of systematic descriptions of facts, and not attempts to explain the principles or philosophical truths of history.

8. Morals.—The home life presents the best possible opportunity for conveying definite ideas about affection, self-sacrifice, considerateness, kindness, generosity, justice, rights, and duties. At first the teaching should be of a concrete kind, and only in the higher classes ought there to be any attempt to begin to form anything like systematic abstract ideas about such matters —in other words, to teach ethics.

It must be remembered that it is only the beginnings of knowledge which are to be thus derived from a central topic. It is as the natural, and therefore the most helpful and fruitful, starting point in the beginnings of knowledge that the greatest good can be obtained in this way. It is absolutely essential that the pupil should, as soon as he is able, take interest in, and learn about, facts more and more remote from the home. The development of one subject from another must be elaborated as much as possible.

It must be admitted that the considerations involved in the drawing up of such plans for educational development are of the greatest possible practical importance, and that all the resources of a sound science of education—together with a mastery of, and power in applying, its principles, by a capable expert—are needed for the satisfactory solution of such fundamental issues.

Whatever is achieved in this direction—and much has already been done, and still more made possible, by the great thinkers and writers on education—will put the art of education on a scientific basis, and secure the greatest and the best practical results.

Some General Remarks.—The principles just discussed are recognised in the following quotations from the opinious of practical teachers. The principles of collectivism and individualism are involved in these words of Dr. Abbott: "In a school it is necessary for a class-teacher to consult the interests of the greatest number, slightly sacrificing the very dull, and still more the very clever, for the sake of the commonplace majority, and endeavouring to compensate the two extremes by a little extra attention out of class."

Mr. Landon says: "In order that the instruction given to a class may be so suited to every member of it that no one is unduly pressed, and no one neglected, the level of attainment and of intellectual power must be fairly uniform throughout." (The Principles and Practice of Teaching.) Comenius advises, "that those pupils only be admitted into the same class who are of equal advancement, and that they be admitted at the same time" (Laurie).

Dr. Fitch points out the dangers of too early application of the principle of individualism in the following passages: "Do you not, in looking back on your own mental life, feel thankful that you were forced to learn things for which you had no special appetite, and which a scientific analyst of your yet unformed character and tastes might have declared to be unsuited to you?"

The Rev. M. G. Glazebrook, writing of specialisation, remarks: "When a boy of moderate ability reaches the age of sixteen it is generally clear that he has a preference for some one subject . . . . A little more than half of the school hours should be devoted to the special subject, but the rest should be strictly reserved for supplementary studies. These latter should be so planned as to train different faculties without the distraction caused by multiplicity of subjects" (Thirteen Essays on Education).

Speaking of the advantages of forming good habits in children, Locke says: "By this method we shall see whether what is required of him be adapted to his capacity, any way suited to the child's natural genius and constitution: for that too must be considered in a right education."

In condensing Pestalozzi's ideas into educational maxims, Morf gives this as one of them: "The individuality of a child is sacred." Comenius has the following practical rules, which are clearly based on collectivism: "Let there be only one teacher for a school, or at least for a class. In one subject, let there be but one author (i.e., let "all be taught from the same books"). Let one and the same labour be expended on the whole of the pupils present (i.e., let "all the scholars . . . . do the same thing at the same time"). Let all disciplines and tongues be taught according to one and the same method" (Laurie).

The principle of proportion is set forth by Mr. Landon thus: "The teacher must work with the pupil, not for him. Take his hand, beguile the tediousness of the way, allow proper rest, and do not hurry or overstrain him; but see that he walks, do not carry him." Nicole (15th century) one of the Port-Royalists writes : " The greatest minds have but a limited range of intelligence. In all of them there are regions of twilight and shadow ; but the intelligence of the child is almost wholly pervaded by shadows; he catches glimpses of but few rays of light. So everything depends on managing these rays, on increasing them, and on exposing to them whatever we wish to have the child comprehend " (Compayré).

Comenius suggests the principle of proportion in the following maxim : "Nature preserves, between root and branches, a true proportion in respect of quantity and quality" (Laurie). And Quintilian shrewdly remarks : " We can scarcely believe how progress in reading is retarded by attempting to go too fast."

That we ought not to press the principle of analysis and synthesis too far is implied by Canon Daniel when he says : "There are many facts which admit of no explanation ; there are others which, if taught to children at all, must be received by them, at first, on authority." Of the need for alternation of work and play, the same writer remarks : "We are too apt to look upon recreation as a mere concession to the weakness of children. As a matter of fact, it is as much a part of education as school work is . . . . If work and play be well proportioned, each will be a recreation to the other." And the limits of the principle of nourishment are indicated by him in these words : " Teachers will do well to remember that it is expedient for children to leave off a mental, as a bodily meal, with an appetite, and that in this, as in many other matters, 'the half is more than the whole.'"

Plato has expressed the influence of the environment in these words: "Let our artists be rather those who are gifted to discern the true nature of the beautiful and graceful; then will our youth dwell in a land of health, amid fair sights and sounds, and receive the good in everything; and beauty, the effluence of fair works, shall flow into the eye and ear, like a health-giving breeze from a purer region, and insensibly draw the soul from earliest years into likeness and sympathy with the beauty of reason."

We should again remind ourselves that the foregoing discussions are but outlines of the matters with which they deal. Our aim has been rather to indicate the science and its most important constituent units than to attempt even a fairly full treatment of any one item. The relations of education to ethics, logic, and physiology have been deliberately excluded, except in so far as incidental references were demanded by the topic in hand.

It must be remembered that education is the science, and teaching the art. One may be a good teacher and a poor educationist, or a good educationist and a poor teacher. He who would have true excellence in either must be sound in both.

Education, like all other sciences, is progressive. We are constantly obtaining more profound, extensive, and accurate knowledge about human beings in particular, and also about things in general. There is, therefore, always the occasion and need for investigating the educational significance of new ideas. This must ever be so, for the activities of the universe are constantly producing fresh modifications of the total complex. Science knows nothing of finality, except as annihilation, and it knows nothing of annihilation.

APPENDIX

The following short list of books is offered as a suggestion for further reading. It is recommended that the volumes be read in the order in which they are arranged.

Lectures on Teaching. Part I. COMPAYRÉ. *Isbister*, 6s.

The Teacher's Handbook of Psychology. SULLY. *Longmans*, 5s.

Apperception. LANGE. *Isbister*, 3s. 6d.

The Essentials of Method. DE GARMO. *Isbister*, 2s. 6d.

Habit in Education. RADESTOCK. *Isbister*, 2s. 6d.

Outlines of Pedagogics. REIN. *Sonnenschein*, 3s.

Introduction to Herbart's Science and Practice of Education. FELKIN. *Sonnenschein*, 4s. 6d.

The Science of Education. HERBART. *Sonnenschein*, 4s. 6d.

Herbart. DE GARMO. *Heinemann*, 5s.

Elements of General Method. McMURRY. *Kellogg & Co., New York*, 75c.

Education. HERBERT SPENCER. *Williams & Norgate*, 2s. 6d.

Education as a Science. Chapters 1–7. BAIN. *Kegan Paul*, 5s.

Essays on Educational Reformers. QUICK. *Longmans,*
3s. 6d.

The History of Pedagogy. COMPAYRÉ. *Sonnenschein,* 6s.

Institutes of Education. S. S. LAURIE. *Thin,* 5s.

Comenius. S. S. LAURIE. *Clay & Sons,* 3s. 6d.

The Child and Child Nature. BÜLOW. *Sonnenschein,*
3s.

The Student's Froebel. Parts I. and II. HERFORD.
Isbister, 2s. 6d. each.

The Life of Pestalozzi. DE GUIMPS. *Sonnenschein,* 6s.

Émile. ROUSSEAU. *Edward Arnold,* 6s.

Education and Heredity. GUYAU. *Walter Scott,* 3s. 6d.

Education from a National Standpoint. FOUILLÉE.
Edward Arnold, 7s. 6d.

The Philosophy of Education. ROSENKRANZ. *Edward
Arnold,* 6s.

Method in Education. ROSMINI. *Isbister,* 5s.

Levana. RICHTER. *Sonnenschein,* 3s.

First Three Years of Childhood. PEREZ. *Sonnenschein,*
4s. 6d.

The Senses and the Will. PREYER. *Edward Arnold,* 6s.

The Development of the Intellect. PREYER. *Edward
Arnold,* 6s.

Story of Primitive Man. CLODD. *Newnes,* 1s.

Primitive Culture. 2 Volumes. Tylor. *Murray,* 21s.

Folk-lore for Everybody. Cox. *Nutt,* 3s. 6d.

INDEX

A

ABBOTT, DR. : on repetition and preparation, 152
    on words and ideas, 422
    on difficulties in teaching, 432
    on gradation in teaching, 435
    on need of relaxation, 492
    on individual teaching, 518
Abstract, the : in education, 217
    its dependence on the concrete, 218
Action : nature springs of, 127
    development of, 184
    see principle of doing, 224
Adjustment : need of time for, 120
    and habit, 135
Analysis : nature of, 336
    in progress from indefinite to definite, 408
Analysis and synthesis: principle of, 335
Animism : in child and race, 406
Apperception : what it involves, 307
    definition of, 309
    how determined, 310
Apperceptive group : what it is, 310
    domination of an, 311
    forming of, 332
Aristotle : on education, 39
    on leisure, 236
    on overtraining, 267
    on development, 271

Arnold, Matthew : on culture, 490
Ascham, Roger : on preparation, 151
Assimilation : and discrimination, growth of, 106
    need of time for, 120
    what it involves, 291
    deepest forms of, 336
    conditions of, 438
Association : what it is, 71
    what the result of, 71
    and attention, 73
    conditions for force of, 73
    an element of knowing, 73
    of ideas, 278
Attention : nature of, 64
    as mental digestion, 65
    kinds of, 65
    pre-adjustment of, 66
    and association, 73
    its functions, 74
    and assimilation, 307
Average, the : and the normal, 474

B

BABY, THE: some characteristics of, 160, 204, 277, 282, 345
Bain, Dr. : on interest in education, 130
    on progress from known to unknown, 205
    on learning, 228
    on juxtaposition, 338
    on self-effort in education, 345
    on value of information, 413

Printed by BALLANTYNE, HANSON & Co.
London and Edinburgh

www.ingramcontent.com/pod-product-compliance
Lightning Source LLC
Chambersburg PA
CBHW022127020426
42334CB00015B/800